T3-BNR-919

FRACTURED HOMELAND

Bonita Lawrence

FRACTURED HOMELAND

Federal Recognition and Algonquin Identity in Ontario

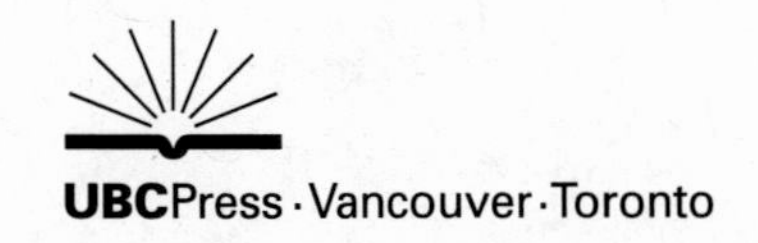

UBCPress · Vancouver · Toronto

21 20 19 18 17 16 15 14 13 12   5 4 3 2 1

Printed in Canada on FSC-certified ancient-forest-free paper (100% post-consumer recycled) that is processed chlorine- and acid-free.

Library and Archives Canada Cataloguing in Publication

Lawrence, Bonita
    Fractured homeland : federal recognition and Algonquin identity in Ontario / Bonita Lawrence.

Includes bibliographical references and index.
Issued also in electronic formats.
ISBN 978-0-7748-2287-9

    1. Algonquin Indians – Ontario – Claims. 2. Algonquin Indians – Ontario – Ethnic identity. 3. Algonquin Indians – Government policy – Canada. I. Title.

E99.A349L39 2012   971.3'0049733   C2011-907993-3

Canadä

UBC Press gratefully acknowledges the financial support for our publishing program of the Government of Canada (through the Canada Book Fund), the Canada Council for the Arts, and the British Columbia Arts Council.

This book has been published with the help of a grant from the Canadian Federation for the Humanities and Social Sciences, through the Aid to Scholarly Publications Program, using funds provided by the Social Sciences and Humanities Research Council of Canada.

Printed and bound in Canada by Friesens
Set in Kozuka Gothic and Minion by Artegraphica Design Co. Ltd.
Copy editor: Deborah Kerr
Proofreader: Steph VanderMeulen
Cartographer: Eric Leinberger

UBC Press
The University of British Columbia
2029 West Mall
Vancouver, BC V6T 1Z2
www.ubcpress.ca

Contents

Part 3: The Bonnechere and Petawawa River Watersheds

Part 4: The Upper Madawaska and York River Watersheds

Part 5: The Kiji Sibi – From Mattawa to Ottawa

Figures

Preface

> Our generation in my family now lives with the repercussions of having been brought up to consider our Native heritage, at very deep levels, to be meaningless. And yet, like a tough weed whose roots are pervasively anchored everywhere in the soil of this land and which therefore *cannot* be uprooted, our Native identity continues to manifest its presence in my family, even after a generation of silencing.
>
> **– Bonita Lawrence, *"Real" Indians and Others***

The issue of ambiguity in Native identity has always interested me, primarily because of my own family's identity struggles. Colonial violence, assimilation pressures, migration, and loss of Indian status have marked my family history and have made recovering a Mi'kmaq identity a difficult process for my generation of my family. Like many urban mixed-bloods, I have struggled to piece together a Native heritage out of family history as my mother's generation (which has now passed on) remembered it, from fragments gleaned from genealogical research, and from elders' accounts. And because of the multiple instances of belonging and not-belonging that I experienced in coming to know myself as a Native person, I decided to focus on urban mixed-blood identity for my PhD research.

In the Toronto urban Native community where I lived during the early 1990s, it seemed that internal divisions defined our lives as Native people, whether it was reserve versus urban, dark-skinned versus light-skinned, or status versus non-status. Of course, these were not neutral binaries. One side of the binary was always "more Indian"; the opposite side was invariably "not Indian enough." And yet, even as these divisions were part of our daily lived experience, most of the Native people around me were uneasy about discussing them. Perhaps this is not surprising. In a city where over 70 percent of the population consists of recent immigrants, the presence of a hundred thousand Native people barely registers. In this context, to be Native is to be heavily minoritized and to continuously encounter widespread ignorance about our very existence. And indeed, in my research, the family histories of almost every participant bore the marks of a tangible legacy of colonial violence and dispossession. Through this work, I began to understand the powerful role that loss of Indian status had played for many of the people that I interviewed, and that a sense of dispossession and homelessness was a common hallmark of urban non-status Native experience.

In 1999, I left Toronto to take up my first academic position at Queen's University in Kingston, Ontario. While modifying my dissertation, which was ultimately published as *"Real" Indians and Others: Mixed-Blood Urban Native Peoples and Indigenous Nationhood* (Lawrence 2004), I became aware of a different kind of non-status experience, one that was rural and associated with a land base. As I became friends with Robert Lovelace, then manager of the Four Directions Aboriginal Student Centre at Queen's, I met people from his community, Ardoch Algonquin First Nation, and began to understand that for many Algonquin people who lacked Indian status, the land anchored them and provided a sense of identity. Like urban non-status Native people, they bore the scars of a history of colonial violence and often struggled with having lost knowledge of language and culture or with not looking "Indian enough." There was one huge difference, however: although the Algonquins I met had been profoundly dispossessed when the settler society appropriated their lands, they could by no stretch of the imagination be conceived of as "homeless," in the manner in which so many non-status urban Native people in Toronto, having lost the ties to their own territories, are homeless.

Gradually, prompted by the friendships that I made among the Algonquins I met in southern Algonquin territory, the idea of conducting research with federally unrecognized Algonquin communities began to grow. In 2003, when I received a tiny grant from Queen's University to "scope out" the nature of such research, I began to interview the leadership of Ardoch and other communities. When I interviewed elder Harold Perry in a canoe as he paddled around the Mud Lake wild rice beds, which for several generations had been his family's responsibility to maintain, I began to see that for the most part,

Algonquins were still living in their own territories and that the land was reflected in their family histories. I also learned that because a comprehensive claim was taking place within the region, they were at risk of losing title to the territory that defined them as a people.

Having acquired a large research grant based on the earlier work, I spent the next seven years interviewing Algonquins from all over the territory. They shared their stories about the past, the land claim struggles that were consuming them in the present, and their hopes and fears about the future. I also made friends with a number of Algonquins who were kind enough to help me, not only by interviewing their friends, but by clearing up multiple misconceptions and clarifying complex issues relating to the history of the land claim. In an act of profound faith, they included me in their e-mail networks so that I became privy to the news and ongoing discussions that were raging throughout Algonquin territory, particularly in the interval between 2004 and 2006, after the land claim regime changed.

Over the years, as I worked on this book and was exposed to the terrible divisions that the land claim was generating among so many Algonquins, as well as their efforts to protect the land, I began to understand the price they were paying to maintain their homeland. I offer this book in humble gratitude for the manner in which so many people shared their stories and their wisdom with me. Ultimately, the knowledge I have received is theirs; only the errors are mine.

Wel'alioq! Um sed nogumak!

Acknowledgments

This book would never have existed without the friendship and assistance of Bob Lovelace. Through his willingness to introduce me to the Ardoch community and other Algonquins, and to share his perspectives in lengthy discussions over the years, Bob has been absolutely essential to the success of this project. The chapters relating to Ardoch were written while Bob was in prison for living up to the responsibilities of Algonquin jurisdiction in order to protect the land. As I worked through the newsletters and leaflets that he had written twenty years earlier, the fact of his incarceration gave the process a poignancy and immediacy that I had not expected to experience in writing about communities other than my own. This was amplified by the fact that for a number of years while at Queen's and during the research process, my own spiritual life was maintained through attending sweat lodges conducted by Bob at his property in the Frontenac highlands. Chi Meegwetch, Bob!

Other individuals from Ardoch, such as Paula Sherman and Harold Perry, played an early and formative role in my understanding of the issues, for which I am very grateful. Meegwetch!

As I struggled to understand the history of the Algonquin land claim, as well as the central role that questions of identity have played in its development, Heather Majaury generously gave her time and energy, offering long (and inevitably humorous) commentary and constantly being willing to help me "fill in the blanks," explaining many dynamics that I would not have otherwise understood. Lynn Gehl also played an important role in my writing. In her tireless research and analysis of the Algonquin land claim, identity, and nationhood, she has constantly challenged Algonquins to rethink, or to think more carefully, about the process in which they are engaging. My own analysis of the land claim and many of the issues faced by contemporary Algonquins therefore owes much to Lynn's work. Finally, my numerous discussions with Bob Majaury enabled me to understand recent developments in Algonquin territory. To all these Algonquins, I offer a heartfelt Chi Meegwetch!

Laura Schwager, a former student of mine from Queen's, was my first research assistant. She provided valuable help during the earliest years of the research when I was struggling, as a new professor, to learn how to run a research project. In later years, her research into her Mohawk family's journey from Akwesasne to off-reserve landlessness intellectually amplified my own work. Niawen!

I also want to thank Brian Murray, who steadfastly typed most of the interviews, despite tremendous difficulties. I want to thank my good friend Jean Murray, who not only typed but carefully coded the work. The countless questions she asked kept me on track throughout the process. Last but not least, I want to thank John Usher, for his work in coding, for his countless efforts to contribute, and for our in-depth arguments about the ethics of the land claim, which, during the early years of the project when I didn't know enough about the issues, kept me honest. Chi Meegwetch!

FRACTURED HOMELAND

Introduction

In 1992, land claim negotiations began between the Algonquins of Pikwakanagan, the only federally recognized Algonquin reserve in Ontario, the Province of Ontario, and the Government of Canada. From the moment that negotiations began – and indeed, from the moment that Pikwakanagan launched the petition to initiate the land claim – the existence of large numbers of Algonquins who had never been federally recognized as Indians rose to the forefront.

This book is about federally unrecognized Algonquins in Ontario. It includes the scattering of historic Algonquin communities whose presence was invisible to outsiders, consisting of networks of families who remained relatively cohesive despite losing most of their land base to settlers and not being recognized under the Indian Act. It also encompasses the even larger numbers of non-status Algonquins scattered across Algonquin territory – as well as outside of it – who were organized by representatives from Pikwakanagan into "area committees" for the purpose of the land claim. Through these organizations, many of these individuals are seeking to re-create organic community-based identities as Algonquins.

Indeed, after years of silence about "Indianness," the land claim has forced many non-status Algonquins to struggle with questions of identity and what constitutes "Algonquinness" and "Indianness." It has also heightened the divisions created by centuries of colonial incursions into Algonquin territory. And yet this book is not primarily concerned with the land claim, but about

Algonquin identity and nationhood. Because the claim affects each community, it will be taken up, but only where it pertains to the efforts of federally unrecognized Algonquins to be reborn as a people after almost two hundred years of settler engulfment of their homeland, the Ottawa River watershed, and a century of erasure as "Indians."

Federally unrecognized Algonquins in Ontario have been invisible in public discourse for over a hundred years. Nonetheless, they have persisted in backwoods settlements and small towns throughout the Ottawa River watershed. Most no longer speak Algonquin, many do not look visibly "Indian," and for many of them, their families have kept silent about their identities for at least a generation, with the result that cultural knowledge is diminished. Unlike non-status Indians in urban settings, however, federally unrecognized Algonquins are anchored by the land in ways that are subtle and yet profound. Connection to the land has enabled some communities to retain aspects of a collective ethos; in other places, the social links that marked Algonquin life have been transformed but not obliterated. For that reason, this book seeks to explore who federally unrecognized Algonquins *are,* in all their diversity, and the differing visions they have of re-creating Algonquin nationhood.

In addressing nationhood, this book does not adopt a post-colonial concern with deconstructing, in an abstract manner, the concept of nationhood. For a people struggling to survive *as* Native people after their collective existence has been continuously under attack for almost three centuries, assertions of nationhood are vital. Indeed, attempting to deconstruct something that is in the process of being reborn is highly inappropriate. And though post-colonial discourse has created a potent body of work addressing nationalism and national identities, as Bonita Lawrence and Enakshi Dua (2005) have noted, for the most part this work is premised upon the same principles of Indigenous non-existence on which colonial discourse rests.

For that reason, the only appropriate definition of "nationhood" relevant in this context is formulated by the United Nations Working Group on Indigenous Peoples:

> Indigenous communities, peoples and nations are those which, having a historical continuity with pre-invasion and pre-colonial societies that developed on their territories, consider themselves distinct from other sectors of society now prevailing in those territories, or parts of them. They form at present non-dominant sectors of society and are determined to preserve, develop, and transmit to future generations their ancestral territories and their ethnic identity, as the basis of their continued existence as peoples, in

> accordance with their own cultural patterns, social institutions and legal systems. (Cobo 1987, quoted in Maaka and Fleras 2005, 30-31)

Nevertheless, because Algonquins sought to re-create their nationhood through the comprehensive claims process, which from the start privileged some Algonquins over others and raised basic ideological questions about the nature of Algonquin identity – indeed, about Indianness itself – this book will explore the views of those involved in the process to tease out the contradictions in the diverse perspectives expressed. The aim is to understand the means through which Algonquins have sought to re-create their identities and their nationhood. I will also attempt to articulate the differing experiences of Algonquinness shaped not only by the presence or lack of Indian status, but by varying experiences of settler incursion in eastern Ontario. In a sense, the book seeks to weave together into a coherent web the stories of nationhood that federally unrecognized Algonquins are grappling with, all across the territory.

In rejecting a reliance on post-colonialism, this book adopts Indigenism as its theoretical approach. Ward Churchill (1992, 403-4) describes this perspective, in bold strokes, as taking the rights of Indigenous peoples as the highest priority, drawing upon the knowledge and values of Indigenous communities, and articulating the spirit of resistance that has marked the history of their fight against colonialism.

And yet, Indigenism has many approaches and many ways of understanding the issues we face. Moreover, as Linda Tuhiwai Smith (1999) writes, Indigenous people's experiences of colonization have of necessity been understood through multivariate exposures to the discourses of other colonized and oppressed people around the world. As a result, there is no "purist" lens of resistance that has not been influenced by struggles elsewhere; nevertheless, the perspectives we develop synthesize these outlooks into viewpoints that are of primary relevance to Indigenous people. In an oft-quoted paragraph, Smith (ibid., 38) addresses this reality:

> The development of theories by Indigenous scholars which attempt to explain our existence in contemporary society (as opposed to the "traditional" society constructed under modernism) has only just begun. Not all these theories claim to be derived from some "pure" sense of what it means to be Indigenous, nor do they claim to be theories which have been developed in a vacuum separated from any association with civil and human rights movements, other nationalist struggles, or other theoretical approaches. What is claimed, however, is that new ways of theorizing by Indigenous scholars are

> grounded in a real sense of, and sensitivity towards, what it means to be an Indigenous person ... Contained within this imperative is a sense of being able to determine priorities, to bring to the centre those issues of our own choosing, and to discuss them amongst ourselves.

Most of my writing might be viewed as the particular strand of Indigenism that addresses the effects of identity legislation and other histories of genocidal pressures on Indigenous people, and the "modern" ways they seek to re-create traditional values. That being said, what I have attempted to develop in this book, above all, is clarity about the colonization processes that Algonquins have experienced and continue to experience in Canada, and how Indigenous people themselves can become implicated in these processes as they search for ways of resisting colonialist assault. Because of this, the diverse paths they have taken toward decolonization are central to this discussion.

Defining "Federal Recognition"

It is important to clarify what is meant by "federal recognition," particularly in Canada, where this term is rarely used. "Unrecognized" Indigenous people are not perceived as being Indigenous by the nation-state in which they are situated. Bruce Miller (2003) has addressed the fact that Indigenous people exist around the world who, for a wide variety of reasons, are unrecognized by the states who occupy their territories. Although each group faces different circumstances, denial of recognition is almost always part of a colonial process whereby states gain untrammelled access to their land and resources. At other times, states also employ policies of non-recognition in order to reduce the numbers of individuals with claims to the land. The term "federal recognition" has gained the most attention in the United States, where the federal government's formal acknowledgment of an "Indian tribe" brings a range of rights and possible benefits that greatly increase the abilities of communities to survive as Indians. These benefits may include far higher levels of autonomy from state governments, eligibility for funding, and increased possibilities for generating revenue or acquiring lands. They can also entail the repatriation of sacred artifacts lost to museums, the maintenance of tribal courts, and finally, recognition as "Indian" by other federally recognized tribes.

Because many US Indigenous groups have been recognized by local state governments but not by Washington, or have had their tribal status arbitrarily "terminated," they can avail themselves of formal mechanisms to *become* federally recognized, provided they can fulfill certain requirements related to proving tribal histories and lineages. In both the United States and Canada, federal recognition is articulated in legislation and legal decisions defining Native identity. In both countries, recognition is therefore intimately tied to both legal and conceptual notions of "who is an Indian." However, in Canada, historically, there is only one means of recognition of Indianness – to be registered as a status Indian within the meaning of the Indian Act.[1]

In Canada, to be federally unrecognized is both an individual and a collective condition. *Individuals* are "non-status" for a variety of reasons. Either they or their ancestors once held Indian status but lost it due to certain stipulations under the Indian Act, or they never acquired it because their ancestors for various reasons were left off the list of band members developed by Indian agents or were classified as "half-breed" during the treaty process and therefore legally excluded from Indianness. *Groups* usually lack federal recognition because they were left out of treaty negotiations – the band simply was not present and was therefore not included. In areas where no treaties were signed, reserves were sometimes set aside, and some Native people who occupied the land now designated as reserves or who were present when the lists of registered Indians were drawn up by the Indian agent appointed for each reserve became federally recognized. However, those whose lands were too quickly consumed by the juggernaut of colonial settlement were frequently not assigned reserves; from then on, they were no longer recognized as Indians. This is the situation for the majority of Algonquins in Ontario.

In Canada, unlike in the United States, the legacy of British colonialism has meant that though the courts might recognize the limited rights of Indigenous peoples to *use* certain territories, the groups themselves are never perceived as nations (not even as "domestic dependent nations," which legally defined Native American tribes in the 1830s). In Canada, at best, a group is designated as an Indian band according to the lists drawn up by treaty officials when treaties were signed. These bands are small subsets of pre-existing nations; as a result, instead of acknowledging the existence of fifty-odd Indigenous nations across the land, Canada recognizes over six hundred tiny subgroups of these nations as Indian bands (now designated as "First Nations"). Until 1985, band membership was determined solely by Ottawa, which decided what individuals belonged to what bands. Because Indian status is bestowed only upon those whose ancestors were granted it, Indigenous people who lack Indian status have no formal means through which to attain it (though, until 1985, non-Indian women who married Indian men acquired Indian status). In a rare measure, after the Newfoundland Mi'kmaq were denied recognition when Newfoundland joined Canada in 1949, they were subsequently brought under the Indian Act to rectify this omission. However, in most instances, the boundaries of who is legally an Indian in Canada cannot be redrawn once they are established.

Through a land claim, however, a people *can* gain recognition as Indigenous, though this, too, is very rare. For the most part, comprehensive claims are negotiated only with those whom Canada already recognizes as Indian (in some land claim processes, a few claimants are recognized as Metis). For that reason, the Ontario Algonquin land claim, where most of those negotiating have never been recognized as Indian and are seeking formal recognition *through* the claim, is highly anomalous.

In speaking of federally unrecognized Algonquins in Ontario, I am referring first of all to communities – to the networks of families that have persisted in the Ottawa Valley in places such as Ardoch, Baptiste Lake, Mattawa, Sharbot Lake, Whitney, and Allumette Island (whose residents were generally displaced to the town of Pembroke). These communities today are descended from the families who managed to remain within their traditional territories, even as their lands were overrun by settlers. They maintained close ties with each other and, over the years, held on to certain collective practices and values that set them apart from the white settlers around them. In some areas, such as Ardoch, these families were forced to develop modern organizations to represent them, before the land claim even began. Indeed, some of the divisions that currently plague some of the federally unrecognized Algonquin communities originated when the land claim negotiators from Pikwakanagan disregarded the organizations that pre-dated the land claim and instead set up separate area committees in their territories to represent them within the land claim. In other areas, such as Bancroft, the land claim was the vehicle that formally organized existing informal networks of communities.

Although those whose ancestors managed to remain in their traditional territories were able to survive as small, cohesive communities, many other Algonquins survived the onslaught of settlers only through relocation. As families and individuals were scattered across Algonquin territory (including Quebec), they survived as best they could. Sometimes, they left the territory altogether; more commonly, however, they travelled around eking out a marginal survival through seasonal work in resource industries and wherever other work could be found. Their descendants were therefore not affiliated with any Algonquin community until the advent of the land claim, when representatives from Pikwakanagan organized them into area committees. In some instances, these area committees have acted as focal points, gathering large numbers of unaffiliated Algonquins scattered throughout the territory, becoming "mega-communities" in the process, with little collective focus or cohesion. Finally, the fragmentation produced by the land claim has brought about a seemingly endless proliferation of newer communities splitting off from older ones.

The only organic way to make sense of these multiple experiences is by understanding that, regardless of whether communities are historical remnants of ancient bands or originated as area committees, most federally unrecognized Algonquin communities are still located within the watersheds where historic Algonquin communities were situated. The rivers fed the people and provided transportation, linking each community into the larger confederacy that historically constituted Algonquin nationhood. This book follows this organization, focusing on contemporary communities according to the watersheds in which they are situated. This approach also enables an exploration of the diverse ways in which the communities of each watershed represent differing contemporary manifestations of a broader and more cohesive past.

A final note should be made concerning federal recognition. In order to negotiate a comprehensive claim in a context where the majority of Algonquins are not federally recognized, Canada has been forced to *provisionally* recognize an entity known as the Algonquin Nation Tribal Council, which represents non-status Algonquins, in order to negotiate with them. However, this entity has no formal federal recognition *outside* of this process. For example, if the negotiations were to break down for good, the Algonquin Nation Tribal Council and its constituent communities could not make other claims on Canada or the provinces as federally recognized Algonquins. For non-status Algonquins, then, federal recognition depends on the successful conclusion of the comprehensive claims process.

Structure of the Book

In order to focus on identity, in an organic sense, for federally unrecognized Algonquins, *Fractured Homeland* is organized into parts that correspond to the various Ontario watersheds in which Algonquins live. Part 1, however, is a general overview, exploring the questions of history and identity with which resurgent groups must grapple in their effort to reconstitute themselves as peoples. Chapter 1 engages with the collective history shared by all Algonquins. It sketches the parameters of their historical existence in their entire homeland, when the Kiji Sibi (now known as the Ottawa River) was the centre of their identity, rather than the site of their division into Quebec and Ontario Algonquins; the chapter also discusses how they struggled against encroaching

Europeans. Chapter 2 examines the colonial divisions experienced by Algonquins, including the effects of the partition of their territory into two provinces and their subsequent categorization into status Indians and non-status Algonquins. In the interests of clarity, Chapter 3 focuses on the underlying framework of Canadian constitutional and policy issues that define what Algonquins have at stake in terms of their rights as Indigenous people in negotiating a comprehensive claim with Canada. Concepts of Aboriginal rights and title, the meaning of treaties, and the comprehensive claims process itself are scrutinized here.

Chapter 4 provides both a brief history of the Algonquin land claim, as the means by which Ontario Algonquins have attempted to reclaim their homeland, and an overview of the divisions created in the process. Chapter 5 then takes up questions of identity more broadly, exploring the parameters of resurgence for non-status Algonquins who are struggling to understand themselves as Indian under the extreme pressure of a major land claim despite generations of silence in their families about Indigenous identity.

The next four parts of the book, based primarily on interviews and existing literature, explore contemporary Algonquin communities in four different watersheds in Ontario. Part 2 focuses on the southeastern region of the territory, where three rivers – the Mississippi, the Rideau, and the lower Madawaska – draw together. This area, one of the first to face settler encroachment in the early eighteen hundreds, was also the first site where Ontario Algonquins were promised a land base. Although this land base was not subsequently surveyed and was then overrun by settlers, this region is home to one of the oldest and best-documented of the federally unrecognized communities – Ardoch Algonquin First Nation. As this community has engaged in several efforts to protect the land, its history will be extensively examined, as will that of more recent communities in the watershed, which have formed in reaction to the land claim. Indeed, Part 2 provides a virtual case study on how the land claim has divided the people of this region, with the most complete articulation of how divisions within and between communities have been created and maintained.

Part 3 examines the communities located in the watersheds of the Bonnechere and Petawawa Rivers. This area contains the federally recognized reserve known as Pikwakanagan (initially called Golden Lake) as well as three federally unrecognized communities. Although the unrecognized communities encompass many individuals whose ancestors did not move to Pikwakanagan and who were therefore never granted Indian status, there is also a sizeable number of individuals in these communities whose ancestors were members of

Pikwakanagan and who lost their status primarily because of gender discrimination in the Indian Act.[2] The tensions between these communities and Pikwakanagan are therefore all the more poignant for these individuals, who feel rejected by their "real" community, Pikwakanagan, simply because, under the complexities of identity legislation in the Indian Act, they cannot regain their Indian status.

Part 4 looks at the last Algonquins to face settler encroachment in the Ottawa Valley, who were granted land in the headlands of their traditional territory, the upper Madawaska River, but were subsequently forced out when a huge provincial park, ironically named Algonquin Park, was created there. The communities they later formed along the Madawaska and York Rivers will be explored here.

Part 5 examines the Algonquins whose families were historically situated along the Ottawa River itself and who today live in small towns on either side of the river. At Mattawa, along the northwestern section of the river (which also encompasses the northern boundary of the land claim), there are two Algonquin communities – one that predates the land claim and one that originated as an area committee. This area is also unique in that it contains a distinct historical Metis community that was central to defining Metis rights under the *Powley* case.[3] In a context where Pikwakanagan has frequently dismissed the claims of non-status Algonquins by asserting that they are "really" Metis, the distinctive differences manifested between Metis and Algonquins in this region are important. Near the southeast end of the river, in Ottawa itself, is a small community of Algonquins who have been drawn into Ottawa to work and live. And around Pembroke, near Morrison's Island, where the ancient Kichesipirini Algonquins were once powerful enough to demand tolls from anybody who wished to travel along the Ottawa River, the descendants of the "people of the island" have re-formed into a community, part of whose homeland now comes under the Province of Quebec but who mostly live in Ontario. Because the Ottawa River forms the provincial boundary between Quebec and Ontario, the communities along it live daily with the fracturing of their homeland into the two provinces, since their membership (and sometimes their territories) spans both sides of the river. They are also aware that the river itself cannot be protected when jurisdictional boundaries place it between current Algonquin land claims in both Ontario and Quebec.

The final chapter of this book focuses broadly on Algonquinness itself and on what can be generalized about Algonquin identity and nationhood. From their initial encounter with Samuel de Champlain in 1603, Algonquins have experienced over four hundred years of extensive contact, first with missionaries and explorers, then with fur traders, lumbermen, settlers, and miners, and finally with those involved in hydro and nuclear development. In Ontario particularly, they have faced a settler society that developed during the early days of Canada's formation and that has enveloped them almost entirely for nearly two centuries. The truly amazing reality that the research reveals is that despite the changes wrought by settlers, a distinct non-status Algonquin identity remains in Ontario today.

Research and the Literature

This book is the result of seven years of research and seventy-odd interviews conducted with federally unrecognized Algonquins in Ontario. It also includes a handful of interviews with non-status Algonquins living in Quebec. In the interests of hearing divergent perspectives, interviews were also conducted with Algonquins who have status, primarily from Pikwakanagan, but also with individuals originating from Quebec reserves who reside in Ontario.

It is important to address some of the methodological issues that arose during this project. The first problem is the profoundly fragmented nature of the research. Most academics have focused on Quebec Algonquins. Perhaps this is not surprising: as northern land-based people, many of whom have retained their language, Quebec Algonquins are more "interesting" to anthropologists than those in Ontario, most of whom speak only English and are more dependent on a wage economy. However, anthropological interest has generally been quite site-specific, featuring in-depth research with a handful of Quebec communities. There are no comparative studies of Algonquins in different communities, even across Quebec, let alone across the provincial boundary. Furthermore, the sporadic references to urban non-status Algonquins in Quebec within the literature inevitably describe them as "Metis" and portray them as simply being acculturated and therefore "less Algonquin," rather than suggesting that they might represent a different experience of Algonquinness than their reserve-based status Indian counterparts.

All of the published work on Ontario Algonquins concentrates on Pikwakanagan, as the only federally recognized Algonquin reserve in the province, and has therefore reproduced the colonial categories that render non-status Algonquins invisible. However, recent primary research has provided valuable data addressing the histories of some of the federally unrecognized communities. One example is the eight-volume report on the Golden Lake land claim that was prepared by Joan Holmes and Associates in 1993 for the Ontario Native Secretariat. Ostensibly about Pikwakanagan, the report includes such wide-ranging research on the entire Algonquin Nation, particularly from government archives, that it has unwittingly provided significant details on the histories of many federally unrecognized communities. *Fractured Homeland* is the first publication to extensively utilize the historical data from this report.

Additional unpublished documents exist for only one federally unrecognized community: a number of graduate dissertations have focused on the histories, identities, and land-based struggles of Ardoch Algonquin First Nation. None of the other federally unrecognized communities have been researched by academics, although the Bonnechere Algonquin Community conducted its own oral history research and produced a slim volume of these histories in the late 1990s. Reports on Algonquin Park archaeological sites were provided to me by members of the Whitney community, and information about the Bancroft community was available online.

Other primary documents were shared by the communities themselves. The website for the Algonquins and Nipissings of Greater Golden Lake routinely posts crucial primary material relating to the land claim, including handbills, reports of public meetings, and newspaper articles, which supplied valuable information. The Sharbot Lake community provided me with a number of newspaper clippings relating to its activities in 2003 (when I interviewed the leader of the community). However, by far the greatest number of primary documents came from the personal files of Harold Perry and Robert Lovelace of Ardoch Algonquin First Nation. By 2004, they had accumulated drawers of file folders containing newsletters, reports of meetings dating back over twenty years, newspaper and magazine clippings on the "rice war" of 1982, transcripts of testimony at trials and hearings in which Ardoch had taken part, and general documents relating to the land claim. These primary sources furnished much of the information about the early years of the claim (prior to 2002) as well as a wealth of material about Ardoch's history. Ultimately, far more written information was available for Ardoch than for the other federally unrecognized communities. As a result, for most of the other communities, I have had to rely solely on my interviews and a few written sources, with the inevitable consequence that the information is sketchier for these communities.

A second problem was the intensity of the meaning of Indian status for many Algonquins. Most individuals whom I interviewed at Pikwakanagan requested anonymity because they wished to avoid community censure for going "on record" as questioning the meaning of Indian status or expressing sympathy for the concerns of non-status Algonquins. Pikwakanagan's leader, Kirby Whiteduck, agreed to be interviewed but clearly saw me as potentially biased against Pikwakanagan because of my interest in the federally unrecognized communities; nevertheless, he provided valuable information about Pikwakanagan itself.

I encountered a third difficulty, which proved insurmountable, when I attempted to expand my research into Quebec. Two leaders of Quebec reserves expressed skepticism regarding my work with the Ontario non-status communities; in their view, the only "real" Algonquins in Ontario lived at Pikwakanagan. Ultimately, the two tribal councils in Quebec, each for very different reasons, denied me permission to extend my research into the nine Quebec First Nations that they represented. In any case, given the size of the Algonquin territory there, the language differences, and the number of communities involved, doing an adequate job would have been a daunting task that would have demanded several additional years of research. Nevertheless, the work suffers by its truncation at the Ontario-Quebec border. It is my hope that other Indigenous researchers will focus on the rebuilding of Algonquin nationhood in Quebec and that their work, in conjunction with this book, will provide a much expanded and clearer picture of Algonquin people today and of their beautiful – if fractured – homeland.

Finally, Algonquin resurgence in Ontario, involving a struggle for federal recognition through a land claim, has brought about its own kind of fragmentation. This affected the research in a number of ways. First, the Tri-Council Policy on Research with Aboriginal People required me, as a funded researcher, to obtain the approval of the Aboriginal leadership in each community before I began research within the community.[4] It also suggests that researchers should, wherever possible, submit their results to the leadership of each community before publishing, to ensure that they have not inadvertently caused problems for the community. However, this policy, developed with federally recognized Aboriginal communities in mind who increasingly have developed straightforward research protocols for researchers to follow, was of little assistance when conducting research with non-status communities involved in a land claim. In many instances, the research involved multiple new communities that were internally fragmented and sometimes in opposition to each other or divided within themselves. Furthermore, in most of the communities that were created for the purpose of the land claim, one individual typically represents several hundred people and sometimes close to a thousand. For many of these communities, multiple dissident voices opposed the policies and practices of their appointed leaders. In such a context, privileging the perspectives of individual leaders within the communities was not possible; I did interview the leaders first, but there was no question of their providing final permission relating to what I published.

A second land-claim-related problem arose when four community leaders whom I interviewed in 2003 subsequently became Algonquin negotiation representatives (ANRs) when the land claim resumed in 2004. Because all communications relating to the claim must go through the claim's chief negotiator, Bob Potts, ANRs are not permitted to speak with researchers, and researchers therefore cannot quote individual ANRs relating to the land claim. Given that the interviews with these community leaders focused entirely on the land claim, I was therefore unable to include any quotes from these individuals at all, or indeed, to contact them about the research that I had conducted. Although I have paraphrased some aspects of their words and included information that they shared with me, the usual research process of seeking permission from these individuals on behalf of their communities could not be followed in this instance. This stipulation also meant that I could not interview the leaders of two other communities – one in Bancroft and one in Mattawa.[5] Because of this, my ability to interview members of their communities was compromised. This major gap in the research was mitigated to some extent by individuals residing in Toronto who were knowledgeable members of the two communities in question and who were willing to provide me with information. My writing concerning these communities therefore relies primarily on historical documentation supplemented by a handful of interviews.

As an outsider, I could not have obtained in-depth interviews with many activists, elders, and community people had I not been assisted by two Algonquin individuals – Heather Majaury and Paula LaPierre – who worked on the project as research assistants in 2005. An additional important source of information came from the informal e-mail networks of concerned Algonquins, to which a number of individuals kindly gave me access. Algonquins use these networks to share an extensive array of detailed information – from copies of their correspondence with the chief negotiator Bob Potts and the responses they received, to the latest events in their communities. Some shared how they had broken away from their communities and formed new entities, having the requisite 125 members required to constitute a community under the land claim. Still others circulated documents (including the letters they had received from the leader of their land claim community formally expelling them as dissidents). Others wrote vociferously and tirelessly on the claim process and shared their newspaper and academic articles relating to the subject. For a specific interval, particularly when the land claim changed from its pre-2004 format to the contemporary framework of negotiations, this e-mail network provided articulate arguments, passionate oratory, and the most up-to-date news about the ever-changing claim developments across the territory. Although a condition of being privy to this information was that I would not replicate it, it contributed valuable background material that is central to this book. These e-mails supplied tangible evidence of how difficult the land claim is for Algonquins and of the resultant divisions in various communities, but it also revealed that though those who negotiated the claim sometimes seemed to speak with a uniform voice, regardless of which community they claimed to represent, the discourse *within* the communities themselves came from intensely local experiences and concerns, varying broadly throughout the region. In this respect, although e-mail consists of text, the immediacy through which it traded news and the vocal and articulate commentary that accompanied it showed that contemporary Algonquins are using e-mail to preserve community life across distances – in essence, to revive and maintain a part of their oral tradition.

The intensifying pressures facing communities due to the land claim affected my research in both subtle and obvious ways. For example, while the project was under way, many community members became increasingly reluctant to talk to outsiders. In 2003, when the land claim was in abeyance, individuals were quite eager to be interviewed; in 2004, they were also eager to be interviewed to discuss the changes in the regime. The willingness of community people to speak with outsiders began to diminish in 2005, as conflicts relating to the land claim intensified. By 2006, most of the people I interviewed were either dissidents seeking alternatives to the direction their community or the land claim was taking or were urban individuals discussing their understandings of their Algonquinness. In 2007 and 2008, only a handful of new individuals consented to be interviewed. In the years after that, most of the research concentrated on updating material via discussions with many people who had been interviewed much earlier. With a handful of new interviews conducted in late 2009, seven years of research were concluded.

This temporal process has had a regional effect as well. The communities in southeastern and southcentral Ontario, which lie relatively close to urban centres and where a network of individuals referred me to other individuals, were relatively well interviewed. However, this was not the case in other areas, particularly around Algonquin Park, at Mattawa and in Bancroft, where very few people consented to be interviewed, and those who did subsequently changed their mind. As a result, in some locations, only the broadest parameters of community experience are described in rudimentary ways, whereas in other areas, the nuances and complexities of local community life are more clearly delineated.

Finally, some communities are described in depth over time, due to my ongoing connections with them, whereas others are presented only at the specific moment when a small range of interviews took place. In many respects, then, this book constitutes a series of snapshots of an evolving people at particular phases of their development and cannot claim to be a comprehensive overview, either spatially or temporally. Nevertheless, it does attempt to sketch a range of experiences and contemporary meanings of Algonquinness for those people whose homelands are on the Ontario side of the Kiji Sibi, whose ancestors fought so hard to survive in the face of settler engulfment, and who are currently struggling with a high-stakes process – a comprehensive claim – that will profoundly affect their futures.

PART 1

Algonquin Survival and Resurgence

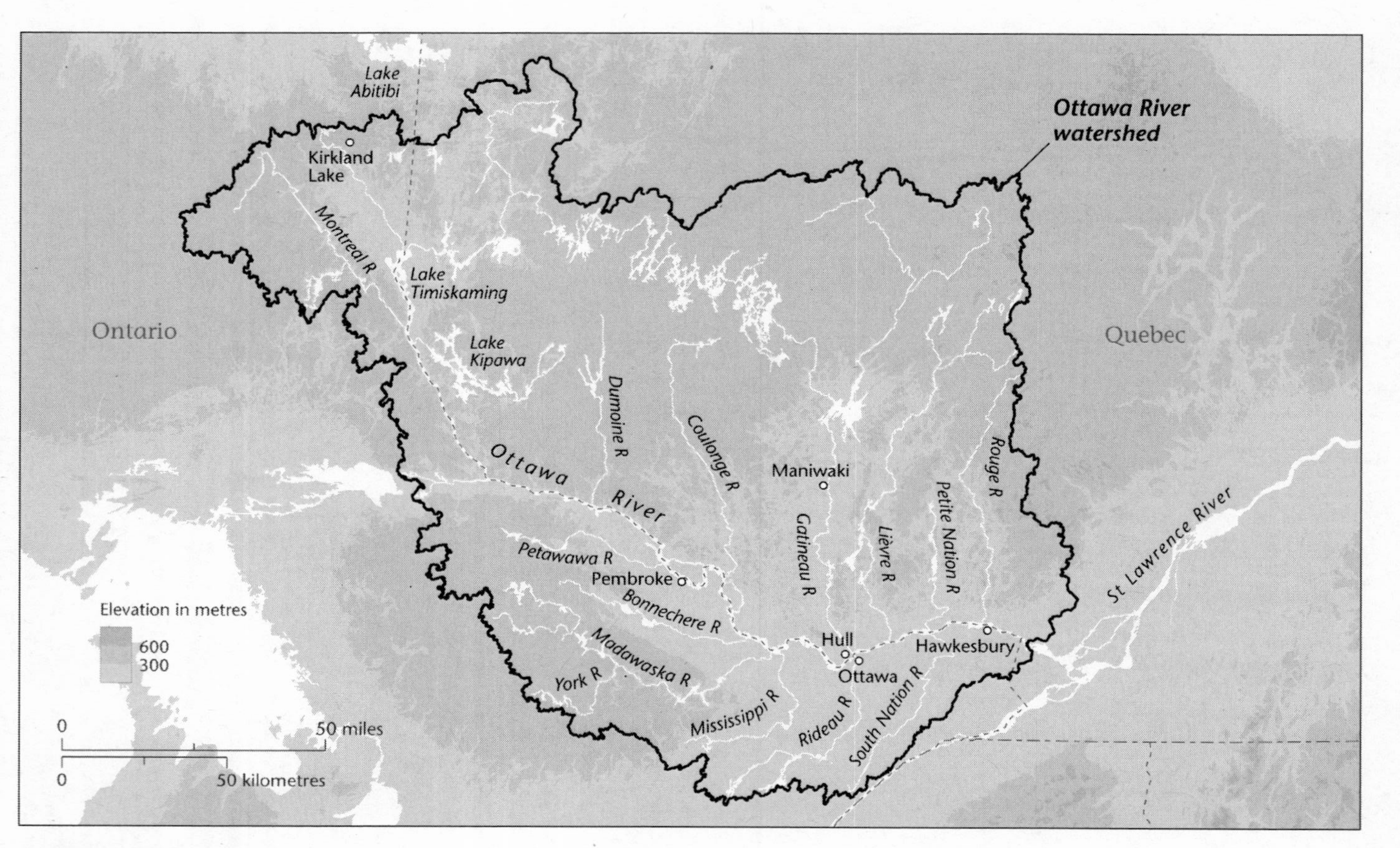

The Ottawa River watershed

1

Diplomacy, Resistance, and Dispossession

The Kiji Sibi, which the French correctly called the Great River of the Algonquins and the English misnamed the Ottawa River, has one of the largest natural watersheds in Eastern Canada, covering approximately 148,000 square kilometres (Ottawa River Regulation Planning Board 1984). The people of the Great River, today named Algonquins,[1] have occupied the watershed since time immemorial.[2] Although their territories have been extensive, those living in the lower Ottawa River watershed have gradually come to refer to themselves as the Omamiwininiwak, the "downriver" people (Morrison 2005, 26). Their territory, stretching south from Mattawa to Point L'Orignal near present-day Hawkesbury and encompassing all the lands drained by the Ottawa River and its tributaries, is included in the Ontario land claim. The Algonquins upriver, along the northern tributaries of the Ottawa as well as the upper Ottawa itself, generally refer to themselves as the Anishnabeg, or sometimes the Irini (now Inini).[3] For example, the Timiskaming Algonquins call themselves Saugeen Anishnabeg, and the Algonquins of Barriere Lake still call themselves Mitcikinabik Inik, named after the "place of the stone fence or weir," which the French called Barriere Lake (ibid., 20-21).

Prior to the advent of Europeans, Algonquins controlled the Kiji Sibi, a strategic point on the routes linking the St. Lawrence River to Hudson and Ungava Bays and to the Great Lakes. Thus, they were centrally involved in wide-ranging trade networks that extended from the Gulf of Mexico to Hudson Bay and from the Atlantic coast to the Rockies (Hessel 1993; Côté 1996).[4] Indeed, we can only conjecture that the language group known as Algonquian

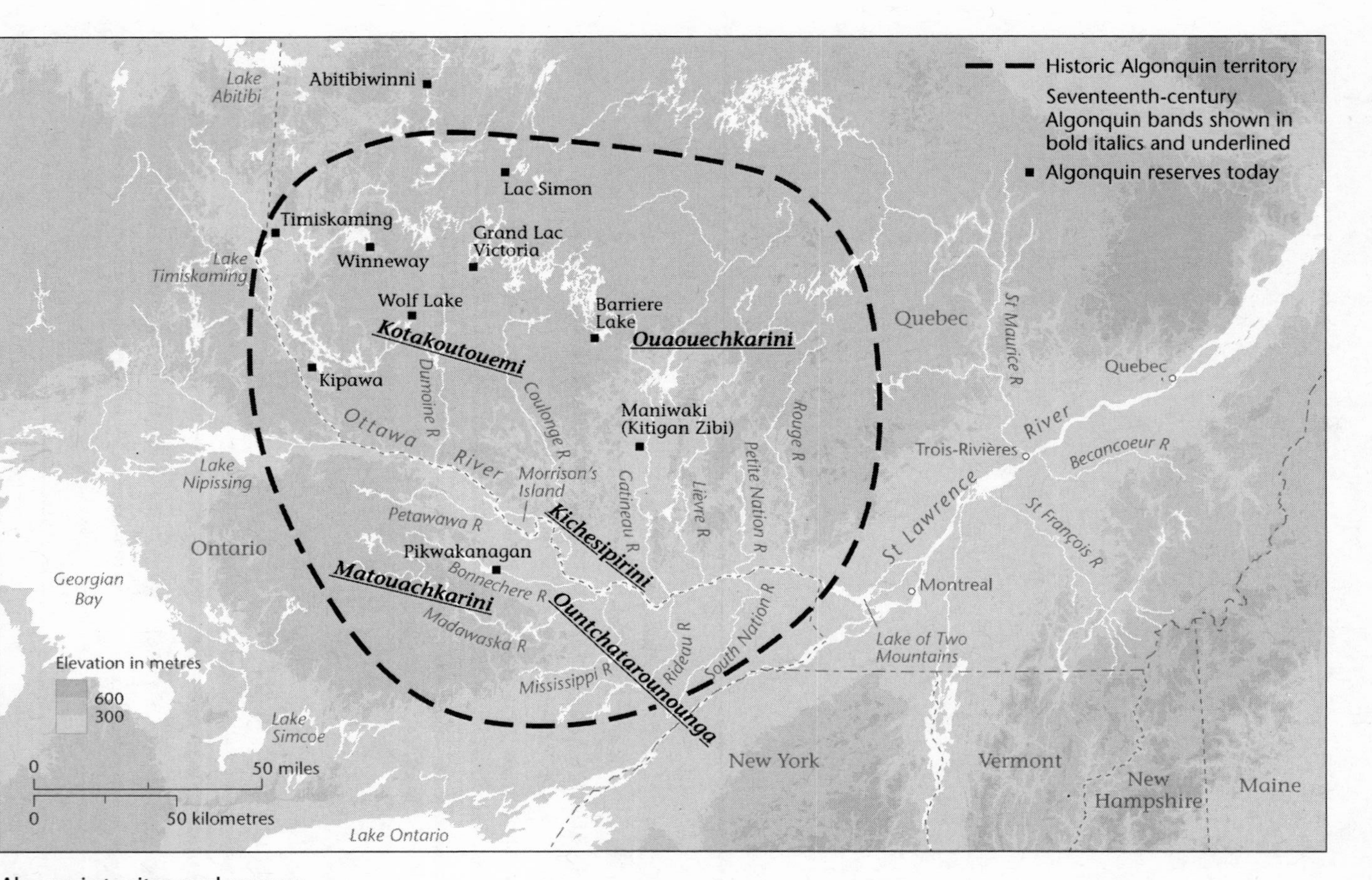

Algonquin territory and reserves

may have been given its name by Europeans precisely because of the key trade role played by Algonquins for thousands of years.

If one looks at the Ottawa River watershed today, often described as part of Canada's "heartland," the Algonquin presence seems to have been entirely erased. Only Mattawa retains its Algonquin name, Matawang, "where the rivers divide" (there, the upper Ottawa River joins the Mattawa River to form the lower Ottawa). Further south, lower Ottawa River names such as Long Sault, La Chaudière, and Calumet and Allumette Islands reflect the long years of French colonization. And yet, as James Morrison (2005) points out, most of these names are actually French translations of Algonquin words. For example, Champlain chose "Sault de la Chaudière" as the name for the rapids near Ottawa because the churning water resembles a boiling kettle. This name is a translation of the Algonquin *asticou,* or *akikok,* which means "boiler."[5] Similarly, the twenty kilometres of rapids near Lake of Two Mountains, known to the Algonquins as Quenechouan or Kindodjiwan (the long rapids), was renamed Long Sault. The rapids that Algonquins called Opwagani pawatik, or "pipe rapids," because the area yielded a stone suitable for making tobacco pipes, were renamed by Champlain Sault des Calumets, or the Calumet Rapids (*calumet* is the French word for the Algonquin ceremonial pipe). Allumette Island (*allumette* is French for matches) refers to the reeds, used as tapers by the Algonquins, that grow abundantly at the island (Bond 1966, 5). Despite the renaming of the Kiji Sibi landmarks and the imposition of an anglicized or gallicized settler veneer on the watershed, the land remains Algonquin, and an abiding Algonquin presence and sense of place survives that more than four hundred years of colonial incursion has never succeeded in uprooting or destroying.

To address the history of Algonquin relations with Canada is to address the formation of Canada itself, for the Ottawa River became a vitally strategic route between French fur traders on the St. Lawrence River and the Native groups to the north and west of the Ottawa Valley. Subsequently, the river became the boundary line between French and English settlement. In a sense, the Ottawa Valley, with the St. Lawrence, was central to the colonization project of both the French and British regimes.

The French Regime in Algonquin Country

Samuel de Champlain first encountered Algonquins in the Ottawa River watershed in 1603, and his journals document his subsequent visits to their villages in 1613. His writing reveals that distinct Algonquin groups lived throughout the watershed: these included the Kichesipirini on Morrison's and Allumette Islands near the present-day town of Pembroke; the Ouaouechkarini (or Weskarini), who lived along the Lievre, Petite Nation, and Rouge Rivers; the Kotakoutouemi, who occupied the Coulonge and Dumoine watersheds; the Kinouchepirini, or Quenongebin, whose territory was between the Petawawa and Bonnechere Rivers; the Matouachkarini (or Matouweskarini), who occupied the Madawaska River region; and the Ountchatarounounga (or Onontchataronon), who lived along the Mississippi, Rideau, and South Nation Rivers.[6] The Native people around Lakes Abitibi, Timiskaming, and Nipissing were mentioned as early as 1640 by the *Jesuit Relations* (Joan Holmes and Associates 1993, 2:27) and were subsequently acknowledged as speaking a language in common with other Algonquins (Laflamme 1979, 2). Although Nipissing chiefs represented distinct Nipissing communities during the summer social, spiritual, and political gatherings at Lake of Two Mountains, both the Algonquin and Nipissing Nations were closely linked culturally and politically, so that in later struggles to assert territorial rights over the lower Ottawa River, the term "Algonquin" applied to both Algonquin and Nipissing rights (Sarazin 1989, 171-72).

According to Gilles Havard (2001, 27, 30-31), two Indigenous-European alliance networks developed in seventeenth-century eastern North America, reflecting previous Indigenous alliance patterns. Based in what is now upstate New York, the Iroquois Confederacy allied with the Dutch when they claimed what is now New York City; after the English took over, the confederacy formed an alliance with them through a series of 1677 treaties at Albany known as the Covenant Chain. The French maintained several Algonquian allies, ranging from the Wabanaki Confederacy in the Maritimes, to the Montagnais and Algonquins north of the St. Lawrence, to the Great Lakes nations including the Nipissings, Odawas, Ojibways, Pottawatomis, Miamis, Illinois, Sauks, Foxes, Mascoutens, Kickapoos, and Winnebagos.

Although Indigenous people resorted to warfare when diplomacy failed, most clashes were minor, brief, and strategic; similarly, when vendettas occurred between clans or nations to appease honour, they were small-scale and highly symbolic. The alliances cemented with Europeans, however, transformed this pattern so that warfare became large-scale and deadly, utilizing European weapons and amplified by rivalries between Britain and France. In such a context, the British and the French encouraged or even fomented wars between their respective allies in order to weaken each other's foothold in the territories (since neither could maintain their North American colonies without

Native allies). This tremendous breakdown in diplomacy affected all Indigenous nations, but those of the Iroquois Confederacy, particularly the Mohawks, who occupied the buffer zone between the British and the French, were overwhelmingly embroiled in warfare on a continuous basis. Because of this, they increasingly attacked other nations, primarily to obtain captives to replace individuals lost in warfare with Britain's enemies. Indeed, basing his estimate on numerous accounts, Havard (2001, 49) suggests that by the 1660s, two-thirds of some Iroquois Confederacy nations were composed of captives who had become naturalized members of the confederacy through adoption into the matrilineal clan systems.

For French explorers, missionaries, and fur traders, a central figure – indeed, a central obstacle in accessing Indigenous territories – was Tessouat, the leader of the Kichesipirini Algonquins of Morrison's and Allumette Islands. For twenty years, until his death in 1636, Tessouat and the Kichesipirini confounded the desires of the French to use the Ottawa River to penetrate further north into Huron/Wendat territory and ultimately onward to the Great Lakes in order to establish their own trading forts. For the Algonquins, allowing the French to use their lands as a conduit to other nations represented a violation of their territorial integrity. Because the Kichesipirini held the narrows of the Ottawa at the fortress-like Morrison's Island as well as Allumette Island, Tessouat was able to assert a monopoly on the trade passing through his territory. The Kichesipirini were so important to the French that in 1620 Champlain sent the young Jean Nicollet to live with them and attempted unsuccessfully to persuade Tessouat to support the French.

But Tessouat's focus was broader than simply amplifying Kichesipirini power. Aware that the connections with the French had resulted in the collapse of Indigenous diplomacy and recognizing that conversion to Christianity threatened the ability of Algonquins – and indeed of other Indigenous nations – to resist the French presence, Tessouat strategized to stop the spread of the militaristic Jesuit order north of Algonquin territory by attempting to undermine its conversion efforts among the Huron/Wendat. Master strategists themselves, the Jesuits laboured unsuccessfully to promote Tessouat's acceptance of a French presence in the Algonquin homeland (Jury 2000).

However, the Algonquins could not indefinitely stop the spread of French influence through their territory. Shortly after Tessouat's death, the French, who had ostensibly been allies of the Algonquins against the nations of the Iroquois Confederacy, negotiated a separate peace with the Mohawks at Trois-Rivières (Havard 2001, 54). Through this alliance, the French were able to rely on the Iroquois, traditionally their enemies, to attack the Algonquins, who, though nominally their allies, had for too long kept the French from expanding up the Ottawa River. The 1647 massacre of the Kichesipirini broke the Algonquin stronghold; the defences of Morrison's Island could no longer impede the French. Nor could the Iroquois attacks be held back; from 1650 until about 1675, due to the intensity of attacks, primarily by the Mohawks, numerous Algonquins were forced to vacate their homelands. Many sought shelter at Trois-Rivières on the St. Maurice River or with the Sulpician mission in Montreal (which was eventually relocated to Oka at Lake of Two Mountains) (Trigger 1994, 794). Others sought the more remote and inaccessible parts of their territory. While the Algonquins were in disarray, the French managed to obtain a toehold in their territory, establishing posts at Lake Timiskaming, Fort Coulonge, and the mouth of the Dumoine River (Joan Holmes and Associates 1993, 2:20). When the Algonquins were able to reoccupy their entire homeland and their populations recovered, they reasserted their control over the Ottawa and its tributaries but could not completely close the river to Europeans. Still, years would pass before Europeans managed to penetrate the many rivers that fed the Ottawa.

One result of the forced migration in the 1650s is that a number of Algonquins remained in permanent alliance with the Montagnais and therefore continued to share the edge of Montagnais territory between the St. Maurice River and the Ottawa River watershed. An 1849 estimate noted that about a thousand Algonquin families (four to five thousand individuals) utilized the tributaries of the St. Maurice as their hunting grounds (ibid., 129-30). Another result is that Algonquin communities as far north as the height of land (the elevation dividing the Arctic watershed from that of the St. Lawrence/Great Lakes) still maintain oral histories of their seventeenth-century encounters with the Iroquois (Emmaline McPherson, Beaverhouse First Nation, author interview, July 2003).

Ultimately, the Iroquois Confederacy and many Algonquian nations, devastated by years of warfare, began pursuing initiatives to overcome the breakdown of Indigenous diplomacy that had developed with the European presence. At the same time, as continuous warfare among Indigenous nations began to interfere with French trading, particularly along the Great Lakes, the French, too, began to explore the possibilities of peace. Havard (2001, 71, 122) suggests, however, that the French sought a peace treaty to pre-empt the possibility that a large-scale Indigenous alliance might develop independently of their influence. The Great Peace of Montreal in 1701 brought together thirteen hundred representatives of forty Indigenous nations. The leader who signed on behalf of the Algonquins, using the Crane symbol, had defeated the

Onondagas in one of the last battles between the Algonquins and the Iroquois before the Great Peace.

Interpreting Algonquin History

One difficulty encountered by contemporary Algonquins in their attempts to re-create their nationhood is the lack of widely available, cohesive knowledge of what *historical* Algonquin nationhood looked like. From the earliest days of European contact, missionaries wrote extensively about the Algonquins; these included Gabriel Sagard, a lay brother in the Recollets, and the Jesuits, who, between 1611 and 1760, travelled throughout Algonquin country in the course of their mission work.[7] These, as well as fur traders and other visitors, provided descriptions (albeit through Eurocentric eyes) of Algonquins at the time of contact and during the subsequent period in which trade with Europeans, warfare, and disease became regular features of their lives. From these accounts, a number of anthropologists and historians have attempted to theorize the Algonquin past.

Unfortunately for Algonquins, European biases about the "primitive" nature of Algonquian societies permeate the primary documents. In general, Europeans perceived the more sedentary Native groups such as the Iroquoians as more civilized than the Algonquians. The Iroquoians cultivated large fields and had obvious fixed territories and visibly structured forms of governance, whereas most Algonquians, as so-called hunter-gatherer bands, were often depicted as lacking even territorial boundaries and certainly as lacking higher-order governance. Due to these biases, early Europeans failed to realize that the Algonquins had a social order that allowed them to maintain internal relations throughout the Ottawa River watershed; nor did they perceive that the Algonquin Nation had consistent diplomatic goals with nations located outside the watershed. Secondary sources often absorb these assumptions without questioning them. Gordon Day (1979), for example, notes, "It is doubtful that there was ever a politically united Algonquin nation – even in Champlain's time there were several Algonquin bands, each with its own chief." Relying on the journals of Champlain, Bruce Trigger (1985, 175-81) assumes that the Algonquin social order had not progressed beyond the band level and depicts Algonquin interactions with the French as those of small groups, each pursuing its own short-sighted economic goals as it competed with other groups for the French trade. By comparison, Trigger portrays the Wendat more sympathetically, presumably because they were Iroquoians who farmed large fields, maintained permanent villages, and had a formal confederacy structure with a higher-order council of fifty chiefs, and thus their values and way of life resembled those of European nation-states more closely than did those of any of the Algonquian peoples.

Fortunately, recent research by Meyer and Thistle (1995), David Meyer (1985), and Meyer, Gibson, and Russell (2008) conducted with various Algonquian communities in northern Ontario and Manitoba has improved our understanding of how nationhood was historically maintained among many Algonquian peoples. The research demonstrates that, because of their reliance on hunting, governance for many Algonquian peoples was maintained on three distinct levels – family, band, and nation, depending on the time of year. In the winter, extended family groups, consisting of related adults and their kin, retreated to their family hunting territory (and later the traplines) for survival. This extended family group controlled a specific territory; thus, it was bound to observe ecological practices to avoid over-hunting or over-trapping and therefore collapsing the local ecosystem upon which it relied for survival.

In the early spring, the larger band, whose jurisdiction was a specific region in the watershed, generally assembled for the goose hunt and remained together for fishing runs and the plentiful gathering of different foods from early to mid-summer. Often the larger band would also meet in the fall, to engage in wild rice harvesting (where applicable) and to ensure that resources were coordinated and shared among families that were ill or infirm, had lost their hunters, or whose territories had been devastated by fire or flood. In general, relations between families were dealt with at the band level, as were celebrations of the winter's births and mourning the winter's deaths.

Finally, the constituent bands were part of a confederated gathering of bands that formed a nation, which generally met for several weeks or at times even for a couple of months in midsummer to address internal diplomatic relations among the bands as well as external diplomatic relations and treaty making with other nations. These nations were therefore essentially federations of bands, who together controlled a specific region, generally a larger watershed. The larger national gatherings often took place at sacred sites and generally lasted for several weeks. At these gatherings, ceremonies were also conducted to observe sacred events, marriage partners were obtained and marriages effected, and the stories and songs that preserved the collective knowledge base of the nation were sung and performed. Games and feasting occurred at these gatherings, as did hosting other nations for trade and treaty making. As Meyer and Thistle (1995, 406) summarize it, these gatherings enabled nations to maintain complex social, spiritual, political, and economic functions even though their members were dispersed for much of the year. They were the means by which a sense of community and cultural oneness within the nation were maintained.

This picture of historical Algonquian governance developed by the above writers appears applicable to Algonquins. Like early fur traders, explorers, and missionaries who noted the existence of cohesive bands in each region of the Algonquin homeland, historical sources such as James Morrison (2005) and Meredith Jean Black (1993) have also described how the Algonquin bands who occupied specific territories regularly gathered together in the summer months. This suggests that, due to their reliance on different parts of their territories and various modes of subsistence at differing times of the year, nationhood for Algonquins functioned temporally rather than spatially, along the model of a confederated structure. Territories were held by families and in total by the band, which in turn gathered together at the nation level. Orators spoke at the nation level, and when pressing affairs with other nations arose, gatherings to decide on diplomatic stances could last a very long time. For Algonquins, affiliations at the clan level also bound members of different bands together in ceremonial functions, which allowed more cohesiveness within the larger nation than could always be maintained through semi-annual or annual meetings.

With the European presence and its associated pressures, many of the best Algonquin orators became known more formally as grand chiefs who spoke for the entire nation in international contexts; however, they spoke only after considerable and careful consultation at all levels across the region, depending again on the richness and size of their watersheds.

Meyer and Russell (2004) have rejected the standard anthropological definitions of Algonquians as being "hunter-gatherer bands," a term that implies a lack of political sophistication. They have categorized collectivities of these "bands" as "nations" despite their small size because they represented distinct sociopolitical units that occupied particular territories and maintained formal diplomatic relations with other nations. Moreover, the historical records clearly labelled these Indigenous peoples as "nations," reflecting not only how other Native groups perceived them, but how Europeans saw such entities themselves. For example, the Great Peace of Montreal in 1701 involved forty nations – France and thirty-nine Indigenous nations that gathered in Montreal to negotiate peace (Havard 2001, 111). Also, at the 1764 Conference of Foreign Nations at Niagara, the British invited the twenty-four Indigenous nations that had sided with them or with the French during the Seven Years' War to attend (Borrows 1997, 162).

In sociology and political theory, the term "nation" is often restricted to those bodies wielding the powers of states – that is, asserting sovereign authority over specific territories, maintaining a monopoly on the use of coercive force, and imposing order through a formal system of laws (Alfred 1999, 47-49, 57). Indeed, it was precisely the absence of such formal leadership structures and the coercive powers vested in European nation-states that enabled many Europeans to deny that Indigenous people *had* governments (Maaka and Fleras 2005, 191). Despite these Eurocentric understandings of nationhood and despite the fact that traditionally, the Algonquin nations maintained a flexible and minimal form of governance, with leaders who could only persuade rather than coerce, the reality was that the bands scattered across the territory conferred together at the national level to address the concerns of each community. Moreover, most Algonquian nations maintained (and still attempt to maintain) social balance through their cultural practices. Below, Plains Cree Metis writer Wanda McCaslin (2005, 88) addresses the relationship between law, language, and social practices in contemporary Indigenous nations:

> Law is embedded in our ways of thinking, living and being. For Indigenous peoples law is far more than rules to be obeyed. Law is found within our language, customs, and practices. It is found within the carefully balanced relations of our clan systems and our extended families. It is also found in ceremonies and rituals. Law is a whole way of life. Through countless means, our traditions teach us how to be respectful of others and mindful of how our actions affect them.
>
> In other words, to exist as Indigenous peoples is to live our law, which holds us in balance. Our communities are a part of the law, and our community members – be they Elders, respected leaders, family, or even our youth – protect law by preserving our cultures' worldviews and ways. These are not passed on through lectures or written codes. Instead, law is modelled for us daily through our languages, customs, behaviours and relationships. The closer we stay to our traditional ways, the more we internalize our law and its values, so that they exist among us as a natural, everyday expectation of what it means to "be a good relative" – not only with each other but with all beings.

For Indigenous peoples, then, nationhood was (and is) not a matter of size or of maintaining a formal government structure or a coercive state apparatus – it is a matter of the cohesiveness and respectful relations maintained internally through cultural practices and language.

In examining Algonquin contexts, one soon realizes that the bands referred to by Champlain and the Jesuits, including the Ouaouechkarini, the Kichesipirini, the Kotakoutouemi, the Kinouchepirini, the Matouachkarini, and the Ountchatarounounga, all of whom occupied the same territories as today's federally unrecognized Algonquins, were part of a larger Algonquin Nation that functioned primarily as a confederacy and gathered during the summer to share the collective business of the nation. These bands also maintained clans that cut across band structures and linked the people of the Ottawa River watershed in complex ways.

A number of sacred sites are known within the Ottawa River watershed – at Rock Lake in Algonquin Park, at Obadjiwan at the narrows of Lake Timiskaming, in the Baptiste Lake region on the York River system, and at Mazinaw Lake (to name only a few). Other gathering places undoubtedly included the spots where the French subsequently established trading posts (or missions) such as at Lake of Two Mountains. However, the sacred sites were probably the most extensively used areas for ceremonial gatherings.

It is essential to theorize about early Algonquin social organization because doing so challenges the historians and anthropologists who have uncritically relied on the primary sources to portray Algonquins as "primitive" bands and who have not perceived that Algonquin social order was complex and organized temporally, according to seasons, rather than spatially. Furthermore, theorizing about early Algonquin social organization provides a means of envisioning ways of re-creating nationhood. From the first, the land claim proceeded as if a singular centralized government would constitute the Algonquin Nation. A more appropriate approach might be to construct the re-created Algonquin Nation along the model of a treaty federation, with communities maintaining a certain degree of autonomy to allow for their distinct circumstances but gathering to sort out commonalities. However, such flexible governance forms would require a retraditionalization of Algonquin society, a possibility that will be explored later in a number of chapters.

Other aspects of historical writing about Algonquins also need revisiting to avoid the automatic adoption of colonialist assumptions. For example, in examining the writings of early missionaries and traders, Algonquin scholars such as Kirby Whiteduck have traced cultural continuities between seventeenth-century Algonquins and those of the nineteenth and even twentieth centuries. However, most commentators who interpret the early writings have not questioned common assumptions about the inevitable demise of Native societies in the face of "civilization" and so have tended to emphasize discontinuity and cultural loss for most Native peoples who encountered Europeans during this period. For federally unrecognized Algonquins in particular, their work enhances present-day colonial divisions rather than deconstructing them.

For instance, both Maurice Ratelle and Peter Hessel, discussing the brief interval during the seventeenth century when Algonquins were forced to vacate much of the Ottawa River watershed, have suggested that Algonquin nationhood was permanently broken at this time and that the nation never effectively reoccupied its homeland afterward. Relying entirely on missionary records, Ratelle (1996) asserts that, when peace was negotiated, warfare and disease had so diminished the Algonquins that they constituted only two small communities, one at Trois-Rivières and one at Lake of Two Mountains, which were subsequently removed to the Timiskaming, Maniwaki, and Golden Lake reserves. For his part, Hessel (1993, 58) sympathetically mourns "the extinction" of the communities along the Bonnechere, Madawaska, Mattawa, Mississippi, Rideau, and other rivers after 1650. The result is that both these historians – and others who make similar claims – replicate colonial divisions by implying that the only Algonquins currently in existence are those whose ancestors moved to today's reserves after surviving the seventeenth-century Iroquois wars. Such writings expunge federally unrecognized Algonquins from the historical record as effectively as the Department of Indian Affairs purged them from its official files.[8]

To interpret the seventeenth-century European documents as Ratelle and Hessel do depends on contemporary modernist assumptions that connections to place are trivial and truncated, and that the bonds between Algonquins and their family territories were therefore minor and easily relinquished. The reality is that complex technologies of adaptation are required for societies to flourish on the land. While conducting ethnobotanical research during the 1960s among four Algonquin communities in subarctic Quebec, where plant variety is very limited, Meredith Jean Black (1980, 65) learned that even after centuries of forced change under colonialism, the communities still consumed approximately forty local plants on a regular basis and that these plants comprised 98 percent of the vegetable foods they ate as well as 95 percent of their medicines. Robert Lovelace (2008) of Ardoch Algonquin First Nation in southeastern Ontario has noted that, with much greater levels of biodiversity at their disposal, the Algonquins of the southerly Ottawa River regions traditionally used over 240 local plants for food or medicine. The division of the watersheds into family territories was not solely for hunting – each area required local knowledge of the waterways where various types of fish were available and of the woodland sites where ash, birch, and cedar for basketry and canoes could be found and where sugar maples were plentiful for the sugar camps. It necessitated a careful knowledge not only of the areas where berries and wild roots were abundant, but where medicinal plants flourished and in what seasons. Finally, most families tended wild rice beds, which fed both themselves and the geese and ducks who congregated there and in turn provided another source of food. Clearly, Algonquins not only "occupied" these regions, they modified them according to their needs and were in turn *adapted* to them at every level. No band or family group would give up its territory lightly.

Indeed, historian James Morrison (2005) argues in support of a continuous presence of Algonquins in the watershed but suggests that throughout the eighteenth century, their identity became more complex. Those who gathered annually at Lake of Two Mountains eventually became Christianized and had strong ties to the Sulpician mission there, yet they remained there only during the summer months. Throughout the rest of the year, they joined those who never went to the mission – band members who resisted Christianization and who gathered at sacred sites rather than at the Sulpician mission, spending most of their time within their traditional territories. Morrison (ibid., 29) cites the example of the Wolf Lake First Nation (formerly the Dumoine band), whose membership traces its lineage equally from the non-Christian Anishnabeg on the upper Dumoine and Kipawa Rivers in the eighteenth century and the Otickwagamik (including several prominent chiefs) from the Nipissing village at Lake of Two Mountains.

Meredith Jean Black (1993) also supports this notion of changes to Algonquin identity with the appearance of the mission at Lake of Two Mountains. However, she posits that the Algonquins who spent their summers at the mission developed a sense of pan-Algonquin identity that they carried back to the non-Christian bands in the watersheds where they hunted throughout the year. Black writes that this may have helped to diminish the sense of identity at the band level (and presumably at the clan level) in favour of a more monolithic identity as Algonquins.

For people who rely on the land for their livelihood and have done so for millennia, connections to place are profound. Language, stories, and the sacred – even something as personal as immediate family histories – are tied to specific sites, which for many Algonquins still exist today.[9] Although the survivors of the seventeenth-century wars and epidemics were not as powerful or as numerous as formerly, and though a Christian influence undoubtedly began to affect their clan structure, they *did* return to the territories that they had traditionally occupied. And in every petition, appeal, and resolution that the Algonquins collectively addressed to the British Crown between 1791 and

1851, they always referred to the entire Ottawa River watershed as being divided into the territories of various families and communities.

By the mid-eighteenth century, as warfare between the British and the French intensified, the Great Peace of Montreal, which had been negotiated in 1701, had disintegrated. However, when the British and their Indian allies attacked the French at Montreal, Sir William Johnson, who became the first superintendent of Indian Affairs, asked the Algonquins to "stand aside." They did so, thereby establishing firm political relations between themselves and the British at the time of the French defeat (Sarazin 1989, 172).

Attempting to consolidate their hold over the territory that France was vacating, the British issued the Royal Proclamation of 1763. With this declaration, Britain established its claim to territories ranging from Florida and the Caribbean to Acadia and Quebec, and set out large sites of land to be awarded to its officers and troops (from five thousand acres for each officer down to fifty acres for each enlisted man). Although it acknowledged Native peoples' possession of their territories, it nevertheless claimed them as British but asserted that Britain could acquire them only via purchase or if their owners ceded them. The Royal Proclamation has been alternately viewed as a treaty, as the Crown's first acknowledgment of Indigenous landholding, and as a unilateral declaration that established the means by which Britain would be able to acquire Indigenous land.

However, regardless of colonial proclamations asserted in Britain, "on the ground" local British and French officials had long been required to observe Native forms of diplomacy, which were often exacting in detail and both costly and time consuming. In particular, the protocols for the use of wampum were very comprehensive. As Havard (2001, 22-23) notes, wampum conveyed voice and word; its purpose was to affirm and validate, in a ritualized way, the messages to be transmitted. No diplomacy could take place without it, and the acceptance or rejection of wampum signified the making or breaking of treaties. At treaty negotiations, orators could not address the group without first presenting strings of wampum. The strings were the simplest of offerings in diplomacy; for significant treaties, woven belts were given, with intricate patterns that symbolized the meaning of the treaty.

In 1763, with peacetime, the first order of business for British officials was to deal with the repercussions of the warfare that had afflicted Indigenous territories for a number of years. In preparation for the Conference of Foreign Nations, held at Niagara in 1764, the Algonquins and Nipissings visited the twenty-four Indigenous nations that had warred with either the British or the French to invite them to this peace conference. They took wampum strings and a printed copy of the Royal Proclamation with them (Borrows 1997, 162). At the Niagara conference, the question of trade on the Kiji Sibi, the "Great River of the Algonquins" as it was still known, was central, so the Algonquins figured heavily in the negotiations. To affirm their relationships with the Algonquins and other Indigenous nations that had been Britain's allies or enemies during its wars with France, the British gave three wampum belts to each nation in attendance. The British and Great Lakes Covenant Chain Confederacy Wampum Belt represented the covenant between Britain and the Great Lakes nations (including the Iroquois Confederacy, the Anishinabeg nations, the Wendat Nation, and many others that had been involved in conflicts with European powers). The Twenty-Four Nations Wampum Belt depicted the Anishinabeg nations (including the Algonquin) drawing a British vessel laden with presents across the Atlantic and anchoring it to North America. In accepting the two belts from the British, the Anishinabeg nations bound the British Crown to a promise that these alliances would be life giving and sustaining, not impoverishing (ibid., 163). The Gus Wen Tah, or the Two Row Wampum Belt, had been created for an early-seventeenth-century treaty between the Dutch and the Iroquois Confederacy to represent how the European and Indigenous nations would share the land, with respect and friendship, but with non-interference in each other's affairs. The Two Row Wampum had subsequently been negotiated with the British when they took over the Dutch territorial possession known as New Amsterdam. In 1764, Sir William Johnson renewed this promise to the Iroquois Confederacy and extended it to the Anishinabeg nations (ibid., 164-65). At Niagara, copies of each belt, woven by Haudenosaunee women, were given to each nation with which the British covenanted.

Below are new editions of the three belts, created by Algonquin scholar Lynn Gehl with guidance from elders. Lynn holds the Two Row Wampum belt in her left hand and points to the British and Great Lakes Covenant Chain Confederacy Wampum Belt. She wears the Twenty-Four Nations Wampum Belt around her neck.

The British Regime and Colonial Incursion

Despite the promises made at the Niagara conference, the disparity between British diplomatic efforts and their trade practices, the expulsion of other European powers from North America, and the press of settlers south of the Great Lakes combined to create a military alliance between a number of Indigenous nations under the Odawa leader Pontiac, who attempted to drive

Lynn Gehl with her Treaty of Niagara bundle, containing the Anishinabe wampum belts that she re-created. Photo by Nikolaus K. Gehl, 2009. © Lynn Gehl

the British out of the Great Lakes region. During the subsequent peace settlements, the Odawas asserted that their territory was part of the Great River of the Algonquins. Although the British knew that the watershed belonged to the Algonquins, when the territory was mapped in 1791, the Kiji Sibi was referred to erroneously as the "Ottawahs River" (Joan Holmes and Associates 1993, 2:33), a usage that persisted, with the result that the river became known as the Ottawa.

This misrecognition of Algonquin territory may have been deliberate, for bypassing those who held title to the land would facilitate the removal of resources from their territory. From 1793 onward, Britain's economy was largely focused on its twenty-two-year war against France, and the forests of North America supplied large quantities of pine for masts and oak for decking for

British ships. The Ottawa River watershed had the finest white pine forests in North America (Ottawa River Heritage Designation Committee 2005b, 89). Squared timber was required in massive amounts. In their haste to secure as much white pine as possible, it is not surprising that the British ignored treaty relations on the Ottawa even while they signed treaties along the St. Lawrence and Lake Ontario waterfront areas to provide settlements for United Empire Loyalists.

In 1791, the British drove a territorial marker through the heart of the Algonquin homeland via the Constitutional Act of that year. The act divided Quebec into Upper and Lower Canada, with the Ottawa River as the boundary line. Thereafter, Lower Canada, which lay north of the Ottawa, would be administered separately from Upper Canada, which was situated on the south side of the river. The Algonquins would be listed as "domiciled" at Lake of Two Mountains, which fell within Lower Canada, and their occupancy of the Ottawa River watershed would be ignored. The convenient fact that many Algonquins met annually in Lower Canada rather than Upper Canada also enabled the British to ignore the question of their title in Upper Canada. From 1791 until 1840, during which much of the Ottawa Valley on the Ontario side was surveyed and settled by whites, the Algonquins had no voice in Upper Canada at all (Joan Holmes and Associates 1993, 1:5-6).

From the 1770s until the 1820s, Algonquins struggled to resist British ascendency in their territories in a variety of ways, involving both claims on friendship and open resistance. For example, after unsuccessfully petitioning the British to stop traders from bringing alcohol into their territories, the Algonquins threatened to close the river to all trade until the rum trade was stopped (ibid., 2:33-34). This strategy proved effective: in 1776, the British passed an ordinance prohibiting the taking of liquor into Indian villages (Sarazin 1989, 173). The Algonquins also sought to bind the British to them in networks of obligation; for that reason, they fought as British allies against the Americans during the American Revolution and in the War of 1812. In 1794, the British did acknowledge that title to the Ottawa River had not been settled. Lord Dorchester met with the Algonquin and Nipissing chiefs that year and promised to rectify the matter, assuring them that the Crown would not take their lands.

During the long interlude in which the fur trade was of prime importance to Europeans, settler incursion had been discouraged in Eastern Canada. However, after the American Revolution, this began to change. In Upper Canada, the fur trade was in decline, and by the end of the eighteenth century, Britain was concentrating on bringing in settlers to establish a beachhead against potential American invasion. For this reason, the British focused their immediate treaty-making process on the Mississaugas, who occupied the land north of the Great Lakes. And yet, the first Loyalist settlers were granted the most immediately available land, along the boundary between Upper and Lower Canada, which Britain had obtained via the Crawford Purchase of 1783 and the Oswegatchie Purchase of 1784, negotiated with the Mississaugas and the Mohawks, respectively. Both treaties encroached, to the north, on the Ottawa River watershed and Algonquin territory (Joan Holmes and Associates 1993, 2:37).

By 1791, the Algonquin and Nipissing chiefs were complaining about the Iroquois presence on their hunting grounds, which the Oswegatchie Purchase had enabled, and about logging on the Rideau River. In 1798, the chiefs petitioned and met with Sir William Johnson to protest more particularly against the Crawford and Oswegatchie Purchases and the Loyalist settlers who were being brought into the southernmost reaches of Algonquin territory (ibid., 38-42). And yet, even as these petitions addressed what was occurring south of the Ottawa River, the nation continued to face incursions north of the river as well. Thus, the Algonquins were caught in a desperate circumstance whereby two different colonial governments were denuding different parts of their territories of its trees and negotiating land cessions without their consent.[10]

By 1829, although some British administrators strongly argued the Algonquin cause, the British authorities had usurped legal jurisdiction over the territory, so that Algonquins who attempted to evict squatters from their land were threatened with legal reprisals (Sarazin 1989, 176). By 1839, Algonquin claims to traditional lands were flatly denied by order of the Executive Council of Upper Canada.[11] And in subsequent years, the Ontario government would refer to the Algonquins of Golden Lake as remnants of itinerant bands who had no treaty rights at all.[12]

Between 1791 and 1851, as the white pine forests continued to be depleted for British shipbuilding, at least twenty-eight petitions were directed to successive colonial administrations on both sides of the Ottawa River in a vain effort to force the British to honour the terms of their own Royal Proclamation of 1763.[13] Most were signed by Algonquin and Nipissing grand chiefs as well as by the various chiefs of specific bands in the territories, a practice that adhered to traditional Algonquin protocol. Leaders must attain consensus from those whom they represent, and families, not the chiefs themselves, hold jurisdiction over specific lands; the leaders speak for them only with their authorization.[14]

In the early 1850s, as New England's forests became increasingly exhausted, the timber demands of the American market began to compete with those of Britain. Americans wanted sawn lumber. As a result, the squared timber market along the Ottawa River watershed declined after 1870, to be supplanted by a lucrative sawn lumber trade with the United States (Ottawa River Heritage Designation Committee 2005b, 98-100). More than any other development, this spurred the era of railroad building in the Ottawa River watershed, which in turn facilitated the penetration of the Madawaska and Bonnechere River areas for large-scale logging (Kennedy 1970, 171). Once again, respecting the rights of the Algonquins of the Ottawa watershed was simply not expedient for the colonial government.

Possibly because of this, when the Robinson-Huron Treaty was signed in 1850, the government chose simply to incorporate all remaining unsurrendered territory south of the height of land – including that of the Algonquins – in the treaty (Sarazin 1989, 183). Subsequently, between 1866 and 1878, a number of Chippewa and Mississauga communities in eastern and southern Ontario who had not signed the Robinson-Huron Treaty claimed land in their traditional territories. Only the Mississaugas of Alnwick claimed land within the Ottawa watershed. Indeed, in 1881, the chiefs and counsellors of the Chippewas of Christian Island, Georgina Island, and Rama, and the Mississaugas of Rice Lake, Mud Lake, and Scugog collectively sent a letter to Sir John A. Macdonald specifying that their claim extended *only* to the watershed and therefore not inside Algonquin territory (Joan Holmes and Associates 1993, 2:166-67). Although these communities received some reimbursement from the treaty monies that had been paid to others since 1850, the matter would not be settled until 1923, with the Williams Treaties.[15]

2

The Fracturing of the Algonquin Homeland

We are a people divided by many layers of colonial history ... We are divided first of all by provincial lines, artificially drawn on a map of our territory making the Ottawa (Kiji sibi) River, which divides Ontario and Quebec, into a significant symbol of separation where it was once the heart of our territory ... The provincial division has created a language division. There are few people still speaking our language and most speakers come from the Quebec side of the territory. Few Algonquins in Ontario speak anything but English. Many Algonquins in Quebec speak only French ... Perhaps the most potent symbol of our disempowerment is the manner in which Canada has not only disregarded our nationhood to the point where it appropriated our lands to build its capital city on, but has absolutely refused to address this in the land claim talks that have been going on for the past ten years ... For me, the Parliament Buildings are a constant reminder of injustice perpetuated by bitter division and the illegal and immoral domination of one nation over another.

– Heather Majaury, "Living Inside Layers of Colonial Division: A Part of the Algonquin Story"

As inroads on Algonquin territory continued, and as logging progressively destroyed the Algonquin way of life, the ability of the Algonquin Nation to respond cohesively began to fracture. From 1842 onward, petitions for lands began to come directly from the spokespersons for specific bands. Seeing their traditional grounds overrun by settlers, various groups petitioned to protect at least part of them for their own needs. Most of these petitions came from

Ontario, where, within a few decades, Algonquins were facing the virtual obliteration of their traditional lands as loggers and settlers pushed them to the margins. The first petitions concerned land on Bob's Lake, in the area drained by the Rideau River in the southeastern part of the territory, which had been surveyed as Bedford, Oso, and South Sherbrooke Townships, where Algonquin land was almost entirely logged out. Next came petitions for land at Allumette Island on the Ottawa River itself, for land at Clear Lake and Golden Lake in the Bonnechere watershed, surveyed as Sebastopol and South Algona Townships respectively, and at the headwaters of the Madawaska River, for land surveyed as Lawrence, Nightingale, and Sabine Townships.

In Quebec, the primary pressure from loggers, squatters, and settlers was along the Ottawa River itself and up into the Gatineau River watershed.[1] Thus, in 1847 and 1849, petitions were mounted for a grant of land to be set aside in the Gatineau region. In 1881, a group of Algonquins on the Rouge and Petite Nation Rivers petitioned for land after their traditional hunting grounds were thickly settled by squatters. They requested 2,000 acres in what was now the Township of Labelle, in Ottawa County, as well as assistance with farming (Joan Holmes and Associates 1993, 2:166).

The Establishment of Reserves (1851-73)

As plans intensified to extend logging throughout the territory, the government of Lower Canada decided to create two reserves. The first was at Maniwaki, on Rivière Désert. And because the Saguenay and St. Maurice Rivers, where thousands of Algonquins lived, were also being logged (ibid., 196-97), the second reserve was sited at Timiskaming, where all the Native people in the Quebec interior would be gathered together. The two reserves were established in 1851.

On the whole, however, despite the logging on certain rivers, Algonquins in the less accessible parts of the Quebec interior could still secure their livelihood by trapping and hunting. Because of this, they felt no need, initially, to settle on the new reserves. Unfortunately, the loggers and prospectors perceived the lucrativeness of trapping and began to scout the remote territories. As a result, the beaver were almost extirpated in some areas, causing great hardship. Indeed, in certain places, such as the St. Maurice watershed, whites were soon bringing in the majority of furs (ibid., 198). Conditions became so dire for Algonquins in some locales that legislation limiting beaver trapping was introduced in 1876 (ibid., 162); not surprisingly, the Algonquins from those territories were among the first to settle on the reserve at Maniwaki.

In Ontario, despite pressures from Native people in many parts of the watershed, only one small reserve was created, at Golden Lake, in 1873. With the establishment of the three reserves, all other Algonquins seeking settlements in Ontario were advised to go either to Golden Lake or Maniwaki if they wanted a secure territory to live on. Those whose traditional territories were along the Gatineau, in Quebec, where logging and squatters were rapidly making life impossible, or along the Bonnechere and Petawawa Rivers in Ontario, which were close to Golden Lake, generally chose to go to Maniwaki or Golden Lake respectively. However, most of those whose territories were much further away refused to uproot themselves, even as their lands were opened up for logging and settlement. The lands promised to Algonquin communities in Bedford Township and Lawrence Township were never surveyed, and ultimately those who had devoted decades of work to clearing their own acreage in the interests of settling there were driven off by loggers, squatters, and settlers.

Nonetheless, even those who accepted the necessity of living on reserves had no intention of residing there full-time, particularly in Quebec. From Gaston Carrière, whose writings span the 1850s to the 1870s, we get a picture of Algonquin life in Quebec as hundreds of families still utilized their traditional lands on the waterways of the interior, trapping for the fur trade and hunting for food (Joan Holmes and Associates 1993, 2:159-60). They inevitably lived near the trading posts of the Hudson's Bay Company. For example, at Lake Abitibi, which was north of the height of land, in Cree territory, more than 100 Algonquin and Cree families gathered near the post there. Well over 100 families lived near the trading posts on the Noire and Dumoine Rivers (this band had merged with the Fort William band of the Coulonge River by the turn of the century), and another 90 families lived near the trading post at Mattawagamangue. Smaller settlements existed at Grand Lac Victoria (20 families), Lac la Truite (25 families), and Barriere Lake (15 families). Near Maniwaki and Rivière Désert, on the Gatineau and Lievre Rivers, there were about 180 families, including a number from north of the St. Maurice River. Acknowledging the vast distances between the trading post settlements and the two Quebec reserves, the Department of Indian Affairs decided that, initially, the reserves would be limited to providing religious instruction and schooling, and would house a mission (ibid., 139-40, 209-10). Clearly, at that point, it was generally accepted that most Algonquins in Quebec would not be settling on the reserves.

And yet, Carrière's writing also reveals that Christian priests made considerable attempts to interfere with and change Algonquin life on the land. For example, in 1875, the Oblate priest at Maniwaki convinced Indian Affairs to stop annuities to the reserve, claiming that the "mixed-bloods" (whom he characterized as drunken and degenerate) had taken it over and were pushing out the "full-bloods" (whom he portrayed as moral and pure). The Algonquins appealed directly to Superintendent General of Indian Affairs Duncan Campbell Scott, blaming the priest for meddling in their lives. In addition, during the 1870s, Father Gueguen at Timiskaming described two groups of Algonquins at Grand Lac Victoria – those who had hunted inside the Ottawa River watershed, whom he considered "civilized," educated, and non-drinking, and those who hunted north of the watershed, whom he regarded as wild, drunken, avoiding missionaries, and "given up to trickery and polygamy" (Carrière 1957-75, 136-37, quoted in Holmes 1993, 2:159-64). Carrière's writing demonstrates that religious authorities were attempting to impose on the Algonquins a range of stereotypical attributes juxtaposing authentic full-bloods and impure mixed-bloods.

Carrière's work also shows that Indian agents exerted themselves to change Algonquin ways. Sometimes Algonquins who had accepted a European lifestyle aided them in their efforts, and sometimes they met considerable resistance. For example, after the Maniwaki reserve was founded, a quarter of its more than four hundred registered Algonquin band members were absent from the reserve for several years, and in the winter, three-quarters of them were off-reserve, hunting in their territories as they always had. However, in 1878, the son-in-law of a hereditary chief began working with the Indian agent, attempting to stop the annuity payments to off-reserve families, in hopes that this would induce them to settle permanently at Maniwaki in order to receive the payments (Joan Holmes and Associates 1993, 2:164, 171). Because this traditional leader had worked with the Indian agent and had become an "Indian Act" chief, the sacred wampum belts of the Algonquins, which were in his possession, were removed from Maniwaki to Barriere Lake at about this time.[2]

This was a significant and powerful statement of resistance from Algonquins who, despite the changes forced upon them, still observed their ancient ways. In an interview conducted by Pauline Joly de Lotbiniere (1996, 105-10) with the late William Commanda, known to many Algonquins as Grandfather Commanda in recognition of his role as spiritual leader, Commanda explained why the wampum belts were relocated. When the man who was working with the Indian Agent was visited by one of the little people, he became frightened and shot him.[3] Because this man had rejected his family's leadership responsibilities in favour of becoming an Indian Act chief and had then shot one of the little people, whose presence may have already signified that Algonquins were in a time of crisis, he was considered to have forfeited his right to be a leader. Therefore, it was no longer appropriate for him to hold the wampum belts that signified the sacred promises made by the Algonquins as a people, and they were moved to the more traditional community of Barriere Lake, where Algonquin values would be respected.

The significance of the wampum belts, particularly at a time when Algonquin life was being disrupted by the imposition of provincial boundaries and the Indian Act, was that they clearly represented that Algonquins, despite a century of territorial violation, still constituted a nation.

The pressure exerted on Quebec Algonquins to settle full-time on reserves was repeated, though unsuccessfully, by Indian agents and missionaries at the Golden Lake reserve in Ontario. The small size of the reserve helped to frustrate their efforts: it was tiny, consisting originally of 1,561 acres.[4] By 1880, it comprised only 1,400 acres, of which 120 were cultivated, 120 were pasture, and the rest were woodlands. On the entire reserve, there were only seven log houses, sixteen wigwams or shanties, and thirteen barns and stables. In such a small area, only a mixed economy of farming and hunting would enable families to survive; however, because of the presence of loggers and settlers all around them, they were forced to venture further and further north to hunt. As a result, many attempted to retain the seasonal migrations between winter camps and summer camps, with only periodic residence on the reserve. In fact, it would not be settled full-time until the 1920s.

Provincial Development and Restrictive Legislation

Algonquin lands in Ontario lay directly in the path of Canadian nation building. Because of this, the pace of colonization was brutally swift, so that by the 1870s every Algonquin community had faced the devastation of logging and displacement by squatters and settlers. By 1924, as Ontario hunting grounds became impossibly far apart and increasingly settled by whites, formerly scattered band members from Golden Lake had begun to live full-time on its reserve. Within two decades, the number of Algonquins at Golden Lake increased from 86 to 164, particularly as they began to feel the punitive force of provincial law, as hunting regulations were imposed.

Many non-status Algonquins whose traditional territories lay along the Bonnechere and Petawawa Rivers had generally hunted and fished in the Golden Lake territory, so that the Golden Lake Indian agent worked with the police to clarify who were "bona fide" Indians and who were not. Increasingly, this was used to force the Golden Lake Algonquins to reside full-time on the reserve, as those who refused to do so were considered to be off-reserve and therefore non-status. By 1935, only seventeen families lived outside the reserve, and they occasionally appeared in court for trespassing in Algonquin Park (ibid., 217, 223). In Ontario, then, it appears that the police used the presence of non-status Algonquins to coerce the people of Golden Lake to live permanently on the reserve rather than risk losing the limited recognition and benefits available to them as status Indians.

In Quebec, it was not until the early twentieth century, when provincial resource development made life on the land too difficult in some regions, that some Algonquins began to consider the option of living on the reserves. For example, in the 1860s, despite the efforts of Indian agents and their collaborators to force people to settle permanently at Maniwaki, a number of families from that community had moved up the Gatineau River and settled around Baskatong, a favourite area for wild geese, where the river never froze for more than four or five days at a time. In 1929 they paid a terrible price for this move, when the Mercier hydroelectric dam was constructed on the Gatineau, which created a reservoir of about 260 square kilometres. The flooding submerged Baskatong, and a number of Algonquins perished (Jen Meunier, pers. comm., 2006); others escaped but mourned their ancestors' graves, which had also been inundated. Today, Baskatong lies thirty feet below the Mercier reservoir, and the bodies buried there, as well as those who died there, have been retrieved and taken to Grand Remous for reburial (Joan Holmes and Associates 1993, 2:196, 216). Other communities were affected more indirectly. When the Cabonga Reservoir was created, the water level of Cabonga Lake rose twenty-two feet higher than the normal level. This massive flooding was disastrous for wildlife and for those who depended upon it for their livelihood (Matachewan 1989, 147-48).

As the fur trade declined and the interior was opened for logging and settlement, a number of communities around Hudson Bay posts that had for years depended on the fur trade began to petition for reserves in the interior. In 1913, the Long Point community requested land south of Lake Kewegama, but as the lands and waters subsequently came under timber and fishing licences, its request was denied. The Wolf Lake band also asked for a reserve in 1921; when the request was denied most of its members moved to Long Point within the next decade (ibid., 210). Another band, at Lac Simon (formerly part of the Grand Lac Victoria band), suffered terribly from the demise of the beaver, particularly as the mining and timber industries began pushing into the area (ibid., 244). However, not until 1962 did Quebec's Lands and Forests

Act authorize the creation of reserves, utilizing up to 133,650 hectares of provincial Crown land for the purpose. Two were set up for Algonquins – a tiny reserve at Lac Rapide for the Barriere Lake band and the Lac Simon reserve for the Lac Simon band (ibid., 216).

In the 1920s, Quebec Algonquins began to feel the effects of Quebec nationalism. During this interval, the provincial government began a campaign to gallicize the names of geographic locations; as a result, most Algonquin names were deleted from provincial maps and replaced with French names (Joan Holmes and Associates 1993, 2:193-95). French-language instruction for Native people living near settlements also intensified at this point.

From 1919 until the 1940s, despite the imposition of a ban on beaver trapping due to declining numbers, Algonquin communities in Quebec continued to suffer incursions from white trappers. They constantly mounted petitions to have the trappers removed or to grant Algonquins new grounds where whites could not trap. With a few exceptions, white inroads were not seriously policed; by contrast, a number of Quebec Algonquins were arrested for hunting or trapping without licences (ibid., 209-14).

In Ontario, this process of criminalization proceeded full-force for a number of decades. Between 1902 and 1940, dozens of Ontario Algonquins, status and non-status, were charged with hunting and trapping violations. Unable to find employment, they could not afford to buy licences and so were reduced to hunting and trapping at night. Some individuals served three-month sentences at Burwash prison for trapping inside Algonquin Park, and with each arrest, their traps, guns, and game were confiscated. Indeed, much of the work of the Golden Lake Indian agent during this period revolved around efforts to have the confiscated guns returned to their owners. For non-status Algonquins, there was no expectation that confiscated equipment would ever be returned (ibid., 199-236).

By the 1930s, with the intensive criminalization and the diminishment of places to hunt or trap, many Ontario Algonquins began hunting and trapping in Quebec. They observed the proper traditional protocols by requesting permission from local Algonquin communities whose lands they wished to use. However, to protect themselves from arrest by Quebec game wardens, some Golden Lake Algonquins asked Indian Affairs for formal permission to hunt and trap in Quebec. This was supported by the 1931 grand council held at Maniwaki, where the chiefs of the Golden Lake, Barriere Lake, Oka, and Maniwaki bands passed a resolution to ask Indian Affairs to help them obtain hunting privileges (ibid., 219-21). Subsequently, the Golden Lake Indian agent issued letters confirming the Indian status of each Golden Lake member who wished to trap in Quebec, yet another means through which status and non-status distinctions were created by the federal government. Although non-status Indians continued to risk being arrested by Quebec game wardens, no Indian agent was called to act on their behalf, and Indian Affairs kept no records as to how many were arrested.

Hunting in Quebec was soon threatened, however. In 1928, the provincial government had approved a policy that hunting reserves would be established in unsettled areas to allow Indians to trap. However, within a decade, the new Abitibi Game Preserve was opened to whites, and 1940 saw the creation of the Mont-Laurier-Senneterre Fish and Game Reserve, a hunting reserve corridor along the highway cutting through the Grand Lac Victoria Hunting Preserve. Many of the Grand Lac Victoria and Lac Simon Algonquins lost their hunting grounds, as did some members of the Barriere Lake band. With the new hydro site at Cadillac, and with logging, pulp and paper mills, mining, and settlement continuing to expand in every direction, people from those communities had few other places in which to trap (ibid., 226-27, 238-39).

Given the size of the Algonquin population that depended on that land at that time, these threats to Algonquin hunters and trappers were extremely serious. By the late 1930s, when these pressures began to accelerate, there were approximately eight thousand Algonquin trappers in Quebec (ibid., 238-39). Most Algonquins used family traplines until 1945, when the province began a system of licensing traplines on a first-come, first-served basis. Although some Algonquins managed to obtain licences, the areas allotted them differed from their traditional territories. Families who had previously spent their winters on a trapline could not continue this custom if their new provincial traplines were located far from their communities. Nor did the new system take their conservation practices into account; family traplines had been managed with sustainability and long-term use in mind (ibid., 204), whereas opening traplines to non-Natives who had no vested long-term interest in an area simply encouraged over-trapping.

In Ontario, very few Algonquins were able to make a living through trapping. In 1940, a move was made to allot Crown land around Algonquin Park for trapping licences, but almost all were given to white settlers. Not until 1954 was the eastern half of Algonquin Park opened to trappers from Golden Lake (and only to them); since then, some Golden Lake trappers have been able to maintain a living with trapping.

In 1978, as the Golden Lake reserve was rediscovering that title to the Ottawa River watershed had never been ceded and was preparing research toward a land claim, Quebec Native people were experiencing another set of land incursions, with the creation of a system of ZECs – Zone d'Exploration Controlée – which accelerated hydro development and logging (Matachewan 1989, 158-62). This sparked a series of land-based protests, which increasingly occupied Quebec Algonquins in wholesale blockades to protect the land and have characterized the struggles of many Quebec Algonquins, notably at Barriere Lake, ever since.[5]

Algonquin systems of land tenure (like those of most Indigenous people) are organized around watersheds rather than the rivers that run through them. In this way of thinking, the natural divisions between territories are the high grounds that divide watersheds. For Europeans, where rivers are merely lines on a map, the river itself becomes the boundary between territories. Thus, when the British chose the Ottawa River as the border between Upper and Lower Canada, they drew an artificial line through the territories of those whose lands had been situated on both sides of the Ottawa River, with the result that the boundary ruptured family and band territories. Communities were forced to adapt as the people settled on one side of the river or the other and began to deal with two different provincial administrations – and were then treated as different communities.

For many years, Indian Affairs administrators dealt with the vagaries imposed by this provincial border. For example, the Quebec communities of Kipawa and Wolf Lake, at the south end of Lake Timiskaming, often received services from Mattawa, Ontario, whereas the Algonquins of Abitibi, many of whom had residences in Ontario, were administered through the North Témiskaming agency in Quebec. For the communities themselves, however, the provincial border created enormous difficulties: on the two sides of the river, two different agencies controlled access to hunting, trapping, fishing, and most other fundamental aspects of their livelihoods. The provincial approach to development also differed, as the Ontario government focused entirely on settlement, whereas the Quebec government viewed Algonquin land primarily as a vast unspoiled region for the use of tourists, miners, the forestry and pulp and paper industries, and ultimately for hydroelectric projects. Because of this, Algonquins on either side of the border began to live somewhat differently from each other. Finally, even the language of colonization differed across the border: on the Quebec side, French was forced on people who primarily spoke Algonquin; in Ontario, Algonquin was dying out through intensive settlement pressures, and the use of English was enforced. Thus, the Algonquin homeland was effectively fragmented, its people divided into Quebec Algonquins and Ontario Algonquins.

Another Fracture: The Exclusion of Non-Status Algonquins

In Ontario, once the reserve was established at Golden Lake, the Department of Indian Affairs washed its hands of any other Indian presence in the Ottawa Valley. Subsequently, the only Algonquins acknowledged in Ontario were those registered as members of Golden Lake. Although settler histories continue to attest to the presence of Algonquins living around white settlements, those who did not move to Golden Lake became almost invisible in official records.

And yet, for a number of years, as Indian Affairs wrestled with the exigencies of colonial administration, small anomalies existed, through which we can occasionally see the traces of a federally unrecognized Algonquin presence. For example, Indian Affairs files from the 1920s and 1930s contain several requests about hunting and fishing violations in the Ottawa Valley from individuals who were simply described as "Indians" and were *not* referred to the Golden Lake Indian agent (for examples, see Joan Holmes and Associates 1993, 2:209, 217, 222). Clearly, these Indians were not affiliated with a reserve and thus were not formally recognized as Indians under the Indian Act.

Another anomaly appears in the historical records of 1926, when the Children's Aid Society in Renfrew informed Indian Affairs that it would be meeting with the minister of lands and forests regarding the need to enable Indians to hunt and fish in Algonquin Park. Presumably, the intent of this was to end the criminalization of Indian fathers who hunted illegally in the park and whose children were taken into care as a result. However, Children's Aid Societies had no authority over status Indians until 1951, which would suggest that the children who were being brought into care in numbers large enough to warrant official intervention were non-status.[6] Needless to say, Indian Affairs did not act on the society's letter.

Furthermore, in 1938, when Chief Tenniscoe of Golden Lake asked that Golden Lake Algonquins who wished to trap be protected against prosecution, he was advised by Indian Affairs to submit a list of the trappers to the Indian agent, who would provide them with certificates of Indian status. Indian Agent Farrell then forwarded the list of twenty trappers to Indian Affairs (ibid., 230). The necessity of issuing these certificates to Golden Lake trappers suggests that non-status Algonquin trappers were also being arrested; the certificates would enable game wardens and police to distinguish between the Indians whom they apprehended: for those with a certificate, they would contact the Golden Lake agent; those without a certificate would simply be criminalized for trapping without a licence.

Moreover, in 1940, when the Golden Lake agent attempted to acquire traplines near Algonquin Park for Golden Lake residents, the forestry department informed him of its concern that only "bona fide" Indians should be given traplines. This response implies that non-status Madawaska River Indians who had been promised land in Lawrence Township, which had subsequently become part of Algonquin Park, were still trapping in their traditional areas. However, Algonquins who were not perceived as bona fide – that is, who were not federally recognized – received no consideration for traplines at all.

It is clear that the official division between status and non-status Algonquins evolved gradually, through specific incidents and practices, and was not initially a hard-and-fast matter, as tends to be assumed today. Indian Affairs documents reveal that for years, a number of Indians who agreed to be listed as members of Golden Lake never moved to the reserve – many resided full-time in small communities across the province, near the areas in which they traditionally trapped, where they mingled with their federally unrecognized relatives. Later, as Indian Affairs tightened its control, the off-reserve membership was increasingly divested of the benefits accruing to those who lived on the reserve full-time. In 1939, when Indian Affairs sent a cheque for $180 to Indian Agent Farrell to cover the cost of purchasing thirty hunting and trapping licences and accompanying gun permits, off-reserve Golden Lake members were denied access to them (Joan Holmes and Associates 1993, 2:235-36). Increasingly, from this point onward, off-reserve Golden Lake members were treated as if they no longer had Indian status. This points to a reality that I will discuss in Chapter 10 – that, even after the reserve was created, distinctions between status and non-status Algonquins, which today have been normalized as long-standing divisions, were probably minimal before the 1940s.

The histories of some non-status Algonquin families can also be found in municipal and provincial land records, although by the 1920s most Algonquins had been dispossessed of any land for which they had managed to obtain fee simple deeds. As the twentieth century proceeded, and Indian Affairs consolidated its hold over status Indians and ignored the rest, these records are almost the only sources through which one can ascertain the ongoing presence of non-status Algonquins. They counteract the erasure that, for almost a century, typifies official discourse in Ontario, from the final denial of the Lawrence Township claim in 1899 until the acceptance of the Ontario land claim in 1991.

In Quebec, the presence of non-status Algonquins is clearly indicated at certain times. For example, in 1942, many Algonquins had become so destitute that Indian Affairs offered reduced prices for Indian hunting and gun permits. When the department stipulated that "half-breeds and whites" must pay full price, whereas "Indians" would pay only a dollar, Indian Agent Gendron, stationed at Maniwaki, asked how he was to treat the "unlisted" Indians: "We have here quite a few Indians who for some reasons or other are not on the list, and they like the others are requesting trapping licenses at $1.00 a license, which are issued to Indians. There is no doubt that these Indians are in many instances as pure blood as any other who are on the list, and I am wondering what to do with them. At first I have issued some licenses to that particular kind of Indians, but since I have received the latest circular, I have not issued one to those Indians" (quoted in Joan Holmes and Associates 1993, 2:242-43).

D.J. Allan, superintendent, reserves and trusts, responded to Gendron on 15 January 1943, stating that issuing an Indian licence would depend on whether the recipient were a bona fide Indian. He offered the following advice, stating that regardless of whether they were "pure-blooded," federally unrecognized Algonquins would not receive the benefits that accrued to their officially recognized counterparts: "As a guide I would say that any person accepted by the Department for relief, medical services, and schooling can be accepted as an Indian for license purposes regardless of whether or not he participates in interest or treaty payments. If a person does not qualify as an Indian under these conditions he should be refused a license and instructed to purchase a regular 'white' license from the local Provincial Warden" (quoted in ibid., 242).

And yet, despite these sporadic references from Quebec officials to a non-status Algonquin presence, it is likely that far fewer Algonquins are non-status in Quebec. Although many Algonquins in the interior of Quebec were able to remain on the land, trapping until the early twentieth century, a colonial apparatus of priests and Indian agents was gradually created to administer and control them. Because of this, Quebec Algonquins did not have to move to a reserve in order to be recognized as Indian. Nevertheless, there *are* federally unrecognized Algonquins scattered along the Quebec side of the Ottawa River, primarily ones who lost their lands to squatters in the same manner as their Ontario Algonquin neighbours did. Quebec First Nations, however, do not recognize their existence. Thus, an additional fracture exists in the Algonquin Nation, as, on both sides of the river, those who are not federally recognized are ignored by the First Nations leadership in both provinces and are, for the most part, seen as external to Algonquinness.

Dispossessing Federally Unrecognized Algonquins

As the Indian Act began to control the lives of status Indians, it provided the vehicle through which additional lands could be expropriated and identities transformed in multiple ways. For federally unrecognized Algonquins, however, other, primarily provincial, laws were crucial to their disempowerment and loss of land.

Settlers in Ontario were first encouraged onto Algonquin territory via provincial legislation. The 1841 and 1849 Public Land Acts enabled a free allotment of no more than 50 acres to settlers along roads in any new settlement area (Leslie and Maguire 1979, 18). Settlers also received the right to purchase an additional 150 acres after they had occupied the initial 50 and cleared and cultivated 12 of them. Before they could receive a patent for the land, they were required to "improve" it (Nuttall 1980, 13-18). Subsequently, in 1853, as new colonization roads were built and lots surveyed, the free allotment was increased to 100 acres for land along colonization roads for every 10 acres cleared within five years as well as the construction of a sixteen- by twenty-foot house (Nuttall 1982, 50). Generally, as the roads were built, but before the land was surveyed into lots, lumber companies were allowed to log it. The one exception was the upper Madawaska River watershed, which, because of its topography, remained largely untouched by loggers and settlers until the 1850s when the Opeongo Colonization Road was constructed. The building of the Ottawa, Arnprior and Parry Sound Railway subsequently opened the area to wholesale white incursion (Kennedy 1970, 146-71).

For most other regions of the Ottawa Valley, the colonization roads policy opened "the frontier" to European settlement. The requirement that settlers must improve their free acreage if they wished to keep it prompted habitat destruction, with the result that survival on the land became increasingly difficult for Algonquins. Moreover, the demand for improvement made it difficult for those Algonquins who did begin clearing land to persist with the mixed-mode livelihood they preferred, where small-scale agriculture was supplemented by hunting. Finally, since fee simple title was frequently denied to Indians, they had little incentive to clear the land. In the instances where lots *were* set aside for Algonquins, surveying, which made the process legal, was typically not done, so whatever improvements they might make, they ultimately lost the land to white squatters or saw it absorbed into provincial parks. (This subject will be explored more closely in Chapters 6 and 11.)

In 1860, the Agricultural Loans Act enabled the Agricultural Association of Canada to acquire land by mortgage as a security for loans or debts. Indian families who did manage to attain fee simple title but who maintained a subsistence economy would inevitably assume a taxation debt; this act ensured that their property would be sold. Indeed, local interests (township boards, local officials) were given considerable power over the granting of landholdings and the seizure of real estate for nonpayment of taxes (Huitema 2000, 51). In a context where no federal records existed for non-status Algonquins, only those local individuals who had the authority to decide which debts to call and which to ignore knew who was, and who was not, an Indian. As Indians were not citizens and were generally viewed by settlers as expendable, this simply hastened the loss of their land.

In 1868, in recognition of the difficulty of establishing farms in eastern Ontario, where much of the land was rock and swamp, the Free Grants and Homestead Act was implemented. This extended the free grant area to 200 acres, provided that 15 were cleared and at least 2 more subsequently; settlers were also required to reside continuously on the land for five years and were not allowed to leave their homestead for longer than six months at a time. This act made it virtually impossible for Algonquins to acquire settlement land, as they typically spent much of their time on the land hunting, trapping, or fishing. Local land agents, moreover, had full powers to judge who was of "moral character" and deserving of land. In this context, Algonquins had almost no chance of being approved for a homestead (ibid., 56-58).

The Indian Act, created in 1876, contained a clause stipulating that off-reserve Indians would be subject to the same taxes for real or personal property as settlers if it were held under lease or fee simple (ibid., 59-60). At the time, various groups of off-reserve Algonquins were petitioning for fee simple title to parts of their traditional hunting grounds, and Crown lands agents were uncertain whether an Algonquin claim should be granted in recognition of the group's ancestral rights to the territory or as an individual claim identical to that of a settler. This clause in the Indian Act ensured that claims based on the notion of justice would not be granted; only if Algonquins made claims as viable as those of white homesteaders would they be allowed to acquire fee simple land. The combined effect of the above acts was that although non-status Algonquins struggled for years to acquire fee simple title to at least some of their traditional lands, by the 1920s, their inability to pay the associated taxes and to satisfy legal requirements that were designed with European settlers in mind meant that they had lost most of the land they acquired. At this point, their dispossession was complete.

A Fractured Homeland

As large numbers of non-status Ontario Algonquins were rendered landless and officially invisible in their own territories, even to status Algonquins, the fracturing of the nation's homeland along the Quebec-Ontario border was increasingly manifested through growing divergences between Ontario and Quebec Algonquins. In Ontario, the surveying of Algonquin territory into townships, its licensing to logging companies, and the incursion of masses of white settlers from the British Isles proceeded almost continuously from 1800 onward, so that by the 1870s, Algonquins had faced displacement in every part of their territories. The Canadian nation-building exercise, which originated in Ontario, fuelled a massive and accelerated expansion northward around the Great Lakes and then westward into the prairies. In this process, only pockets of "wilderness" remained on the Ontario side of the Ottawa River watershed, so Algonquins were increasingly reduced to eking out a precarious existence, hunting and trapping "illegally," and non-status Algonquins barely survived on marginal lands in areas too poor for farming. For both status and non-status Algonquins, partial adaptation to white society – through jobs, schooling, and, most of all, through church attendance – was fundamental to survival. With this, they gradually lost their language and the stories and songs that went with it.

It's important to note that despite this partial adaptation to white society, Algonquin values were not lost. Instead, as their relationship to the land was transformed, Algonquin traditional ways were modified to enable families to preserve an Algonquin identity and yet survive as landless people. Most profoundly, with changes in their circumstances came a silence about Algonquin identity. Over the years this often included a forced forgetting of much of the painful history they had endured since their land was taken by white settlers.

In Quebec, by comparison, the colonization process was organized differently, particularly in the interior of Algonquin territory. Because the fur trade, which required pristine forests, was still viable throughout the nineteenth century, the surveying of large blocks of forest within the interior for timber leases did not begin until the fur trade gradually declined in economic importance in the late nineteenth century, and was outstripped by the economic interests associated with forestry. And although squatters seized land along the Ottawa River itself in the early 1800s, settlement in the interior began only after some of the forests were logged, in the 1860s. Furthermore, the reserves at Maniwaki and Timiskaming augmented the mission process already under way at some trading posts through the constant intercession of priests attempting to shape Algonquin life in the interior and preserve Algonquins from the "corrupting" presence of settlers. Thus, for many years, it was possible for Quebec Algonquins to retain their family trapping territories, the traditional practices of a life lived directly on the land, their language, and the songs and stories that were vested in it. For these reasons, Algonquin ways of life in Quebec began gradually to diverge from those in Ontario.[7]

And yet, Algonquins in Quebec did experience pressure from white society. Under a nascent Québécois nationalism intent on claiming the provincial land base as Québécois, asserting Aboriginal rights would become increasingly difficult for Quebec Algonquins. Furthermore, with globalization, the wholesale looting of natural resources has accelerated into the present, and so Quebec Algonquins currently face direct threats to their survival and pressures to finally give up life on the land.

Ironically, it was the Province of Ontario, the chief agent of much of the devastation and fracturing of the Algonquin Nation, that provided the last official recognition of its fundamental wholeness. In 1898, the Province submitted a brief to the tribunal established to settle claims against the old Province of Canada, which included the following passage: "The Algonquin claim to the north, or Lower Canada, side of the Ottawa, which is admitted, is no stronger, nor founded on any better, or any different evidence, than that which goes to establish their claim to the south side: they are not two claims but only one claim, whole and indivisible; that by parity of reasoning, the admission of the claim to the north side, involves and compels the admission of their claim to the south, or Upper Canada side; the evidence that supports the one maintains also the other" (quoted in Joan Holmes and Associates 1993, 2:186).

Unfortunately, as we shall see in Chapter 4, when Algonquins finally gained the means to resist the tide of destruction by asserting their jurisdiction over the land, the long years of division between Quebec and Ontario Algonquins, and between status and non-status Algonquins, particularly in Ontario, simply furthered the fracturing of their homeland.

3

Aboriginal Title and the Comprehensive Claims Process

Self-government is not an Indian idea. It originates in the minds of non-Indians who have reduced the traditional ways to dust, or believe they have, and now wish to give, as a gift, a limited measure of local control and responsibility.

– **Vine Deloria Jr. and Clifford M. Lytle, *The Nations Within***

The Algonquin land claim was made possible through the 1973 *Calder* decision, in which the Supreme Court of Canada stated that Aboriginal peoples have a pre-existing title to their traditional land base, which exists wherever it has not been formally extinguished (Monture-Angus 1999, 66). *Calder* finally refuted the 1885 *St. Catherines Milling and Lumber* decision, which, as part of a dispute between Ontario and Canada over timber rights, had asserted that land title in Canada lay with the Crown and that Indian rights to land were merely usufructory and premised entirely upon the benevolence of the Crown (ibid., 68-71). Based on a court case to determine the existence of Nisga'a title to traditional lands, *Calder,* and others leading up to it, such as *R. v. White* (which ruled in 1964 that treaties should be given their widest meaning in favour of Native people), enabled many Indigenous people to feel a sense of possibility for the first time. After a century of extensive land loss and oppressive legal controls, Indigenous nations might finally have a chance to do more than barely survive. The Algonquin land claim was initiated during this period of hopefulness for Aboriginal people.

In this chapter, I will explore the context in which the Algonquin land claim exists – the Supreme Court decisions that have shaped, and ultimately constrained, concepts of Aboriginal rights and title, and the two federal government policies regarding self-government and comprehensive claims that have been implemented in view of them. In such a context, we can see the limitations that Algonquin people face in negotiating a comprehensive claim.

Legal Framework

Aboriginal Rights

Although *Calder* asserted the existence of Aboriginal title, which stemmed from Aboriginal peoples' prior occupancy of the land, Canadian law was unclear as to what Aboriginal title actually *was* and about how to determine whether it had been extinguished. In *Calder,* Justice Emmett Hall proposed that the onus for proving that the Crown had intended to extinguish title lay with the Crown itself and that intention to extinguish must be "clear and plain," but not until the court affirmed this in the 1990 *Sparrow* decision could some determination be made as to when title had been extinguished in specific locales (Monture-Angus 1999, 76). And yet, Aboriginal title was not legally defined until the *Delgamuukw* decision in 1998. *Sparrow* also constituted another form of test case, in that it was the first to address the meaning of Aboriginal rights. In 1982, the Constitution Act had declared, in section 35(1), that "the existing aboriginal and treaty rights of the aboriginal peoples of Canada are hereby recognized and affirmed." The *Sparrow* case involved a fisherman from the Musqueam Nation, Ronald Sparrow, who was charged with violating British Columbia fishing regulations. In his defence, Sparrow asserted that he was exercising an Aboriginal right to fish where his people had fished for generations. *Sparrow* was referred to the Supreme Court in 1990, where it became the court's first pronouncement on the meaning of section 35(1).

In *Sparrow,* Justice Antonio Lamer acknowledged the reality that "Aboriginal rights exist because of one simple fact: when Europeans arrived in North America, Aboriginal peoples were already here, living in communities on the land and participating in distinct cultures, as they had done for centuries" (Borrows 2002, 59). According to John Borrows (ibid., 59-60), this should have led Lamer to a definition of Aboriginal rights in which the tenets of Indigenous law were combined with those of the Crown. But Lamer stepped back from this recognition, arguing instead that the rights affirmed by section 35(1) must be directed toward the reconciliation of the pre-existence of

Aboriginal societies with the sovereignty of the Crown. Michael Asch and Patrick Macklem (1991, 507) explain the implications for Aboriginal people: "The Court unquestioningly accepted that the British Crown, and thereafter Canada, obtained territorial sovereignty over the land mass that is now Canada by the mere fact of European settlement. The Court's acceptance of the settlement thesis appears to exclude any possibility of the recognition and affirmation of a constitutional right to aboriginal sovereignty." Patricia Monture-Angus (1999, 95), however, notes that regardless of Lamer's ruling, Aboriginal rights by definition do *not* flow from the Crown or from provincial, territorial, or federal statutory regimes; thus, the assumption that these regimes have the authority to regulate Aboriginal rights is only presumed and is therefore without clear foundation in Canadian law.

Indeed, the *Sparrow* decision could have explored the extent to which Canada's existing legal and constitutional framework infringes upon Aboriginal rights. For example, if self-government is an Aboriginal right, sections 91 and 92 of the Constitution, which divide all legislative authority between the federal and provincial governments, leaving no space for Aboriginal jurisdiction, absolutely infringe upon that right. However, because *Sparrow* sidestepped the possibility that Aboriginal rights could require any adjustment to the federal-provincial constitutional relationship, self-government as an Aboriginal right was left with no venue to exercise power except at the level of a municipality – a travesty of nationhood.

Sparrow also provided a test to establish when Ottawa or the provinces could infringe on Aboriginal rights, thus creating an escape clause for them. Furthermore, the *Sparrow* decision introduced the "culturalization" of Aboriginal rights – so that the Aboriginal right to fish for food, which should have simply been a question of survival for contemporary Aboriginal people, is defined as an Aboriginal right because it is "distinctive to the Aboriginal culture claiming the right" (Borrows 2002, 60). Nonetheless, the *Sparrow* ruling was positive in some ways, particularly in that it asserted that the section 35(1) phrase "existing Aboriginal rights" must be interpreted flexibly so as to permit the rights to evolve over time.

However, in 1996, *Van der Peet,* a crucial Supreme Court decision, fundamentally changed how Aboriginal rights were viewed in Canada. Like *Sparrow,* the case revolved around the Aboriginal right to fish, this time relating to selling fish caught under a food-fishing licence. In his decision, Justice Lamer set down an extensive test to determine the existence of Aboriginal rights, which is summarized below (Borrows 2002, 62-66):

1. The court must consider the perspectives of Aboriginal peoples; however, the Aboriginal perspective must be framed in terms cognizable to the Canadian legal and constitutional structure.
2. The precise nature of the claim being made must be determined – including the nature of the action taken in claiming an Aboriginal right, the government regulation that is claimed to violate that right, and the tradition, custom, or practice relied upon to establish that right.
3. The centrality of the practice to the group claiming the right must be determined, as to whether or not the practice is an integral part of the distinctive custom in question.
4. An Aboriginal right is integral to a distinctive culture if it has continuity with activities that existed prior to the arrival of Europeans.
5. Given the difficulty in establishing definitively what a pre-contact practice was, the court should not undervalue the evidence presented in establishing continuity with pre-contact cultural practices.
6. Aboriginal rights are not general or universal but relate to the specific history of the group claiming the right.
7. The practice being claimed as a right must be independently significant to the community and not merely incidental relating to another more integral tradition – so that incidental practices, customs, and traditions cannot be piggybacked on integral practices to make them part of Aboriginal rights.
8. The practice being claimed as integral cannot be one that arises in response to European influences.
9. The practice being claimed can arise separately from the group's relationship to the land.

As Borrows (ibid., 61-63) observes, the net effect of the *Van der Peet* test is to heavily circumscribe Aboriginal rights. It establishes non-Aboriginal characterizations of aboriginality, evidence, and law as the standards by which Aboriginal rights shall be evaluated. *Sparrow* had argued for the flexibility of the phrase "existing Aboriginal rights" to permit the evolution of the rights, and it viewed the exercise of rights necessary for physical and cultural survival as the test for what was "integral" to a culture. In *Van der Peet,* however, being "integral" to the culture meant integral to the group's "cultural distinctiveness," with the pre-contact culture as the standard of what was distinctive. Moreover, according to *Van der Peet,* Aboriginal rights exist *not* to ensure the physical and cultural survival of contemporary Indigenous people but to preserve the distinctive elements of their pre-contact culture.

Borrows also takes issue with Lamer's ruling that Aboriginal rights are not general but must be established on a case-by-case basis, since this means that claimants cannot rely on analogies with other claimant groups. The ruling means that Aboriginal people cannot build jurisprudence in this area, as is customary in Canadian case law, since each group must prove its case uniquely and cannot premise it on other decisions. In addition, the ruling ignores the global basis of Aboriginal rights, whose source is an overarching First Nations jurisprudence that existed when Europeans arrived. Borrows (ibid., 65) asserts that the organization and laws of Aboriginal peoples should be universally protected as entities that each group can successfully claim, even though their content will vary from group to group.

Another Supreme Court decision of 1996 – *R. v. Pamajewon* – ruled on self-government as an Aboriginal right. It dealt with the casinos on two Ojibway reserves, at Shawanaga and Eagle Lake, and whether an Aboriginal right to self-government included being able to operate high-stakes gambling. Here Justice Lamer rejected the understanding of the two Aboriginal communities, which saw the establishment of casinos in terms of their survival and future livelihood. Instead, he held that because pre-contact Ojibway gambling took place on a small scale and because casinos were definitely a twentieth-century phenomenon, operating a casino was not congruent with Ojibway gaming at the time of contact. Therefore, Aboriginal self-government did not include the right to operate a casino. Furthermore, Lamer ruled that self-government claims were required to undergo a test like the one given in *Van der Peet*. As Kent McNeil (2002, 3) points out, with *Pamajewon*, self-government rights exist only in relation to matters that were integral to specific Aboriginal societies and regulated by them prior to being influenced by Europeans, which in some parts of Canada was four hundred years ago. This test would successfully eliminate most claims relating to many matters that have become the business of First Nations governments in recent times. It would hamper their capacity to function effectively in the modern world and would certainly offer them no protection as self-governing nations. As John Borrows (2002, 68) succinctly remarks, Canadians are lucky that their current rights do not depend on what their ancestors did three hundred years ago.

In both *Van der Peet* and *Pamajewon*, some justices dissented from the opinion of the others, asserting that Aboriginal rights should be rooted not in the distant past but in the laws and customs of Indigenous peoples today and in the extent to which such rights assist them in surviving and thriving. One can only hope that future court decisions will ignore the majority opinion and take this dissenting view as a precedent. As the situation stands, however, "freezing" Aboriginal rights according to pre-contact practices, especially in matters of self-government, means that Aboriginal people cannot compete as equals in Canadian society, as European laws are allowed to advance and change, whereas theirs are not (ibid., 71).

Gladstone constituted a final blow to Aboriginal rights, greatly enhancing Ottawa's power to infringe on them in a variety of ways. This 1996 Supreme Court case addressed the Heiltsuk people's right to sell herring spawn on kelp, which had been their practice since time immemorial. Its effect is particularly problematic, given the rationale that *Sparrow* had provided for reviewing infringements of Aboriginal rights. *Gladstone* affords an example of how various factors, such as those relating to Aboriginal people's rights to engage in a commercial fishery, could be introduced to enable a broader rationale for infringing on the right in question (Mainville 2001, 79-81).

Russell Barsh and James Youngblood Henderson (1997, 1004) characterize the *Sparrow, Van der Peet,* and *Gladstone* decisions (in which Justice Lamer played a significant role) as a form of "naive colonialism." In examining how these three decisions have affected the ability of Aboriginal people to actually claim Aboriginal rights, they conclude,

> If all the hurdles announced by *Sparrow, Van der Peet* and *Gladstone* are assembled, they form a formidable and intimidating barrier: The Aboriginal practice at issue must be shown to be pre-existing and central; it must be shown never to have been extinguished by the Crown prior to 1982; it must have been infringed upon by government action after 1982; the government action must be shown to have lacked adequate justification; and it must be shown to go beyond the reasonable discretion enjoyed by the Crown as a "fiduciary" to determine whether the Aboriginal community concerned has been given an adequate "priority" in the enjoyment of the resources it has traditionally utilized. All of this translates to a heavier evidentiary burden at trial, more expense, and greater risk of an adverse ruling, amounting to a present-day extinguishment of the rights asserted.

Aboriginal Title

As mentioned above, though *Sparrow* had established that the test for extinguishment of Aboriginal title was the unambiguous articulation of intent to do so and that the burden of proof rested with the government, Canadian law was unclear regarding the actual nature and scope of Aboriginal title.

It is important to understand the hope that the 1973 *Calder* decision had engendered in many Aboriginal people. Indigenous nations whose lands had been taken without a treaty process and with no hope of recompense saw in *Calder* a way toward recognition of their historic and ongoing relationship to their territories; these expectations were heightened in 1982, when Aboriginal rights were entrenched in section 35(1) of the Constitution. As many Indigenous people saw it, Aboriginal title was a means of asserting their sovereignty over their lands, as well as receiving at least some compensation for the tremendous loss of land and resources that had impoverished them while enriching Canada.

By far the most powerful expression of these aspirations in the wake of *Calder* was *Delgamuukw,* a case launched by the Gitksan and Wet'suwet'en, who together claimed ownership and jurisdiction over fifty-eight thousand square kilometres in northern British Columbia. During the trial, the leaders of the two nations sought to prove their ownership and jurisdiction on Indigenous terms by demonstrating the songs, stories, crests, and names that justified the claims of the seventy-one houses who between them had held responsibility for 133 territories that stretched back twelve thousand years. However, the trial judge, Justice McEachern, rejected these claims to ownership and jurisdiction as unprovable compared to the written legislation in British Columbia, which dated back to 1846. He rejected the Indigenous claims as inconsistent with the division of powers between Canada and British Columbia under section 91(24) of the Constitution, stating that "all legislative jurisdiction was divided between Canada and the province and there was no room for Aboriginal jurisdiction or sovereignty which would be recognized by the law or the courts" (quoted in Persky 1998, 210). In the BC Court of Appeal, Justice McFarlane affirmed the trial court's decision, stating that

> the Gitksan and Wet'suwet'en people did not need a Court decision to permit internal self-regulation, if they consent to be governed. However, the rights of self-government encompassing the power to make general laws governing the land, resources, and people in the territory are legislative powers that cannot be awarded by the courts. Such jurisdiction is inconsistent with the *Constitution Act, 1982* and its division of powers. When the Crown imposed English law on all the inhabitants of the colony and when British Columbia entered Confederation, the Aboriginal people became subject to Canadian (and provincial) legislative authority. For this reason, the claim to jurisdiction failed. (ibid., 32)

As Monture-Angus (1999, 117) notes, this ruling underlines the tiny space of self-government that Canada is willing to allow Aboriginal people: the right to administer themselves under Canadian and provincial law.

When *Delgamuukw* went to the Supreme Court of Canada, the main issues to be determined were whether the court had the power to decide on the claims for Aboriginal title and self-government, and whether it could interfere with the factual findings made by Justice McEachern. Although the court could have dispensed with *Delgamuukw* once those rulings were made, Chief Justice Lamer took it upon himself to address the content of Aboriginal title. Given that his *Van der Peet, Pamajewon,* and *Gladstone* definitions had already seriously limited the content and extent of Aboriginal rights, it is particularly unfortunate that he decided to rule on Aboriginal title in *Delgamuukw.*

In discussing the findings of McEachern, Lamer examined the issue of oral testimony. He observed that the appellants had utilized every possible means of proving their ancient occupation of the territory, including stories, songs, and dances, and that by his own test for Aboriginal rights, this oral history must be accommodated and placed on an equal footing with the more familiar types of historical evidence that are presented in court (Persky 1998, 16-18). Because McEachern had given no credence to the oral histories, Lamer made a judgment of a "palpable and overriding error" in his findings.

Lamer's findings were that Aboriginal title was a right to land, conferring the right to use the land for a variety of practices, not all of which need be integral to the distinctive culture of Aboriginal societies. However, land under Aboriginal title was not to be used in a manner that was irreconcilable with the nature of Aboriginal peoples' attachment to it. Lamer's test for proof of Aboriginal title was as follows:

1 The land must have been occupied prior to Crown sovereignty being asserted.
2 There must be a continuity between the present and pre-sovereignty occupation.
3 At the assertion of Crown sovereignty, that occupation must have been exclusive (Borrows 2002, 101).

Finally, Lamer ruled that even though Aboriginal title is recognized and protected by the Constitution, it is not absolute. Indeed, he provided a list of conditions in which the infringement of title was justified: "In my opinion, the development of agriculture, forestry, mining, and hydroelectric power, the general economic development of the interior of British Columbia, protection of the environment or endangered species, the building of infrastructure and the settlement of foreign populations to support these aims, are the kinds of objectives that ... can justify the infringement of Aboriginal title. Whether a particular measure or government act can be explained by reference to one of these objectives, however, is ultimately a question of fact that will have to be examined on a case by case basis" (quoted in Persky 1998, 20). Lamer added, however, that infringement of title would be restrained by the duty to consult and that the honour of the Crown demanded fair compensation whenever infringement occurred (Persky 1998, 20).

The *Delgamuukw* decision was greeted with some jubilation in British Columbia simply because of the Province's long history of denying the existence of Aboriginal title, but commentary has been far less sanguine elsewhere in Canada. Patricia Monture-Angus (1999, 126-27, emphasis in original) stated,

> In my opinion, the clearest danger to Aboriginal understanding of our self-government responsibilities lies in the "inherent limit" on the "range of uses," such that the use cannot be "irreconcilable with the nature of the attachment to the land." The interesting question, and it is a question that directly impacts on self-government, is *who* has the ability to decide if the use is not irreconcilable with the attachment to the land? There is no obvious answer to this question and several possibilities. Is this an articulation of the self-governing powers of First Nations? Is it a power of the federal Crown? The provincial Crown? And if so, what is the source of that power? If it is a power of the federal (or provincial) Crown, it is absolutely likely that this power will interfere with Aboriginally defined beliefs about self-government and internal community control. Or perhaps Lamer was articulating on behalf of the courts a new role for judicial scrutiny. If so, this is a very unusual role for courts who would normally shy away from a responsibility that is ongoing and indefinable.

John Borrows (2002, 96-97) addresses the fact that the problems of *Van der Peet,* as relating to Aboriginal rights, reoccur in *Delgamuukw* in that Indigenous perspectives must be reconciled with British assertions of sovereignty, though not in ways that genuinely merge the two systems of law. This enables some aspects of Aboriginal legal and political rights to exist within the Canadian system but absolutely subordinates and limits Aboriginal perspectives to Canadian constitutional and legal frameworks. As Borrows (ibid., 97) concludes, "The court's approach to reconciliation thus forcibly includes non-treaty Aboriginal peoples within Canadian society and subjects them to an alien sovereignty, even though most have never consented to such an arrangement. This inclusion subordinates Aboriginal legal systems and limits the uses to which Aboriginal peoples can put their lands. The implications of this approach deeply undermine original Aboriginal entitlements – on grounds none other than self-assertion."

Policy Framework

The inherent right to self-government policy and the comprehensive claims policy were both created by Ottawa in response to constitutional changes and Supreme Court decisions that addressed Aboriginal rights and title. Both documents suggest that, within the implementation of these policies, everything is negotiable. Unfortunately, the reality is that the colonialist assumptions informing the Supreme Court decisions that constrain Aboriginal rights and title have moulded these policies as well. Both policies clearly articulate that Aboriginal laws and traditional jurisdictions cannot be part of negotiations relating to self-government or comprehensive claims, that Canada can unilaterally decide what constitutes an "integral" aspect of Aboriginal culture, that discussions on self-government will remain separate from those regarding territory (as if governance is not associated with territory), and above all, that questions of compensation will not be addressed. This last stipulation sidesteps any recognition that Canada's wealth has come (and continues to come) from appropriating Native peoples' lands and resources, and that Native poverty is therefore a direct result of Canada's wealth. Moreover, the Supreme Court decisions discussed above limit what is possible to achieve by litigation, leaving Native people no other option but to negotiate with Ottawa, inevitably from a position of weakness.

When Aboriginal rights were first entrenched in the Constitution, many Native people believed that at least some aspects of their control over their own affairs would be "on the table" as part of asserting a right to self-government or making a claim based on Aboriginal title. But in 2002, when talks on a number of comprehensive claims were proceeding under this assumption, Ottawa walked away from several negotiating tables across the country, labelling them "unproductive." These tables – 30 of approximately 170 – dealt with various matters ranging from specific claims, to self-government negotiations, to comprehensive claims within the British Columbia treaty process. When interviewed by the CBC, then Indian Affairs minister Robert Nault stated that he had discontinued negotiation with certain tables because Native leaders had made excessive demands. These included issues relating to Aboriginal jurisdiction and the right to enact certain laws and to resist having Ottawa delegate authority over all matters relating to self-government (Nahwegahbow 2002, 2).

In an environment where the Supreme Court decisions regarding Aboriginal rights and title have essentially predetermined what is open to negotiation, it is perhaps not surprising that Aboriginal leaders who attempt to infuse Indigenous frameworks of understanding into Canadian processes are characterized as unreasonable and acting in bad faith. Nevertheless, it is important to explore the self-government and comprehensive claims policies in some detail, to understand these processes more clearly.

The Inherent Right to Self-Government Policy

In 1995, the federal government released its Approach to Implementation of the Inherent Right and the Negotiation of Aboriginal Self-Government Policy. The document clearly states that recognition of inherent right is based on the view that the Aboriginal peoples of Canada have the right to govern themselves in relation to matters that are internal to their communities, integral to their unique cultures, identities, traditions, languages, and institutions, and with respect to their special relationship to their land and their resources (Canada 1995). The language here is virtually identical to that of *Van der Peet, Pamajewon,* and *Delgamuukw* in that it limits self-government to purely internal matters and "culturalizes" Aboriginal rights, so that what is to be protected are not the existence, needs, and livelihoods of Aboriginal peoples, but their pre-contact cultures. The policy explicitly states that the inherent right of self-government does not include a right of sovereignty in the international sense and will not result in sovereign independent Aboriginal nations. Instead, the participation of Aboriginal peoples in the Canadian federation will be enhanced, and they and their governments will not exist in isolation, separate and apart from the rest of Canadian society. By suggesting that Aboriginal perspectives lead only to total independence from Canada, the policy ignores any notion that these perspectives should be part of the dialogue about *how* Indigenous people are to participate within Canada.

Negotiations relating to self-government are tripartite, involving the First Nation, Ottawa, and the relevant province or territory. The policy indicates that Aboriginal jurisdictions and authorities should work in harmony with those of other governments, which suggests that some "give" is expected from the provinces in the matter of jurisdiction. However, should an

Aboriginal government's law conflict with any of the laws of the province or territory, it will be overridden by provincial or territorial law. Moreover, only matters considered internal to the group, integral to its distinct Aboriginal culture, and essential to its operation as a government can be part of self-government.

Although these limitations are extremely troubling, Aboriginal people are even more concerned about the financial aspects of the negotiations. The fact that no separate funds have been provided for implementation means that the considerable costs of transitioning to self-government must come from existing federal expenditures, which will depend on available resources. Second, although the policy suggests that self-government will ensure a stable source of funding for Aboriginal governments, there are no provisions to constitutionally protect transfer payments from Ottawa to First Nations in the manner in which provinces are constitutionally protected (McNeil 2002, 32). This leaves First Nations in a very vulnerable position, particularly given Canada's history of significantly underfunding Aboriginal infrastructure and services relating to basic needs such as housing, clean water, sanitation, and accessible health care. Third, Ottawa's fiduciary obligations may diminish if bands take on some level of control of their own lands.[1] In general, the new Aboriginal governments created under this policy would be significantly impoverished unless Ottawa chose to contribute the necessary funding.

As of September 2011, two BC bands (Sechelt and Westbank First Nations) had negotiated self-government agreements, and nine Yukon First Nations had negotiated a self-government agreement as part of their comprehensive claim (AAND 2011). An examination of these agreements reveals that all generally adhere to a template, suggesting that the policy framework and process determined what was to be discussed. Notably, divisions between status and non-status Indians are maintained: Canada will continue to fund services for status Indians who come under self-government agreements but will not do the same for non-status or Metis groups, who must seek funding agreements with their relevant provinces in order to obtain self-government. Perhaps not surprisingly, although urban communities, Metis groups, and other non-band organizations can negotiate self-government agreements, none have done so to date. Indeed, very few bands appear to have completed their negotiations, although most First Nations across Canada are involved in at least some aspects of self-government negotiation.

Criticism of the self-government policy has been extensive. For the most part, echoing the critiques of *Pamajewon,* it has asserted that the policy is permeated by colonial control. David Nahwegahbow (2002, 10) offers some perspective by taking a historical approach. He notes that Ottawa did not recognize the right to self-government until 1993, despite the 1983 Penner report, which recommended that it do so and, more importantly, stated that legislation be passed to preclude the application of provincial laws in all areas of jurisdiction necessary to permit First Nations to govern themselves effectively. Furthermore, in 1990, the Royal Commission on Aboriginal Peoples had articulated the need for an Aboriginal Nations Recognition and Government Act, an Aboriginal government transition centre for capacity building, and a new Department of Aboriginal Relations to oversee the self-government process. Significantly, both the Penner and royal commission reports, which both advocated creating significant levels of controls for Aboriginal governments, maintained that federal governmental structures related to Aboriginal governments should be located outside the Department of Indian Affairs (ibid., 11).

Other criticism of the self-government policy focused on the First Nations Governance Act, which was derided because the rights it conferred were virtually synonymous with those already obtainable under the Indian Act. As Kent McNeil (2002, 19-23) suggests, if self-government is to involve more than a simple devolution of Indian Act rights, it must be more clearly tied to territorial issues. He adds that the inherent right to self-government must be seen as having two dimensions, one territorial and one personal. The former embodies the government that exercises authority over a specific geographical area. The latter involves authority over persons, who are usually citizens of a nation or residents of the territory over which the government has jurisdiction. In this framing, the inherent right of self-government is understood as conferring residual government authority over all aspects of Aboriginal life. The territorial dimension allows the nation to make and enforce laws related to land use and environmental protection, as well as hunting and fishing rights. The personal dimension involves jurisdiction over family law, marriage, adoption, and citizenship. McNeil notes in particular that the existence of a statutory definition of an "Indian" erodes the authority of Indigenous nations to determine their own citizenship according to their own rules, and that much research is needed in this area, considering what is at stake for First Nations.

Another criticism of the self-government policy relates to its mandatory inclusion of the Charter of Rights and Freedoms as part of self-government. McNeil (2002, 26) states that more is at stake here than the Charter's section 25 protection of Aboriginal rights. As Kerry Wilkins (1999, 119) explains, the Charter would affect traditional practices:

> The hope was that the Charter would ensure the courts of ways of protecting vulnerable individuals living within [self-governing] communities, and that its application would ensure an essential consistency to the notion of Canadian citizenship. Applied full-strength to inherent-right communities, however, the Charter stands to endanger the traditional foundations of order and authority which their own sense of integrity provides; in doing so, it most probably would disrupt the traditional ways of protecting the vulnerable and frustrate and discourage their own traditional notions of citizenship. None of the Charter's own mechanisms for mitigating these effects is especially satisfactory.

The most problematic issue, however, and one that applies equally to self-government and the comprehensive claims process, is identifying who has the right to self-government. The Royal Commission on Aboriginal Peoples carefully distinguished between Indigenous nations and local communities. It identified an Indigenous nation as a sizeable body of Indigenous people who share a sense of national identity and who constitute the predominant population in a territory or collection of territories. Local communities, on the other hand, are the smaller groupings of Indigenous people that are not themselves nations but are part of nations. The royal commission estimated that there are probably between fifty and eighty Indigenous nations in Canada and approximately a thousand local communities (RCAP 1996b, 178-81).

McNeil (2002, 28) points out that due to the fragmenting effect of the Indian Act's band system, many Aboriginal communities are most comfortable dealing at the band level, or at most the tribal council level, and have little skill or experience in working at the nation level. Added to this actuality is the fact that treaties and provincial boundaries bisect Indigenous nations, dividing them into different jurisdictions, with the result that envisioning a reunited nation is difficult. McNeil suggests that this fundamental area needs significant research to address ways of overcoming these divisions.

The Comprehensive Claims Policy

Federal policy assigns Aboriginal land claims to one of two broad categories. Comprehensive claims are based on the assertion of continuing Aboriginal rights and title that are not covered by a treaty or other legal vehicle. Specific claims arise from non-fulfillment of treaties or other legal obligations, or from the improper administration of lands or assets under the Indian Act or other formal agreement (Hurley 2009, 1). Despite the stipulations of its own policy,

Ottawa has agreed to negotiate a few comprehensive claims in areas governed by treaties. For example, in the Northwest Territories, it accepted the Dene and Metis claims in locations covered by Treaties 8 and 11 because the land provisions of the treaties had not been properly implemented (Turtle Island Native Network 2001). On the other hand, in areas administered by Peace and Friendship treaties – eighteenth-century agreements that ended the warfare between Indigenous nations and Britain – the question of title has never been addressed. Although the Mi'kmaq Nation in the Maritimes and southeastern Quebec signed Peace and Friendship treaties, Canada has refused to negotiate a comprehensive claim, stating that Aboriginal title in these regions was simply "superseded by law" without land cession treaties ever being negotiated (Marshall, Denny, and Marshall 1989, 101).

Modern Canadian treaty making was ushered in with the James Bay and Northern Quebec Agreement, a document of more than eight hundred pages, which was negotiated in 1975 between Quebec, its provincial energy corporation Hydro-Quebec, and a handful of Cree and Inuit communities who had always lived on the land, many of whom spoke little English or French. When the Cree and Inuit learned from outside sources (they were not even directly informed) of Hydro-Quebec's plans to construct a massive hydroelectric development on their traditional lands, they took the government to court. After six months of borrowing money and taking elders to testify in a Montreal courtroom a thousand miles to the south, the Cree and Inuit won an injunction, only to see it overturned in less than six hours. Ultimately, knowing that the La Grande Project would be completed before they could get a Supreme Court hearing, and fearing for its outcome, the Cree and Inuit were forced to negotiate an agreement. As Matthew Coon Come (2004, 156-57) describes it, naked power imbalances marked the process from beginning to end:

> Canada refused to intervene on our behalf, and Hydro-Quebec held a gun to our heads – the destruction of our lands and rivers continued daily while we negotiated. Thus it was that on 11 November, 1975 we signed the James Bay and Northern Quebec Agreement ... Over the last nearly thirty years since signing the JBNQA we have learned the many ways in which this was not a good agreement. We have been in and out of courts since 1975 to get the government to implement it. They still refuse and delay, and many of the benefits we were promised have failed to materialize. These benefits are things that all who live in Canada enjoy as a right. My people had to bargain for clean water supplies and sanitation, for clinics and schools, for our rights and our way of life.

The experience of the James Bay Cree with the first "modern treaty" reveals that, in terms of power relations, little distinguishes the new treaties from their historical counterparts.

All modern treaties, otherwise known as land claim agreements, are negotiated through the comprehensive claims policy, which came into existence in 1973 as a result of the *Calder* decision. Between 1973 and 2009, twenty-three comprehensive claims have been settled (Hurley 2009, 1-2). However, to truly understand the comprehensive claims process, we must examine how a claim is negotiated.

Negotiating a Comprehensive Claim

Before the negotiation process can begin, a First Nation is required to submit a statement of claim, which must include "a statement that the claimant group has not previously adhered to a treaty; a documented statement from the claimant group that it has traditionally used and occupied the territory in question and that this use and occupation continues; a description of the extent and location of such land use and occupancy, together with a map outlining the approximate boundaries; and, identification of the claimant group including the names of the bands, tribes or communities on whose behalf the claim is being made, the claimant's linguistic and cultural affiliation, and approximate population figures of the claimant group" (Canada 1987).

The federal government funds the research stage of the process, and if the land claim is accepted, First Nations must annually secure loans or grants from Ottawa to finance their participation in the negotiations. Claims are accepted only if the Indian Affairs minister deems that they have a high probability of success. Once a claim is accepted, the minister appoints a senior federal negotiator, who receives his or her mandate from Ottawa.

The parties then enter into preliminary negotiations, outlining areas to be discussed. It is important to understand that the "Scope of Negotiations" in the comprehensive claims policy establishes very strict parameters concerning what can be put on the table, in terms of land rights, waters, fisheries, subsurface royalties, and sacred sites. It rejects concepts such as co-management or sharing environmental management with First Nations. It also establishes fiscal caps and sets limits on royalties and revenue sharing – indeed, on most areas under discussion. Perhaps most importantly, it maintains the existing constitutional division of power between Ottawa and the provinces (ibid.). Clearly, control of the process is firmly in the hands of the federal government.

The first crucial issue to consider here is the power imbalance relating to funding. Because they are borrowing money from Ottawa, Native people who launch a claim are aware that during every day of the negotiations, their debt is mounting and that it will ultimately be deducted from the final settlement. Nor are these amounts trivial. According to an Indian Affairs estimate, the cost of negotiating a land claim can range from $15 to $50 million (INAC 2003, 22). Once this amount has been deducted from the cash settlement, the actual monies received will be significantly reduced. Although Ottawa has forgiven some of these loans, the general rule is that they must be paid, and so the first "gun" held to the head of Indigenous people is the pressure to negotiate fast before the debt piles up. And since Ottawa controls funding, the possibility that funding may be withdrawn if agreements are not forthcoming represents an additional set of pressures.

Of course, the irony of these pressure tactics is that the poverty of Native communities, which makes them dependent on government loans for land claim negotiations, exists precisely because their wealth has been expropriated via the colonial process. In seeking title to the land, they are forced to borrow money from the very government that appropriated their land and resources in the first place. The funding issue highlights the fact that modern treaty negotiations are built upon a negation of the living reality of colonial history and the power it has granted Canada. For example, Canada continually denies that it should pay compensation for centuries of occupying people's land and usurping their resources. Its negotiators repeatedly insist that "history has been dealt with" via the apology to victims of residential schooling and the $350 million healing fund, and that the cash component of treaty settlements is an exchange of "value for value" (de Costa 2002a, 8).

In this manner, power relations can remain hidden, and compensation levels can be kept abysmally low. In the case of the Nisga'a, for example, it was determined that the damages they had sustained in over a century of occupation and resource theft amounted to $4.3 billion, yet their settlement involved $240 million (Gehl 2006). Of course, the millions of dollars that the Nisga'a had borrowed during their twenty-five years of claim negotiation were deducted from this settlement.

However, the biggest government pressure tactic is that untrammelled resource development continues while the treaty is being negotiated. For many Native people, the fact that clear cutting continues to devastate their homeland or that mines are being created on their territories while they sit in negotiations are powerful incentives to keep negotiations brief and accept whatever terms are offered.

The extinguishment of title is perhaps the most crucial concern for many Aboriginal people. Critics of the comprehensive claims process have suggested that the government should not seek to extinguish Aboriginal title: instead, it should specify which rights it is seeking from Native people to develop and use land and resources (Conseil Attikamek Montagnais et al. 1986). However, given the power imbalance that permeates the comprehensive claims policy, negotiations are grounded in either the full extinguishment of title or a specification of exactly what rights Aboriginal people will retain in the land.

The 1973 comprehensive claims policy contained what were referred to as "blanket extinguishment" provisions in that Indigenous people were to "cede, release and surrender" all Aboriginal rights and interests in and to the settlement area in exchange for the benefits provided by the settlement agreement. When Indigenous people's dissatisfaction regarding this requirement was obviously impeding the progress of claims, Canada adopted a new approach in 1986. This consisted of two alternatives – modified rights and non-asserted rights. In the former, which was first employed during the Nisga'a negotiations, Aboriginal rights are modified rather than extinguished, becoming solely the rights enshrined in the treaty. Under the latter, Aboriginal rights remain unextinguished, but Indigenous groups agree not to exercise them, confining themselves solely to the rights articulated and defined in the treaty. The 1986 policy allowed for the retention of Aboriginal rights on land that Indigenous people will hold once their claim is settled, but only insofar as such rights are not inconsistent with the treaty. Since the implementation of the 1995 comprehensive claims policy, Canada has continued to explore new approaches to achieving its primary goal – "certainty" with regard to lands and resources – without requiring outright surrender of Aboriginal land rights. For example, the Tlicho Agreement, which came into effect in 2005, distinguishes between land rights and non-land rights. Finality is achieved for land rights, and clarity and predictability for non-land rights. The agreement applies the non-assertion approach, whereby the Tlicho agree not to exercise or assert any rights other than those set out in the agreement.

Ravi de Costa (2002b, 8-9), in a trenchant criticism of the concept of "certainty" as expressed by the federal government, has commented,

> Certainty is best understood as working out what happens after treaties are concluded ... A small industry has evolved to take extinguishment phrases out of the argot of agreement-making in Canada. From "Cede, release and surrender" – the earliest phrasing – to the language of the James Bay and Northern Quebec Agreement, in which First Nations "release" and then are "granted-back" their rights, this has been a productive field. The current orthodoxy is "Modify and release," which has operated since 1998 and is the

> approach taken in the Nisga'a Final Agreement. Yet sections 26-31 of the Nisga'a Final Agreement may make this all a mere exercise in semantics. Here the two governments are "released from future claims"; they have "a duty to consult" only under the terms of the Agreement itself; they receive an indemnity against all "acts or omissions" that may have infringed aboriginal title "before the effective date"; and are provided with an indemnity against any infringements of still existing rights not protected and set out in the NFA. This is what governments call non-extinguishment ... It is clear that no concept in Indigenous-settler relations is more fetishised than certainty, but the treaty process lays bare the question: is "certainty" the recognition of Indigenous rights, or an indemnity against their assertion?

De Costa's comments are echoed by Stephen Aronson and Ronald Maguire (1996, 59, 64), who suggest that the differences between the original extinguishment clauses in the 1973 policy and the current approaches in the 1996 policy are "modest" in nature. They observe that modern-day settlements are similar to "private real estate transactions" in that "the only right Indigenous people have is the right to surrender lands and resources to the Crown."

If comprehensive claims are really modern treaties, it is clear that at the heart of treaty making, past and present, lies the assumption of Crown sovereignty. Indeed, as Kent McNeil (2002) demonstrates, jurisprudence in this area is instructive. McNeil compares four Supreme Court cases – *Simon, Sioui, Sparrow,* and *Delgamuukw* – to reveal the inconsistencies in the establishment of sovereignty. The *Simon* case of 1985 considered the rights accrued under the 1752 Treaty of Peace and Friendship between the Mi'kmaq and Britain; *Sioui,* which dates from 1990, involved a 1760 treaty between the Hurons of Lorette and Britain. The court viewed the Mi'kmaq and the Hurons as "quasi-sovereign nations" who were treaty signatories with Britain, and it recognized a range of rights under the two treaties. By comparison, in *Sparrow* and *Delgamuukw,* the court saw the Musqueam, the Gitksan, and the Wet'suwet'en as having been subjugated simply because Britain had asserted sovereignty over British Columbia in 1846. McNeil highlights the contradictions here: According to the court, British sovereignty at the time of the two eighteenth-century treaties was not yet established in Eastern Canada, even though the British had been in the area for over a century. But in 1846, when a treaty between Britain and the United States established the forty-ninth parallel as the boundary between their respective western possessions, it conclusively proclaimed British sovereignty over the whole of British Columbia, even though the British had barely entered the west coast at this time. McNeil emphasizes the necessity of conducting research into how British sovereignty can supersede Indigenous jurisdiction – how it is that European settlement automatically confers Crown sovereignty, and indeed, how sovereignty can be asserted when no treaties are established with Indigenous people.

Although Crown sovereignty lies at the heart of the treaty relationship between Aboriginal people and the Crown, sacredness has been central to treaties between Aboriginal peoples themselves. According to the report of the Royal Commission on Aboriginal Peoples (RCAP 1996a, 68-69), treaties were of the highest order of diplomatic relations across the continent and were maintained through the use of ceremony, replete with rituals, oratory, and specific protocols such as the exchange of wampum belts and smoking the sacred pipe, all of which were conscientiously observed by treaty partners. Indigenous terminology relating to treaties reveals an extraordinary attention to detail and to the various types of treaties. In the Ojibwa language, for example, there is a difference between *Chi-debahk-(in)-Nee-Gay-Win,* an open agreement with matters to be added to it, such as the Lake Huron Treaty of 1850, and *Bug-in-Ee-Gay,* which relates to "letting it go" – treaties requiring no further terms. However, treaties were always regarded as living entities to be renewed in ceremonies, which in turn renewed relationships. Nations cemented treaties with each other for purposes of trade, peace, neutrality, alliance, the use of territories and resources, and protection, resulting in far-reaching geopolitical alliances ranging from the Wendat Confederacy, which united four nations of similar dialects, to the Wabanaki Confederacy, the Iroquois Confederacy, and the Blackfoot Confederacy, each of which united diverse nations with many languages. Once formed, these confederacies were strengthened by the demands of the fur trade and became mechanisms for dealing with European colonists.

During the fur trade, Europeans entered into treaties according to Indigenous protocols, but this dynamic changed once Native people began to lose control of their territories. Particularly in Eastern Canada, the waning of the fur trade and its replacement with settlement policies, the drastic decline in Indigenous populations due to epidemics and warfare, and the growth of internecine divisions brought about by religious conversion and other destabilizing factors all contributed to this loss of power for Indigenous nations in their dealings with Europeans (Lawrence 2002, 41). In this situation, it was all too easy for Europeans to negotiate treaties that were ostensibly about peace and trade but were subsequently revealed to focus on land cession (ibid.). As a result, between 1781 and 1830, most of southern Ontario was surrendered to Europeans. Between 1814 until the census of 1851, the white population of what is now southern Ontario multiplied by a factor of ten, from 95,000 to 952,000 (J.R. Miller 2009, 94). Given the attenuated power that Native peoples now commanded, the old alliances between themselves and Europeans were abandoned.

With Confederation and the increasing power of the Canadian state came an accelerated process of land acquisition treaties in Western Canada and the North, so that in less than fifty years, eleven numbered treaties had been signed, claiming all the land stretching from Lake Superior to the Rockies and north to the Arctic Ocean.

Lynn Gehl (2009, 5) has compared these historic treaties with the modern treaties of the comprehensive claims policy. She has discovered that, with the exception of the Nunavut settlement, the modern treaties involved First Nations obtaining self-government powers only at the level of a municipality.[2] In examining the numbered treaties, she also found that Treaties 1, 2, and 5 allocated 32 acres per person, whereas the other numbered treaties apportioned 120 acres per person. Under the terms of the Nisga'a Agreement, each individual received 80 acres.

And yet, this does not compare with the situation of the Lheidli T'enneh, a band near Prince George. With a traditional territory of 10,000 square kilometres, the band was offered 29 square kilometres, 7 of which were reserve lands that it already held. This band, whose land borders Treaty 8 territory, would have been entitled to 140 square kilometres had it signed that treaty a hundred years ago (de Costa 2002a, 4). In April 2007, it voted to reject the treaty that it had spent thirteen years and $1 billion negotiating with the federal and provincial governments. Only 47 percent of its 234 members voted in favour of the treaty. In general, it appears that modern treaties, at least those south of the sixtieth parallel, seek to leave Native people with less land than the historic treaties ever did.

In fact, more than any other aspect of Canadian policy, treaties grounded in European terms, both historically and in the modern era via the comprehensive claims policy, reveal the ongoing colonialism at the heart of Canadian society. It is not merely that Canada assumed sovereignty over the land with no clear basis under its own laws, it is also the hostile and mean-spirited attitude that Canada displays regarding any notion that it should now share the land in the traditional Aboriginal manner of negotiating treaties. Indeed, Canada appears determined to keep the door slammed shut on any possibility of real Native participation in activities on traditional lands. Ultimately, there is little difference between, on the one hand, historical treaty making and policies based on assimilation, and on the other, modern treaty making and policies based on containment and the notion that Native peoples will be domesticated through subordination to Canadian authority and therefore finally neutralized as sovereign entities.

Perhaps not surprisingly, the comprehensive claims policy has been challenged on a number of levels. For example, John Olthuis and Roger Townshend (1996), who voice many criticisms of the policy, assert that equity and compensation must be assessed according to the value of the assets on the date they are restored, not on the date in which they were improperly taken.

The British Columbia Treaty Process

Since 1871, when British Columbia joined Confederation, the province has consistently refused to recognize that Aboriginal peoples have any rights requiring recognition by "civilized law" (Culhane 1998, 27). Because of this, when Canada set up the comprehensive claims process in 1973, the British Columbia government refused to recognize that most of the province had outstanding claims: its position was that Aboriginal title did not exist and that therefore it had no need to negotiate land claims (ibid.). However, by 1983, Native people had responded by blockading highways, railroad lines, and forestry access roads, as well as seeking and receiving injunctions to stop resource development throughout the province. Many cut logs "illegally" from the logging operations working without benefit to them on their land (de Costa 2002b, 3).

British Columbia is hugely dependent on its resource extraction industries. At the time of the blockades, 100,000 of the province's 1.9 million labour force worked directly in forestry and forest products, which provided British Columbia with approximately $1.6 billion in export revenue. This comprised 50 percent of provincial exports and nearly 5 percent of total exports from Canada as a whole (de Costa 2002a, 2).

Native activism represented a profound threat to the provincial economy, so the British Columbia Claims Task Force was set up in 1990; its report, approved the following year, suggested that the Province enter into negotiations with BC First Nations. Within two years, the British Columbia Treaty Commission Agreement was signed between Canada, British Columbia, and the First Nations Summit, a peak body of a majority of BC Native groups in the province. The agreement was enacted as legislation in 1993, creating the British Columbia Treaty Commission.

The fundamental goals of treaty making in British Columbia were to deal with outstanding land claims through a negotiation process, to define Aboriginal rights and title, and to create a "new relationship" between Aboriginal people and settlers, many of them working in resource industries. Negotiation would be patterned after the comprehensive claims process, but with the obvious power that BC First Nations had demonstrated in forcing this issue, Ottawa initially exerted much less overall control. Shepherding a claim through the British Columbia Treaty Process involves six steps (de Costa 2008):

1. Submitting a statement of intent to negotiate a treaty, which includes a rough indication of their traditional territory and a sense of who they are and how they are organized.
2. Preparing for negotiations and demonstrating "table readiness": Here all parties have to demonstrate their "mandate," their capacity to negotiate and ratify agreements, and what measures for public observation of treaties and consultation are to be put in place.
3. Framework agreement negotiations: These relate generally to the structure of the negotiations involving a broad indication of the issues that each party wishes to discuss. The framework agreement is then ratified according to the processes set out in step 2.
4. Agreement in principle negotiations: These are the first substantive negotiations on the topics the three parties wish to discuss. The aim is to agree on drafts of chapters that are to become the final text and therefore receive constitutional protection. Ratification at this stage requires the Province to obtain cabinet approval.
5. Negotiating a final agreement involves discussions to agree on final texts. Here constitutional and legal reviews must be undertaken. Once a final agreement is reached, it must be ratified by all three parties. Subsequently a community referendum must take place within the First Nation involved, which enables the community to accept or reject the agreement. If the community indicates its acceptance, the agreement must then obtain the approval of both the British Columbia legislature and the Parliament of Canada. On the "effective date" negotiated, this agreement becomes a treaty under the terms of section 35 of the Constitution Act of 1982.
6. Implementation: This involves the transfer of cash and authority over lands and resources as indicated in the final agreement. At this point, the First Nation will no longer be administered under the Indian Act but under terms of its own making.

The British Columbia Treaty Commission began accepting statements of intent from First Nations in December 1993. Originally, it assumed that about twenty tables would be established, but by late 1993, it had received forty-three statements of intent, and by 2002, forty-nine First Nations were sitting at forty tables.

A number of issues arose, some immediately, and some only after much time and money had been spent. These are enumerated below:

a In the loan system, loans are due seven years after the table reaches an agreement in principle or twelve years after the first loan if talks break down. Most First Nations objected to having to borrow money to negotiate. As they saw it, this involved impoverished Native people incurring debt so that the settler governments could rationalize Indigenous rights into the dominant political system.

b In the haste to set up the system, nobody addressed the question of who actually had the right to negotiate in connection with a territory. The Indian Act had added multiple levels of Native governance, including tribal councils and bands, to the existing traditional frameworks. A complete lack of clarity regarding who possessed Aboriginal title was revealed at the negotiation tables, a problem that was thrown into sharp relief by developments subsequent to the Nisga'a Agreement. After the agreement was ratified, the Gitanyow and Gitksan hereditary chiefs insisted that it incorporated part of their lands and they took the case to court (de Costa 2002b, 6).

c For most Native people, land was the central issue, and reclaiming authority over as much as possible was their primary goal. However, the federal negotiators tried to apply guidelines resembling those of the comprehensive claims process – rejecting co-management and shared jurisdiction on non-settlement lands. Indeed, Ottawa and Victoria were reluctant even to discuss "quantum" – the package they were "buying" for the jurisdictional certainty they desired, in terms of settlement lands and cash – until negotiations had been under way for some time. Most First Nations, on the other hand, wanted a sense of the quantum early in the process, before they had borrowed large sums of money only to finally receive an unacceptable offer. Many have walked away from the process because they were not offered appropriate levels of jurisdiction over their traditional land. Indeed, after a number of years, many First Nations concluded that the quantum being offered by Victoria and Ottawa was calculated formulaically, so that $60,000-$65,000 per person in land and cash was all that would ever be offered.

d With so many tables, the resources of the Province were immensely stretched, with few trained negotiators. A decade after the process began, most tables were commonly granted only one day of negotiation every six weeks (de Costa 2002a, 2). As their debt piled up and logging continued on their traditional territories, First Nations repeatedly asked that interim measures be implemented – in particular, a moratorium on resource development for the duration of negotiations. Instead, they were commonly offered palliative measures to ameliorate the terrible lack of services in their communities. In conversations with Robert Lovelace, he has referred to this tactic as "deliberate famine," in which First Nations are intentionally underserviced and denied the basic necessities that Canadians take for granted, in the hopes that they will surrender, in exchange for basic services, what Canada most values – the title to their lands.

e As is the case with the comprehensive claims process, Canada refused to accept the notion of compensation, whereas British Columbia insisted that cash payments would be for "economic development." However, by 2002, the First Nations Summit had passed a motion that all final agreements must deal explicitly with compensation (ibid.).

f Like land, self-government was a key issue. Many BC First Nations absolutely rejected the notion of being reduced to municipalities. Instead, they asserted the need for governance of an entirely different order, constituting a new branch of Canadian sovereignty (ibid., 4).

By the end of 2000, BC First Nations were $150 million in debt, with little to show for it. The *Delgamuukw* decision had expanded the nature of Aboriginal title in law, but the actions of the British Columbia Treaty Commission did not reflect this. Some First Nations began considering abandoning the treaty process and instead beginning litigation, whereas others felt that perhaps the burden of proving rights to ownership and jurisdiction over their traditional lands should rest with settler governments and not with themselves. Many concluded that they should simply exercise their rights on their traditional territories regardless of recognition, engaging in what some have referred to as the Gisday process (de Costa 2002b, 10).[3]

At the time of writing, very few treaties have been ratified. The Maa-nulth First Nations, of Vancouver Island, had their treaty ratified in mid-2009 (BC Treaty Commission 2006), and the Tsawwassen First Nation's treaty of April 2009 had not yet been ratified by the band. The Lheidli T'enneh Nation signed an agreement, but during the community ratification process, the band rejected it in March 2007 (Brethour 2007, 1). Agreements in principle have been reached with the In-SHUCH-ch Nation, Sliammon First Nation, Yale First Nation, Yekoche First Nation, and Sechelt Indian band. All were signed between 1999 and 2007, but none have reached the level of a final agreement.[4]

Writing about the BC treaty process, Taiaiake Alfred (1999, xiii-xix) stated in no uncertain terms that it enables Canada to retain the land base that is the foundation of its power, while devolving the more onerous details of administration to First Nations, granting them powers akin to those of a municipality and enforcing compliance with provincial regulations in exchange for a cash settlement, greater control over their former reserves, areas of shared jurisdiction, and a permanent surrender of all Aboriginal title to traditional lands. Indeed, the process that most Native people first viewed as central to asserting title has become the primary means through which title is surrendered.

Rejecting the Politics of Recognition

A number of Aboriginal scholars have questioned the entire process of seeking recognition from settler governments. Glen Coulthard (2008, 188) notes that for the past thirty years, the self-determination efforts of Indigenous people in Canada have increasingly been cast in the language of "recognition." Coulthard applies the term "politics of recognition" to various recognition-based models of liberal pluralism that seek to reconcile Indigenous claims to nationhood with Crown sovereignty via the accommodation of Indigenous identities in some form of renewed relationship with the Canadian state. This may involve the delegation of land, capital, and political power from the state to Indigenous communities, generally through land claim agreements, economic development initiatives, and self-government packages. Coulthard argues that instead of establishing co-existence grounded on the ideal of mutuality, the politics of recognition in its contemporary form is reproducing the configurations of colonial power that Indigenous struggles for recognition sought to transcend in the first place.

In noting that our identities – as individuals and as groups – do not exist in isolation, Coulthard (ibid., 196) suggests that if our identities are shaped by recognition, they can also be distorted by misrecognition, so that distorting representations of Indigeneity serve to damage Aboriginal people and prevent them from flourishing. In an analysis based on the work of Frantz Fanon, Coulthard observes that the long-term stability of a colonial structure of dominance depends as much on the "internalization" of racist forms of asymmetrical and non-mutual modes of recognition as it does on brute force.

According to Fanon, a colonial configuration of power must be attacked at two levels if one hopes to transform it; these are the objective level, where power is maintained through the appropriation of land and resources, and the subjective level, where ideological structures of dominance are ensconced in racist "recognition."

From this perspective, the politics of recognition can address colonial injustice only in reformist terms. The promotion of state redistribution schemes that grant certain "cultural rights" and economic concessions to Indigenous communities through land claims and self-government agreements fails to address the objective level of power that colonialist states have accrued via land and resource theft. The liberal recognition paradigm enables colonialist states to maintain power by "managing" land claims to their own benefit.

The second problem with the recognition paradigm relates to the subjective realm of power relations. Most recognition-based proposals rest on the problematic assumption that the flourishing of Indigenous peoples as distinct and self-determining is dependent on being recognized by the settler state. For Fanon, only resistance struggles – Coulthard calls them "transformative practices," such as struggles for cultural regeneration – are capable of enabling subjugated people to deconstruct the racist misrecognition that is so harmful.

When recognition is not accompanied by the transformative practice of cultural resistance, the fundamental self-transformation that comes with decolonization cannot occur. Under the politics of recognition, the colonized may receive constitutionally protected rights but cannot challenge the subjugation of their sovereign rights that is inherent in the process of delegating power. Indeed, those who engage in the politics of recognition must accept the infantilization and belittling of Indigenous societies that ensues when colonizers define the "integral" aspects of their "special cultures," delegating self-government that does not entail real Indigenous control and structuring land claims so as to permit no self-determination. In addition, Coulthard suggests that Indigenous people who work within the politics of recognition are in grave danger of adopting the limited and structurally contained terms of recognition as their own, so that in effect they identify with what he calls "white liberty" and "white justice."

As Coulthard (ibid., 195) points out,

> Anybody familiar with the power dynamics that currently structure the Aboriginal rights movement in Canada should immediately see the applicability of Fanon's insights here. Indeed, one need not expend much effort at

> all to elicit the countless ways in which the liberal discourse of recognition has been limited and constrained by the state, politicians, corporations and the courts in ways that pose no fundamental challenge to the colonial relationship. With respect to the law, for example, over the last thirty years the Supreme Court of Canada has consistently refused to recognize Indigenous peoples' equal and self-determining status, based on the Court's adherence to legal precedent founded on the white supremacist myth that Indigenous societies were too primitive to bear fundamental political rights when they first encountered European powers. Thus, even though the Court has secured an unprecedented degree of recognition for certain "cultural" practices within the colonial state, it has nonetheless failed to challenge the racist origin of Canada's assumed authority over Indigenous peoples and their territories.

Coulthard's arguments reveal that, far from being liberatory, the politics of recognition is increasingly what Canada *needs* in order to absorb an Indigenous presence into its liberal democratic framework and to convince the world that it is *not* a colonial state. It seeks to demonstrate that "its" Indigenous peoples – tamed and domesticated – have become reconciled with the state and are happily co-existing within it, now that Canada protects its "special" cultures. For Indigenous people to step back from the politics of recognition – to refuse to be "reconciled" to Canada under such terms, and instead, to seek strength in their own traditions and their own land-based practices – may not challenge the brute force of colonial power, but it does delegitimate it.

Coulthard's reasoning is supported by Taiaiake Alfred (2005), who asserts that the large-scale "statist" solutions offered by Canada, such as land claim negotiations and self-government, merely provide a good living for those who represent their people in such contexts. At the same time, however, the great majority of Native people do not benefit from such practices, and indeed, are bearing the brunt of a racist society that denigrates their identities as Indigenous people and has done its best to erode and destroy Indigenous peoples' traditional frameworks of identity as ensconced in language and relationship to the land. The result is weakened and isolated people, too often consumed by addictions and tremendously unhealthy. Alfred suggests that a strategic focus on self-help for many Native people who are struggling with addiction and poor health is fundamentally necessary for decolonization, whereas those who are stronger and able to engage in critical resistance should concentrate on delegitimizing Canada's liberal democratic facade and reclaiming traditional practices on the land.

This understanding of legal decisions, self-government policies, and the comprehensive claim process – which can be summed up as the politics of recognition – provides a background for the issues entailed in the Algonquin land claim, the subject of the next chapter.

4

The Algonquin Land Claim

In the previous chapter, we learned how legal and policy frameworks seriously diminished the promise of Aboriginal rights and title that marked the 1970s and early 1980s in Canada. Moreover, we saw that the Indian Act has created significant confusion as to which levels of government – traditional clan governance, Indian Act governments, or tribal councils – actually possess the authority to assert Aboriginal title.

What we have not considered is the extent to which this situation can profoundly divide communities. A case in point is the Ontario Algonquin land claim, which reveals much about the long-term fragmenting effects created by the provincial boundary running through the heart of the territory. However, it reveals still more about the rupturing of Algonquin identity through the Indian Act and the multiple and ongoing ways in which a comprehensive land claim can intensify conflicts within and between communities.

Beginning the Process

In 1976, Chief Dan Tennisco of Golden Lake (which was subsequently renamed Pikwakanagan) asked the Rights and Treaty Research Programme of the Union of Ontario Indians to examine the federal government's taking of railway rights-of-way on the Golden Lake reserve. This necessitated an inquiry into the establishment of the reserve and the settlement of the area, which soon revealed that no evidence for the surrender of Algonquin territory existed (Sarazin 1989,

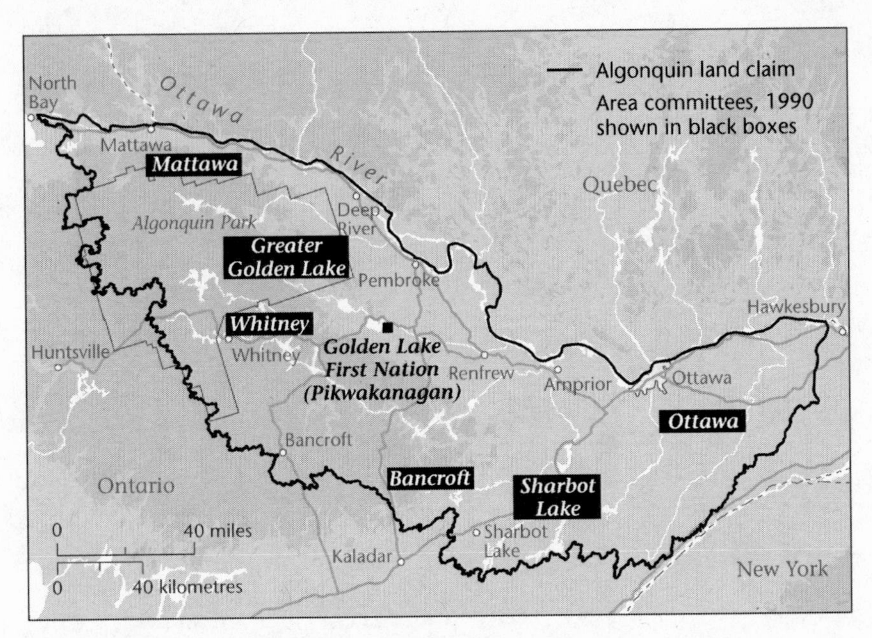

The Algonquin land claim and area committees, 1990

191). Given this, the Algonquins were in a position to assert Aboriginal title to their traditional land base, the Ottawa River watershed.

However, if title had never been surrendered, the immediate question, of course, was who should assert it? Initial discussions involved the federally recognized communities in both provinces: one in Ontario – Pikwakanagan, with a population of under four hundred at the time – and nine in Quebec, where two-thirds of Algonquin traditional territory lies. Living under the Indian Act had undoubtedly bound these communities together, but to suggest that this was sufficient to unite them is to ignore deeper complexities. As mentioned above, their histories had begun to diverge during the nineteenth century as large numbers of Quebec Algonquins maintained both their language and a life on the land, whereas their Ontario counterparts, overwhelmed by settlers, lost their language and were systematically deprived of their lands except for the small reserve at Golden Lake. In addition, Quebec Algonquins faced a provincial regime that viewed any assertions of Aboriginal rights or title as an affront to its own assertions of sovereignty and that had expressed its extreme nationalist sentiments through creating large development projects in Algonquin territory. Inevitably, support for land claim research in Quebec would take a back seat to stopping clear cutting and hydroelectric projects.

Ultimately, given the different circumstances they faced, the communities decided to proceed with their respective research toward establishing a collective claim to the entire land base.

It is unclear whether the parties in discussion ever gave thought to the Quebec and Ontario Algonquins who lacked Indian status. Even if some individuals knew of their existence, the band leadership was almost certainly unaware of the full extent of Algonquin dispossession that had been brought about by the denial of recognition of non-status Algonquins.

In 1978, a meeting between Pikwakanagan and the Quebec communities revealed that although Pikwakanagan had almost finished the necessary research for a statement of intent, the Quebec communities had not. Some were engaged in efforts to protect the land or were organizing against the ongoing criminalization of hunting, and still others were struggling to acquire formal reserves (Matachewan 1989, 148, 156-64). As a result, Pikwakanagan decided to pursue its own claim. One can only conjecture what would have happened if Pikwakanagan had chosen to assert Algonquin jurisdiction by ignoring the provincial boundary and engaging in a pan-Algonquin struggle to protect the land, rather than undertaking a land claim alone. Nor was there apparently much thought taken as to whether, in forging ahead with a separate claim, Pikwakanagan would permanently sever the Algonquin Nation. In many respects, had Ontario Algonquins focused on building stronger bonds with the Quebec reserves and on reclaiming language and healing many of the fractures of the Algonquin Nation that colonization had brought, asserting Algonquin nationhood through the comprehensive claims process would have fundamentally changed their circumstances.

Instead, Pikwakanagan claimed the Algonquin territory on the southern side of the Ottawa River, whereas the Quebec communities concentrated on the northern side. The bands had agreed that, should any negotiations occur, one designated representative from each side of the river would be invited to attend meetings on the other side, and all research would be shared (Sarazin 1989, 191). Accordingly, in 1983, Pikwakanagan delivered a petition to Ottawa, dictated by protocol and signed by almost all its adult population. The petition cited at least twenty-three previous petitions and formally requested immediate recognition that all Ontario Crown land in the Ottawa River watershed below Mattawa belonged to the Algonquin Nation, as represented by Pikwakanagan (ibid., 192). By this action, Pikwakanagan explicitly claimed the right to speak on behalf of all Algonquins in Ontario; implicitly, then, other Algonquins would be expected to join the land claim under its terms.

An indication of the unequal power relations between the Algonquins and Ottawa is apparent in Canada's delay in even responding to the claim. Although its own policy specified that it must formally respond within twelve months after a claim was submitted, nine years elapsed before Ottawa finally joined the Ontario government and Pikwakanagan in land claim discussions (Sarazin 1989, 200). Indeed, five years after the claim was submitted, massive combined action from Pikwakanagan and non-status Algonquins across the territory was required to stop Ontario's plans for fast-tracking development in the Ottawa Valley and to bring the Ontario government to the table (ibid., 194).

At this juncture, the Algonquins could have proposed a natural resources accord to provide a form of funding independent of government loans. In an interview conducted by Heather Majaury with long-time Aboriginal rights activist Bob Lavalley in 2005, he stated that accessing the income from resource development would provide an economic base that would enable the Algonquins to undertake some necessary nation-building tasks in preparation for negotiation. Even an accord that granted a small percentage of profits from resource development in the watershed would significantly change the negotiation process.

For 150 years, logging in the Ottawa Valley had created enormous fortunes, first in timber, then in pulp and paper. During the 1980s, while the Algonquins were waiting for Ottawa to respond to their 1983 petition, the forest industry was generating $573 million every year on the Ontario side of the watershed alone (Ottawa River Heritage Designation Committee 2005b, 102). Pulp and paper had stimulated the construction of hydro dams, and hydroelectric projects between the 1880s and 1960s had radically changed the Ottawa River. They had flooded lands and built dams that created a physical barrier to river life (Ottawa River Heritage Designation Committee 2005a, 118, 124), submerging Algonquin villages and sacred sites and radically disrupting the ability to rely on the river for food and transportation. Indeed, the 1984 value of the electricity generated by the Ottawa River was about $1 million per day (Ottawa River Regulation Planning Board 1984). The wealth of Canadian society is clearly predicated on many years of Algonquin impoverishment.

Although the comprehensive claims policy had been modified by 1992 and stipulated what Algonquins could and could not claim, limited resource sharing *was* on the table and could have been approached as an interim measure, given the unique circumstances of the Algonquin land claim. Nor were the Algonquins alone in advocating this approach. In 2007, the Canadian Centre for Policy Alternatives examined the 130 British Columbia forest accords negotiated in recent years, particularly the $2 billion that Victoria collected in stumpage fees – the monies paid by forest companies to the government when cutting trees on Crown land. The centre concluded that Victoria should forward all the fees to Aboriginal communities, noting that though they received a portion of the fees, this amounted to only 3.5 percent, or $35 million annually (*Windspeaker Business Quarterly* 2007, 9). Had the Ontario Algonquins succeeded in negotiating even 3.5 percent of provincial stumpage fees, their ability to conduct negotiations would have been greatly aided. And perhaps more importantly, their greatest obstacle – the difficulty of speaking with one voice when two very distinct experiences of on-reserve status Indians and federally unrecognized Algonquins were involved – could have been overcome through utilizing some of the funds for oral research into the histories of the non-status communities. Lack of recognition meant that the identities of non-status Algonquins had never been documented, and oral histories were probably the only means of clearly distinguishing the genealogies of today's non-status Algonquins without crude reliance on blood quantum. It also meant that funds could have been devoted toward consultation with Quebec communities, and ways of at least addressing jurisdictional overlap and perhaps ultimately bringing both provinces to the table could have been explored. But none of this could be even entertained, since a natural resource agreement was not, apparently, sought.

In 1992, Ottawa finally began negotiations. At the table, Pikwakanagan identified four issues for discussion:

- The need to establish an adequate Algonquin land base, to be made up of unoccupied Crown land
- Settling questions of natural resource use to reflect both Algonquin and non-Algonquin concerns in the territory
- Recognition and reaffirmation of the Algonquins' inherent right to complete jurisdiction over their land and people
- Obtaining fair compensation for past, present, and future use of Algonquin territory and its natural resources (Algonquin Golden Lake First Nation 1992b).

On 25 August 1994, a framework for negotiations was signed at Pikwakanagan. With this, the substantive negotiations of the claim could begin in earnest. If all went well, the process would move on to discuss an agreement in principle, which would detail the contents of a final settlement. The ultimate step would be the final agreement itself and its ratification and implementation.

Federally Unrecognized Algonquins Enter the Picture

According to Greg Sarazin (1998, 1), who was the first land claim negotiator, a number of reasons prompted Pikwakanagan to bring non-status Algonquins into the claim. First was its awareness that despite Indian Act categories, Algonquin history far predated the creation of the Golden Lake reserve and was shared by all Algonquin communities, whether federally recognized or not. Second, Pikwakanagan knew that, if federally unrecognized Algonquin communities organized independently of the reserve, Canada or Ontario could use any allegation of overlapping claims to potentially delay the negotiations. Thus, registering all Algonquins in the claim, status and non-status, was politically expedient. Finally, Pikwakanagan believed that alliances with other legitimate Algonquin groups in Ontario, even if they were federally unrecognized, would strengthen the numbers and the moral authority of the claim.

The word "legitimate" is important here, suggesting that a straightforward and singular standard exists to define who is Algonquin and who is not. Given the many levels of transformation endured by Ontario Algonquins during almost two hundred years of settler engulfment, and the differing colonial pressures faced by status and non-status Algonquins, this expectation was not realistic. Indeed, it lay at the root of the problems that subsequently arose.

In 1986 and 1987, Pikwakanagan Algonquins began trying to contact the descendants of the historical Algonquin settlements. Documents written at the time indicate that they could not easily recognize what Algonquinness looked like when it was non-status.[1] They assumed not only that non-status Algonquins would "look like Indians," but more importantly, they certainly expected that non-status settlements would be clearly delineated, as reserves are. No member of the Pikwakanagan negotiating team was familiar with the histories of dispersal experienced by federally unrecognized Algonquins when their land base was logged out and granted to settlers, which meant that even in cohesive communities people lived far apart and scattered among white people. Not until Pikwakanagan representatives began to inquire about current land use did the Algonquinness of those who lacked Indian status finally become somewhat visible to them.[2]

In 1990, Chief Kirby Whiteduck began meeting on behalf of Pikwakanagan with non-status Algonquin people in the areas of Bancroft/Baptiste Lake, Mattawa/North Bay, Sharbot Lake/Calabogie, and Whitney/Lake St. Peter. The intent of these meetings was first of all to form these networks of Algonquins into "area committees" and then to enable everyone to decide, by consensus, how the leadership of their area committee was to be selected –

generally by open nominations from the floor followed by secret ballots (Sarazin 1998, 2).

What this process ignored was that, prior to Canada's acceptance of the land claim, a handful of federally unrecognized Algonquin communities had already created modern organizations to represent themselves. Some had been engaged in active community building since the 1982 Constitution Act had enabled them to make claims on the state, despite lacking Indian status. Others, such as Ardoch, had developed a formal organization to protect its wild rice beds when the provincial government attempted to take them over in 1979. These communities, in which a strong leadership already existed, were not invited to participate in the meetings between Pikwakanagan and the non-status Algonquins; instead, unaffiliated individuals in their territories were asked to create separate area committees.

For example, the Pikwakanagan organizers initially overlooked a network of Algonquin families that had struggled for empowerment under the Ontario Metis and Non-Status Indian Association for the communities of Madawaska, Whitney, and Sabine. In his 2005 interview with Heather Majaury, Bob Lavalley, who had led this group for a number of years, explained that he had approached Pikwakanagan upon learning about the land claim and insisted that the Algonquins in his area should be included in it. A strong-minded individual with twenty years of activism relating to non-status Native rights, Lavalley was eventually brought in.

Although Lavalley and the Whitney, Madawaska, and Sabine families were included in the claim, three other federally unrecognized communities that had self-organized before negotiations began were not. The Antoine First Nation, Ardoch Algonquin First Nation, and the Bonnechere Algonquin Community were not invited to send representatives from their organizations. Instead, separate area committees were set up in their traditional territories, and band members were asked to leave their own organizations behind and enrol in them *as individuals* (Ardoch Algonquin First Nation and Allies 1996a).

Pikwakanagan faced some very real difficulties in the negotiations with respect to these federally unrecognized communities. It had struggled for nine years to be accepted as the First Nation claiming the entire Ontario territory, and its leadership clearly feared that bringing in federally unrecognized communities who already had a history of self-organizing and whose experienced leaders would expect a voice in the process might derail the claim by presenting alternative positions at the negotiating table. Canada and Ontario undoubtedly expected the Algonquins to speak with one voice, and Pikwakanagan had assumed that non-status Algonquins would rely on it to lead the process.

In such a precarious situation, it is perhaps unsurprising that Pikwakanagan opted for non-status Algonquins who were unaffiliated with any community in the areas where these organized committees existed. Unaffiliated individuals would presumably be grateful that Pikwakanagan had recognized them as Algonquins, which would make them more malleable and unlikely to assert their own views after being incorporated into the negotiation process. Once Pikwakanagan was forced to accept the Whitney, Madawaska, and Sabine communities as part of the claim, its leadership had no wish to bring in other strong non-status voices that might challenge its control.

For Antoine, Ardoch, and Bonnechere, however, effectively disbanding and joining a new Pikwakanagan-created area committee was to entirely undermine what made them Algonquin. Ardoch, in particular, could trace its lineage back to the early nineteenth century, when its traditional land base was being lost. To Ardoch members, this history and their long affiliation with their territories made them Algonquin. To join an area committee involved denying this history and being reduced to non-status individuals waiting for recognition by Pikwakanagan in order to "become" Algonquin.

Each side had its own reasons for adhering to its opposing positions. Nevertheless, this did not change the fact that the council of Pikwakanagan had been accepted to represent Ontario Algonquins or that the hegemony of Indian status worked in its favour. And although status Algonquins, whose identities had been defined by the Indian Act for over a century, had no clear notion of what a "legitimate" non-status Algonquin was, they had a great deal of authority in determining who would be accepted as Algonquin.

In terms of Indian Act norms or Ottawa's expectations regarding the parameters of the land claim, the three excluded communities could be considered anomalous in some way. Ardoch was considered anomalous in two ways – it had rejected the "chief and council" mode of governance created by the Indian Act, choosing instead to be ruled by a traditional "heads of families" government, where each family had representation. Moreover, it had sometimes used custom adoption to take in Native people from other nations, which has been a time-honoured practice among most Indigenous nations. Although traditional governments were now allowed under the Indian Act, Ottawa tended to distrust them, particularly if they voiced perspectives that challenged its authority. And in a 1992 meeting with Ardoch, Pikwakanagan's leadership voiced its concern about the presence of non-Algonquin Native people within the community, even though Pikwakanagan's membership contained many Native women from other nations who had become "naturalized" as Algonquins under the Indian Act as it existed prior to 1985 (Algonquin Golden Lake First Nation 1992a).

The Bonnechere Algonquin Community had started out as the Bonnechere Metis and Non-Status Indian Association. Although its leadership had conducted genealogical research to prove the Algonquin heritage of all community members, Bonnechere had accepted "Metis" funding in order to accomplish many of its goals. It could therefore be easily dismissed as Metis rather than Algonquin.

And finally, the Antoine community at Mattawa traced its lineage from historical bands on both sides of the Ottawa River, and some of its members lived in Quebec. Given that only the Ontario side of the territory was being included in the claim, the issues of traditional territories and membership that overlapped the Quebec-Ontario border were ample grounds to assert Antoine's non-compatibility with the claim.

However, a number of the community leaders whom I interviewed, particularly from Ardoch, were firm in their beliefs that Pikwakanagan had excluded the three communities primarily because, with a tradition and therefore an expectation of self-representation, they each had strong leaders with extensive experience of struggling for Native rights. Like Lavalley, who had fought to have Whitney, Madawaska, and Sabine included in the claim, the leaders of Antoine, Ardoch, and Bonnechere were cognizant of the Aboriginal rights of federally unrecognized communities and were certainly not "grateful outsiders" to Indianness. Thus, each of the three excluded communities had the potential to challenge the automatic assumption of Pikwakanagan's leadership or the notion that only Pikwakanagan should define who was Algonquin.

At the heart of the matter was the fact that Pikwakanagan did not really perceive any of the informal networks of non-status Algonquins that existed across the watershed, whether area committees or independently organized, as having any real connection to place. It did not see these informal networks of Algonquins as being historically connected to the lands that their ancestors had used. Although most non-status Algonquins were widely scattered throughout their ancestral territories, they still maintained close networks of relations, and for many, their grandparents' "Indianness," although poorly conceptualized at the time, was still clearly connected to specific practices in specific places. If Pikwakanagan had taken connections to place into account, the question of "who were the legitimate Algonquins" could have been answered fairly clearly by referring to many of the Algonquin elders at the time. Moreover, in the small towns of rural eastern Ontario where non-status Algonquins lived, even the older white people still had very clear notions as to which families were "Indian." This was perhaps most obvious in Pembroke, where a racially based class structure had segregated Algonquins, many of whom had been displaced from Allumette Island, from the settler society so that it was very clear who was Indian and who was not. But in the interviews I conducted, many individuals spoke of their parents' and grandparents' experiences of segregation in places such as Mattawa and Bancroft.

In the late 1980s and early 1990s, when Pikwakanagan first began wrestling with the issue of how to define what a non-status Algonquin was, many of these elders, Native and white, were still alive. Their recollections would have brought a degree of clarity in defining which non-status Algonquin families had maintained some aspect of Algonquin identity. Furthermore, other individuals who did not live in the territory could be evaluated through their connections to relatives. Proving connections to historical lineages would then have helped to anchor the identities of these networks of families, rather than functioning as the sole criterion in defining Algonquinness. Relying on the memories of elders, amplified by historical records, would also have prevented the inclusion of large numbers of Algonquins whose families had so intensively intermarried with settlers that they had abandoned their ancestral Native identity generations earlier but who wanted to claim a distant Algonquin lineage solely to gain hunting rights.

However, conducting oral histories with elders would have required time and money – a necessary investment if non-status Algonquin identity were to be properly addressed by the land claim. None of the federal government funding for preliminary research on the claim had been devoted to this task, which meant that during the nine years in which Pikwakanagan attempted to get Canada to the table, the existence of non-status Algonquins was ignored. Once Canada agreed to negotiate, Pikwakanagan apparently did not consider it necessary to request monies to address non-status Algonquin identity in any depth. In the intensely refracted world of Pikwakanagan, where being Algonquin meant having Indian status, the identities of non-status Algonquins may not have seemed important enough to warrant attention, except to bolster numbers in the land claim. The negotiators may also have been under great pressure from Canada to proceed quickly.

When Pikwakanagan created the area committees, then, it clearly viewed them as serving locales where non-status Algonquins now happened to reside, as if they had no historical rooting in any specific region. In essence, for non-status Algonquins, Pikwakanagan separated the question of non-status Algonquin identity from questions of place. As a result, a struggle ensued about blood quantum as being the defining characteristic of who was a legitimate Algonquin – ignoring the reality that what generally delineates Indigenous communities, federally recognized or not, is connection to place.

In October 1994, once the area committees had been created – with Antoine, Ardoch, and Bonnechere still excluded – the chief and council of Pikwakanagan invited them to a meeting to discuss how each would provide input into the negotiations. It was decided that the larger issues would be addressed by an Algonquin Nation Circle, which consisted of representatives from Pikwakanagan and the area committees, and that the shorter-term, more immediate issues would be handled by a smaller group, the Algonquin Management Circle (Sarazin 1998, 2). The chief and council of Pikwakanagan had the same function and status as an area committee representative in both the nation circle and the management circle. In February 1995, this process was implemented.

Lack of understanding of the issue of place was not the only problem created by the negotiations. It is almost certain that the Pikwakanagan status Indians, who were used to dominating the process, had little awareness of how to work across the very real differences in the community structures and legal regimes governing status and non-status Algonquins. Unfortunately, due to the exclusion of Antoine, Ardoch, and Bonnechere, a number of politically savvy leaders who were accustomed to working with both status and non-status Indians were also excluded. This was particularly regrettable because the divisive legacy created by the Indian Act and the exclusion of the majority of Algonquins from federal recognition meant that both sides were susceptible to significant mutual distrust and suspicion.

This was heightened by a lack of familiarity with each other, particularly on the part of Pikwakanagan. Although several non-status Algonquin leaders had a long-term involvement in Native politics and were therefore conversant with the political regimes faced by status Indians, most belonged to communities that had been excluded from the land claim. Within the claim, only Bob Lavalley was well versed in the politics of both status and non-status communities. The leadership of Pikwakanagan, on the other hand, worked solely with other status Indians and thus too frequently assumed that Indian identity was limited to those who held a status card. Knowing nothing about non-status Indians, it was ill-prepared to work across the differences separating the two groups.

By 1993, in consultation with the fledgling area committees, Pikwakanagan had produced a first draft of an Algonquin enrolment law. Once ratified, this was to be used only to determine who was entitled to *participate* in land claim negotiations. It included a Schedule A, a list of historically known Algonquins, which would be used as the basis for tracing lineage and thus determining who among the non-status should be included in the claim (Kanatiio 1998a, 3).

Although the enrolment law was intended to move beyond the Indian Act to include Algonquins who lacked Indian status, it sparked a great deal of controversy. The issue that dogged the footsteps of all involved and prompted considerable cynicism among non-status Algonquins was the fact that the Indian Act rules with which Pikwakanagan was accustomed to working continually appeared "behind the backs" of those concerned. For example, Pikwakanagan initially formulated a one-quarter blood quantum requirement (normative under the Indian Act) for non-status enrolment (so that anybody seeking enrolment who was not already registered under the Indian Act must be able to prove one-quarter descent from a known Algonquin from the Schedule A list). After much resistance from the area committees, this was subsequently reduced to one-eighth (Sarazin 1998, 2). By relying on blood quantum, the enrolment law denied the possibility that any non-status Algonquins had maintained a solid identity as Algonquins, or connections to place. In formulating this law, Pikwakanagan thus denied that federally unrecognized communities should have the fundamental right that First Nations had asserted since 1985: the right to determine their own membership.

In 1994, when the Algonquin enrolment law was ratified, the area committees were still being set up, Antoine, Ardoch, and Bonnechere remained excluded from the process, and an agreed-upon mechanism for working with non-status Algonquins had not yet been ironed out. In some sense, Pikwakanagan's haste to establish the enrolment law was deliberate. To accept potentially thousands of non-status people, many of whom had little sense of what being Algonquin meant, ran the risk of creating what some have referred to as "paper Indians" – individuals who are legally recognized (on a piece of paper) as Algonquin because they are of proven Algonquin descent but who have no real affiliation with other Algonquins, no knowledge of their own culture or heritage, and no desire to learn about being Algonquin. Indeed, the worst-case scenario regarding paper Indians was the possible inclusion of those who identified strongly with white society and who might, on the basis of minimal Algonquin descent, fabricate an Algonquin identity in order to become beneficiaries of the land claim – or simply to acquire hunting rights without buying a licence.

However, once again, it is difficult to determine where legitimate concerns end and stereotypes begin. In 1985, Bill C-31 had amended the Indian Act, with the result that many Indigenous people regained Indian status. During a 2005 interview, Kirby Whiteduck recounted that after Bill C-31 the Pikwakanagan membership had more than tripled within a year, increasing from fewer than four hundred to thirteen hundred people, most of them off-reserve. Thus, by 1993, Pikwakanagan had already accommodated hundreds of "new Indians," as those who regained their status under Bill C-31 were frequently called. Many at Pikwakanagan were understandably quite nervous about the implications of expanding definitions of Algonquinness to admit non-status individuals, particularly those whose understanding of their own Native identities was ambiguous. Because many at Pikwakanagan saw Indian status as the sole indicator of who was Algonquin, such a fundamental broadening of Algonquinness threatened to dissolve the firm parameters of identity upon which some colonized people rely to keep some boundary between themselves and a hostile colonizing society and to maintain their sense of self.

Even the leadership from Pikwakanagan who did see the Indian Act as colonial legislation found it difficult to understand the nuances of non-status Algonquin identity. Some individuals of Algonquin descent *had* long since renounced any connection with their heritage, and their inclusion in the nation might be problematic. And yet, for every so-called paper Indian who enrolled in the land claim simply to acquire hunting rights, many others had never lost their sense of Algonquin identity. And probably most numerous were the thousands of non-status Algonquins whose parents or grandparents, although maintaining connections to place, had been silent about Algonquin identity. These individuals were being forced to cope, almost overnight, with the complexities of Native identity and the rewriting of their sense of self as Indian. No one who was motivated purely by gain would be willing to take up the challenging and psychologically intense struggle to reclaim an identity that has been historically so marginalized, with boundaries that are so disputed. Many non-status Algonquins willingly made the journey into "Indianness," despite its difficulties – not for personal gain but because their families, landless and living in racist environments, had been unable to either wholly claim an Algonquin identity or entirely leave it behind.

Lacking an understanding of these subtleties, the Pikwakanagan leadership attempted to narrow the parameters defining Algonquinness as quickly as possible in order to shut out the paper Indians and to create a nation of "real" Algonquins. In doing so, it unwittingly foreclosed on the necessary process of identity building among non-status Algonquins that is fundamental to truly re-creating Algonquin nationhood.

Schedule A of the enrolment law caused further problems. To be included in the land claim, non-status Algonquins were required to demonstrate a one-eighth blood quantum descent from an individual who was listed in the schedule as a "known" Algonquin. In creating this condition, the Pikwakanagan negotiators, all of whom were male, had not taken gender-based discrimination into account. Because of the patriarchal attitudes of European census-takers, very few women were listed in the schedule, with the result that non-status people who traced their descent from female ancestors did not figure into the equation. As Lynn Gehl (2003, 66) writes, "I find this practice of using Schedule A to determine who is an Algonquin very disconcerting because it is derived from 19th century census records and petitions which are inherently patriarchal in that they are based on European standards. For example, [on the census records] it was a common practice for women to be listed as 'wife,' as they were considered mere chattels of their husbands. Thus, in many instances, no names were provided for these mothers of the present Algonquin nation."

Nor did the negotiators take into consideration that many ancestors of contemporary non-status Algonquins were not listed in Indian registries, because they had refused to move to Golden Lake when the reserve was created; they, too, would not be included in Schedule A (Ardoch Algonquin First Nation and Allies 1994). In the tiny backwoods towns where many non-status Algonquins had eked out precarious lives on the edge of settler society, few had left many records of their existence for their descendants to utilize.

Finally ratified in 1994, the enrolment law was ultimately a vehicle whereby the Pikwakanagan representatives successfully pushed through their vision of who would be recognized as Algonquin. Based on the false assumption that Aboriginal rights were a matter of bloodline, much as the Indian Act had asserted for over a century, it ensured that federally unrecognized Algonquins who could not prove a one-eighth blood quantum would become external to the nascent Algonquin Nation that they hoped could be reborn through the land claim.

Because Pikwakanagan had proceeded with land claim discussions while the enrolment law and representation issues were being addressed, a large backlog of issues awaited ratification by the Algonquin Nation Circle and the Algonquin Management Circle when these two bodies were finally created. For example, in May 1995, the Algonquin Forestry Proposal was ratified. In June 1995, the Algonquin Management Circle directed that a land proposal should be developed. In July and August 1995, the Algonquin enrolment law came under review for proposed amendment and ratification. In September

1995, the Algonquin Interim Hunting Agreement was brought to the Algonquin Management Circle for input, review, and ratification. Via this agreement, non-status Algonquins who were affiliated with an area committee attained the same hunting rights as those enjoyed by Pikwakanagan, provided they remained affiliated with a land claim community. In October 1995, specific and focused land consultations with the broader Algonquin community commenced under the direction of the Algonquin Management Circle. In November 1995, the circle received, discussed, amended, and ratified the first Algonquin Land Proposal. It also approved a questionnaire to provide broad community input into the more detailed Algonquin Land Proposal and directed the method of data collection. In December 1995, the circle intervened in *Harold Perry v. the Queen*, a case mounted by Ardoch that dealt with the hunting rights of all non-status Algonquins, which will be explored in Chapter 6 (Sarazin 1998, 2).

For the federally unrecognized Algonquins, all this occurred at a phenomenally accelerated pace. Their area committee representatives were brought into an extant land claim and asked to work in tandem with the Pikwakanagan negotiators, who already had a certain vision of themselves as Algonquins as well as governance processes and procedural rules under the Indian Act, which forced the pace for them and did not allow them to engage in real community building. For their communities – in many instances composed of individuals who worked in resource industries and who thus lacked much formal education – having to provide input into complex legal documents without being given time to understand the process was a guaranteed recipe for fear, confusion, and ultimately resentment. Moreover, though some leaders had political experience, others were neophytes, and of necessity, most were still engaging with basic issues of Algonquin identity while a land claim was being negotiated "over their heads."[3] And indeed, the process of "finding" Algonquins – in which people of Algonquin ancestry were solicited to contact other individuals whom they knew to be Algonquin – continued throughout most of the next decade.

But it is clear that, given this pace, trouble was brewing in the negotiations. A sore point for Pikwakanagan was when the federally unrecognized communities were granted hunting rights under its own hunting agreement. This raised the ire of some Pikwakanagan members, who felt that the non-status Algonquins should not have automatic access to an agreement initially negotiated only by Pikwakanagan; they pressured their leadership regarding the issue, which only heightened the tensions within the negotiations. Then, in July 1997, a survey questionnaire about a proposed new Algonquin citizenship law was sent to all those who were registered according to the Algonquin enrolment law (Kanatiio 1998c, 3-4). The survey was complex, asking extensive questions about who should be entitled to Algonquin citizenship, which verged very closely on questions regarding entitlement to Indian status. Because such a questionnaire had been sent only to those people who had been selected via a process of differentiating between Algonquins, it seemed highly likely that the citizenship law would simply perpetuate the exclusions of the enrolment law. It could be expected to unquestioningly accept Pikwakanagan members, including white women who had married status Indians before 1985, and to accept only those non-status Algonquins who could satisfy the minimum one-eighth blood quantum requirement, regardless of community recognition. This angered a number of federally unrecognized Algonquins, who saw that, once again, many of their members were being excluded despite being recognized as Algonquin by other non-status Algonquins.

In October 1997, the Algonquin Government Task Force was established, consisting of four individuals drawn from Pikwakanagan and the area committees to seek input from the various communities on the desired structures, mandates, and accountability of an Algonquin government. Its final report proposed a model of governance, the Algonquin Nation Council, to represent seven regions: Algonquins of Pikwakanagan, Bancroft/Baptiste Lake, Greater Golden Lake, Mattawa/North Bay, Ottawa, Sharbot Lake, and Whitney. Each community would be governed by a three-person area council, except for Pikwakanagan, which was mandated under the Indian Act as having band governance consisting of a chief and six councillors. The seven communities would each send one representative to the Algonquin Nation Council, which, as a body, would replace the Algonquin Nation Circle and the Algonquin Management Circle (Kanatiio 1998b, 2). During the implementation of the Algonquin Nation Council, the Algonquin Nation Circle became known as the Algonquin Negotiations Interim Directorate.

In many respects, the implementation of such a circle would have addressed the primary weakness of the area committees: overwhelmingly they each had only one leader, whose primary goal was generally to focus on the land claim. Having a three-person council in each community would have enabled actual community building to take place and would have prevented the concentrations of power that are so prevalent among the non-status communities. However, the system was never implemented due to other developments, which will be explored below.

When Antoine, Ardoch, and Bonnechere found themselves still excluded from this proposed model, they mounted a legal challenge to the land claim process. In July 1999, their representatives met with the Algonquin Negotiations Interim Directorate and asked for equal representation at the negotiating table (Ardoch Algonquin First Nation 1999). They also noted that since the Algonquins had already incurred a $3.5 million debt for the cost of conducting the claim, pressures were mounting for the negotiation team to complete the process regardless of the outcome. They asserted that good faith dialogue could not occur under such terms and that the Algonquins, who were the true "landlords" of the watershed, were being treated as if they were tenants. Indeed, the more politically astute leaders had always insisted that resource revenue sharing must be in place before substantive negotiations could begin, so that Algonquins could come to the table with their own monies and could take the time to achieve consensus on issues of identity, membership, and representation. However, though Antoine, Ardoch, and Bonnechere were ultimately brought into the land claim process, none of these suggestions were taken up. Tensions therefore continued to grow within the negotiating team, as the strain of dealing with poorly understood and for the most part unacknowledged divisions built up.

During the summer of 2000, in an effort to address the increasing disunity among Algonquins, Pikwakanagan held a national assembly, with the theme "Honouring the Spirit of Tessouat – Uniting all Algonquins." All Algonquins, including those from Quebec and the non-status communities in Ontario, were invited to attend the one-day event, featuring workshops and speeches. And yet, even this – a process intended to build bridges between Algonquins – was marked by divisions around Indian status. For example, at the assembly an Algonquin-language kit was distributed gratis to status Algonquins. Non-status Algonquins were required to pay for it.

A number of non-status Algonquins who attended the assembly have mentioned that buying the kit made them feel like outsiders to the Algonquin Nation. Lynn Gehl (2003, 69), whose *kokomis* (grandmother) was from Pikwakanagan and who has mounted both section 15 Charter and section 35 constitutional challenges to her denial of Indian status, describes her experience: "In the afternoon, while I attended a workshop titled Unity ... I raised the issue of language kit distribution, specifically why they were provided at no charge to status members, yet a charge was applicable to non-status members. If true unity is sought, I asked, why are non-status individuals charged a fee whereas status individuals are not? My question was answered in terms of funding, specifically, who provided the funds – Indian Affairs. Based on this, the band decided to provide these kits to all status members yet sell them to non-status members."

Although the intent of the Indian Affairs funding was to supply kits to the status Algonquins, surely a fundamental requirement of a unity conference between status and non-status individuals would be a willingness, on the part of status Indians, not to perpetuate the divisions created by the Indian Act. Had the kits been distributed among status and non-status Algonquins alike until they ran out, or if alternative funds had been sought to ensure that the non-status also received the kits for free, colonial divisions would not have been maintained and goodwill would have been engendered among the non-status Algonquins. Falling back on economic arguments and accepting preferential treatment on the basis of status simply highlighted differences and, whether inadvertently or not, externalized non-status Algonquins.

At this point, the divisions between the status and non-status Algonquins began to manifest themselves in a dramatic fashion. If non-status Algonquins were to assume greater responsibilities within the negotiation process, they needed to share the legal and financial obligations associated with the debt that Pikwakanagan had been carrying since the claim's inception (Kanatiio 1998b, 4). To this end, a corporation called the Algonquin Nation Negotiations Directorate (ANND) was founded under the laws of Ontario to administer the legal and financial responsibilities of the claim. The tensions that ultimately exploded between Pikwakanagan and the non-status communities had complex roots, but the creation of ANND intensified pressures almost to the breaking point. The chief problems lay with the loss of independent political status for Pikwakanagan within the negotiations due to the structure of ANND as an Ontario corporation, as well as the fact that Pikwakanagan was so greatly outnumbered by non-status Algonquins.

The immediate flashpoint that brought both of these points together, however, and resulted in a breakdown of negotiations, was the moose hunt. Hunting is a way of life for many Algonquins in the Ottawa River watershed, and as such has always been a contentious issue between status and non-status Algonquins. The Algonquin Hunting Agreement, which had been negotiated in 1992 between the Ministry of Natural Resources and Pikwakanagan, had been extended to Algonquins who were part of the area committees, providing them with hunting rights at the same level as Pikwakanagan. When ANND was created, Pikwakanagan's independent political voice in the negotiations was superseded by it; moreover, as an Ontario corporation, ANND had no framework to enable Pikwakanagan to continue to extend its hunting rights to the non-status communities. Because of this, a separate hunting agreement for non-status Algonquins was needed, and so an interim hunting agreement was signed between ANND and the Ministry of Natural Resources in 2001.[4]

Hunting for the land claim communities was now regulated by two separate agreements. Pikwakanagan was governed by its 1992 agreement with the Ministry of Natural Resources, in which it regulated its own membership through Algonquin law and maintained a tribunal to try violators. The non-status Algonquins came under the interim hunting agreement between ANND and the ministry. They had no bodies to oversee the hunt (and indeed, as an Ontario corporation, ANND did not have the jurisdiction to set hunting regulations). When the moose allocations for the 2001 hunting season were divided equally between status and non-status Algonquins – so that forty-eight moose went to Pikwakanagan and forty-eight were to be divided among all of the non-status communities – an uproar ensued from Pikwakanagan, even though on a per capita basis it had received far more moose than the vastly more numerous non-status Algonquins (Tennescoe 2002).

Ultimately, the issues driving the Pikwakanagan backlash went much deeper than hunting, as was revealed by "21st Century Algonquin Moose War" (Algonquin Golden Lake First Nation 2001), a document that circulated unofficially at Pikwakanagan. Signed by sixty adult members of Pikwakanagan's approximately three hundred on-reserve residents, it demonstrated that the anger and fear of a number of status Algonquins was fuelled by concerns that the rights and privileges attached to a status card were being eroded and subsumed by the community membership cards issued by the non-status communities to enable their members to hunt. The signatories asserted that the only reliable arbiter of Algonquinness was the Indian Act, that non-status Algonquins were "not really Indian," that an auditor must be hired to investigate the Algonquin enrolment law (even though Pikwakanagan had created it), and that a genealogist must be employed to re-examine the ancestry of all the non-status people who had been recognized as Algonquin through that law. The anger emanating from Pikwakanagan regarding the large numbers of non-status Algonquins who were being registered and the notion that all of them should have Aboriginal rights was clearly expressed in this document. The result was a call for concrete measures to reduce the numbers of non-status Algonquins being recognized under the enrolment law and for Pikwakanagan to sever connections with ANND.

On 16 November 2001, the Council of the Algonquins of Pikwakanagan directed that its chief, Lisa Ozawanimke, and her council alternate resign from ANND. It took the position that Pikwakanagan's chief and council should become the sole negotiating body for the land claim, representing all Algonquins who were status Indians (Ozawanimke 2001). The fact that Pikwakanagan had unilaterally passed the enrolment law before the non-status communities had sorted out their representation now worked in its favour. What had been unilaterally passed could be unilaterally repealed. Moreover, since according to Pikwakanagan there were now legally no Algonquins except those with Indian status, Pikwakanagan could resume its sole place at the table and "get down to business" in the land claim (Ozawanimke 2001). At that point, the negotiations ground to a halt.

Pikwakanagan's explosion of anger at the federally unrecognized Algonquins was partially based in impatience with the difficulties of conducting a land claim across the barriers separating status from non-status Indians. However, it blamed the federally unrecognized Algonquins for slowing down negotiations, a stance grounded in the normativity of Indian status. The history of non-recognition of those Algonquins who had historically refused to move to reserves was seen as incidental to the real history of Algonquins – those who were reserve-based. The fact that the definition of Algonquinness extended no further than adherence to Schedule A was not seen as problematic at Pikwakanagan and nor was its failure to conduct oral histories to determine the parameters of non-status Algonquin identity. Moreover, in some respects, the non-status Algonquins were blamed for problems in the negotiations that may have had much more to do with Canada or Ontario.

For the non-status Algonquins, the truly stunning thing about the position of the Pikwakanagan leadership was its flat refusal to acknowledge them as kin in any meaningful way. Even more problematic for some was the leadership's assumption that since Canada had "made" Indians via the Indian Act, Ottawa was responsible for developing the federal recognition that would enable non-status Algonquins to participate in the land claim. Until it did, the non-status Algonquins were not Algonquins and therefore should not take part.

Many non-status Algonquins who had been involved in the land claim since the area committees were formed had assumed that the Pikwakanagan leadership knew that Algonquinness entailed more than an Indian status card. For them, the leadership's hardline stance was shocking. For others, the uncritical reliance on both the Indian Act and Ottawa as final arbiters of Algonquinness was not surprising. What it *did* reveal was that Pikwakanagan's claims regarding Algonquin self-determination had degenerated to mere rhetoric: in insisting that only Canada could make Indians, it had jettisoned any notion of Algonquins as being truly self-determining.

On 6 March 2002, ANND, in its turn, insisted that because it had been created by both status and non-status communities, and because the chief and council of Pikwakanagan had formally transferred the negotiation process over to it in May 2001, it could not be "unmade" by Pikwakanagan's refusal to recognize non-status Algonquins. ANND therefore created an entity known as the Algonquin Nation Tribal Council (ANTC), whose purpose was to provide political representation for the non-status communities, to work to resolve the ruptures in the Algonquin Nation, and to continue to represent the Algonquin people of the region (Algonquin Nation Negotiations Directorate 2002). On 8 August 2002, the Ministry of Natural Resources signed a protocol with the ANTC, which recognized the separate hunting rights of non-status Algonquins involved in the land claim (Algonquin Nation Tribal Council 2002).[5]

Despite the hardline stance of the Pikwakanagan administration, Chief Negotiator Greg Sarazin, himself an on-reserve member of Pikwakanagan, maintained neutrality regarding its position. He continued to recognize ANND, indicated his willingness to acknowledge the ANTC, and persistently urged Pikwakanagan to return to the table (Peplinskie 2002). Moreover, some on-reserve community members stood apart from Chief Lisa Ozawanimke's position. Indeed, on behalf of "concerned elders and band members," six individuals publicly signed a letter asserting that she was not listening to band members, that no meetings were being held to update the community, and that the chief had openly disregarded advice from elders (*Eganville Leader* 2002).

In 2002, Canada and Ontario retained an independent facilitator, Eva Marszewski, who recommended that both parties, Pikwakanagan and ANND, should have a joint negotiator to represent them in the claim. Over the next year, various processes of consultation and facilitation were employed, with differing degrees of success. In August 2003, the parties retained the services of a lawyer, Bob Potts, from the Bay Street law firm of Blaney McMurtry, to attempt to resolve their differences and to lobby the government to continue negotiations. Finally, in March 2004, they reached an agreement.

The protocol agreement signed by Pikwakanagan and ANND on 25 March 2004 fundamentally changed the land claim process. Initially, it had been at least grassroots-inspired and led by an Algonquin chief negotiator who respected Algonquin traditions and genuinely desired to rebuild Algonquin nationhood, which he saw as consisting of both status and non-status Algonquins. With the new regime, a non-Native lawyer, Bob Potts, was appointed as chief negotiator and senior legal counsel to take instructions from "both sides." On one side was Pikwakanagan, representing its fifteen hundred status Indians; on the other was ANND, with the ANTC politically representing approximately five thousand Algonquins, status and non-status.[6]

Under the new regime, though the Algonquin enrolment law of 1995 was immediately reinstated, there would be no further talk of nation building or of creating an Algonquin government to promote the interests of the nation. Instead, in a process curiously analogous to that of the 1869 Gradual Enfranchisement Act, which formally ended Canada's recognition of any Indigenous government larger than community-scale (Lawrence 2004, 33), the focus shifted to individual Algonquin "communities" and to negotiation representatives for each one (Potts 2004).

In a similar manner, since "nationhood" was no longer a topic for discussion, no further references were made to "citizenship"; instead of citizens, there would be "electors" and "beneficiaries." In place of an organized Algonquin political representation, attempting to speak with one voice, a team of Algonquin negotiation representatives (ANRs) would be established. The ANRs were not required to have any qualifications, such as education or experience, other than being nominated by 10 recognized Algonquins and proving affiliation with 125 other Algonquins (Potts 2005). Notably, their creation bypassed the ANTC as an independent body consisting of the leaders of the land claim communities. Furthermore, Pikwakanagan was granted the privileged position of having seven representatives – the chief and the entire council – whereas each non-status community would have one.

The Fragmentation of the Non-Status Communities

For the non-status communities, the new regime under Blaney McMurtry created a process almost guaranteed to produce not only extreme and undemocratic concentrations of power but, ultimately, extreme fragmentation. The leaders of the area committees originally formed by Pikwakanagan to organize the non-status Algonquins into communities had de facto become the board members of ANND. When they created the ANTC, they automatically became the "chiefs" of their communities, which were then labelled "First Nations." Under the process created in 2004, the ANTC chiefs had access to community membership lists, a fact that positioned them to be elected as ANRs.[7] Indeed, in the 2005 elections that selected the first ANRs, several of the chiefs deliberately changed the wording on the election notices, calling the Algonquin negotiation representative the "Algonquin Nation representative" and putting the word "chief" in front of their name so that voters would assume they were incumbents who were merely continuing their position as community leaders (Hendry 2006). In almost all the non-status land claim communities, a single person controls the monies received for the claim under

ANND and is simultaneously an ANTC chief and an ANR. Since 2004, most of these individuals have concentrated their energies on the negotiations, with the result that community building occurs in a piecemeal and secondary fashion.

Still more problematically, no mechanism exists to enable communities to depose an ANR if they are dissatisfied with him or her or if they wish to opt out of the claim and the ANR does not, an eventuality that will be explored in Chapter 7. Nor, in a situation where an ANR also holds the community membership lists as an ANTC chief, can individuals scattered across a region easily run against him or her. Perhaps not surprisingly, given the control afforded by these positions, no new ANRs have ever been elected for any community unless in a rare instance the incumbent walks away from the table, as happened with the Ottawa community in 2007. Indeed, most of the existing ANRs are the same individuals who started out as area committee representatives in 1996.[8] On the other hand, under the Blaney McMurtry regime, new non-status communities can be created by any individual who is nominated by 10 Algonquins and who represents 125 Algonquins (Potts 2004). Although this process is to be commended for its inclusiveness, the result is that numerous land claim communities can be created within each Algonquin territory. In many respects, this fragmentation was itself the product of the new land claim regime: under its rules, opposing the leadership in most communities is virtually impossible; thus, in most contexts, the only solution is for individuals to form new communities. This is a recipe for both extreme factionalism and extreme fragmentation. Whereas new groupings of people who were previously excluded can certainly join, existing communities can splinter extremely easily. This is particularly the case for communities that wish to question or critique the fundamental assumptions of the land claim.

As communities have split and multiplied without reference to any cohesive non-status Algonquin government entity, non-status Algonquins can no longer exercise any collective voice within the land claim process. However, the factionalism and fragmentation that the new regime has helped to create are for the most part being ignored by the lawyers on the negotiating team, since the divisions no longer affect Pikwakanagan, but are now primarily confined *among* the non-status communities themselves.

One of the first mandates of the renewed land claim process was to hold meetings in Algonquin communities with the primary goal of establishing a beneficiary list.[9] At the first meeting, it became obvious that many of the non-status Algonquins had not been adequately informed by their leadership about the new regime to which they were now subject. Many did not understand the original dispute between Pikwakanagan and ANND. Increasing numbers, who had clearly been inspired by the nation-building process that the land claim could potentially enable, spoke with hope of the need to rebuild the Algonquin Nation, to strengthen Algonquin culture and communities, and to provide venues for out-of-territory Algonquins to participate.[10]

At subsequent meetings, divisions sharpened. A group of concerned Algonquins known as TANAC (the Algonquin Nation Advisory Committee), consisting of members from Ardoch, Bancroft, Bonnechere, the communities of Whitney, Madawaska, and Sabine (unified as "Whimasab"), a new community at Maynooth, and Ottawa, had prepared a statement, challenging a number of the ANTC chiefs as not adequately representing their communities. In fact, almost all the ANTC chiefs were challenged by their communities as lacking the authority to represent them (Ardoch Algonquin First Nation 2004).

Even more alarming is that, after these meetings, ongoing attempts at intercession by community members, in the form of letters and e-mails to Chief Negotiator Bob Potts and other administrators in the land claim, achieved little. In general, the negotiators dismissed each petition as arising from "petty internecine squabbles" rather than seeing these reactions as genuine outrage at the power vested in ANTC chiefs (which they carried over into their positions as ANRs), the potential for abuses and arbitrary exercise of that power, and the lack of attention to community building by leaders who appear obsessed with the land claim to the exclusion of everything else.[11] Having ironed out many of the fundamental differences between status and non-status Algonquins, the negotiators seem determined to ignore the divisions that affect non-status Algonquins. In the rush to proceed with the land claim, these are brushed off as irrelevant. Some ANTC chiefs (now ANRs) have long characterized those who criticize their governance, no matter how constructively, as "ankle-biters," thus dismissing all dissent as petty carping.

In contexts of oppression, where all avenues for expressing dissent are marginalized, the Internet is often employed as a tool to promote empowerment. Indeed, federally unrecognized peoples around the world are using the Internet as both a means of communication and a site to post genealogical information and their own histories that colonialism has helped to erase or distort – erasures or distortions that, too often, scholarly discourses have maintained as "truths." Writing about Trinidadian Carib peoples, Maximilian Forte (2006b, 253) notes that the phrase "I went on the internet to find out who I am" is a common articulation of identity struggles among persons of Aboriginal descent. Through the Internet, they find ancestors, acquire a counter-hegemonic education about Indigenous identity, and ultimately come to understand themselves as Indigenous. Indeed, the Internet is particularly useful to federally unrecognized people who are geographically scattered and who may have difficulty in otherwise communicating with one another. Moreover, in a context where many are struggling to find a voice *as* an Indigenous person, the Internet can assist in articulating these identities. Forte (ibid., 257, 259) also contends that as individuals challenge and engage each other through websites, the sense of community developed on-line may be far less fictive than more established forms of nationalism. He asserts that where groups are having difficulty achieving federal recognition, the Internet can help to embody and embed those identities. He cautions us, however, that though the Internet can assist individuals in positioning themselves and rearticulating their identities, inequalities in access to cyberspace can limit the ability of many to participate in on-line community building. Finally, the connection to land, so central to Indigenous struggles, cannot be created on-line.

Many Algonquin communities post information on websites. Unfortunately, most sites have become venues for the leadership's involvement with the land claim, with the result that the webmaster presents the information supplied by the leadership, and no other voices are heard. Counter-hegemonically, however, many non-status Algonquins have generated a vast network of e-mail contacts, which provides them with an alternative venue to critique events, relay news from their communities, and share valuable information across the territory. For many concerned Algonquins, e-mail has facilitated a tremendous level of nation building.

However, one must wonder how the land claim will evolve under its new leadership. When I interviewed her in 2005, Lynn Gehl offered the following insights:

> I think that the Algonquin people do not have enough knowledge about the land claims and self-government process – it is very complex – and I'm disturbed by how the leadership manipulates this ignorance. And I am also concerned about the fact that hunting and men are dominating the process.
>
> I also think the federal and provincial governments are directing the process. The federal and provincial governments should be ashamed of themselves, negotiating with unqualified leaders and uninformed people! And our own negotiator tells us that we shouldn't worry, that the Algonquin negotiation representative positions require no qualifications as though he's doing us a favour ... What many don't realize is that this is what the government wants. The government wants to deal with unqualified Algonquin

> leaders at the negotiation table ... Is this how treaty making in Canada is done? Do the governments of Canada allow unqualified people to negotiate a treaty?
>
> As I see it, our negotiator is also a problem. He doesn't understand an Indigenous world view. He doesn't understand that we have a different relationship with the land ... I don't think he knows anything about Indigenous philosophy, just as a lot of Algonquins don't. And we should be negotiating on a nation-to-nation basis, which means negotiating through our paradigm. And it should not simply be about negotiating how much money we're going to get. I don't think we should be giving up any more of our land ...
>
> The way things are going, we are going to get ripped off. We're probably going to get two hundred million dollars, like the Nisga'a received, and maybe we'll get 3 or 4 percent of our land. We won't get a cut of the subsurface rights, and we won't get a cut of the hydroelectric power that is generated from our rivers, as we should for time immemorial.
>
> I think it could be an opportunity to begin nation building, provided they give Algonquins our cut of all the resources and don't force us to extinguish our [title to] the land base. But if we go to table with these unqualified people who don't have the necessary skills and don't know what policies to move in and out of, they're going to be easily robbed.

Despite the flaws of the process, an indubitable reality for many Algonquins is that without the land claim, they would have had no venue for recognition of themselves as Algonquin. During one of my interviews with Bob Majaury, which took place in 2005, he addressed what many Algonquins believe: "In terms of land claims negotiations – there's been nothing positive there, in terms of progress. But in terms of identity, I think there has been a lot of positive developments coming out of that. Like healing ... there probably has been some of that – because just for somebody to say 'I'm Algonquin' is an accomplishment. When I filled out my census form, I put down 'Algonquin' – that had to be quite a big moment for me."

And yet, ironically, those who speak out about being Algonquin are still subjected to racism and harassment. As some individuals stated during their interviews, when the land claim reached the negotiation stage, Algonquins in government positions began to face considerable discrimination from non-Native co-workers, including acts that might have potentially endangered them. For non-status Algonquins, the land claim has provided a venue to address their identities, but it has also polarized the opinions of some local whites against Algonquins.

To a significant extent, then, the land claim process has generated profound changes in how non-status Algonquins see themselves. In the next chapter, we will explore this issue in depth.

5

Reclaiming Algonquin Identity

> Okay, so now you're part Indian and you can prove it. But then you're sitting there, with reserve people especially, and their mythology – I don't like using the word mythology but I'm gonna use mythology for this, their mythology is that all those new Algonquin people never knew they were Indian until the land claim ... But that's not true. It's more that the process of assimilation put us in a situation where we could neither assert our identities nor prove them – and we were not allowed to talk about it. And then the land claim allowed us to prove it and gave us a context through which we could assert it.
>
> **– Heather Majaury, "Living Inside Layers of Colonial Division"**

Federally unrecognized Algonquins in the Ottawa River watershed have had to prove their identities as Algonquins in order to assert their very existence in their homeland. If the land claim has provided them with a venue to prove that existence, it has also forced a brutal pace of development on them, demanding not only proof of Indigenous identity but a constant justification of their right to assume it. For some, particularly those involved in negotiations through the claim, this may involve a *performance* of "Indian" identity, which can actually obscure the daily lived social practices, transformed and muted by colonization but maintained through connections to the land, that have held non-status Algonquins together through more than a century of extreme colonial pressures. For others, the erosion and transformation of traditional

Algonquin practices have led to ongoing attempts at cultural reclamation by practising ceremonies and relearning traditional Algonquin teachings.

At the same time, the threat that the land claim leadership will surrender Aboriginal title and rights to their traditional territory has created a profound polarization among federally unrecognized Algonquins. They must therefore grapple with the larger questions that have divided Indigenous communities throughout centuries of colonization. These issues – about the meaning of being Indigenous, of land versus money, of faith in "progress" versus faith in the ancestors – are being raised at a time when many are struggling to understand what an Indigenous identity *means* to them personally, given the heritage of silence and loss that has characterized their ancestors' experiences.

Federally unrecognized Algonquins are, in fact, part of a particular Indigenous experience, globally – as a people for whom the juggernaut of colonial history involved such fracturing and scattering that only a handful of remnant communities survived it. For them, the violence of colonial destruction has been supplemented by the violence of being considered non-existent by the settler societies that displaced them. This has affected Indigenous communities around the world in various ways. In a number of areas, including the Caribbean, Tasmania, and Newfoundland, colonial discourses have asserted that Indigenous peoples died out during the colonization process. In other areas, as with the Ottawa Valley Algonquins, denial of recognition is more selective; certain groups, usually those who conform to colonial requirements, are accepted as "Indian," whereas the remainder are considered non-existent. In all cases, the underlying colonial assumption that "real" Indigenous peoples cannot survive contact with European civilization, but must inevitably vanish (Brantlinger 2003), means that the survivors of this brutal experience of colonization are frequently dismissed as "inauthentic" – too "mixed-blood," too "acculturated."

In Canada, individuals and communities can lose (or not acquire) Indian status in a variety of ways (Lawrence 2004). However, unlike in the United States, where formal processes of federal acknowledgment exist, in Canada there is no explicit legal text or formal means whereby an unrecognized nation can gain federal recognition (Bruce Miller 2003, 138). Existing Indian bands can be amalgamated or divided, and new bands can be declared into existence by government action; however, in the latter case, all the membership must have Indian status. Many federally unrecognized communities have some members whose ancestors acquired status through membership in a federally recognized Indian band, but most consist of people who have never had status and will therefore never be eligible to attain it. For this reason, the land claim represents the only means through which non-status Algonquins can gain federal recognition as Algonquin people.

Globally, Indigenous peoples are most commonly denied recognition so that unrestrained economic development can proceed in their territories (Bruce Miller 2003, 8) or settlement policies can be seamlessly imposed without the bother of negotiating treaties. In general, however, federal recognition or non-recognition is also part of a process whereby states manage their relations with Indigenous people by reducing their numbers, often through enforcing definitions of Indianness linked to blood quantum, which facilitate Indigenous "vanishing" through bureaucratic sleight of hand (ibid., 14-15). The ancestors of today's federally unrecognized Algonquins faced multiple episodes of all these experiences as people lost their land and starved or were dispersed across the territory in an effort to survive. Once their numbers were drastically reduced, their presence could be officially ignored, whereas the few who settled on the single small reserve that Ontario provided were recognized as Indian.

As colonial governments reorganized Indigenous people through identity legislation, recognizing some but not others, Native people inevitably resisted the imposition of such categories. In many respects, however, their ability to resist is directly connected to the colonial history they have experienced. We can see this manifested in the types of struggles in which various communities have engaged to protect their lands. For example, at the same time that the Algonquin land claim was being launched, the Gitksan and Wet'suwet'en in northern British Columbia were claiming ownership and jurisdiction over their traditional territory through the *Delgamuukw* case. With less than 150 years of colonial presence in their territories, and relative isolation in a number of regions, their traditional cultural frameworks were still so active, even with the genocidal impact of residential schooling, that they were able to argue their claim in an entirely traditional manner, through the songs, dances, and stories – all told in their Indigenous languages – that demonstrated the affiliation of their clan and house leaders to every inch of their territory (Monet and Skanu'u 1992). Although the divisions imposed by the Indian Act were real, the traditional framework that underlay it retained a viable resonance and vigour for the Gitksan and Wet'suwet'en.

By comparison, the Algonquins of the Ottawa River watershed have borne the brunt of contact with two colonial regimes for more than 400 years, and their lands on the Ontario side have been almost entirely overrun with settlers for over 150 years. Although the familial social ties that bound their communities together did survive, the overarching framework of geopolitical/

spiritual structures that had maintained cohesion for the people as a whole had long been shattered. In such a context, where traditional culture has been transformed and eroded, and where language use has been minimized and almost lost for *both* status and non-status Algonquins, the sheer intensity of the hegemonic assumptions about Indianness that pervade settler society has been difficult to resist. As we saw in the previous chapter, Algonquin attempts to assert title to the Ottawa River watershed ran head-on into questions of entitlement under the Indian Act, with hegemonic divisions between status and non-status Algonquins effectively derailing their ability to speak with one voice and therefore limiting what they could achieve with a divided negotiating process.

According to William Roseberry (1994), the reality of hegemony is that despite inevitable differences in the world views of subordinated and dominant groups, the very process of domination forces subordinate groups to accept the material and meaningful framework generated from the dominant group, not only in order to resist oppression but for their own understandings of who they are. Whereas some status Algonquins have clearly internalized the notion that Indian status is an acceptable means of distinguishing between Algonquins and non-Algonquins, others, through having been forced to accept the framework of the Indian Act, must resist within its parameters; to act otherwise is to risk destabilizing the very structure that defines their collective identity as Algonquins.

The Indian Act's identity section is grounded in a potent British colonial discourse about "primitive" peoples that invokes notions of a "true" type of savage who must inevitably die out in the face of civilization, whereas the "impure" types – the irrevocably changed mixed-blood descendants of true Indians – survive but no longer as Indians. This primitivist discourse is deeply engrained in the primarily British settlers who have long maintained ruling positions in Canada. Indeed, Patricia Bartko's (1999-2000) exploration of the signing of Treaty 8 at Fort Resolution in 1900 provides an excellent example of how these stereotypes permeated British and Canadian attitudes toward Native people. During negotiations, the treaty commissioners expressed considerable disappointment at their first sight of the Dene people of Lesser Slave Lake:

> The crowd of Indians ranged before the marquee had lost all semblance of wildness of the true type ... It was plain that these people had achieved, without any treaty at all, a stage of civilization distinctly in advance of many of our treaty Indians to the south after twenty-five years of education. Instead

> of paint and feathers, the scalp-lock, the breech-clout, and the buffalo robe, there presented itself a body of respectable-looking men, as well-dressed and evidently quite as independent in their feelings as any like number of average pioneers in the East ... One was prepared, in this wild region of forest, to behold some savage types of men; indeed, I craved to renew the vanished scenes of old. But, alas! One beheld, instead, men with well-washed, unpainted faces ... It was not what was expected. (quoted in Bartko 1999-2000, 264)

These stereotypes exercised a profound effect on how the Dene were perceived. Because they had taken up European dress, they were seen as lacking the "true type" of wildness that would have marked them as Indian. Therefore, the commissioners generally viewed them as half-breeds. Commissioner O.C. Edwards complained, "I have not seen an Indian as he is popularly known or depicted since I left Calgary. These so-called Indians of the north are all half-breeds" (quoted in Leonard and Whalen 1999, 53).

The prevalence of these assumptions about the pure wildness of "real" Indians who must inevitably die out and be replaced by mixed-bloods whose entitlement to Indianness is highly suspect has spawned a body of stereotypes about Indianness at all levels, ranging from Hollywood films, to Canadian national policies about blood purity and degrees of civilization as maintained through the Indian Act, to local racist stereotypes by rural whites in the Ottawa Valley, who argued at the advent of the land claim that contemporary Algonquins – status or non-status – did not deserve hunting rights because they were not "pure" Indians. From all quarters of Canadian society, the hegemonic view is that Indianness is biological, defined solely by blood and regulated through the Indian Act, and that degrees of Indian blood correspond with Indian status, which in turn corresponds with degrees of cultural purity. The role of gender in delineating who is defined as Indian under the Indian Act has complicated these dynamics, but the basic belief that Indian status secures full-bloodedness and cultural purity has been widespread in Canadian society. We should not be surprised that being forced to live under Indian Act dictates has meant that many reserve residents not only utilize this framework to understand their own identities, but engage with it to resist domination.

In many respects, the definition of Indigenous peoples articulated by the International Working Group on Indigenous Peoples does not help federally unrecognized groups to resist this stereotyping, in that the definition assumes that cultural distinctiveness and historical continuity are fundamental aspects of their identity. And yet as Bruce Miller (2003, 64-65) points out, federally unrecognized Native people are often unable to establish historical continuity and may lack overt physical or cultural distinctiveness.

For most, then, survival as Indigenous people involves a process of *resurgence*. Writing about Caribbean Indigenous peoples, who continuously have to fight the myth of their own extinction, Maximilian Forte (2006a, 13-14) cautions us that some who speak in terms of "resurgence" may simply be revealing that, having recently removed their blinders, they are now capable of perceiving the Indigeneity that always existed. However, resurgence also refers to the intensified struggles of unrecognized Indigenous people to assert their identities, to learn more about their own traditions, and to develop pride in themselves.

The central issue faced by federally unrecognized Algonquins is the hegemonic power of the Canadian state, which dichotomizes the "pure" Indian and the dubiously Native mixed-blood, and then organizes this dichotomy along the lines of Indian status. In this respect, the land claim represents a contradiction. On the one hand, it has provided a number of Algonquins with a framework through which to begin actualizing a Native identity. On the other hand, however, that actualization is occurring within a hegemonic norm that privileges Indian status and therefore renders them already inherently inauthentic. Below, I will address how these issues affect non-status Algonquins, particularly in the context of the legacy of silence about Indigenous identity that so many of them must negotiate.

Identity Struggles of Federally Unrecognized Algonquins

> Literature written by contemporary Indian authors commonly includes characters who face the dilemma of an identity constructed within the authoritative discourse of the non-Indian world. In order to be recognized, to claim authenticity in the world – *to be seen at all* – they must conform to an identity imposed from outside.
>
> – **Louis Owens, *Mixedblood Messages***

Few issues relating to non-status Algonquin identity are as complex as the silence that so many individuals describe within their families about being Algonquin. For those wishing to challenge whether non-status Algonquins are "Indian enough" to consider themselves truly Algonquin, a simplified picture is often presented of opportunistic individuals who, through their silence about Algonquinness, have been able to enjoy the benefits of being part of the settler culture but who are now claiming Indianness because it might benefit them through the land claim. However, the interviews conducted showed a much more complex picture of how rural and urban non-status Algonquins experienced silence in their families about Algonquin identity – and the various reasons for the silence.

The interviews clarified that, for the most part, this silence should more properly be interpreted as *silencing* – a result of the tremendous difficulties faced by Algonquins after their traditional lands were flooded with settlers. Robert Lovelace (2006) discusses the situation in the southern part of the territory, where Algonquin lands were almost completely lost by the 1870s: "The racism expressed by the settler population toward Indian people was crushing. Indian men were denied respectable labour and women were relegated to being chore girls and worse. In the early twentieth century, Algonquin homes were burnt and occupants forced out of settler communities. Children were taken by child welfare authorities and placed as indentured servants and field hands at farms around Kingston and Amherstview." In a context of settler violence, silence was forced upon Algonquins. Survival was precarious, and to openly express any aspect of an Algonquin identity – through language, song, or story – was enough to provoke further violence from settlers. To pass this knowledge along to one's children was thus to potentially endanger them.

For example, one individual interviewed by Laura Schwager in 2004 described how her family members became silent about their identities after leaving their community. Her grandparents, despite difficult lives, had lived on the land within their traditional community and had openly maintained an Algonquin cultural identity. However, for her mother, who lived and worked in Kingston, being silent about Native identity was the only means of coping with the racism she encountered in town. For this individual, the only time she learned anything about an Algonquin identity was during the summers when she accompanied her mother back to the community to help her grandparents. This interview demonstrated clearly that for some Algonquins, silence about their identities began with no longer living on the land.

Other interviews also clarified that with land loss, silence was also a function of grief and numbness. One individual, interviewed by Laura Schwager in 2004, recounted a story addressing her family's attempt to obtain fee simple title to parts of their traditional land. This individual's grandmother had been a traditional healer and midwife for many years, and had managed, through great struggle, to pay the required taxes to enable her to keep the land. However, when the woman's grandmother died, her mother, while struggling with grief and loss, was presented with a bill for ninety-nine dollars in taxes if she wished to keep her mother's house. Unable to raise the money, she lost the land, which she had always counted on as her foundation in life. After enduring this trauma, and without land to sustain herself, she was forced to move to Kingston, where she simply turned her back on the past, as too painful to acknowledge. Her family was therefore raised with little knowledge of their own history.

For the most part, then, non-status Algonquins did not choose silence – rather, they were silenced. Others became silent through grief and numbness. But did this silence mean that they discarded their Algonquin values? Many interviews revealed that grandparents and parents struggled hard to live according to Algonquin ideals, even as they were surrounded by settlers. Many were unable to conform easily to the very different values of settler society. Ardoch elder Carol Bate, interviewed in 2005, described her father's experience:

> My father had one foot permanently in two worlds and he suffered hugely about it. Because he tried to live with one foot in the world that said if you're an honest man and a generous man you're a good man, and with the other foot in the world that said if you're a competitive cutthroat who cheats people and you get a big house and fill it full of fancy furniture, then you're a good man. And I watched him struggle all his life about this. People said many things about him – that he couldn't hang onto his money, all these things. But he lived a good life, so that at the end of it he had enough to feed his family and he had given us all you need for children to grow up ... and certainly lots of pleasures too, not just the necessities. He had been a man I could be proud of. But as he was dying, he turned to me and said, "I'm really sorry I don't have anything to leave you." And I thought, "This is 100 percent against what you've believed all your life – that we shouldn't be focusing just on acquiring money, that we should be thinking about more important things in life. And here you are, two days from death and all of a sudden it's gotten you again and you're all tangled between the two worlds again."
>
> I don't know what I said to him at the time but I'm sure I said, as gently as I could, that we were fine, that he did indeed leave us a lot of things that were more important than money. I have his picture in my wallet. Everything I do is for that man's sake, because he was hopelessly ill-fitted to live in two worlds. Often he was in pain, from conflict, but didn't know if it was him or the world going the wrong way.

Another important factor to consider in looking at Algonquin histories is that experiences of colonization varied widely across the territory, not only between Quebec and Ontario but between differing regions of Ontario. For example, while many Ardoch families were migrating to find work, Algonquins further north were still able to rely on the land for their livelihoods, although this involved accommodating the presence of logging in their territory. Individuals with lands around the Petawawa River were still able to rely on hunting and trapping during the 1930s and 1940s, for food and for skins to sell for supplies (as well as making moccasins, gloves, and other articles of clothing for the family).

Even in this context, silencing still occurred, though on a more subtle level. Some individuals spoke of a reluctance on the part of their grandparents to tell them the stories and histories from the past. Clearly, some elders saw ahead to a time when their grandchildren would be required to adapt entirely to the white world; they may have decided that passing on an Algonquin oral tradition might only burden their grandchildren, who above all had to survive.

While those living along the Petawawa River and further north in Mattawa were still able to rely on the land for sustenance, Algonquins from Allumette Island were being forced off their land. Most moved to Pembroke, just across the river from their homes. Segregated into the poorer parts of town and facing terrible poverty, they nevertheless fought hard to survive with dignity and to maintain a strong level of cohesiveness within their families. In a 2005 interview, Dennis Timms described Algonquin life in Pembroke as he was growing up:

> The housing was so bad. If somebody had a garage or shed, there would be whole families living there. And they had shacks downtown. You know, the shack town down there around Everett Street and Hollywood? And Giroux Ville, and Stafford? That's where I spent most of my time. And no, you couldn't cross the boundaries. I remember going to school with patches on my clothes. And you weren't ashamed of it then. But I was clean – I mean, those people were so strict about being clean, I remember that. Even with the poor housing. Women used to go to the river and beat the clothes on washboards. And around Black Bay sometimes, if they didn't have a washboard, they'd beat the clothes on rocks – I've seen that a couple of times.
>
> In winter, they'd bank sand around their shacks. Used to build a little barrier and fill it up with sand. Bank the place for the winter, and then when the snow came, you'd bank it with snow. Right up against the house. It was survival, but I mean, the reason why they were living substandard is because they were left behind and they never got any formal education and so, once

> you were twelve, you had to go to work. In order to survive. I remember us going to the dump, waiting to see what people threw out. Whatever we could get, we would use. It was survival, of the fittest ...
>
> I remember Jean Avenue ... There was a dump there, and a big sand pit ... Those weren't meant to be playgrounds but that was where we played. And I know people that when they were between jobs, or just totally destitute, they lived in those sand pits. That's where they lived. That's where they slept. That's where they had their campfire and they ate. That was the place. And out in the country, by the time you'd get in Black Bay, there were people living in lean-to's, you'd find roofs, built right into the ground – they were using the ground as insulation.

Timms remembered the effort to keep body and soul together in hard times, and how cohesive the community was. However, a younger Algonquin woman, who remembered how her grandparents had struggled to maintain family and community cohesiveness in her childhood, recalled as a teenager how alcohol slowly invaded the Pembroke community, until by the 1970s many families had become dysfunctional. Algonquin boys were particularly targeted in schools as "troublemakers" and sent to reformatories; in this manner a whole generation of Algonquin men was criminalized. She also spoke of the violent brawls that sometimes took place in the West End, where Algonquins were segregated.

Others from Pembroke, remembering the terrible breakdown in social relations that came with alcohol, spoke about their families' efforts to break free of the cycles of despair and dysfunction that had begun to shape their lives. In some instances, people were forced to turn their backs on family members who lived in poverty and destitution, in order to raise their children without exposure to the pain that they remembered from their own childhoods.

When being Algonquin became too associated with alcoholism, racism, and violence, some families attempted to suppress any expressions of their identity. The results included internalized racism, particularly against dark-skinned family members, and the intensely dysfunctional relations that arise when people deny who they are and can find no other target for their anger than their kin.

The interviews demonstrated that the grandparents and parents of today's federally unrecognized Algonquins came from a range of rural and urban experiences, and that silence around identity had everything to do with whether their families had retained connections to land or had been forced to migrate to work, whether they had lived in isolated towns surrounded by racist whites or were ghettoized together into substandard urban conditions, and whether they were able to maintain collective values or faced family breakdown, alcoholism, violence, and despair. The results can be summed up as a collective experience of silencing, brought about by a profound experience of colonial violence. The result, however, for their descendants has been confusion and sometimes ambivalence about Algonquin identity.

It's important to realize that the resulting confusion about identity that many non-status Algonquins struggle with also comes from having to reconstruct an Indigenous identity in the face of the stereotypes about Indianness that fill the dominant society. In such a context, it is not enough simply to prove one's ancestry – one must also conform to stereotypes relating to phenotype, knowledge of culture, and above all, Indian status. During a 2005 interview, Heather Majaury described the "identity crisis" that can result when non-status Algonquins attempt to actualize their silenced Native identity:

> I've seen people come in to the offices in the midst of their identity crisis, which I can relate to. They start off with "I'm white, but part Indian but I can't prove it." Which means they're completely disenfranchised as far as a personal voice goes, right? Then it's, "I've found some records! I can prove who I am." The next thing they get is a mittful of cards – because everybody and their brother has set up an organization where they can give out membership cards ... So everybody's got their cards. And what you're looking at is a situation where a lot of people are confronted with an identity crisis and are trying to deal with it through having a card ... This is how I see it ...
>
> And I mean, if people on reserves put so much stock in having an Indian card, then why shouldn't the non-status people embrace the community cards that they get when they have established their heritage? Are they expecting the non-status Algonquins to be superhuman? ... But the reality is, the only system people are really aware of is the colonial system that identified people as Indians in the first place. The Indian card is the only one that really matters, as far as the government and the reserve people believe. It's been very confusing.

To make matters worse, though the land claim has enabled many non-status Algonquins to reclaim their identity because they have found records to prove it and have received an identity card, it has also periodically withdrawn that recognition. Since 2001, when the numbers of non-status Algonquins enumerated for the purposes of the land claim began to expand exponentially, there have been numerous calls from the band council at Pikwakanagan for "recounts." Because of this, membership files have been reopened and reverified – first by Joan Holmes in 2004 (which resulted in only minimal denials of enrolment), and later, through a constant re-evaluation, and in some instances removal, of individuals who were accepted into the land claim as Algonquins through an appeal board. These people, who had proven Native ancestry but had not been able to prove that this ancestry was Algonquin, therefore had their ability to be counted as Algonquin evaluated before a board.

It is important to contextualize this. First of all, though undoubtedly most of the people who were dispossessed and struggling to survive the onslaught of the colonial process in the Ottawa River watershed were Algonquin, it is equally likely that at least some individuals came from the surrounding Indigenous nations also facing settler encroachment, who may have cast in their lot with the Algonquins as the tide of colonization swept across the land. With the establishment of the reserve at Golden Lake, Indianness, not Algonquinness, was the salient factor that Indian Affairs administrators were concerned with; because of this, the individuals who settled at Golden Lake were not required to prove their Algonquinness – they simply had to be Indian.

Second, until 1985, any woman who married a Pikwakanagan man became legally Algonquin; because of this, many Native women from other nations (as well as non-Native women) have been "naturalized" as Algonquins simply because of Indian Act rules.

Finally, when the Algonquin enrolment law was being created, a number of the root ancestors who were classified as known Algonquins on Schedule A had similar descriptors in the historical records as those Algonquins whose ancestors were simply listed as "Indian." For this reason, an appeal board was created to evaluate the files of those individuals whose ancestors were listed simply as Indian, to acknowledge the limitations of the colonial record keeping system, and to allow Algonquins to determine who were Algonquins based on wider criteria, such as kinship and oral accounts. It was understood that in such circumstances, no single factor would determine identity; instead, a comprehensive picture would be drawn from all available evidence and would acknowledge that colonialism had forced Algonquin families to assimilate. Through these wider criteria, the appeal board would be able to determine which root ancestors identified after the Algonquin enrolment law was created in 1993 should be added to Schedule A. At the time, the distinction between Schedule A and "board files" merely meant that certain cases were evaluated on an individual basis. When people were enrolled via an appeal board evaluation rather than because their ancestors were listed in Schedule A, they had simply taken a different route to the same conclusion.

But as the possibility of reaching a settlement becomes more real, the decisions made under the Algonquin enrolment law are being revisited, and families who were once considered Algonquin are now being subjected to increasing scrutiny, for the purposes of exclusion. For example, in 2010, two members of the Pikwakanagan council appealed the enrolment law registration of four people whose root ancestors were Margaret Thomas and Hannah Mannell, claiming that Thomas and Mannell, though Native, were not Algonquin. The enrolment review board, consisting of five members from non-status communities, considered the case, and though it agreed that Thomas and Mannell were probably Cree, it nonetheless dismissed the appeal on 22 November 2010. Its reasoning hinged on two factors: the registration of the four individuals from the Thomas-Foy and Hannah Mannell lines had been accepted by the appeal board in 1994, and the registration had survived the ninety-day interval when new registrations could be challenged, as required under the enrolment law. Thus, to question their status now would be to undermine the Algonquin enrolment laws of 1994 and 2004. The majority decision was to deny the appeal and maintain the enrolment of the four individuals as well as others who were descended from Thomas and Mannell. However, the enrolment review board did suggest that no more enrolments be accepted from those who traced their ancestry via the Thomas-Foy or Hannah Mannell lines.

This decision was subsequently overruled by the Algonquin negotiation representatives, who removed the four individuals and everyone else who had been registered because they were descended from Thomas or Mannell. Between five and six hundred people were thus de-enrolled from the land claim. At present they are mounting a court case to challenge their exclusion.

In conversations with Heather Majaury in July 2011, she noted that the process is backward, in that though the reserve is willing to *consult* with non-status Algonquins about the negotiations, their actual *acceptance* as possible beneficiaries is a different matter, especially for those whose enrolment was via the board system. For several years, non-status Algonquins have been able to vote for their representatives in the negotiating party, a political body that both Ottawa and Ontario have recognized as legitimate. However, this may not necessarily make them beneficiaries of a final agreement; as a result, many individuals who have struggled long and hard in connection with the land claim may ultimately be excluded from voting on it or from being a beneficiary.

These exclusionary processes are shaped by the fact that in the comprehensive claims process, Canada will not entertain questions of compensation for loss or damage. Instead, its emphasis on the idea of "beneficiaries" suggests that Algonquins are getting a deal, rather than something that is deserved or inherent. If compensation is deserved or inherent, all Algonquins, whether status or non-status, board file or schedule A, are entitled to it. If there are only beneficiaries, those who potentially do not "deserve" benefits *should* be excluded as not being bona fide Algonquins.

On 31 March 2011, the Algonquin Agreement-in-Principle Ratification Committee finally released its preliminary voters list. Not only did it exclude members of the Thomas-Foy and Hannah Mannell lines, it permitted the enrolment of everyone on the list to be challenged. The families of some individuals who have been deleted from the list have lived in the Ottawa River watershed for over two hundred years, which means that their Native ancestors, whether Algonquin or not, lived under Algonquin law, since at the turn of the nineteenth century, the Algonquin Nation still maintained control over the entire watershed. As individuals are struck off the voters list, their ability to be beneficiaries is correspondingly affected.

Culture and Authenticity

> Beads and buckskin, sacred pipes, wise elders, prayers to "mother earth" and so on – we all recognize these signifiers of essentialist authoritative discourse in the realm of Native American literature. Although such signifiers have crucial and invaluable meaning to Native people, from the Euroamerican perspective this is merely a surface discourse established from a cultural glance by the dominant European-American culture over several hundred years of colonization to define the distinct "otherness" of Indigenous Americans. To go beyond such facile cultural discourse to the deeper and irreplaceable role such signifiers play in specific Native cultures would be to recognize the humanity of the colonized, a move certain to make a difficult task of cultural erasure more difficult still.
>
> – **Louis Owens, *Mixedblood Messages***

Some Algonquins whom I interviewed addressed questions of cultural resurgence, which, for many, are far more important than any other issue raised by the land claim. Others discussed the difficulty that Algonquins can face when their real cultural heritage – transformed by colonization and maintained in subtle but definite ways – is not acknowledged unless it is accompanied by a performance of "Indianness" that is recognizable to the mainstream. Heather Majaury has commented that non-status Algonquins seeking validation of their identities often feel pressured to claim "traditional" cultural knowledge:

> As I have grown in my understanding, I would suggest that while Algonquin people didn't grow up with what would be considered the bells and whistles of formal ceremonies, there were patterns of ways of being or living that were deeply connected to the land and cycles of life. It just seems to me that there is pressure to put on the beads and feathers to be considered legitimate or to live up to a Western idealized way of being Indian. There is nothing wrong with either – it's an adaptation. The problem is in a nation that bore the brunt of colonization there has to be some realistic ideas of cultural adaptation and respect for the strength of that when confronted with the dominance of the hegemonic systems that have occupied the land, our bodies, and our minds. As it stands, collectively we have to prove a cultural cohesion that is impossible through the history we have had or to perform to the colonial gaze for recognition. We can't just be who we are. But I also think that reclaiming culture and re-educating ourselves and learning is valuable and important. I think there is a paradox here.

In this context, non-status Algonquins are in a lose-lose situation. Having to weigh their identity claims against those of Pikwakanagan, which are validated by an "Indian" card, they are inevitably minimized. Thus, many are forced to claim that they possess a seamless (pre-colonial) font of cultural knowledge, and in doing so, deny the legacy that they *have* inherited, which outsiders cannot recognize as Indian because it is not dressed in beads and feathers.

This issue lies at the heart of the recognition paradigm. The reality for all federally unrecognized Indigenous communities is that, in essence, winning such recognition forces them to lie about the experiences of colonization and genocide that have indubitably shaped who they are today. In a sense, it violates the lived experiences of individuals and demands a false conformity with stereotypes about Indianness.

This process is most visible with the Honey Lake Maidu, a northern California tribe that is seeking federal recognition. Its documented history – in which band members were murdered by settlers, and children were rounded up by the military and sold into slavery on local farms – attests to the bitterness of the tribe's past and the miracle of its survival. Only two of the band's six original lineages still exist, and the community is dispersed throughout the region (Tolley 2006, 25-33). Although their history has been marked by genocide, the Maidu must deny it if they wish to achieve federal recognition: they must assert that they have maintained a historical continuity as a tribe and geographical cohesion in their homelands, that they represent a good percentage of their original tribal lineages, and that they have maintained culturally specific traditional practices (ibid., 36). Federally unrecognized Algonquins in Ontario have encountered a similar dynamic; the land claim process requires them to deny their history of government-sanctioned policies of genocide and erasure and the profound silencing that ensued in order to assert that they exist at all and should have Aboriginal rights.

Local Meanings of Indianness and Metisness

An additional complexity confronting all Native people in Canada is the historical existence of mixed-blood people during the fur trade and their subsequent categorization, under the 1982 Constitution Act, as irrevocably "different" from Indians. Olive Dickason (1985, 29-30) has posited that distinct "Metis" communities were created due to their occupational segregation during the fur trade, and that in areas where the fur trade was undeveloped, such as the east coast, mixed-bloods simply remained part of Native communities. Regardless of why such communities came into existence and of how Metis people understand themselves to be Metis, the formal definitions of "Metis" and "Indian" as rigidly distinct categories are grounded in colonialism and do not reflect the true complexity of people's lives.

Because those classified as "half-breed" were excluded from the Indian Act, and because the Ottawa River was a key corridor for the development of the fur trade in Western Canada, it is important to take up the question of "Metisness" in the Ottawa River watershed, particularly because the term is frequently used by individuals from Pikwakanagan to dismiss the Algonquinness of non-status Algonquins. In this discussion, I distinguish between "Metisness," referring to individuals who define themselves as members of culturally distinct communities within a Metis Nation or whose lineage comes from historical "halfbreed" communities, and those who do not identify as Metis but who are referred to by status Indians as "metis" as a means of denying their Indianness. In a conversation with Heather Majaury in August 2011, she indicated that the use of the word "metis" to refer to mixed-bloods who lack Indian status, which is now common in southern Ontario generally and the Ottawa Valley in particular, originated in the 1970s. Thus, it may be an artifact of the 1969 White Paper, Canada's attempt to unilaterally terminate the legal category of "Indian." In the wake of the White Paper, the primary concern of status Indian organizations became to protect Indian status at all cost. Labelling those who lack it as "metis" was a good way of establishing firm parameters around Indianness and excluding those who lacked Indian status.

In this way of thinking, who is – or is not – metis? In southern Ontario reserve communities, the word has had multiple meanings. For example, when Indian women married white men and lost their status, their mixed-blood children were almost always seen as metis. Conversely, the mixed-blood children of white women who married Indian men and lived on-reserve were uncategorically Indian. They had Indian status and thus were not seen as metis. Historically, many non-status Algonquins who knew themselves to be Algonquin were nonetheless considered metis by status Indians if they were visibly mixed-blood. If, however, they looked Native (which, with growing contemporary levels of intermarriage, was more common a generation ago than it is now), they were generally referred to as non-status Indians.

The logic of these assumptions is pervasive and still holds true in many southern Ontario reserve communities, where, unlike in northern Ontario and Western Canada, the term "metis" is not seen as referring to culturally distinct hybrid people. In southern Ontario, the word simply signifies a lesser category of Native people who are "not Indian enough" by both status and blood. In this way of thinking, "metis" are not to be confused with "non-status Indians," who look Native and who therefore are presumed to be Indian.

As the above definitions suggest, the categories of "metis" and "non-status Indian" were somewhat nebulous in southern Ontario prior to 1982, and for this reason, early organizations such as OMNSIA, the Ontario Metis and Non-Status Indian Association, did not generally distinguish between them, particularly in the Ottawa Valley. However, when the 1982 Constitution Act officially recognized the Metis as an Aboriginal people, questions intensified about Metis identity and Metis ethnogenesis (which associated "Metis" with a people or a nation, not with an individual condition of mixed-bloodedness). These issues of ethnogenesis were extremely pertinent not only in Western Canada but also in northern Ontario and a scattering of communities around the Great Lakes, where culturally hybrid and distinct groups who had always considered themselves to be Metis could finally have their aboriginality recognized.

With this development, however, being "non-status" and being "metis" in the Ottawa Valley were no longer nebulous categories with definitions that were somewhat blurred; instead, they began to accrue distinctly different sets of meanings – with powerfully different repercussions for how identity and nationhood were understood. At Pikwakanagan, definitions of "metis" meaning "mixed-blood" remain prevalent. However, outside the reserve, as non-status Algonquins struggle to define themselves, they understand "Metis" in its more contemporary meaning – as distinct and culturally hybrid people who refer to themselves as a nation – which clearly has nothing to do with being Algonquin. Very little cultural hybridity exists in most non-status Algonquin lineages, particularly in the inland communities along the tributaries of the Ottawa River. For the most part, Algonquins in these communities view themselves simply as the descendants of both Algonquins and Europeans who have struggled to remain, if not on the land, at least within their traditional territories.

Algonquins from this background almost unanimously reject the label "Metis," not because they deny being of mixed blood, but because they deny the disconnection to Algonquin territory and heritage that the word has implied since the 1982 recognition of the Metis as a distinct people. Most do not see their mixed blood as connecting them to a larger Metis Nation – they see themselves as mixed-blood Algonquins whose affiliations are to the Algonquin territory of their ancestors and to the Algonquin Nation.

It's important to note that even those families whose non-Native members were part of the early fur trade do not consider themselves to be Metis, particularly if they live far inland from the Ottawa River. In many cases, when seventeenth-century fur traders allied themselves with Algonquins, they married into their families, learned their language, and lived in their world. Many Algonquins whose ancestors were involved in the fur trade have been rooted in the Ottawa Valley for more than two hundred years, far longer than Pikwakanagan has been in existence. They see themselves as Algonquin, not Metis, regardless of how Pikwakanagan labels them.

On the other hand, some individuals from communities along the edge of the Ottawa River, where the imprint of the fur trade can still be felt, have expressed a hybridized Metis identity that is nevertheless deeply imbued with pride in Algonquin identity. For example, a number of Algonquins living in Pembroke defined themselves as being *both* Algonquin and Metis. These individuals spoke of traditional Algonquin values but simultaneously expressed tremendous pride in the amalgamation of French and Algonquin elements that to them represented Metis culture. They spoke about the celebratory nature of Metis gatherings, with food, dance, drink, and music to acclaim life in all its wonder, where gatherings were not only social but political, in that they enabled men and women to discuss important issues. For these individuals, their vision of Metisness was strongly informed by Algonquin values and had both "mixed-blood" and "cultural" overtones, so that being Metis was seen as a distinct identity that was nevertheless not incompatible with being Algonquin.

Other individuals from small communities along the banks of the Ottawa River disagreed with this perspective, distinguishing between "Algonquin" and "Metis" ways. In their view, Metisness was a cultural identity descended from the lively, extroverted, and adaptable lifestyles produced by Native and primarily French intermarriages during the fur trade. Being Metis meant being forced to carve a niche in the in-between world of the fur trade and therefore being constantly on the move. As a result, Metis men generally accepted whatever survival opportunities came their way, expressing the pain of their rootlessness through music and driving it away with revelry. And yet many individuals from this heritage also saw themselves as Algonquin because they had an Algonquin background, because Metis men generally married Algonquin women, and because their families had lived in Algonquin territory for generations.

Only one person suggested that the *real* Algonquin values, which were strongly connected to the land and resistant to change, were in some danger of being supplanted by the more flexible Metis values.

It is difficult to address the reality of cultural change and its manifestations, given the colonial categories underpinning contemporary definitions of both "Indian" and "Metis." As individuals utilize various definitions to explain their complex identities, these categories can obscure more than they illuminate. Defining "Indianness" as rooted to the land and "Metisness" as transitory belies the history of Algonquin dispossession, as Algonquin men were forced into a lifetime of transience working within resource industries, and were forced to live apart from their families for years at a time. For instance, one interview subject, an elderly man who had survived by working in lumbering and other resource industries his entire life, demonstrated a deep acceptance of change and transience as well as the concomitant loss of community and a corresponding lack of ties to specific places. He lived on the Quebec side of the river and tended to speak French more often than English; moreover, he clearly loved the celebrations that maintained community and saw Native people who were connected to the land as being the "wild" ones, more Indian than himself. All of this would seem to suggest that he self-identified as Metis, but he referred to himself as unequivocally "Indian" throughout the interview.

In general, questions about the meaning of Metis and Algonquin heritages arose only where Algonquins lived along the Ottawa River itself. Later, we shall see that in the town of Mattawa, at the northern edge of the watershed, both Algonquins and Metis are very clear regarding what the differences are between Algonquins and Metis in a more northern context. Although both groups have been consigned to the "Indian" part of town, the older folks know who is Algonquin and who is Metis. It is also clear, however, that with acculturation, the youth are losing a sense of these distinctions due to pressures of assimilation.

In general, to embrace hard-and-fast and often intensely ideological definitions of non-status Algonquins as *either* non-status Indian *or* Metis generally does not reflect the complex realities in the Ottawa River watershed. Ultimately, the driving force for the insistence that non-status Algonquins are "really" metis is Pikwakanagan's contention that anyone who is not legally defined as Indian must be metis. The variations in individuals' understandings of their identities – as rooted in the fur trade, as arising from intermarriage with settlers, as culturally hybrid, and as Algonquin rather than Metis – reveal the complexities of actual lived experience in the Ottawa Valley; in such a context, where many non-status Algonquins are struggling to understand and express their Algonquinness, it is perhaps premature to embrace such divisions and differentiate between "Algonquin" and "Metis."

Having gained a general sense of the identity issues that confront non-status Algonquins, we must remember that for many individuals, Algonquin identity is tied to place. Thus, the remainder of this book will explore the histories and experiences of Algonquin communities according to how they have always lived – in specific watersheds. It will provide a snapshot of the complexity of Algonquin identity and lives over the interval between 2003 and 2009, when interviews were being conducted across the watershed, during the seven years following the resumption of the land claim negotiations. What I hope will be revealed in the following chapters are both the tremendous efforts of people who are attempting to honour their ancestors by rebuilding a nation and the immense contradictions they face as they utilize a comprehensive claims process that is designed to bypass just such an eventuality. I will begin with an in-depth look at the communities of the Mississippi, Rideau, and lower Madawaska watersheds, the profound divisions they have suffered, and their efforts to protect the land.

PART 2

The Mississippi, Rideau, and Lower Madawaska River Watersheds

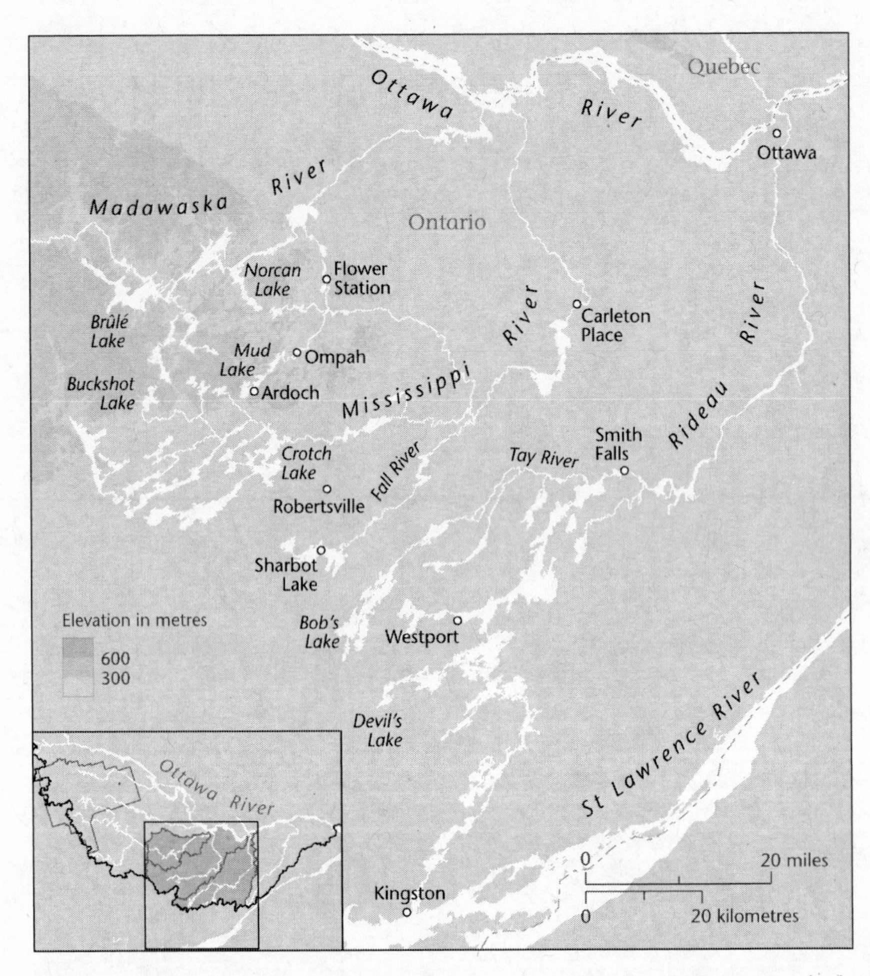

Algonquin communities in the Mississippi, Rideau, and lower Madawaska River watersheds

6

The Development of Ardoch Algonquin First Nation

The people whose traditional land base is in the watersheds of the Mississippi, Rideau, and lower Madawaska Rivers were among the first Algonquins to see their lands overrun by settlers. For that reason, they were also the first to petition for and have lands set aside for them. Although incursions by loggers and white squatters rapidly made the land unviable for their use, their descendants managed to survive and remain in their ancestral territories. The community was drawn into collective action during the early 1980s to defend its wild rice beds. Needing a formal structure to address this concern, it amalgamated to form one of the earliest of the modern federally unrecognized Algonquin communities, at Ardoch. The land claim subsequently divided this community, as a group broke away from Ardoch to form the Sharbot Lake area committee, now Shabot Obaadjiwan First Nation. Dissatisfied with Shabot Obaadjiwan, a third group later formed, to focus on cultural revival – Pasapkedjiwanong Algonquin First Nation.

In many respects, the relations between these three groups illustrate most of the conflicts that have sprung up within and between communities as a result of the land claim. For that reason, the following three chapters will explore these issues in detail. The potential for such divisions to escalate is always present in other watersheds, and where other issues may be paramount, the divisions that occurred in this region offer a case study of the pressures that the land claim can generate.

This chapter will describe the history of settler incursion and dispossession in this region and the development of Ardoch Algonquin First Nation. Ardoch has always existed as a community of allied families working together to ensure their survival. Its core families maintained a connection to their lands throughout the settlement process, even as settlers appropriated most of their territory. In the early 1980s, they formally organized themselves, not because of the land claim but in an unprecedented resistance to provincial government attempts to take over their wild rice crop. Protecting the land and focusing on community building and strengthening Algonquin identity have been Ardoch's priorities since that time. Ardoch is also unique in that, more than any Ottawa River watershed community, it has voiced the most critical and sustained analysis of the land claim. Finally, Ardoch has mounted a number of important court cases to advance the rights of non-status Algonquins. Because of these factors, a number of scholars have focused on Ardoch rather than the other communities. For all these reasons, the present chapter will detail Ardoch's development; the following chapter will focus on the effects of the land claim and provide an overview of Shabot Obaadjiwan and Pasapkedjiwanong; and the third chapter will discuss the ongoing issue of uranium exploration in the region and the need to protect the traditional land base.

Historical Occupation and Dispossession

In southeastern Ontario, the Mississippi, Rideau, and lower Madawaska watersheds have been occupied by Algonquins since time immemorial – originally as the Ountchatarounounga band, and by the late eighteenth century, after a hundred years of trade and colonial warfare, as an amalgamation of the surviving families who had remained on their traditional territories. However, only when settlers began to overrun their lands in the early nineteenth century did the people of this region enter into official records. Their leader, Peter Shawinapinessi, was born around 1780, during the first decades of British occupation when Algonquin resistance was strong. A few years later, parts of his people's traditional hunting territories were erroneously included in the Crawford Purchase, the 1783 Mississauga surrender of land to the government. Between 1819 and 1822, the remainder of the land was erroneously included in the Rideau Purchase, another Mississauga surrender. The area was soon surveyed into townships – Bedford, at the head of the Rideau River system, Oso, in the Mississippi system, and South Sherbrooke, which spanned both river systems (Joan Holmes and Associates 1995, 8).

By 1823, settler encroachment had begun to impoverish Peter Shawinapinessi's band. Because of this, he frequently travelled to Lake of Two Mountains, where he met with the leaders and grand chiefs from other territories, reported on the situation, strategized, and received "presents" from the British on behalf of his people. Some Mississaugas, whose territories bordered on those of the Algonquins, joined the band at this time by marrying into its families. When the Mississaugas were forced to relocate to a reserve at Alnwick, some of these people chose to stay with their Algonquin families. During this period, the Algonquins utilized the land around Bob's Lake, Crotch Lake, Mud Lake, and Sharbot Lake.

Between the 1840s and the 1870s, the northern parts of what are now Frontenac and Lanark Counties were intensively settled. Large tracts of land were awarded to timber companies during the 1840s, and the tall pines of Bedford, Clarendon, and Miller Townships soon vanished to provide masts for British ships (Huitema 2000, 147-48). In 1856, the Frontenac Colonization Road was surveyed and built (Delisle 2001, 77); as it brought settlers northward, the Algonquins retreated to the margins of settlement areas, attempting to establish new camps and family territories (Huitema 2000, 145). Here, they encountered more lumber camps as well as squatters who were moving north to claim land. Violent dispossession – rape, beatings, theft, expropriation of land, and the diminishment of wildlife – all became part of the lives of Shawinapinessi's band.

On 17 July 1842, Shawinapinessi petitioned the governor general for 2,000 acres to be set aside in Bedford, Oso, and South Sherbrooke Townships. The proposed tract was bounded by lakes, although the soil was poor. In March 1844, Order-in-Council 1467 granted Shawinapinessi a licence of occupation for land near Bob's Lake, though "only during the pleasure of the Crown," and it was accordingly removed from public sale (Joan Holmes and Associates 1993, 2:106-7). However, the Department of Crown Lands soon disregarded this process and issued timber licences for the area. By 1845, the Algonquins had cleared approximately ten acres and had constructed two log houses and a number of outbuildings; however, the settlement was surrounded by lumber operations, so Shawinapinessi petitioned the governor general in 1846 to ask for protection from the loggers and requested that the proceeds from the cut timber be granted to Algonquins. He also requested information as to when the land would be surveyed, as surveying was already a year overdue.

In 1861, Shawinapinessi complained to the superintendent of Indian Affairs that seventeen white persons had settled or squatted on the Bedford tract (ibid.,

118-19). Their activities – clearing and burning the bush, and driving cattle onto the land to forage – made life increasingly difficult for the Algonquins. The squatters not only relied on Indian land, they used the Indian trails between the Madawaska and Mississippi River systems, continuing to do so until more roads were built.

Although the Algonquins needed the Bedford tract for camping and small-scale farming, their hunting, trapping, and gathering territories included other parts of Bedford, Oso, and South Sherbrooke Townships as well as areas north of the Rideau River system. During this time, they regularly travelled to Westport, in North Crosby Township, to Perth, in Drummond Township, and to Kingston (Joan Holmes and Associates 1995, 12). By the 1870s, however, as loggers and squatters made it impossible for them to use the Bedford tract and relentlessly foreclosed on many lands that supplied them with food, local Algonquins began to experience tremendous poverty and forced change. The death toll, particularly from tuberculosis, was high (Huitema 2000, 162).

Clarendon Township, where Ardoch is located, became a free grant area in 1868. Settlers surged in, each claiming 100 acres. Until this time, and indeed until the 1890s in some locations, the families now recorded on the provincial census as Antoine, Charles, Cota/Pesendawatj, Mitchell, Sharbot, and Whiteduck were still supporting themselves by hunting, trapping, fishing, and minor agriculture (Joan Holmes and Associates 1995, 14). Increasingly, however, though some families did maintain at least a winter or a summer campsite or sporadic access to their sugar or wild rice harvesting areas, many of the men were forced to leave their families and hunt further and further north, in Lanark and Renfrew Counties, or to seek work in the logging camps. Invariably, their wives and children stayed in the traditional hunting grounds, fending for themselves, gathering plants, roots, berries, and wild rice, and performing menial chores for white families in exchange for handouts.

During a 2003 interview, Harold Perry, a respected Ardoch elder, spoke about his family's history:

> My family – they were here when the white people came, and of course because Indian people weren't allowed to have land ... So they took all this land that we were using and gave it to the settlers, when they came in. And then, around Ardoch, when they did the first agricultural census, it showed where my great-grandfather had made maple syrup, up there. And then, from what I can gather, they took that lot, and sold it off, gave it to the settlers when they came in. And then my great-grandfather – he had to turn around and get permission to go on his own land.

By the 1880s, as the logging industry denuded the territory and large tracts of land were burned to enable the establishment of settler farms, thick black smoke hung in the region, and the wildlife had almost vanished. Death and disease took their toll on family structures and slowly undermined Algonquin spiritual processes. Algonquins were increasingly forced to rely on Christian churches to build at least some form of relationship between themselves and the settler society displacing them (Huitema 2000, 170).[1]

Although contact between Euro-Canadians and Algonquins was initiated for economic, social, and religious reasons, the Algonquins may have embraced Christianity because religious allegiance allowed them more freedom than the political system of the colonial government, which largely curtailed their liberty. Given that death and disease had taken a toll on their elders, destabilizing kinship structures and making spiritual practices difficult (particularly in urban settings), attending church may have served spiritual needs as well as helping them to interpret the coerced changes in their belief systems. In this respect, church attendance was definitely part of an adaptive strategy.

More pragmatically, participating in European religious observance provided possible inroads into the Euro-Canadian economic system, for the clergy took an interest in the well-being of their Algonquin parishioners to encourage the conversion of community members. Finally, since Algonquin men were frequently absent for long periods while they worked as loggers, many Algonquin women were employed by settler families. In a context where sexual abuse at the hands of employers was always a threat, Algonquin women may have sought out the church in hopes that it might censure men who abused them.

By the 1890s, a few Algonquins were sporadically listed on land registries as occupying land in Clarendon Township. Most relied on a mixed economy, subsisting in the dwindling areas where wild rice harvesting, fishing, trapping, and hunting remained viable but increasingly finding small niches in the settler society where they could trade goods, sell crafts, or perform odd jobs to survive.

By the turn of the century, survival had become increasingly difficult, as land alienation removed even more significant territories (Huitema 2000, 174-78). By then, lumber mills, railroads, productive farms, and hundreds of mines existed in the region (Lovelace 2006). The descendants of those who had occupied the Mississippi, Rideau, and lower Madawaska watersheds had been erased from official recognition as Indians. Ignored by Indian Affairs and driven from their land, they nonetheless maintained a presence around Ardoch and Sharbot Lake, and church and census records refer to the families who are the recognized ancestors of today's Ardoch community – the Antoines, the Beavers, the Cota/Pesendawatjs, the Mitchells, the Sharbots, and the White-ducks (Perrys) (Joan Holmes and Associates 1995, 16). The families were joined by marriage and close residence as well as mutual social, religious, and economic support. They hunted and trapped in adjacent townships and up the lower Madawaska River, particularly around Brule Lake, Buckshot Creek, Buckshot Lake, Crotch Lake, Devil's Lake, Flower Station, the small lakes and streams at Mud Lake, Norcan Lake, Ompah, and Sharbot Lake (ibid., 17).

After the 1920s, younger Algonquins were increasingly forced to travel to large towns and cities in search of work. They continued to view the small towns that had displaced them on their territories – particularly Ardoch as well as Sharbot Lake – as their homes. Hunting, fishing, and wild rice gathering became important supplements to a precarious existence obtained through wage labour (Huitema 2000, 196-98). Banding together to work collectively on food production, to address the issues affecting them, and simply to maintain social ties continued to be central to their survival.

Below, Harold Perry described life at Ardoch in the 1920s and 1930s, when he was young:

> During the First World War, a lot of our people went into the war, and they all got gassed, the men, eh? So the women kind of took over and ran things, you know. I remember, them smoking fish, at the point, at my place. People would gather there. When I was growing up, the women were running things ... I remember Indian people coming and having meetings. I don't know what the meetings were about, but they would have meetings. And then after the meetings, the music would come out, and it would be happy times. It felt like happy times. I guess that would be in the mid-thirties ...
>
> The generation before me – they must have had it hard – because any good land got taken for farming, and they couldn't have it ... You couldn't even get across the land to trap. I had that happen to me, years ago – tried to get across the land to go where I used to trap, had to cross some farmer's land. He says, "You can't go," eh? That's hard to take. It's something you don't forget, either. Then you have to sneak around, to hunt and trap. That's basically why, I think, they have so many suicides in the Aboriginal communities. It's things like that. These things don't sound like much, but they're very aggressive. You can only take it so long, eh? The world just gets too hard, it's time to go.

Manoomin Keezis

In 1957, Harold Perry obtained a patent to a small part of his family's traditional territory at Mud Lake (Huitema 2000, 199). It had been occupied by his great-grandparents, Mary Buckshot and Joseph Whiteduck (Lovelace 1982, 29). This small but symbolic reacquisition of Algonquin territory, and the practice of wild ricing that was associated with it, became the nucleus of the modern Ardoch community.

During the 1880s, at the darkest time for Ardoch when survival itself seemed impossible, Mary Buckshot brought wild rice, or *manoomin,* from Rice Lake and planted it at Mud Lake. As the white settlements grew, the Rice Lake manoomin beds were extinguished by the construction of the Trent Canal (ibid.), but the stand at Mud Lake remained. Its hereditary guardianship was passed in a continuous line from Mary Buckshot to her daughter Henrietta Whiteduck, to her grandson Richard Perry, and subsequently to her great-grandson Harold Perry. In the late 1970s, a commercial operation obtained a licence to harvest the Mud Lake wild rice, a development that galvanized the small informal community into taking a stand to protect it and ultimately created the modern community of Ardoch Algonquin First Nation.

What has been called the "rice war" arose from a number of issues. The first was the Ontario government's attempt to consolidate its control over wild rice, having recently discovered that it could be exploited as a lucrative resource. The second issue was the importance of the rice to Ardoch: reclaiming jurisdiction over the rice beds was an essential process for regaining cultural knowledge. The third, and related, issue was how this process changed the way in which the people saw themselves. After decades of silence about their Algonquin identity, in a world where being Indian meant living under the Indian Act, the Ardoch people knew themselves to be of Native heritage but had no real name for themselves. By the end of the struggle, they had begun to explore their identities as Algonquins.

The Rice War

For Aboriginal people, manoomin is a spiritual gift of the Creator that nourishes their spirits. A self-seeding annual, wild rice is actually an aquatic grain rather than a true rice and is unique to North America. It grows in flowing water, primarily in sandy soils, forming dense beds at river banks and in shallow lakes. Vulnerable to fluctuations in water level, it can be drowned if the water rises too high. Its seed ripens over a period of days, shatters, and drops into the water, where it generates new plants for the next year. Aboriginal peoples have been planting, maintaining, and harvesting manoomin beds since time immemorial (Delisle 2001, 37-38). Its planting, harvesting, processing, preparation, and consumption are all heavily imbued with cultural and spiritual significance – indeed, the Anishinabeg calendar refers to the time of the rice harvest as manoomin keezis (wild rice moon). Wild rice figures centrally in diet, and its harvest brings together individuals, families, and communities in a collective relationship rich with story, song, and local history. Thus, the Ontario government's attempt to appropriate manoomin as a "resource" represented a cultural violation for the Native people who rely on it.

In 1960, Ontario passed the Wild Rice Harvesting Act, which unilaterally asserted its authority over rice harvesting and instigated a system of harvesting licences, enforcements, and penalties (ibid., 45). In recognition of manoomin's importance to Native people, a large region was set aside in northwestern Ontario for the Ojibways of the Treaty 3 area. However, as wild rice became increasingly sought-after by non-Native consumers and prices rose to nearly twenty dollars per pound of cleaned rice, local businessmen began lobbying the Ontario government to open the Treaty 3 area to non-Natives. In 1977, Ontario proposed to open all areas to non-Native businessmen, but instead, in response to the Royal Commission on the Northern Environment, it granted a five-year moratorium on wild rice licences to non-Natives. The moratorium applied to non-status Indians because they were not defined as Indian under the Indian Act (ibid., 48-50).

The resistance mounted at Mud Lake in 1982 was therefore tied to – and crucial to the outcome of – a much larger struggle between the Treaty 3 First Nations and the Ontario government over control of the wild rice harvest. For Native people in both regions, the stakes were high. For the Treaty 3 nations, who had been devastated by years of clear cutting and mercury contamination, manoomin constituted "the last stand" in repelling the absolute commodification of their way of life and in terms of developing a viable Native-controlled rice industry (ibid., 44). For the federally unrecognized Algonquin community at Ardoch, manoomin represented an Algonquin practice that had maintained the community and connected it to a heritage and spirituality that had been drastically curtailed when settlers took their hunting grounds and the land set aside for them in Bedford Township. In short, the Mud Lake manoomin beds were central to their cultural survival.

In 1979, when a licence was issued to a private harvester, Lanark Wild Rice Company, a public meeting was held at Ompah, where over a hundred people, Native and non-Native, turned out to inform the Ministry of Natural Resources (MNR) that they were opposed to the commercial harvesting of wild rice. As a result, when the company applied for a licence in 1980, it was turned down. Lanark Wild Rice then appealed the decision to the MNR deputy minister, who held a hearing at Sharbot Lake at which local Algonquins, Alderville and Curve Lake Mississaugas, and settlers all testified to the importance of wild rice in their lives.[2] The deputy minister honoured the moratorium and refused to grant the licence, but the decision was unilaterally overturned by the MNR minister. Mud Lake was to be zoned into commercial and local usages, which would make it impossible for the Perry family to maintain the manoomin in a healthy state (Lovelace 1982, 28-32).

Harold Perry notified the chiefs of the local reserves as well as the Union of Ontario Indians and the Ontario Metis and Non-Status Indian Association (OMNSIA). Despite their unified protest at the MNR office in Tweed, the situation remained unchanged. Thus, the Native and non-Native communities coordinated their efforts and, with the organizational support of the Union of Ontario Indians and OMNSIA, established a round-the-clock blockade of the lake. When the Ontario Provincial Police (OPP) attempted to escort the company employees and their mechanical harvester to the lake, they were stopped by a roadblock of thirty residents (ibid., 32-33).

Next day, the company employees, their tow trucks, and the mechanical harvester were attended by twenty-seven OPP cruisers, seven MNR boats, and two helicopters as well as other vehicles (Delisle 2001, 115). The police rammed their way through the roadblock, pushing aside those who refused to move, some of whom sustained minor injuries, and detaining two residents for the duration of the blockade (ibid.). When residents took to boats to protect the rice beds, they were pursued by the MNR boats. With over a hundred local people involved, and the police occasionally jamming their CB radios, the resistance was spiritually and physically held together by Harold Perry (Pawlick 1982, 41). The OPP also invaded the hall at Ompah, evicted a local conservation group, and turned it into a command post (Lovelace 1982, 34).

Eventually, because the road to the lake intruded onto private property by just under a metre, and the property owner denied them access, the police were forced to retreat because they lacked a legal means of reaching the lake (Delisle 2001, 114-15). Unwilling to experience a second invasion the following day, Ardoch's residents dug up the access roads to the lake, and a twenty-seven-day stand-off ensued while local people negotiated with the Province. From this, a formal alliance was established between the Algonquins of Ardoch, other local Aboriginal communities, and the settlers of the Ardoch area. Called IMSet (Indian, Metis and Settlers Wild Rice Association), it enabled the people to focus more proactively on how to protect the wild rice for the future. It became obvious that they needed to consult with academic professionals, to prove legal and moral rights, and to build community awareness programs to maintain connections that had been built during the struggle.

In hearings and negotiations with the MNR, IMSet proposed that Mud Lake be reserved solely for domestic harvest (Lovelace 1982, 38-39). In this plan, IMSet would ensure that the rice was managed sustainably and would coordinate the harvest; should a surplus occur, it would also engage in job creation, with harvesting, processing, and marketing as potential job positions, and would address community needs through training and other local initiatives. Finally, it would safeguard the traditions relating to manoomin and would advance cultural traditions generally in the community (Delisle 2001, 131-32).

The MNR rejected this proposal, insisting that provincial jurisdiction must be maintained, that 70 percent of the rice would be licensed for local users and 30 percent would go to commercial harvesters, and that it would continue to set harvesting quotas. IMSet sought a way of working with the government without endangering the rice beds, but when the MNR refused to grant any of the suggested concessions, the community withdrew its own concessions and asserted Aboriginal and community authority over the Mud Lake manoomin. The process ultimately resulted in a stalemate: the ministry continued to assert that it had legal authority over the wild rice at Mud Lake but was unable to apply it. It ultimately withdrew its involvement in the management and harvesting decisions relating to the rice.

The provincial government's reaction to the wild rice issue had been so precipitous, so extreme, and so inconsistent with the actual value of the crop that it led OMNSIA representative Duke Redbird to suggest that the attempt to control the Mud Lake manoomin was a test case for the larger issue of Aboriginal rights (Willsey 1981). Had Ontario managed to claim the Mud Lake rice beds, its efforts to claim the rich rice beds of northwestern Ontario would undoubtedly have been aided. In the end, although Indigenous jurisdiction was not recognized, the local community maintained functional authority "until some later date." Given the respective power of the MNR and the people of Ardoch, this represented a resounding victory (Delisle 2001, 134-38).

With the creation of IMSet, it became obvious that the Ardoch Algonquins needed a formal body of their own, which would represent them within IMSet. They therefore incorporated as an organization called Manoomin Keezis, which soon became a focus for community building and education around Algonquin identity – from sponsoring craft development and showing films about Native culture to holding community gatherings and organizing the annual Wild Rice Festival. In 1985, when IMSet (and Manoomin Keezis) ceased to be formally active (Darwell 1998, 71), the community-building process continued on a more informal basis.

The rice war, then, was intrinsic to the development of Ardoch. In taking a stand to protect the manoomin, it challenged the centuries-long process of land encroachment, the theft of territories that enabled survival, and the collective trauma – starvation, disease, rape, and other forms of settler violence – that this encroachment had entailed, as well as the subsequent denial of their existence as Indians by the Department of Indian Affairs. Standing against this process represented a profound opportunity for collective healing; it is no accident, therefore, that the rice war provided the impetus for a community to rebuild.

During interviews, Ardoch Algonquins who take part in harvesting wild rice described the importance of ricing as a cultural activity. They spoke in detail about the beauty of days spent on the rice beds and the connections within and between families who are out there together. Ultimately, ricing is a strong collective cultural experience for those who take part.

The history of the resistance is also important. The pride and integrity that the rice war represents to the community was most clearly articulated by Art Cota III, a young man of Ardoch, more than twenty-five years after it began:

> I always smile when I talk about this. It's a very proud thing for our community. Like, we always refer to it as the rice war. And it's, "Oh, wow! We won the rice war." I remember when I was in high school, there was actually a monument erected at Ardoch right at the river ... and it's been over twenty-five years now, people have always looked back on that and been really happy. It's been kind of a victory, a smallish victory within a larger struggle. I think it's knowing that the rice war happened and that we were successful at it, that kind of gives us hope for the other struggles that are happening and that are going to happen. And that really brought us together as a community ... And it also kind of set up the conditions in which the local community kind of saw Ardoch. We were not only a community that saw itself as a community but the other people, the settlers, if you will, also came to see Ardoch as a community on its own. And so, I feel that that was an important step, too, in the rice war. Sure, it was getting to keep the wild rice and no one was going to take it away, but it was also ... we kind of came into our own, I think, in many ways. That was a very important kind of a milestone in terms of our group and it's our identity.

Connecting Past and Future: The Birth of Ardoch Algonquin First Nation and Allies

For ten years after the rice war, Harold Perry and Bob Lovelace worked to bring the community together and to research the history and genealogies of the Algonquin people at Ardoch. At a fundamental level, the leadership had to teach, encourage, and promote an understanding of what it meant to be Algonquin.

During an interview, Ardoch elder Carol Bate discussed this process:

> I knew nothing about Algonquin history, nothing about Algonquin land, nothing about anything ... Then I started visiting people and I would say something about "Your people are Indian," and I would get these wonderful answers like, "No, well, my grandmother was but we aren't." And I began to catch on that there was a tremendous identity problem. It's not that long ago that no one wanted to know if there was "Indian" in the family. Then I began to talk to older people that I hadn't seen for many, many years or that I had just met and they were as bewildered as I was. And I had thought that they would understand, they would know because they were in their eighties, nineties. I thought they'd know. No they weren't too sure about Algonquins or Indians ... So I just started poking around a lot ...
>
> They talk about identity theft? The biggest identity theft in this country was going on when they hid our nationality. If you weren't on a reserve, 90 percent of us became [officially] white, or became French, which, by the way, to the English was the same thing. So they stole our identities ... We would need a start of twenty years to educate our people, to bring the language back, to clean up history, and to teach our children what it means to respect both sides of their ancestry ... That's how badly we've robbed ourselves and our children of our history.

Examining the history of non-status Algonquins reveals the obvious reasons for such silence. Although Algonquins who refused to move to the reserves in the 1870s managed to avoid starvation and eked out a living in the backwoods, their children, driven off even those marginal lands and lacking the safety of a reserve, were forced to live among whites who despised them. During the 1920s, for non-status Algonquins in the Ardoch area, being Indian meant facing hunger, poverty, humiliation, rape, beatings, eviction, and the forced separation of children from families. Small wonder that silence about Indianness became the norm.

In 1991, Bob Lovelace and Harold Perry attended a national gathering of non-status Indians. They realized that, through its struggles over wild rice and subsequent community building, Ardoch was already a strong, albeit informal, community. When they returned to Ardoch, they called a council, which was attended by over fifty people, to discuss the formation of Ardoch Algonquin First Nation and Allies.[3] It was here that their research into people's Algonquin lineages became essential because it enabled people to establish themselves as extended families organized around shared ancestors; this process revealed that some twelve extended families formed the core of Ardoch.

At the meeting it was decided that a general council, to be held three or four times a year, would be the final arbiter of all business at Ardoch, that decisions would be made by consensus, and that the council would appoint a spokesperson or several spokespersons to represent Ardoch between councils. Although all people of Aboriginal ancestry could speak at the council, only Algonquins would make community decisions. About 95 percent of Ardoch's members were of Algonquin ancestry (Ardoch Algonquin First Nation and Allies 1993, 4).

Ardoch began formally conducting its affairs in 1992. At a summer gathering at Sharbot Lake in 1993, Harold Perry proposed that Ardoch's business should be conducted by heads of families, as this was in keeping with traditional forms of government, and that they should meet regularly as a steering committee (ibid.). In time, the family heads would be referred to as Ka-Pishkawandemin, the traditional government. In this framework, the guidance of elders would be essential, and co-spokespersons from the general council rather than chiefs would represent the community to the outside world (ibid.).

Although Ka-Pishkawandemin was essential to Ardoch's development, its guiding principles were equally important, for they would enable the community to rebuild its relationship with the natural world. The following excerpt from the principles demonstrates what the elders saw as essential: "Algonquin people are the first people of the Kiji Sibi watershed and therefore have a special responsibility to ensure that the land is cared for. Algonquin people can look to no other place in the world to find their origins. Kijimanito created Omàmìwinini (Algonquin) in this valley to give them life and purpose. The creatures with whom we share this valley are our closest relatives. All that is Algonquin, our culture, spiritual practices, language, governance, honour and relationships is the 'story' of this land" (quoted in Sherman 2008b, 119).

From the start, Ardoch involved itself in a range of local activities that focused on community building, practical assistance for its membership, and educational efforts relating to Algonquin identity and culture. It held three major annual festivals – the Winter Social, the Silver Lake Powwow, and the Wild Rice Festival. It circulated a regular newsletter, *Point of Contact,* which featured news, artwork, and articles by the membership, and it organized summer camps, education programs, and Algonquin instruction for young people. It also launched a number of ventures in which it educated local schools about the history of Algonquins in the area. Given the fact that its membership, though centred at Ardoch, was spread throughout the towns and cities of the watershed, such measures were crucial.

Asserting Algonquin Jurisdiction

> [Algonquin jurisdiction] is a reasonable and responsible relationship with the world around you ... It's a sense of responsible relationship between yourself and humans, all of your kinship, and the other parts of Creation ... We look at that more as having responsibility over that territory that we were created in ... Jurisdiction means that your ownership of the land was never surrendered ... Jurisdiction means our right to be there and our right to have a say in what's going on.
>
> **– Excerpts from comments by Ardoch members, quoted in Bettina Koschade, "'The Tay River Watershed Is Our Responsibility'"**

In keeping with its guiding principles, Ardoch has been involved in a number of struggles to protect its territory. The concern for the land is based on a profound familiarity with it, as was demonstrated during a 2007 interview with Art Cota Jr., who had spent a lifetime observing the land:

> I was born just up the road, two miles from here, and I've never left this area my whole life. I know every rock, hill there is for a few square miles around here. Down at the lower end of Sharbot Lake, I've trapped there since I was twelve years old. When I was a kid growing up, all the lakes around here, the snow would go and it would get to be maybe minus five or six at night and then go to plus five or whatever in the daytime. The sun would come out and pretty soon you'd have an inch of water all over top of the ice, but you'd still have a foot or two of ice. And all the old-timers always used to say, the lake's going to go glare. Freeze at night and then thaw in the daytime. That used to be a really good time of the year. You know, you'd say, "I'm going to go fishing trout today." By ten o'clock, you'd be walking around, your boots would be cutting into the ice maybe an inch or so and you'd say, "Well, I guess it's time I go." But now ... the sun is so powerful that the water doesn't lay on top

> of the ice. It makes a million little pinholes in the ice and just as soon as it goes glare, maybe three or four days later, the ice is gone. The whole lake's open. She don't last, because the sun is just more powerful.

Ardoch has worked to protect the land in a number of ways. When development threatened parts of its traditional territory at Norcan Lake and at Buckshot Lake, it was compelled to intervene. It participated in an Ontario Municipal Board hearing to stop a large-scale condominium development at Norcan Lake and succeeded in reducing the size of the project. With Buckshot Lake, Ardoch gained the right to halt all building permits if archaeological sites were found. Furthermore, the objects and artifacts discovered there, archaeological and historical, were to be returned to Algonquin people (Darwell 1998, 139). But it was in connection with hunting rights that Ardoch reached a crossroads, engaging in a struggle – the *Perry* case – that would define the hunting rights of all federally unrecognized Algonquins.

Harold Perry v. the Queen

In 1991, after the *Sparrow* case formally acknowledged that Aboriginal peoples have an Aboriginal right to hunt and fish for food and ceremonial purposes in their traditional territories, the Ontario Ministry of Natural Resources (MNR) created an interim enforcement policy to regulate the application of provincial and federal hunting and fishing laws to Aboriginal people. *Sparrow* had been a test case for Aboriginal rights, as affirmed under the Constitution Act of 1982, and as such, had nothing to do with the Indian Act. Nonetheless, under the interim enforcement policy, only status Indians were exempted from prosecution for violations of provincial hunting and fishing legislation.

For Algonquins, particularly those outside reserves, hunting is not only a necessary provider of food but the primary means through which an Algonquin identity can be lived on the land. For Ardoch, hunting has been essential to its struggle for jurisdiction over its territories.

On 25 September 1993, Harold Perry was arrested by MNR officers for duck hunting without a licence. He had informed the MNR beforehand that he would be hunting for food in his traditional territory, in hopes of generating a test case to determine whether the interim enforcement policy violated section 15(1) of the Charter of Rights and Freedoms. He produced his Ardoch card for identification and was told that he would be charged because the enforcement policy did not exempt non-status Indians from prosecution. When Perry subsequently suffered a major heart attack, Ardoch informed the minister of natural resources and asked that the matter be negotiated rather than prosecuted. This request was not acknowledged, however, and Perry was charged under the Game and Fish Act (Ontario) and the Migratory Birds Convention Act, a federal statute. The case therefore had serious ramifications for the rights of non-status Indians across Canada (Darwell 1998, 123-25).

In December 1995, Justice Paul Cosgrove of the Ontario Court ruled that the interim enforcement policy violated the Charter because it discriminated against non-status Indians solely on the grounds that Ottawa had the right to define which Aboriginal groups could practise their traditions without prosecution. When the provincial government tried to circumvent this ruling by repealing the enforcement policy and replacing it with Aboriginal compliance guidelines (which still discriminated against non-status Indians), Cosgrove had to rule again, on 22 January 1996, that the Province must treat Metis and non-status Indians just as it treated status Indians, and that the enforcement policy should be reinstated, with its discriminatory wording removed (Hogben 1996).

The provincial government tried to block this by claiming that it was already involved with "All Algonquins" in the land claim negotiations initiated by Pikwakanagan (in which Ardoch was not included).[4] This, too, was rejected by the court, which ordered Ontario to negotiate with Ardoch (Darwell 1998, 126-27). After waiting for three months, Ardoch's lawyer asked Cosgrove for an injunction to order the Province to begin negotiations. The judge granted the injunction and imposed a deadline, giving the provincial government thirty days to produce a report indicating that it had conducted meaningful negotiations with Ardoch (Platiel 1996). Ontario then took the issue to the Court of Appeal, where Justice Finlayson ruled that a judge had no authority to order the Province to engage in negotiations. Despite Ardoch's subsequent appeal, the Supreme Court refused to revisit the case (Darwell 1998, 127-29, 131).

Nevertheless, although the court's attempts to force compliance on the provincial government were overturned, Cosgrove's ruling – that Ontario must treat Metis, non-status Indians, and status Indians equally and must negotiate arrangements with Metis and non-status Indian communities to recognize and affirm their hunting rights – has not been challenged. Thus, the hunting rights of non-status Algonquins remain upheld. In September 1996, Ardoch established its own hunting and fishing regulations, appointed a fish and wildlife manager, set out best hunting practices, defined allocations, and established territorial definitions.

During a 2007 interview, conservation officer Art Cota Jr. described Ardoch hunting practices:

> The way we've always done it in Ardoch is we set out our ground rules per se for hunting. The Ardoch group – we don't have as many hunters as some of the other groups. In my eyes, sometimes I believe the reason people want to join other groups is just to get their hunting and fishing card and then walk away. So the way we do it, we harvest what we need. For a few years I tried to keep track – you know, had people phone me and tell me what they'd got. Then we discussed that and we said, "No, that's not the right thing to do either." We tell everyone that they can hunt deer or moose or ducks and take what they need. What we want them to tell us is if one family has twelve people eating at the table and the other family has three, then if they need more game, they're allowed to kill more and get more game. If they don't have hunters in the family, they'll contact someone such as myself or my brother and say, "We could really use a deer. If you could get an extra deer, get it for us." So, you just have to try to keep it within the normal realm of thought. Like, just because you have the right to go and kill an animal, if you don't need that animal to eat, or you don't want that animal to eat, then why would you want to kill it?

Before we examine other issues in which Ardoch has been involved, it is useful to consider the implications of the *Perry* decision in terms of building community. During his 2007 interview, Art Cota III spoke about growing up while *Perry* was unfolding:

> I'm not sure if I can actually remember when the *Perry* case was happening ... I know, even years later, it was definitely a discussion item. Even after it had been won and kind of fleshed out, there were still people talking about it ... sitting around the dinner table, with my family, and in my community. People talking about their frustrations with it ... "O.K. it's been awarded, but now will it be recognized?" Will it actually be put into place? And so that is the frustration, even more than the actual case, for a lot of people and it's still a topic of discussion today. And it's an interesting discussion, but at the same time, it's kind of the springboard for further discussion about who we are ... Who we are as a community. Who we are as a people. And so, as far back as I can remember, that case and then everything that's grown out of those discussions, has been what's informed me about being a member of Ardoch.

The Casino Rama Case

A second court case in which Ardoch was involved almost challenged the Indian Act itself. In 1993, Ontario and representatives from Ontario's First

Nations entered into negotiations with the goal of partnering in the development of the province's first reserve-based commercial casino, which was to become Casino Rama, at Mnjikaning First Nation, near Orillia. Profits from the casino were to be shared among Ontario's First Nations. The casino opened in 1996 and proved so lucrative that it became apparent that about $10 million would be divided annually between Ontario's status First Nations. Because of this, Bob Lovelace, in conjunction with Ardoch, Beaverhouse First Nation, the Bonnechere Metis Association, and other Ontario non-status and Metis communities, challenged their exclusion from a share in the profits.

In 1996, Justice Paul Cosgrove ruled that Ontario Metis and non-status Indians could not be excluded from sharing the profits of the casino (Wong 1996). The case was taken to the Ontario Court of Appeal by Chiefs of Ontario, which represented 133 status Indian bands. The Cosgrove decision was overturned when the court ruled that, under the Charter, discriminating between one disadvantaged group and another was acceptable (Blackwell 1997). Subsequently, *Lovelace* went to the Supreme Court of Canada, which was asked to rule on the following questions:

1 Does the exclusion of the appellant Aboriginal groups from the First Nations Fund of the Casino Rama Project on the grounds that they are not Aboriginal groups registered under the Indian Act violate section 15 of the Charter?
2 If the answer is yes, is the violation demonstrably justified under section 1 of the Charter?
3 Do the Provinces have the authority to exclude the appellant Aboriginal groups from the First Nations Fund of the Casino Rama Project on the grounds that they are not Aboriginal groups registered under the Indian Act?

In *Lovelace,* the court ruled that because the fund was set up to ameliorate the conditions of First Nations under the Indian Act, rather than to ameliorate those of First Nations outside the act, the Charter had not been violated. Ontario had not exceeded its authority, given that it was simply exercising its spending power according to the terms that had been set for the fund.

The decision did recognize the Indian Act as the source of the discrimination between status and non-status First Nations. However, it ultimately upheld notions of a distinct and essential difference between First Nations, Metis, and Inuit, which clouded the issue so that the fund, negotiated in partnership solely with First Nations, could be said to be *meant* to address only their "distinct" circumstances. Thus, it did not discriminate against other categories of Aboriginal people.

The Tay River Environmental Hearings

A third matter in which Ardoch intervened involved protecting the Tay River, part of the Rideau River watershed. In February 2000, a multinational corporation that mined and processed calcium carbonate filed an application to take water from the Tay to its processing plant near Perth, Ontario; the calcium carbonate itself came from the company's mine near Tatlock, north of the plant (Koschade 2003, 70). Despite 283 submissions by concerned citizens, environmentalists, and Ardoch Algonquin First Nation, the Ministry of the Environment issued a "phased" permit to the corporation (ibid., 70-71). Widespread protest ensued, so an environmental review tribunal held hearings between February 2000 and February 2002. In February 2002, the tribunal allowed the appeals, restricting the amount of water that the company could take (ibid., 75).

A crucial issue for Ardoch at the tribunal hearing was that its knowledge of the land was based on its long and unbroken jurisdiction over it. At the tribunal, it had attempted to call elders and others whose familiarity with the Tay ecosystem was based on long-standing practices of living on the land (ibid., 125). However, it had not been permitted to do so, because the tribunal had asserted that addressing Algonquin jurisdiction lay beyond its mandate. As a result, Ardoch was compelled to withdraw from the tribunal and to make a presentation to the tribunal clarifying why it had done so (Koschade and Peters 2006, 306). As explained by Ardoch members who were involved at the time, Algonquin jurisdiction derives from a knowledge of the land, of the teachings related to it, and the duty to be responsible for its welfare (Koschade 2003, 104).

Below, Art Cota III described how individuals still observe each other's hunting and trapping territories despite decades of land loss:

> It's a very wide-ranging territory and most families within the Ardoch community ... have little plots of land where, you know, their fathers and grandfathers traditionally hunted. And a lot of them live on the same land where they hunt, where they hunt for deer. So, certainly ... our people know that this is the area where traditionally the Cotas hunt and this is where the Perrys go and it is the same every year. It's still important to the community today and it's been carried on long before the government became involved.

The Manoomin Centre

Ardoch's focus on community building ultimately led it to plan a community centre – the Manoomin Centre at Pine Lake. Above all, Ardoch wanted a site where it could maintain an office and conduct cultural events, language classes, and ceremonies. Choosing the Pine Lake location after considering it for some years, Ardoch met with North Frontenac Council representatives in June 2006 to apprise them of its plans. It then met with the MNR, informing it that the land would be used as part of Algonquin jurisdiction. When the MNR challenged Ardoch's actions, Ardoch responded that, because the land had never been surrendered, the Province did not have clear title to it. Until a bill of sale was produced to prove its purchase, title remained in Algonquin hands. Although the ministry backed off, in terms of asserting jurisdiction, it continued to apply pressure in the name of *its* responsibilities for the environment.

Although Ardoch has maintained Ka-Pishkawandemin, its traditional government, for many years, and elders and leaders have worked at developing knowledge and pride regarding their Algonquin heritage, they are discovering that the most difficult task is addressing the internal aspects of colonization and imparting a sense of what Algonquin jurisdiction *really* means in the most spiritual sense of the word.

As family head Paula Sherman (2008b, 113-14) observes, the reality that Algonquin territory has been occupied has affected the psyches of community members, who may know intellectually that they are part of the land but who have difficultly feeling this in their hearts, particularly as the Province of Ontario has long asserted its control over the land. During its attempt to establish the Manoomin Centre, Ardoch was repeatedly obliged to counter MNR efforts to undermine the meaning of Algonquin jurisdiction. When Ardoch could not be forced to relinquish it, the ministry tried other tactics to assert its authority: it endeavoured to issue land-use permits so as to "give back" the land to the community, then threatened it with an injunction and charges, and finally offered to donate sewer equipment and logs for the construction process. Sherman (ibid., 114-15) discusses the ministry's motives: "In retrospect, almost every action on the part of the MNR has probably been the result of concise use of government scenarios that test various responses to Aboriginal blockades and processes. Such scenarios have existed for years and were even discussed as part of the testimony on the Ipperwash inquiry in 2005. Some of those scenarios could have been developed by the *Interministerial Committee on Aboriginal Emergencies* known as the 'blockade or barricade committee' among government officials." Sherman also notes that Ardoch members were divided among themselves regarding how to respond to the MNR: some emphasized the importance of building harmony with outsiders, whereas others recognized that failing to rebuff the ministry – whether adversarial or apparently benevolent – would seriously impair their ability to assert Algonquin jurisdiction.

At that point, the ministry's tactics escalated and created significant difficulties for the community. Ardoch had consulted with knowledgeable elders to address possible environmental implications of building the centre and had conducted ceremonies to ask for spiritual guidance. But when it began clearing the trees for the building and powwow grounds, cottagers living nearby suddenly woke up to the fact of Algonquin presence. Ardoch had decided that consulting with the descendants of the settlers who had appropriated its land in the first place was unnecessary, but its traditional responsibilities to maintain good relationships led it to meet with local residents and concerned cottagers to reveal the site plan and building design and to answer questions.

Some local residents were supportive, but others incited resistance through blatantly racist remarks to the effect that they had no wish to spend their summers listening to "wild Indians banging on drums" or "singing and dancing around campfires." One individual even threatened that he would withhold fire services. Although the Ardoch members attempted to explain the history of the area, the cottagers rejected it and viewed them as "squatters" whose claims were worthless because they had been "conquered long ago" (Sherman 2008b, 116-17).

After this, Ardoch decided to hold no further meetings with the cottagers, who, for their part, formed an association to take their concerns to the MNR. The ministry responded by pushing for its own environmental assessment, and the mayor of North Frontenac Township, who had initially been supportive of the centre, was pressured by his council into openly opposing it and insisting that building permits were required for every part of the process.

After Ardoch refused to comply, the cottagers hired a Toronto lawyer to represent their interests. When the lawyer pleaded with the MNR to assert its jurisdiction, the ministry stepped up its demands for an environmental assessment (ibid., 117-18). In response, Ardoch hired a reputable biologist to conduct an assessment. It also retained an architect to develop the plans and visited the North Frontenac Council to inform it that the centre would adhere to building code standards and official plan requirements – in short, it had covered all the bases so that the ministry's demands for an environmental assessment could not be used to delay the process. As Bob Lovelace stated, "We are prepared to work with the government, but we're not prepared to reinforce their denial of history and law" (quoted in Armstrong 2006).

In the end, Ardoch prevailed, but the consequence was tremendous animosity where none had existed before. More profoundly, however, Ardoch members were divided and confused about how they should have responded. Much of this related to the ministry's dismissal of Algonquin principles and its insistence on a "scientific" model of assessment. Some band members declared that Ardoch should have worked with the MNR to avoid conflict regardless of the principles of development that Ardoch had established since its founding, which state that Algonquins must honour their traditional responsibility to protect the land. Others felt that allowing the ministry to establish jurisdiction would have serious implications for the community's ability to assert its own jurisdiction in the future. The Ontario government relies heavily on the notion that a one-time acceptance of provincial jurisdiction can be read as a permanent "surrender" of jurisdiction (Sherman 2008b, 119).

As Paula Sherman (ibid.) suggests, Ardoch's lack of a deep and heartfelt knowledge of its relationship to the land speaks to the larger issue of cultural and linguistic loss. She emphasizes that Ardoch members do not seek to replicate who they were in the past, but to bring forward their traditional teachings, ceremonies, and practices to build a strong base through which to resist ongoing colonialism and destruction of the land. If they wish to stop the process of identity loss, they must observe the principles that define them. Although their efforts to do so are constantly impeded by outside forces such as the MNR, their worst enemy, according to Sherman, is their own lack of confidence in themselves and their defining principles. Noting that the provincial and municipal governments operate on unceded Algonquin land without consent, she addresses the hegemony that they hold in the minds of the community. As a result, despite MNR disrespect for the elders who conducted a traditional environmental assessment, many community members believed that Ardoch should have cooperated with the ministry's demands.

Ultimately, it is this cognitive colonialism, as Sherman (2008b, 118-23) terms it, that lies at the heart of the struggle and makes many Ardoch members unsure of their real relationship to the land. She suggests that Ardoch members need to rebuild their confidence in themselves as Omàmìwinini to honour their side of the ancient wampum belt in building good relations with others. She also asserts that Ardoch's responsibility to maintain good relations with settlers extends only as far as the settlers' willingness to take responsibility for honouring *their* side of the wampum belt, rather than insisting that their institutions outweigh the Aboriginal title and rights of Omàmìwinini.

Ardoch had begun to raise funds for the Manoomin Centre when it was forced to put the project on hold, in order to resist a proposed uranium development on its traditional land (discussed in Chapter 8). In the future, it also hopes to work with tourism operators before the land becomes too depleted of wildlife. During his 2007 interview, Art Cota Jr. mentioned the cumulative damages caused by fishing lodges:

> Fishing now around here is not that good. The lakes are mostly just overfished ... You take Crotch Lake for instance ... I can remember as a kid going back there and staying there with my uncle in his cabin and my dad and we'd fish pickerel in March and have a good time. Now, there's two lodges on Crotch Lake. Between those two lodges, I think there's like three hundred people [who] stay there ... So if half of them fish, that's 150 fish a day, every day, all summer long. And those lodges put nothing back into the lake. So how would you like to have a business that you don't have to actually own the property, you just own the shoreline, but you don't have to put anything back into the water that you rely on? My wife and I went up to camp on Crotch Lake. Well, they've got campsites all over the place. It was our understanding that if you were an Ardoch Algonquin, you could go up there and camp ... But the non-Native man from the lodge went and checked the whole lake to make sure what everybody was doing ... So basically, the people who own the lodges on Crotch Lake own the lake ... and that's right in the middle of Ardoch territory.

For Ardoch, asserting jurisdiction in a region heavily dependent on tourism will mean working with tourism operators to restock lakes and perhaps to develop less ecologically damaging tourism alternatives.

The Youth

Interviews with the younger members of Ardoch revealed the extent to which the community's history and ongoing struggles had enabled some of them to strengthen their sense of identity. As Art Cota III put it,

> As an Algonquin person struggling with identity, there are so many gaps in our history ... If someone asked, "What is your heritage? What events led up to who you are today, as an Algonquin person?" – there are gaps there. I don't necessarily know very much about how much "Native" stuff my great- or great-great-grandparents did because it was never really talked about. It was different for them. They weren't really allowed to be Natives and I feel that there's a gap there. It's kind of a unique situation for us in that here we

are, calling ourselves Algonquin people, we're comfortable with that label that we've given ourselves, but we're here without necessarily the look of an Algonquin person, without the language and without most of the customs. You're thinking, "Where do I fit in?"

I think that a lot of the identity is filled, not by looking into the past and looking to grasp ahold of something and hang onto it, but it's also what we're doing today. It's not necessarily where we come from anymore, because there's no end to what we can do, to what's ahead of us. So our identity is going to be informed, in large part by today and tomorrow – the future.

It's like this summer, with the uranium struggle. I mean if you are an Ardoch Algonquin person, that's part of your identity. It's going to be part of me for the rest of my life, being involved in that struggle. And although it's an unsettling issue, it's very rewarding in some sense, because it does give you a sense of identity, individually and as a community. You know, we're not just what's left over of a culture that's gone. *We are* that culture in this day and age.

Cota added that the current generation of leadership is focusing on the younger people, on developing tomorrow's leaders:

A few young people, myself included, are kind of being drawn in ... I feel I'm kind of kept informed by some of the people and I'm invited to come and be part of things, with the hope, I think, that if I'm doing this now, at twenty-two, then when I'm forty-four I will be that much more involved. And, if the day ever comes that I was required, or maybe wanted to take on a leadership role, I'd be in a position where it would make sense for me to do so. And I think a lot of what Paula [Sherman] and Randy [Cota] are trying to do is to involve young people. I mean they know that they're not going to be around forever and they want the group to continue. And I know, just in assigning tasks and so on, and especially this summer at the Robertsville [uranium] site too, you can kind of see where a lot of younger people probably will continue to be involved. They kind of emerge when they're needed, when there's work to be done. I'm sure that their eyes are on those people, you know.

Ardoch is unique among federally unrecognized Algonquins in its emphasis on building community, on protecting the land, and on taking stands and holding to principles, regardless of cost. In many ways, it has frequently forged ahead and fought for the benefits that other federally unrecognized communities hope will be conferred *on* them via the land claim and without such struggle. Ardoch has followed its own path, seeking to have its rights defined in court, engaging in overt resistance, taking stands, and organizing with others, and has thus won important rights. Moreover, it has retained a clarity about, and a resistance to, the reality of ongoing colonialism.

7

The Effect of the Land Claim in This Region

The land claim has affected the people of the Mississippi, Rideau, and lower Madawaska watersheds in highly particular ways. Ardoch has mounted perhaps the most extensive collective critique of the claim, and it has a history of activism that is not shared by most of the communities of the Algonquin Nation Tribal Council (ANTC). Because of Ardoch's unique history and its framework of leadership, decisions made by other ANTC leaders have at different times run headlong into the principles of its hard-won goals. On two occasions, this forced Ardoch away from the negotiating table, a development that has cost it: first, individuals broke from Ardoch and formed the Sharbot Lake area committee, later known as Shabot Obaadjiwan, to become involved in the land claim. Later, a small breakaway group led by Randy Malcolm claimed to represent Ardoch in the negotiations.

Ardoch and the Land Claim

In 1991, when Pikwakanagan began setting up area committees, it invited families in the Sharbot Lake region to form one, even though a number of individuals in those families were part of Ardoch. During a 2003 interview, Bob Lovelace observed that Ardoch initially supported the development of the area committee as a means of acquiring a voice in the land claim.

Indeed, in 1992, when land claim negotiations started, Ardoch invited Pikwakanagan representatives to attend a general council meeting to discuss the claim. Ardoch's concern was that, due to its proven unbroken jurisdiction over the Mississippi, Rideau, and lower Madawaska watersheds, it needed to be involved to protect its ancestral lands. It feared that Pikwakanagan would "bargain away" Algonquin jurisdiction and that Aboriginal title would be extinguished as part of the claim. As Harold Perry (quoted in Darwell 1998, 134) noted, "Once this claim goes through, that's it. There's no more room for negotiation after that. Not ever – and that's what the government wants. This is unsurrendered Algonquin territory, and it's Ardoch Algonquins who use it."

At the meeting, the Pikwakanagan delegation expressed its concern that some Ardoch members were not of Algonquin descent. Ardoch had requested the right to represent itself, with the provision that only those of Algonquin heritage would be beneficiaries of any settlement. In October 1992, Pikwakanagan representative Clifford Meness wrote to Harold Perry, assuring him that Pikwakanagan would not accept extinguishment of Aboriginal title. He suggested that Ardoch send a list of its Algonquin membership to assist in the enrolment process (Algonquin Golden Lake First Nation 1992a). However, in January 1993, Pikwakanagan refused to recognize Ardoch as a participant in the land claim process and invited individuals from Ardoch to join the area committee that it was setting up at Sharbot Lake. Following this, Ardoch formally issued a declaration that Pikwakanagan represented neither it nor its territory in the claim (Ardoch Algonquin First Nation and Allies 1993).

At this time, a number of Sharbot Lake individuals became involved with the area committee; some had never been formally affiliated with any community, and others had belonged to Ardoch. They subsequently became part of the Algonquin Management Circle set up by Pikwakanagan, as representatives from Sharbot Lake. By 1996, a number of Ardoch members who wished to become involved in the claim had begun to disassociate themselves from Ardoch (Ardoch Algonquin First Nation and Allies 1996b). Because of this, Ardoch polled all its members and asked everyone who wished to remain part of Ardoch to respond and to state clearly that they should be represented by Ardoch, not the management circle through the Sharbot Lake area committee. Three months later, all those who had not responded to the poll were withdrawn from the Ardoch registry (Ardoch Algonquin First Nation and Allies 1996a). Certain families were split as a result of this process. Some members of the Antoine, Bedore, Cota, and Sharbot families chose the Sharbot Lake area committee, whereas other members of these families opted to remain with Ardoch.

The precise feelings and reasons that led some Ardoch members to split from the community are unclear from the outside. As Indigenous groups struggle to survive in a world organized around their disappearance, broad ideological differences typically arise between so-called modernists and traditionalists – those who believe that money and secular forms of power will best facilitate community survival and those who believe that such forces will engineer their downfall. For federally unrecognized Algonquins, such divisions are manifested between those whose sense of identity hinges on government recognition, in a context where the land claim enabled them to assert their Algonquinness for the first time, and those who understand their connection to the land and the ancestors as forming the basis of their identity. The people who first embraced the Sharbot Lake area committee may have done so for myriad reasons – to fight for formal government recognition, in the hope of acquiring money or power, due to fear of being left behind while the claim proceeded without them, or simply because of family loyalty, choosing to follow relatives who left Ardoch. Finally, locating an organization in Sharbot Lake, with its large Algonquin population, provided a venue through which many local Algonquins who had not previously been involved could validate and express their identity. Just as the wild rice issue drew Algonquins into the Ardoch community, the land claim drew previously unaffiliated Algonquins from Sharbot Lake into Shabot Obaadjiwan.

After the formation of Shabot Obaadjiwan, the land claim generated yet another split in the Ardoch community. In 2000, after Ardoch launched a lawsuit to challenge its exclusion from the claim, it was brought into it, along with the Antoine First Nation and the Bonnechere Algonquin Community, which had also been excluded. In 2001, Randy Malcolm, a member of the Whiteduck family who was related to Harold Perry but who had only recently joined Ardoch, became Ardoch's representative on the newly created Algonquin Nation Negotiations Directorate (ANND), the corporation that administered the legal and financial responsibilities of the land claim. When negotiations broke down and ANND created the Algonquin Nation Tribal Council (ANTC) to provide political representation for the non-status communities, its members began calling themselves chiefs. As Ardoch's ANTC representative, Randy Malcolm followed their example, describing himself as the chief of Ardoch, even though this violated the community's governance system, which had been based on consensus and organized through the heads of families since 1993. For the Ardoch leadership and many community members, this traditional governance model was essential to who they were as Algonquins. And though the heads-of-families structure maintained two co-chiefs who functioned as intermediaries between the heads of families and the outside world, their positions had nothing to do with the system of chiefs created by the ANTC.

In addition, Ardoch's position on hunting differed significantly from that of the other ANTC communities. Ardoch had fought and won the *Perry* case, which affirmed that non-status Algonquins had an Aboriginal right to hunt in their traditional territory. Thus, it challenged the manner in which, under the land claim, Algonquins viewed their right to hunt as dependent on agreements with the MNR – first, under the Algonquin Hunting Agreement of 1992 (Sarazin 1997) and subsequently by the 2002 agreement between the ANTC and the MNR (Algonquin Nation Tribal Council 2002).

Because many non-status Algonquins know little about the implications of *Perry* but are centrally concerned with hunting, their decision to become registered in an ANTC community has often been dictated by the fact that doing so enables them to hunt outside of provincial restrictions, particularly for moose. Because this has drawn increasing numbers of Algonquins into the ANTC-affiliated communities, it is in the best interests of these communities *not* to acknowledge the *Perry* decision, for if non-status Algonquins learned that, under *Perry,* they have hunting rights that are independent of the land claim, their reason for joining an ANTC community could potentially diminish.

When the ANTC signed an interim hunting agreement with the MNR in 2002, Ardoch's concern was that, in accepting ministry jurisdiction, the ANTC communities had disregarded a right that they already had, one that Ontario could safely ignore if Algonquins persisted in signing such documents instead of practising their rights. Ardoch members knew that *Sparrow* had forced Canada to recognize Aboriginal harvesting rights and that *Perry* had extended these rights to non-status Indians. They were also aware of Ontario's tendency to view agreements, once implemented, as carved in stone, so that if Algonquins continued to assent to provincial control of their harvesting rights, the *Perry* decision would eventually be considered null and void simply because the majority of Algonquins had never observed it.

On the other hand, the ANTC communities needed the monies they received as part of the hunting agreement, and they craved the provincial recognition that it signified. Heather Majaury, a former member of Sharbot Lake who changed her affiliation to the Ottawa community, was directly involved with the land claim during its early years. She offers her recollection of the situation in 2002:

> The Algonquin Nation Tribal Council was operating from a position of extreme weakness. In the context of the land claim they had veto power that was essentially equal to that of Pikwakanagan – but with no access to

funding and without the pretense of unity, which is hard to achieve in any circumstances, much less so between people of similar origin who have been divided politically through the Indian Act for over a hundred years. The only way that the ANTC had access to any sort of funds to even keep things running was to sign some sort of agreement with the Ministry of Natural Resources, because the MNR agreed to give them money. Just enough to actually cover their newsletter, to inform people of the ANTC political position on such matters as hunting, to let people know how to get their hunting cards, and in general to further the land claim negotiations.

But the other thing was that all of a sudden, through this interim hunting agreement, the Ministry of Natural Resources was acknowledging the Algonquin Nation Tribal Council as an Aboriginal government entity! Think about it – they were acknowledging the Algonquin Nation Tribal Council. You're getting into power relationships at this point, right?

There's a disconnect, beyond the ground reality of actual nation building and political organizing, between what that really is and people's ideas of what that really is. People's ideas of it, I think, come from a place of "Ahhh! Law is God." Nobody's analyzing it through power, nobody's looking at how political structures occur because of power – who has it, who doesn't, and who is willing to work together.

The thing that most Algonquins don't get is that hunting is the one thing that *has* been defined, that the courts have understood – that non-status Algonquins have some form of collective hunting rights! Actually, it's really based on the fact that to not allow people to hunt for food in our homeland would be genocidal, would it not? So that's pretty solid. In fact, I would say that hunting is the foundation of Algonquin culture. And that's why I stand beside our hunters – because it's one of the things [about being Algonquin] that has truly survived. People hunt.

Randy Malcolm signed the ANTC interim hunting agreement on behalf of Ardoch, violating Ardoch's position on the need to exercise Aboriginal rights or risk losing them. When it became obvious that Malcolm was no longer following the dictates of the Ardoch heads-of-families council (as a representative should), he was given a letter of resignation indicating that he no longer spoke for Ardoch on the ANTC and was asked to step down.

At that point, Malcolm announced that a "splinter group" had broken away from the negotiations, but that as chief of Ardoch Algonquin First Nation, he still represented the community. The Crawford family continued to support him, but most Ardoch members did not recognize him as their representative.

In hopes of winning supporters, he encouraged individuals who had not previously been affiliated with Ardoch to sign up to *his version* of the community in order to obtain their hunting cards. Although some hunters left Ardoch to join Malcolm's group, most of them remained with the original community, and Ardoch withdrew from the ANTC.

When I interviewed Randy Malcolm in 2004, he maintained that the entire Ardoch community had stayed with him and that a handful of individuals – a "splinter group" as he termed them – were alone in suggesting that Ardoch should leave the table. His strong belief was that, for Algonquins, the only hope lay in receiving recognition and money from the government. He compared the lack of power of contemporary Algonquins with the authority, recognition, and funding that they would win through the land claim and indicated that he *had* to stay at the table for the sake of Ardoch's future.

Perhaps Randy Malcolm believed that he would gradually sway the main membership of Ardoch into supporting his continued presence at the negotiation table. And he may sincerely have believed that the land claim was Ardoch's only hope. However, Heather Majaury offered an insightful interpretation of his actions, relating them to the pervasive insecurity that afflicts non-status Algonquins:

> At the time, Randy Malcolm and I sat and had coffee, because I was questioning what he was doing. Well, what happened with Randy – and this is the way I see it – was that there were some real serious issues within Ardoch around who was being listened to and who wasn't. Randy Malcolm was having no choice but to come back to his community to say, "This is the hunting agreement the other communities want to sign. Do you want to sign?" They said, "No." Randy Malcolm at that point considered himself to be chief – that's what he called himself ... What he was saying is that he essentially should be considered a chief because he was the spokesperson for the Ardoch community at the ANTC table.
>
> However, that agreement became null and void when the heads of families of Ardoch removed him from that position. And the reason why they removed him from the position was that they were unwilling to sign the interim hunting agreement. So he had a responsibility at that point in time to honour their unwillingness to sign. That's what I think he needed to do.
>
> Now, the ANTC is where each of the community leaders originally on the ANND corporate board had created their meaningful political connections. So Randy had bonded there – he'd built an identity there. I don't think people realize how powerful identity is. And identity does not just come

> from the inside. Identity comes from acceptance by peers. And it comes through recognition by authority and through relationships of likemindedness and contrast.
>
> Now, Randy Malcolm can trace his background to the Whiteducks. So it's not a question that he's not Algonquin. And Ardoch is his historical community. But in my opinion, it wasn't satisfying his need to identify as a leader. But the Algonquin Nation Tribal Council was. Now he had a responsibility to go back to the ANTC leaders and say, "My community will not sign the agreement." And that would have either forced the ANTC into negotiating with the Ardoch heads of family or would have forced them to expel Ardoch. Those would be the two choices. Right?
>
> Now, either way, if the ANTC started negotiating with the heads of families at Ardoch, or expelled Ardoch, Randy Malcolm could no longer be a chief as recognized by the ANTC if all that happened. So instead he decided to do what he did, which was this whole fight over cards, where he had a meeting where individuals from Ardoch could come and get ANTC cards from him. I don't know if individual Algonquins brought up in assimilated circumstances understand the inherent nature of the right to hunt, so it is easy to be manipulated by what seems to be the benefits of affiliation.

While Ardoch's problems were unfolding, the land claim negotiations broke down. However, Doreen Davis, head of ANND and chief of Shabot Obaadjiwan, continued to promote the claim. In doing so, she repeatedly asserted that Randy Malcolm spoke for Ardoch and that Harold Perry, Bob Lovelace, and others constituted a splinter group that had broken away from the "real" Ardoch. Indeed, when I interviewed her in 2003, it was obvious that Malcolm had become "naturalized" within the ANTC as sole leader of Ardoch. It was as if the heads-of-families structure and the entire community, with its twenty years of activism, had never existed.

Randy Malcolm's claim to represent Ardoch and his dismissal of the membership as a splinter group was troublesome enough for Ardoch, but a greater difficulty was the manner in which the *other* ANTC leaders uncritically supported his claim. Particularly trying was the fact that Doreen Davis *knew* the heads of families at Ardoch, as well as their history, having originally come from that community herself. Unequivocally, she was aware that the small minority whom Randy Malcolm represented was not the "real" Ardoch. Furthermore, by accepting him as Ardoch's representative, she validated him to the other ANTC chiefs from outside the territory.

And yet, Algonquin political circles can be very small. Other ANTC chiefs who knew the Ardoch heads of families may have doubted the validity of Malcolm's claims even as they accepted them. Three factors may account for this: First, most ANTC chiefs probably disagreed with Ardoch's commitment to a consensual governance based on heads of families. Except for the leaders of Antoine and Bonnechere, almost every ANTC chief represented a new community that had been formed by Pikwakanagan as area committees solely for the purposes of negotiating the land claim. These communities had only one representative, who spoke for the membership and played multiple roles – as ANTC chief, as member of ANND, and (in 2005, after the talks resumed) as the Algonquin negotiation representative (ANR). With its emphasis on family consultation and consensus, Ardoch simply did not fit into this framework. On the other hand, Randy Malcolm's group *did* fit in with the top-down political process of the ANTC.

Second, pressures around non-status Algonquin identity may have made it easy to dismiss the "real" Ardoch because of the presence of Bob Lovelace as one of its co-chiefs. Lovelace, a Cherokee who had worked for years in Sharbot Lake as a social worker prior to his involvement at Ardoch, had played a decisive role in aiding the wild rice resistance and had subsequently supported the other struggles in which Ardoch engaged. As a result, Lovelace had been formally adopted into an Ardoch family and was frequently invited to be a co-chief, primarily because of his powerful leadership and negotiation skills. This made him an easy target for a whisper campaign to the effect that only Algonquins could build Algonquin nationhood, that he had turned a misguided faction against its own people, and that he constituted a danger to Algonquin unity.

However, hunting was probably the greatest factor that prompted the ANTC chiefs to opt for Randy Malcolm's group. For Ardoch to withdraw from negotiations because it insisted that non-status Algonquins already had the right to hunt and did not need to sign the interim hunting agreement would put a considerable strain on the remaining ANTC leaders. They needed the money that Ontario provided them for administering the terms of the agreement; they needed the moose tags that went with the agreement to draw hunters into their communities who might not have signed up had they known their hunting rights did not depend on ANTC membership; and they needed to present a unified front to both Pikwakanagan and the negotiation team – a unity that Ardoch threatened to upset.

In 2004, when the land claim talks resumed, Bob Crawford was a co-chief of Ardoch, along with Bob Lovelace. The ANR system was to be implemented as soon as elections were held in 2005, and Crawford recommended that Randy Malcolm become Ardoch's ANR. At 2004 meetings held throughout the territory to explain the ANR system to the membership, the ANTC leaders maintained a "closed shop" in asserting that Randy Malcolm was the ANTC chief who represented Ardoch, despite the protests of the Ardoch heads of families. This left Ardoch with few options. After the negotiating team ignored its vociferous commentary at community meetings and it failed to raise the issue with the land claim lawyer, Bob Potts, Ardoch simply continued to work on community building and ignored the negotiations altogether. However, through the four traumatic years that Malcolm sat as Ardoch representative at the land claim table, the community faced the daily reality that he did so without its consent and was capable of signing its rights away should an agreement be reached during his tenure.

In 2007, Randy Malcolm finally bowed to the inevitable and acknowledged that he did not represent Ardoch Algonquin First Nation. He changed the name of the small group that he did represent to Snimikobi First Nation (Ardoch). Since then, it has not engaged in any of the efforts to defend Algonquin territory. For example, though Shabot Obaadjiwan joined Ardoch to resist uranium development in their shared traditional lands, Snimikobi did not involve itself. Because of this, its purpose seems primarily to enable Malcolm to continue to sit at the negotiating table and represent his supporters.

Since 2004, Ardoch has remained outside the land claim. In a 2007 interview, Bob Lovelace stated that its experience convinced the heads of families that, despite initial good intentions, the land claim is a destructive influence, corrupting individuals via the prospect of government recognition, access to money, or superficial notions of power. Unlike most of the communities formed because of the claim, Ardoch has based its sense of Algonquin identity on a relationship to the land. Its ongoing nation-building processes will take place in spite of the land claim, not because of it.

And yet the land claim continues to create strains within the communities because of its hegemonic presence claiming to represent all Algonquins and because of its potential to sign away the community's rights. As Art Cota III explained,

> With the land claim ... nobody knows what will happen ... Everybody seems to know what they want to happen, in an ideal situation, some are sticking to the hard line, which I would say Ardoch's is probably more the hard line and some aren't ... I want to think the reason some of these splits have happened,

> other than just greed, which I think has accounted for most of it, but I want to think that people are hopefully trying to be realistic in saying, "What's likely to happen and what can I salvage from it?" or something like that. And no doubt these people are confused. Everybody's confused. It's so uncertain. There's no real model to go by. We just don't know what's going to happen. And I think people are scared. People are very uncertain. They're thinking, "What's going to happen in my lifetime? What's going to happen in my children's lifetime?" And I think, you know, these splits [in the communities] don't just happen ... I think the government is very happy that the splits are occurring and I don't just think that they're sitting back passively, hoping that groups fragment.

This is particularly an issue for those individuals who have been less active in the community. Many of today's adults have been taught in school that colonialism either never happened or is a thing of the past, and that they can expect justice, democracy, and fairness from Canada, and certainly not racism. They do not share the elders' intimate knowledge from lived experience of racism and ongoing colonization. Indeed, in 2011, as the land claim negotiators began to speak of an agreement in principle, new fractures are threatening the community. Some individuals wish to be registered with the claim to vote "no," which involves registering themselves as "independent" since Ardoch is outside the claim. Others are being swayed by wild promises of money to make a last-ditch attempt to "jump ship" and become involved with the claim by leaving the community. Many others, however, have opted to remain firmly affiliated with Ardoch, though fearing that the negotiators will relinquish Algonquin title to their territory.

Having explored the various splits that the land claim brought to Ardoch, we now turn to the other communities that share its territory – Shabot Obaadjiwan and Pasapkedjiwanong.

Shabot Obaadjiwan First Nation

When I began research with Shabot Obaadjiwan, the structural differences between the ANTC communities and Ardoch became apparent. With Ardoch, because of its lengthy history of community building and activism, many of its members had voluminous files containing leaflets, newsletters, other documents, and ephemera dating back twenty years that provided me with a solid "read" of its history. I also benefited from a substantial body of graduate theses and other scholarly literature, which provided in-depth analyses of key aspects of Ardoch's history. Finally, before I could interview people from Ardoch, I had to attend a meeting of its heads of families; subsequently I was encouraged to approach community members for interviews. As a result, I was able to conduct at least a dozen interviews with a range of Ardoch leaders and community members.

Such was not the case with Shabot Obaadjiwan First Nation, and here I found myself at a considerable disadvantage. In 2003, when I interviewed its leader, Doreen Davis, she was able to supply me with only one thin file composed primarily of archived newspaper articles on local community events. Lacking Ardoch's longevity in community building, Shabot Obaadjiwan simply had not generated the data that could provide a solid "read" of its recent history. It also had no council members with whom I could speak, and though Doreen Davis, a charismatic and persuasive individual, did meet annually with the ANTC communities for weekend events and arranged traditional gatherings, most of her work had taken place in the context of confidential negotiations, which meant that she could divulge little to me regarding the community and its aspirations.

Because Doreen Davis did not offer any suggestions regarding whom I might interview, I was forced to begin with two community members with whom I was familiar and request their referrals to other people. The problem with such "snowball" sampling is that it did not necessarily ensure a balance between supporters and critics of the directions that Shabot Obaadjiwan was taking. My snowball sampling produced four interviews with individuals who, although varying broadly in their ages and basic political views, all strongly challenged aspects of Davis's administration. Although Shabot Obaadjiwan is a large community, and I encountered numerous individuals who plainly supported Davis (mostly young men who were hunters), I had little success in securing interviews with them. As this book approaches publication, I have maintained discussions with several people whom I initially interviewed in 2005, as well as with others who are now members of Pasapkedjiwanong, in an attempt to understand the current issues at work in these communities.

If Ardoch can be characterized by inspired leadership and continuous attention to community building, Shabot Obaadjiwan can be described as having a huge Algonquin presence – some community members estimated that about two thousand Algonquins live in the Sharbot Lake area. Although many community members appear to be somewhat disconnected from the formal leadership due to its prioritization of the land claim, the people with whom I spoke mentioned a tremendous cohesiveness among Algonquins in the community, who demonstrate a sound confidence in their own identities and abilities. Indeed, some interviewees functioned in a de facto manner as grassroots leaders and displayed a sureness in their identities that I did not encounter in most of the other communities that were created because of the land claim.

Chief Doreen Davis has led her community since it incorporated in 1999. She has spent most of her life in the Sharbot Lake area and recalls hearing her great-grandmother speaking Algonquin, but in a context where speaking the language in public could bring trouble to a family, it was not passed on. When Murray Hogben (2000a) interviewed Davis, she remarked that "you couldn't speak your language at home because you might speak it in school and get in trouble." According to her interview with Hogben, she is descended from Chief Francis Sharbot, who was born in Oka and who founded the village of Sharbot Lake.

Davis was originally a member of Ardoch, but when the Sharbot Lake area committee was being created, she left Ardoch to join it. When the committee incorporated as a band in 1999, it called itself the Sharbot Mishigama Algonquin First Nation – "the people of the big water." By 2000, 573 people in Sharbot Lake had completed their genealogies and been registered as community members (ibid.). When I interviewed Davis in 2003, enrolments had reached 800 and were still increasing. Membership in the community is determined according to the Algonquin land claim enrolment requirements, whereby individuals must be of one-eighth blood quantum as traced from the Schedule A list of historically known Algonquins.

Indeed, there are many Algonquins in Sharbot Lake who know that they are Algonquin but cannot prove that they fulfill the requirements for enrolment in the claim. During a 2004 interview, community member Pat Crawford was unequivocal about the extent of the Algonquin presence in Sharbot Lake. Crawford, who has worked at the Katorokwi Native Friendship Centre in Kingston for a number of years, has also been a community nurse at Sharbot Lake. Below she speaks about the connections between Algonquins in her community:

> I'm Algonquin from the Sharbot Lake area. Both my father and my mother were born and raised in that area, there's like six or seven generations ... My community is Sharbot Lake, I was raised there. Our traditional hunting grounds, everything was there. Even though a lot of us don't have status, we still have that ancestry. They tried to starve us out, they tried to kill us off with disease and war, and we're still here. So they might have gotten rid of some of us, but they haven't gotten rid of us all! And they need to realize that

> we're not going away! We're in the business of survival – that's how we lived on this land for so long. Most of the people in the area are related in one way or another; they're either first cousins or second cousins, or whatever.
>
> My dad used to show us stuff, when we'd go through the bush; he'd pick this or that up and chew it ... We would go out every fall and pick wild mushrooms. And we'd freeze them and keep them for the winter. He'd pick morels and go get the leeks, and we fished and hunted for deer.
>
> I'm a community nurse here. So I go to the people's houses and sit and visit with them and we talk politics, and they'll ask about what's going on in the community? And "How's so and so?" And "Have you heard from this one?" You can't get into the nitty-gritty, about everything, but everybody knows everybody else in Sharbot Lake.
>
> I think the main strength of the community is tenacity. Sheer stubbornness. That's a good strength to have, to be able to endure and keep going on ... There will be some times we do the things we do and we don't understand why, but it's been with us for years, and years, and years. And that spirituality, that uniqueness is there. My grandfather once said to me, "You must be an Indian; I see your heart crying."

In many respects, the interviews showed a consistent sense of strength in Algonquin identity at Sharbot Lake that had been sustained for years through the cohesiveness of families and a strong resistance to being further erased as a people. Although individuals had felt the silencing in their families, for many, their knowledge about their identities had gone underground rather than being suppressed. However, this strength is also a function of the remarkable efforts that a number of community members have made to promote Algonquin cultural identity. For years, these people worked very hard – an enterprise that received no economic support from the land claim – to promote pride in identity and encourage the use of Algonquin language and traditions.

Perhaps because Sharbot Lake has such a large Native population, relations between it and local whites have at times been difficult, particularly relating to the long-time Algonquin practice of spear fishing during the spring pickerel runs. A notable incident that Davis described to me took place at Pedherney's Creek in Westport, in April 1999. Normally, in order to avoid attracting attention from potentially hostile whites, band members spear by flashlight after midnight. However, on the night in question, two elders, two adults including Davis, and two youths, a boy and a girl, were fishing, and the elders were teaching the youths how to spear fish. Spear fishing is a complex skill: dressed in chest waders, fishers stand in cold, swift-running water in the middle of the night, holding a flashlight as well as a spear; seeing the pickerel by flashlight is difficult. That evening, a few local white men who had been drinking in a bar until closing time noticed the spear-fishing group. When the Algonquins tried to leave, the men blocked them with a truck, crowding them in an intimidating manner and challenging their right to spear pickerel. Davis took charge, telling the driver to contact the police or the Ministry of Natural Resources if they wished to make a complaint; the truck subsequently drove away.

The next evening, however, seventy Westport men met at the local tavern and marched to the creek. Learning of their presence, Randy Cota, an Ontario Provincial Police constable and co-chief of Ardoch, phoned Doreen Davis to warn her. Since it was too cold for anybody to fish that night, the crowd eventually dispersed (Hogben 2000b). On the next night, however, conditions were good for spearing. When the MNR tried to discourage the Sharbot Lake people from showing up, Davis insisted that they wouldn't be deterred from engaging in a cultural practice that was important to them.

In discussing this event during my interview with her, Davis described how, expecting trouble, she had coordinated who would spear that night. She asked three relatives to accompany her, and Algonquin men from Sharbot Lake drove down to attend in support. Davis's plan was that every spear-fisher, men and women and youth, would take one small male pickerel each to demonstrate that they could distinguish between fish and were not endangering stocks.

About forty police officers arrived at the creek with a large crowd of Westport men. Indeed, rather than protecting the band members, the police initially seemed more intent on taking their identification and documenting who was present. When Davis arrived, she and her three relatives had to walk through the hostile gathering with the police and the ministry officials behind them, rather than in front defending them. A crowd of Westport men lined a nearby bridge, and Davis told her relatives not to respond to any insults and to fish downstream so as not to be hit by beer bottles if the men started throwing them off the bridge.

However, when they entered the water, the men followed them to bar their way. In turn, Algonquin men from Sharbot Lake blocked the Westport men from moving into the water. The police finally intervened and forced the Westport crowd back onto the bridge. While further incidents took place on the bridge itself, the police protected the spear-fishers until the pickerel had been speared and the crowd dispersed.

On the following day, Davis met with spokespersons from various outdoor clubs and other local people from Westport, explaining why Native people spear pickerel – it is a cultural practice involving skills that they wish to maintain, it allows the community to have a pickerel feast in the spring, and it is not about filling everybody's freezer. Although some people remained hostile, Davis gradually developed a working relationship with a number of individuals because of these efforts.

In fact, since then, Charlie Jones, from the Westport and Area Outdoor Association, who had initially been responsible for assembling some of the Westport men to protest spear fishing, now works with Davis and other Sharbot Lake Algonquins to set realistic fishing limits (for non-Natives as well as Natives) and to restock the lakes with pickerel using a hatchery leased from the MNR (Hogben 2000b).

Because of this, some Sharbot Lake Algonquins are making long-handled dip nets in the traditional manner, which they adapted from drawings of old Algonquin nets, so they can check whether the fish are spawning and return them to the stream without spearing them. To avoid straining their relationship, the Algonquins no longer spear-fish at the Pedherney's Creek bridge (ibid.). Indeed, Davis and Jones each won an Environmental Service Award from the Westport Chamber of Commerce for their efforts in educating both the white and Native communities on conservation issues (Hogben 2000c).

Shabot Obaadjiwan also took a stand against the new arrangements in which Ontario devolved responsibility for maintenance of Crown land to municipalities. Without consulting Algonquins, some municipalities started charging fees on access roads to campsites and lakes. Shabot Obaadjiwan refused to pay. Instead, it met with enforcement officers, took them into one of the grounds, built a sacred fire, and spent the day talking with the officers about Algonquin values. After that, Central Frontenac Township developed a policy in which Sharbot Lake Algonquins are exempt from paying the fees.

Shabot Obaadjiwan and the Land Claim

Davis's efforts to smooth relations between local whites and Sharbot Lake Algonquins are highly strategic, given her long involvement with the land claim. When the claim first began, a strong racist backlash developed in white communities, particularly around Golden Lake, where Pikwakanagan is located, spearheaded by the local hunters and anglers' associations, cottagers, and tourist operators. Using what Emma LaRocque (2010) refers to as "civilization-savagery" discourse, these groups asserted that the land claim would allow Algonquins to control all the natural resources and that they would over-fish and over-hunt until the wildlife was gone.[1] In this context, spear fishing was a lightning rod for white anger regarding Aboriginal rights.

At the time of the Westport incident, the land claim was in abeyance. However, as the head of ANND, Davis was aware that involving local Native leaders in conservation work with outdoor clubs would encourage non-Native support, or at least neutrality, in connection with the claim, particularly given that hunters' and anglers' associations are frequently opposed to land claims. Her peacemaking approach both educated whites about spear-fishing practices and helped create a warmer reception for the land claim in towns such as Westport.

Indeed, Davis has a strong vision of how Shabot Obaadjiwan could apply the compensation money awarded for the claim. When Murray Hogben (2000a) interviewed her in 2000, he noted,

> Spread across the walls of the Sharbot First Nation's resource Centre – the former Hinchinbrooke Township building on Highway 38 between Godfrey and Parham – are detailed maps showing the swamps, lakes, rivers and Crown land in the area. There are markers for different land uses, from hunting and fishing to economic initiatives, "reserved lands" and even a casino. The land reserved for future development includes the area between Bob's Lake and Crow Lake, the site of the Bedford Township reserve first offered and rejected in 1844 and another parcel of land west of Bob's Lake. There's also a proposal to buy – with compensation money – 200 surveyed lots along nearby Silver Lake on Highway 7.

When I interviewed Davis in 2003, she was the sole representative for eight hundred people and seemed comfortable with the fact. At the time, the land claim was expected to reach completion relatively quickly, and Davis seemed willing to defer questions of community building until that point. She said that Shabot Obaadjiwan had rejected the "chief and council" form of governance and wished to return to a traditional model. However, most traditional models build in forms of representation by community members. At Shabot Obaadjiwan, Davis appeared to be the only person who was formally invested with a leadership role.

Indeed, despite the strong grassroots community feeling that was obvious in several of the interviews I conducted, it was clear that the grassroots leaders are not connected to the land claim process. In fact, the community's biggest weakness seems to be this lack of a structured representation between the chief and the informal leadership. Undoubtedly, Davis has considerable dynamism.

She has taken on a strong leadership role in the negotiations and appears energetic and willing to work very hard. However, her vision of what a settlement could accomplish for her group has meant that her greatest energies are focused on the land claim.

Some of the people I interviewed described how stressful the process was for community members. For example, Pat Crawford, who was interviewed in 2004, remarked that people were asked to make complex decisions, often without understanding the issues involved:

> I was sitting at a community meeting one time ... We had a motion put through to ask that we not use such big words in our minutes and it was a real eye opener for me ... I realized that a lot of people have very limited reading skills! So how can they ever understand? You know, they have to trust people a lot. And they have to depend that what is written there is what the leaders say is written there.
>
> In a way, it's the same as when the first contact happened, and they wrote treaties. We're still dealing with the same stuff, around literacy. And with the land claim, the government is putting forward documents written by lawyers with legal jargon that the normal lay person cannot understand ... And then they'll say, "You agreed to this." That's what scares me – a lot of the people that have to read this don't bother, because they can't. And they'll just agree because somebody said to, and trust the wrong person, and that's what's scary ...
>
> It's the whole leadership for the land claim that's a problem. It's not just in Sharbot Lake. It's the process itself. You can't sign papers up at that level without bringing it back to the people, and approaching at a level where people understand and feel comfortable with it. That's how it was always done.

Several individuals pointed out that reclaiming Algonquin language and cultural knowledge at the grassroots level, which should have been front and centre within the land claim, has gradually been sidelined. It was not always like that. In the early 1990s, Doreen Davis invited a group of community people to come together to promote social and cultural events. Clearly, she and the group believed in the need for a cultural revival – in fact, the early days of the claim fired a passion in many Algonquins to rediscover their culture and heritage – so the entire group worked extremely hard. Funded only by bake sales and yard sales, it created large gatherings every year. At local and regional fairs and events, it provided visual displays, taught cultural skills and crafts, and hired drummers and dancers as well as encouraging the growth of women's traditional drumming in Sharbot Lake. Gradually, these events became so successful that they drew thousands of people.

However, the group began to find that the more successful it was, and the more that community people became involved in cultural activities, the less support it received from the leadership. A number of reasons could account for this, but it is important to consider the pressures that affect Native people whenever they deal with institutions of colonial power, such as the comprehensive claims process, particularly when they themselves lack colonial signifiers of Indianness (such as a status card). In some respects, the non-status Algonquins at the negotiating table are under pressure to present themselves as knowledgeable cultural leaders in order to authenticate their right to speak as Algonquins. This relates to the issues discussed in Chapter 5 – the difficulty of expressing an Algonquin identity without colonial signifiers such as a status card. As Circe Sturm (2002, 140-41) notes, through her exploration of Cherokee identity, "culture" can validate a Native identity when other signifiers of "Indianness" are absent.

However, after two hundred years of settler incursion, "culture" in the Algonquin context relates more to practices on the land, such as hunting and spear fishing, as well as the socialization that has maintained the collective ethos of communities such as Sharbot Lake. This form of culture is largely unrecognizable to non-Natives, who desire the "beads and feathers" that signify Indianness to outsiders. And though many Algonquins at the grassroots level are now exploring traditional teachings and attempting to relearn ceremonies and language, the non-status ANRs at the negotiating table are operating in a desacralized space where the *symbols* of Indianness, but not the actual ceremonies, are present. In a sense, for the ANRs, "beads and buckskin, sacred pipes, wise elders, prayers to 'mother earth' and so on" (Owens 1998, 12) become the currency that establishes their Algonquinness to the non-Native negotiators. At the same time, the negotiation process separates and isolates them from the grassroots membership of their communities, which is engaging in genuine cultural revival. Furthermore, in the power-driven environment where Algonquins are negotiating with the state, it is difficult to use pan-Indian symbols to promote an Algonquin identity without commodifying them. Reflecting on the intensifying pressures to commodify "Indianness" within high-powered organizations, Louis Owens (ibid., 13) writes that, as "every savvy Indian fund raiser knows, there is nothing like traditional regalia and a drum to get the cash flowing." At home, ANRs may engage in traditional Algonquin social practices, such as hunting or spear fishing and the familial networking that has always maintained a non-status Algonquin identity, but at the negotiating table they must rely on pan-Indian symbols of culture to validate their identity. Conversely, actual cultural gatherings organized by ANTC communities generally focus on discussion of the land claim rather than ceremony and cultural revival. As a result, the grassroots desires of community members to promote knowledge of language and culture are increasingly out of step with the goals of the ANTC leadership who use "culture" to promote the land claim.

Of course, this issue is much larger than Sharbot Lake: it pertains to the relationship between cultural revival and the current land claim administration. It speaks profoundly to the despiritualized approach to treaty making that has marked the negotiations since 2004. Initially, when the land claim was led by Algonquins, it was about regaining land and nationhood, and therefore reinvigorating Algonquin cultural values. The post-2004 claim, which explicitly bypasses discussion of nationhood and maintains a centralized control in the hands of non-Native lawyers, has little connection to a spiritual revival.

Thus, it is perhaps not surprising that local social/cultural venues in Sharbot Lake have had to resist being engulfed by the land claim. This issue was frequently mentioned by the organizers of the Silver Lake Powwow, an annual summer event that has been held in a provincial park near the town of Sharbot Lake for many years. In 2005, while attending the powwow, I spoke with some of the organizers, who described their struggle to ensure that the powwow remains a community event rather than a venue through which Shabot Obaadjiwan promotes the land claim. Indeed, six years later, discussions at the Katorokwi Native Friendship Centre in Kingston with some of the current organizers emphasized that many Sharbot Lake Algonquins who enthusiastically attend the powwow every year remain insistent that it be independent from Shabot Obaadjiwan.

In the summer of 2011, in order to update the information about Sharbot Lake that I had obtained during interviews in 2004 and 2005, I spoke with a number of individuals whom I had interviewed from that time. Additionally, while attending recent Algonquin events, I spoke to other Sharbot Lake individuals about their thoughts relating to the land claim. Some observed that the negotiations did not correspond to Algonquin values. Others were concerned with the process but saw the positive accomplishments of the claim. For her part, Pat Crawford, who was interviewed in 2004 and 2011, was deeply troubled by the divisions created by the claim:

> The government divides and conquers by keeping people fighting amongst themselves. Throw them a bit of money here and a little bit of money there, and the greed will eat them up, and they'll sit back and laugh at us. And that's exactly what's happening. And until we start working together for the good of all the people and not just a few, it'll never change. And if I hear that negotiator [Bob Potts] say "That's just petty differences" one more time!
>
> You know, like, "If it's in the past, it's a petty difference." It's not a petty difference! It's not being petty – there are strong serious issues that have happened, that have split the community. There are reasons for that. And the negotiator is not listening to why those communities have split, that there's a reason why; it's not just personal issues. In a way it is, in another way it's not. It's because there's an ethical way to deal way with people, there's a moral way to deal with people. There's a right and a wrong, and a lot of the stuff that caused the split is because the leadership doesn't listen. They weren't listening to the majority. They only listen to a few; they are making decisions without coming back to the people, and making decisions that are not only going to affect us, but seven generations. And they're not thinking of those seven generations; they're thinking of here and now, and they shouldn't be.

In 2005, when the first ANR elections were held, Melinda Turcotte ran against Doreen Davis but was defeated. Indeed, during the election, a number of community leaders ran for election in their respective communities precisely to address their concerns relating to the negotiation process; all were defeated.

Lynn Gehl (2005a), from the community of Greater Golden Lake, has offered an in-depth analysis of the 2005 ANR elections. Framing everything is the pace imposed on the negotiation process by Bob Potts and his apparent willingness to ignore the protests of non-status community members about the difficulty of dislodging the very individuals who, as members of ANND, created a system to ensure that they stayed in office.[2]

Pasapkedjiwanong Algonquin First Nation

From the late 1990s, a number of people who had been involved in the Sharbot Lake social/cultural events committee became increasingly estranged from the politics of the land claim. They disliked its narrow focus and the despiritualized manner in which the negotiations were taking place. Moreover, they were disturbed by the fact that community members had no voice in the process; instead, it was conducted by leaders who were sworn to secrecy, who occupied positions where all power was centralized, and who were not subject to community control. Because of this, alienation and misgivings regarding the leadership increased within the community.

In 2002, former members of the cultural events committee established the Algonquin First Nation Cultural Circle Committee to bring back and share true knowledge of Algonquin culture and traditions. At the request of elders, approximately two hundred of them formed their own community, Pasapkedjiwanong, which means "the water that runs between the rocks," the Algonquin name for the Rideau River. They were formally incorporated as Pasapkedjiwanong Algonquin First Nation on 19 June 2007.

Mindful of a sense of responsibility to challenge the land claim, Pasapkedjiwanong hired a lawyer to formally incorporate itself as an organization. Despite fulfilling every requirement for involvement in the claim, the group was barred from taking part – in essence, the existing ANRs, which included Doreen Davis, had no intention of allowing a body that had split off from Shabot Obaadjiwan to sit at the table.

However, Pasapkedjiwanong's larger concern was to promote traditional values and to nurture each other's strengths. It relies on its council of elders for leadership. At the elders' suggestion, the community has a council of three chiefs to avoid the possibility that one chief could accrue too much power. The role of the chiefs is to serve Pasapkedjiwanong by implementing the decisions of the elders.

Many Algonquins are so burned out by the land claim, the disharmony it has created, and its "business as usual" focus, that resignation and cynicism have long since replaced the joy that once accompanied their desire for cultural reawakening. In this situation, Pasapkedjiwanong sees its goal as keeping the culture alive, walking the "red road," and nurturing hope and faith in each other as Algonquins.

It's also important to note that, like Ardoch and Shabot Obaadjiwan, Pasapkedjiwanong is rooted in the traditional territory of the region. Indeed, Melinda Turcotte, a member of the council of chiefs, comes from Bob's Lake, the area of the original Bedford tract that was granted to Peter Shawinapinessi's band. For the most part, Pasapkedjiwanong focuses on revitalizing sacred connections to the land and to the language. In this respect, its goals fit well with those of Ardoch, and both are members of the Algonquin Union (an organization of Algonquin communities unaffiliated with the land claim that will be discussed in Chapters 13 and 14). Turcotte herself was often praised by the late William Commanda for her years of work in promoting language and traditional values.

Once occupied by Peter Shawinapinessi's band, the Mississippi, Rideau, and lower Madawaska watersheds are currently occupied by three groups of Algonquins who share common descent from the band. Ardoch first rallied the people into a contemporary organization in order to protect the wild rice, but the land claim split the community and resulted in the creation of Shabot Obaadjiwan. Disheartened by the negativity of the claim, Pasapkedjiwanong then broke from Shabot Obaadjiwan to recover the traditional values that had originally inspired Ardoch. Despite this fragmentation, the watersheds nevertheless remain occupied by one people. Indeed, the three communities were drawn into an alliance when their lands were threatened by plans to drill for uranium.

8

Uranium Resistance: Defending the Land

In October 2006, Frank and Gloria Morrison discovered that a mining company, Frontenac Ventures, had staked part of their property in North Frontenac Township without their consent. In all, the company had staked approximately sixty-nine square kilometres, most of it on unceded Algonquin land, and was about to begin test drilling for uranium, with plans to drill 200 holes. The primary access to the staked area was an old tremolite mine in Robertsville. After months of being stonewalled by various levels and departments of the government, the Morrisons contacted Ardoch Algonquin First Nation in hopes that its Aboriginal rights might enable them to stop the mine.

Ardoch met with Shabot Obaadjiwan First Nation and together the two groups decided to oppose the exploration, basing their stance on the fact that their Aboriginal title and rights had never been signed away and that uranium development would destroy the ecological sustainability of the land. Members of Pasapkedjiwanong, although not yet formally incorporated as a community, took an active part in the resistance. Subsequent meetings were held with non-Native residents of the area to inform them of the situation and to plan resistance.

Robert Lovelace (2009, xii-xiv) characterizes the resistance strategy as involving four key steps – research, community education, legal action, and direct action:

1 Through research, Ardoch learned about the history of uranium mining and the associated social, economic, and environmental consequences.

2 Through community education, Ardoch shared what it was learning with as many people as it could reach via community meetings and speaker series. Because of this, a coalition of activists formed – the Community Coalition against the Mining of Uranium (CCAMU) – which in turn began to educate people across the province about the issue. Ardoch also reached out to other Aboriginal communities facing the threat of mining ventures in their traditional lands.
3 Through legal counsel, Ardoch sought to learn whether court actions might further its cause. Discovering that the *Haida* and *Taku River* Supreme Court decisions had ruled that the federal and provincial Crowns had a duty to consult with Aboriginal people if development were proposed on their traditional territories, Ardoch approached the Ministry of Northern Development and Mines. However, its concerns were ignored.[1]
4 Direct action was finally taken up when Ardoch realized that existing laws did not protect Aboriginal people's interests. While calling on friends and activists both nationally and internationally to support its efforts, Ardoch organized to block the activities of Frontenac Ventures.

Faced with the same constraints, Shabot Obaadjiwan also decided to employ direct action to halt the uranium exploration, although, as a member of the Algonquins of Ontario, as the land claim negotiation team was now called, it sought different legal counsel relating to its rights as a community than Ardoch did. In June 2007, the Ontario Provincial Police's Major Events Liaison Team (MELT) and Aboriginal Relations Team (ART) contacted Ardoch and Shabot Obaadjiwan to ensure that their protest would be peaceful.[2] Both teams became an integral part of the resistance that followed.

The Protest

On 28 June 2007, Ardoch and Shabot Obaadjiwan moved onto the Robertsville site. Almost immediately, local non-Native supporters began organizing with anti-nuclear and environmental activists to support their blockade. National news coverage increased as did the support of activists and leaders, including local Members of Provincial Parliament (MPPs) and the Green Party of Canada. People from Ardoch and Shabot Obaadjiwan, along with other Algonquin supporters, camped inside the gates of the old tremolite mine. In doing so, they risked prosecution for directly interfering with the drilling. The activists were asked to establish a separate camp immediately outside the gate so that they could alert passersby to the presence of the blockade and aid the protestors inside the gate without risk of being charged with trespass. Many supporters from out of town camped along the road to the site, which added to the visibility of the protest.

Art Cota III described Ardoch's experience of working with Shabot Obaadjiwan after the two communities had been separated for over fifteen years:

> When they first found out about the uranium, I believe there were conversations between our leadership and Doreen [Davis] saying, "What are we going to do? We have to act on this uranium thing." It was very, very interesting for me to go and see Doreen sitting up towards the front with Randy and Paula and Bob and Harold and my grandfather and so on. We all, Doreen's group and Ardoch, agreed that we'd have to take this course of action, which is what we ended up doing ... going to the site and protesting and staying there and putting up tents and so on ... But you could always sense that there were Doreen's people and then there were Harold's people ... I mean, if you could kind of get inside those people, see their thinking – if Harold and Doreen, hypothetically, didn't agree on a certain thing, whose course of action would they follow? And so all of us were there doing the same sort of thing, but you knew where their allegiances were ... We weren't fully gelling. We weren't saying, "Well, we're just going to put the groups aside for now." We never were all one people ... When we had to join forces in court, or we had to all stand there and say, "No, you're not coming in," then we were very much together. And we're still together in that we don't want anything to happen to the land – but that's not the only issue that Ardoch's dealing with, and it's not the only issue that Shabot Obaadjiwan's dealing with, and all of these other issues continue. I mean, even any time you start talking about a nation, I guess different people wonder what makes a nation a nation. Would Doreen's group and our group and the other groups necessarily comprise an Algonquin nation? I don't know. And I don't think too many people do know what they think about that ...
>
> My first real interactions with Quebec Algonquins happened just this summer, in terms of some of their people coming to support us, because we had three marches, along Highway[s] 7 and 38 in Sharbot Lake regarding the uranium, and I know that I did meet at least one person, an Algonquin person from Quebec, who had come to support us. I don't know whether that was just something that he felt he wanted to do, or whether he felt that because he was an Algonquin person, it was kind of a duty to come, or whether he felt it was a family thing or something like that. I don't know what the

> connections are, necessarily. I know that this was the first time I had really interacted with the Algonquins on the other side of the river.

In July 2007, Frontenac Ventures filed a lawsuit against the two communities for $77 million; four of the Algonquin leaders – Doreen Davis of Shabot Obaadjiwan and Bob Lovelace, Paula Sherman, and Harold Perry of Ardoch – were also named in the suit. At the end of July, Frontenac Ventures asked the Ontario Superior Court for an injunction to stop the protests immediately. When Justice Cunningham refused to hear evidence relating to the Aboriginal rights of Ardoch and Shabot Obaadjiwan, the two groups refused to participate in the process, since the court was excluding matters relating to their jurisdiction over the land. The judge ruled that by blocking access to the site, they were harming the company's interests, so he granted the interim injunction, which was served at the end of August.

However, after the results of the Ipperwash Inquiry, the Ontario Provincial Police had established their own policies for dealing with non-violent protest to ensure that the situation remained under control.[3] They had engaged in community consultation from the start of the uranium protest and as a result, the opposition had remained peaceful to that point. Knowing that the court decision might inflame a situation that was currently under control, and that the government had not negotiated with the protestors (a repeat of Ipperwash), the OPP refused to observe the injunction.

At the beginning of September, fearing the possibilities of state violence, the Algonquin leadership invited the Christian Peacemakers to send a team to the blockade site. The Peacemakers maintained a continuous presence, and Amnesty International urgently called on Premier Dalton McGuinty to protect the rights of Indigenous people in the province and to support the implementation of the Ipperwash Inquiry recommendations. Messages of support came from Greenpeace, local MPPs, the Green Party of Canada, 81 organizations from twelve countries, and 107 individuals.

At the end of September, the Algonquins undertook a ceremonial descent of the headwaters of the Mississippi watershed, travelling to Parliament Hill by canoe. They brought water from their starting point and poured it onto the steps of the Parliament Buildings to send the message that the waters of the Mississippi are very close to the seat of Canada's government. The Algonquins had prepared a proclamation to the Government of Canada in which they demanded a moratorium on uranium mining, and they presented it to Conservative MP Scott Reid, who represented the riding of Lanark-Frontenac-Lennox and Addington.

At the same time, Ardoch and Shabot Obaadjiwan returned to court. On 27 September, an interlocutory injunction was granted, naming five people – Bob Lovelace, Harold Perry, and Paula Sherman of Ardoch, and Doreen Davis and Earl Badour of Shabot Obaadjiwan – who were ordered to cease their protests or face immediate arrest. Because of the court's unwillingness to address the issue of Indigenous jurisdiction and the provincial government's requirement to consult with Aboriginal people, all five refused to recognize the injunction. Non-Native protestor Frank Morrison, the property owner where Frontenac had staked, and John Hudson and David Milne of the Christian Peacemakers were also charged with contempt of court.

In October, the Algonquin leadership met with Kitchenuhmaykoosib Inninuwug First Nation (formerly known as Big Trout Lake First Nation) in northwestern Ontario, which had been engaged in a two-year struggle with the Ontario government and Platinex Incorporated, a mining company that had staked claims in its territory. Platinex was represented by the same legal team that represented Frontenac Ventures. In both cases, the Ontario government had allowed mineral staking and exploration to occur without any meaningful consultation and accommodation with First Nation communities, in violation of the *Haida* and *Taku River* decisions.

Ardoch and Shabot Obaadjiwan then reached an agreement in principal to engage in mediated negotiations with the provincial government. Negotiations began on 6 January, but after eight weeks of talks, the Algonquin negotiators were informed that the outcomes could not include the possibility that no drilling would take place, and so the process broke down. On 12 February, after Frontenac Ventures filed contempt of court charges against them, Badour, Davis, Lovelace, Perry, and Sherman appeared in court. Doreen Davis and Earl Badour of Shabot Obaadjiwan First Nation agreed to abide by the terms of the 27 September 2007 injunction.

Ardoch was in a different position, however. For over thirty years, it had struggled to exercise Algonquin jurisdiction over the land. Co-chief Paula Sherman and Honorary Chief Harold Perry were charged with contempt, but the particularities of their personal circumstances prevented them from resisting. Perry was seventy-eight and had heart problems, whereas Sherman, a single parent, risked losing custody of her younger children and one grandchild if she went to prison. Both therefore agreed to abide by the terms of the injunction.

The responsibility for asserting Algonquin jurisdiction thereby fell to Robert Lovelace. In response to the charge, he stated that he had no choice but to obey Algonquin law and thus could not submit to the court injunction. On

15 February 2008, he was sentenced to six months in jail for refusing to comply with it. He was taken away in handcuffs to Quinte Detention Centre. After two weeks, he was transferred to the maximum security provincial prison in Lindsay, Ontario. From that point onward, anyone found within 200 metres of the gate to the Robertsville site, or interfering with Frontenac Ventures employees or equipment, was to be arrested and charged with criminal contempt.

Art Cota III described the shock of encountering, for the first time, the ugly face of Canadian racism during the trial:

> This summer I had my eyes opened. I thought that Canada was a country in which we wouldn't necessarily face racism. I'd heard my dad and my grandpa and others talk about racism. I thought, well, you know it's kind of a thing of the past. It's not. And you talk about what it's like to be Algonquin. I guess you've got to start thinking about what it means to be Canadian, too.
>
> I'll never forget this summer, sitting in court, and just thinking, "Man, am I in a time machine, or what? Did I just go back 150 years?" I just felt like that Native sitting in the courtroom and being told that "you have no right to your land. You are a terrible person because you're standing in the way of progress." I just felt ... that Native people were just so belittled ... And for me, I had to look at the question of "How do we – or do we – fit into the Canadian identity? And how do I think of myself as a Canadian? Can I be an Algonquin person at the same time as being a Canadian, and how can I count on those two being balanced? Or will they perpetually be in opposition? Will I always be butting heads?" That's the way that I felt. I felt that the Algonquin people were standing in the way of what Canada wanted ... Like, we're saying, "What gives them the legitimacy, you know; where does their power really lie to tell us what we can and cannot do?" Maybe the power is simply in those military personnel that they keep on hand in case we get out of hand. In order for *us* to exercise what we feel is our sovereignty.

Taking a Stand

After Bob Lovelace was imprisoned, shock and outrage reverberated in progressive circles, with support pouring in from a range of sources, including the Ontario College of Family Physicians, the Union of BC Indian Chiefs, MP Scott Reid and MPP Randy Hillier, David Suzuki, and a host of other national and international figures. A number of cities, including Ottawa, demanded a moratorium on uranium exploration.

On 17 March 2008, eight members of the Kitchenuhmaykoosib Inninuwug First Nation (KI) were charged, and six were sentenced to prison for six months. The protests about Lovelace's imprisonment expanded to support KI. In a brutal demonstration of the differing treatment accorded non-Native and Native people who are involved in environmental struggles, the day after the "KI Six" were jailed, all charges were dropped against the non-Natives involved in the Robertsville protest – John Hudson, David Milne, and Frank Morrison. On that same day, 18 March 2008, Shabot Obaadjiwan issued a press release indicating that it had submitted documents to lay suit against both Frontenac Ventures and the Government of Canada on the basis that they had failed in their "duty to consult" as upheld in numerous Supreme Court rulings.

Although the duty to consult had been clearly established, Ottawa's response is instructive. Rather than upholding the broad duty to consult in order to maintain the "honour of the Crown," as the *Haida* and *Taku River* decisions stipulate, the government set out only the narrow measures required to legally fulfill the obligation.[4] Ottawa is currently working to develop a policy on consultation and accommodation that will address outstanding legal and policy matters, including the scope of the duty, which Crown bodies are involved, the nature and scope of accommodation, the capacity of government and Aboriginal groups to engage in consultation, and the reconciliation of an evolving legal duty with statutory and other legally based obligations (Canada 2011, 6).

As Bob Lovelace and the KI Six remained in prison, the groundswell of protest and support continued across Eastern Canada, including fundraising efforts with well-known artists and performers such as Bruce Cockburn. On 29 May 2008, after a full day of submissions, the Ontario Court of Appeal ordered Lovelace and the KI Six released immediately and stayed their sentences, including fines. The KI Six had served two months in prison, whereas Lovelace had served three and a half. Officially, the court ordered them released for time served but added that it did not consider the sentences or the time served to be appropriate. It blamed Ontario's "sweeping" Mining Act, which allowed mining companies to conduct aggressive exploration, including removing trees, blasting, drilling, trenching, and building roads on First Nations land, without any consultation or environmental assessment. The court also criticized the McGuinty government for ignoring repeated requests by the Algonquins for consultation and instead supporting the jailing of Lovelace and the punitive fines imposed on the community and its leaders. Finally, it expressed serious concern that Justice Cunningham, who had sentenced Lovelace, had ignored numerous Supreme Court decisions that required governments to consult with First Nation communities *before* approving industrial activities that could affect their rights. Cunningham should have ensured that Ontario had consulted with the Algonquins before ordering them to end their protest and then jailing them when they continued to demand consultations in defiance of his injunction (Ardoch Algonquin First Nation 2008).

Perhaps most essential to the stance adopted by Lovelace and the KI Six – who were separated from their families and risked losing homes and jobs because of it – was standing up to prevailing ideology, as expressed in *Haida,* that regardless of whether consultation takes place, development cannot be resisted. Ardoch, Shabot Obaadjiwan, and KI uncategorically rejected this, affirming that First Nations have the right to refuse resource development.

In November 2007, before his imprisonment, I interviewed Bob Lovelace about the uranium situation. He spoke about the troubled relationship between Ardoch and Shabot Obaadjiwan:

> I think it's really important to try to understand the dynamics, certainly the political dynamics of Aboriginal communities. First of all, it's my belief that there's only one community. But the way in which the federal and provincial governments isolate issues for Aboriginal people, it tends to divide our politics so that some people choose to be represented by one kind of governance, Aboriginal governance, and some people decide to be represented by another, and we often aren't given many choices in that regard. If we were an order of governance unto ourselves, then we could sort those things out and accommodate one another to the point where ... we could have enough breadth of governance to be able to accommodate various desires of Aboriginal people. But Sharbot Lake and Ardoch are basically one community. We're all related. Our territories overlap. The big difference comes in that some Algonquins wanted to continue with pursuing a land claim under the comprehensive land claim agreement, and I have my own prejudices about that, and I would say no matter what, no matter how corrupt that process is, no matter how poor of a settlement that can be achieved, that some Algonquins say that that's the only way, the only way that we'll get some peace for our children and our grandchildren and be able to use some of our land.

Splitting the Communities

On 13 June 2008, the Province of Ontario laid charges against Frontenac Ventures and Gemmil Sand and Gravel Limited for breach of environmental regulations, asserting that road construction to access the proposed uranium drill sites had damaged sensitive wetlands and that fill had blocked waterways (*Kingston Whig-Standard* 2008). At that point, Shabot Obaadjiwan indicated its willingness to open consultations with Frontenac Ventures, the provincial government, and the Algonquins of Ontario. On 28 November 2008, Shabot Obaadjiwan, the Algonquins of Ontario, and Randy Malcolm's small group (Snimikobi) signed an agreement with Frontenac Ventures and the Ontario government regarding specific measures to protect health, safety, the environment, and Aboriginal values and interests. In return, the company volunteered to remove some of the lands at issue from its exploration plans, and Ontario withdrew those lands from further mineral staking (Province of Ontario 2008).

However, their concessions soon proved to be meaningless. With respect to the charges relating to breach of environmental regulations, MNR officials ultimately refused to testify, so the court case was dropped. On 12 February 2009, it was confirmed that by late May and early June of 2008, when Frontenac was entering into discussions with Shabot Obaadjiwan, it had already drilled fifteen test holes at the Robertsville site. Indeed, drilling had ceased only on 17 June, four days after negotiation began. And though the Ontario Ministry of Labour had been involved, the ministers of Aboriginal Affairs and Northern Development and Mines, who were participating in the consultation with Shabot Obaadjiwan, indicated that they had known nothing about it.

Frontenac stated that it had not been asked during the negotiation whether it had already undertaken any drilling, and therefore it did not disclose it. It added that the samples had not even been assayed (Green 2009). However, a mere fourteen days later, on 26 February 2009, Frontenac announced that its drilling had discovered a large Alaskite-type uranium deposit extending over a fifteen by eight kilometre area, with an average grade of 1.77 pounds per ton (Frontenac Ventures 2009). Despite its earlier statement, Frontenac must have assayed the first few holes it drilled. Small mining companies do not drill fifteen "blind" holes; instead, they drill a few and assay the samples, examining the drill core to determine the rough outline of the ore body underground. After this, subsequent exploratory drilling takes place at specific sites and at specific angles to outline the geometry of the ore body as well as its size and grade. Thus, when Frontenac volunteered to remove some of the land from its exploration plans, it already knew it was worthless. At the time, Doreen Davis remarked that Frontenac's duplicity had somewhat soured her trust. However, the agreement still stood.

Once Frontenac Ventures, Shabot Obaadjiwan, and the Algonquins of Ontario signed their agreement, the uranium issue became part of the comprehensive claim negotiation. Specific details of negotiations are kept secret, but no information of even the broadest sort is available regarding the "consultation" process with Frontenac Ventures. Indeed, the Shabot Obaadjiwan website has not been updated since 2005 and makes no reference to the struggle to resist uranium exploration. Perhaps, like BC First Nations, who have borrowed millions of dollars only to sit mired in land claim negotiations while their territories are destroyed by logging, Shabot Obaadjiwan is sitting at a table where Frontenac is supposedly engaged in consultation and yet drilling for uranium still continues.

With the release of Lovelace and the KI Six, activist emphasis shifted to changing the Mining Act. This act most clearly exemplifies the reality that Canada's economic growth is based on resource extraction. It enables mining companies to establish their control over virtually any land where minerals may exist. Consultations relating to changes in the Mining Act began in August of 2007, and eight months later, the new Mining Act was introduced. Although it affords more protection to private landowners and claims to recognize Aboriginal rights (Kelly 2009), its notion of "meaningful consultation" with First Nations does not allow them to refuse exploration and mine development on their traditional territories. Three organizations spoke out against the act – Mushkegowuk Council, a tribal council representing seven Cree communities along the west coast of James Bay who face increasing pressures relating to diamond exploration; Kitchenuhmaykoosib Inninuwug; and Ardoch.[5] All addressed the fact that, in a situation where a community cannot say no to mining development, consultation and accommodation are meaningless. These issues were strongly supported by a range of environmental groups as well.

Furthermore, the additional dangers posed by uranium mining are not covered in the Mining Act. Chief Isadore Day of Serpent River First Nation and the Lake Huron treaty commissioner have called on the Province of Ontario to use the act to address the special hazards of uranium mining. In particular, Day noted that a legislative gap exists between provincial regulations on uranium exploration and federally regulated jurisdictions on production and waste management of uranium, which is a huge problem for the communities in which uranium mining occurs. Serpent River is located south of Elliott Lake, which was Ontario's chief uranium producer for a number of years. Day stated that his community is situated near a major lake basin that, between the 1950s and the 1990s, was continuously contaminated by radioactive waste from spills and runoff from mine tailings. He suggested that special triggers be incorporated into the new Mining Act that explicitly defined, determined, and directed appropriate requirements as they pertain to uranium exploration.

He also spoke of the need for harmonization triggers to ensure that a responsible and consistent thread of due diligence linked Ottawa and Ontario (Union of Ontario Indians 2009).

Indeed, in *Dishonour of the Crown: The Ontario Resource Regime in the Valley of the Kiji Sìbì*, Paula Sherman (2008a, 42-47) examines the potential damages of uranium drilling. The first affects water: as groundwater mixes with the water used in the drilling process, it can contaminate aquifers that provide communities with drinking water. The second impact is the release of highly carcinogenic radon gas into the air and groundwater around drill sites. The third entails a range of other damages to the lands and water associated with the site preparation: areas to be drilled must first be clear-cut, and the overburden, the layer of soil covering the rocks, must be removed, generally through blasting with high-pressure hoses run from local swamps, which causes extensive soil runoff into local wetlands and waterways. Finally, parts of the forest must be cleared to enable drilling equipment onto the various sites, which leaves a swath of devastation in its wake.

Overall, however, is the profound disrespect demonstrated by uranium exploration companies, not only to the land but to the Indigenous communities that rely upon it. Sherman notes that there are 595 abandoned uranium exploration sites in Nunavik (northern Quebec), most with derelict buildings and materials, including waste oil and chemical products, that have begun to contaminate land and water as their containers deteriorate, killing local wildlife. Other northern peoples, such as the Dene, have faced similar dangers from contamination due to uranium drilling in sites ranging from northern Saskatchewan to Great Slave Lake. In every case, nothing has been done to remediate these problems.

Sherman (2008a, 47-51) also examines the experiences of Indigenous people in Australia and the United States, noting that uranium damage to land and water, including toxic contamination of aquifers, is a chronic problem for them. She concludes that Indigenous people have little reason to trust resource companies operating in their territories, with their facile promises that uranium exploration will have "no effects."

The tremendous problem for Aboriginal people when industry impinges on their territories is that their interests continue to be viewed as expendable to the "national interest," particularly in the case of energy resources. Whether the issue is hydroelectric development in the James Bay Lowlands (as covered on page 68), oil development on Lubicon Cree lands in northern Alberta, or uranium mining in northern Saskatchewan or Elliott Lake, in all instances, the "greater good" of Canada (to say nothing of the profits of energy corporations) is found to outweigh the sustainability of Indigenous people's way of life and relationship to land.[6] Writing from prison, Bob Lovelace (2009, ix) addresses the "big picture" of what land-based Aboriginal people face as societies with unsustainable appetites for consumption gobble the resources of sustainable communities, thus rendering them unsustainable. He notes that the process is global and that ultimately it involves a totalitarian subjugation of peoples, no matter how much it is couched in the language of accommodation:

> This dilemma in governance arises out of a heritage of colonialism; that is, the process by which a group having exhausted its sustainability options dispossesses another group of its. Using seduction or force, a dominant group undermines the power of multiple others. This is the principal mechanism that separates much of humanity from the sacred relationships with the earth and has become normalized in the governance of nations ... Determinism, progress, and ideological or theological perfectionism are dead-end illusions on a living planet in this galaxy. Here, the highest achievement for humankind is to exercise our innate ability to adapt to the local. In knowing and using the local environment sustainably ... each individual takes a transactional responsibility and experiences immediate consequences. Collectives are supported for what individuals give by way of sustenance and knowledge, not just what they can take away for less than they contribute. The question is, then, how can humankind achieve this state of grace?

For Ardoch, the uranium protest has continued in subtle ways. Pipe ceremonies and teaching circles are held periodically near the site, involving brief forays to the gate for spiritual purposes. On two occasions, large-scale campaigns were mounted for people to gather and pray for the land, with significant participation. Meetings continue to discuss developments and forms of resistance. However, as always, Ardoch has also attended to the community processes – in this case, building the Manoomin Centre – that uranium development temporarily postponed.

Questions Raised

With the campaign to repel uranium exploration in the Mississippi, Rideau, and lower Madawaska watersheds, the differing responses of the leadership, both to resource development and ultimately to questions of the land claim, reflect a deeper ideological/philosophical/spiritual divergence regarding the relationship between Indigenous people and their traditional lands. This divergence is not unique. Indeed, it appears in Indigenous communities around the globe, where it is expressed in two basic approaches: the first resists what are perceived as alien and predatory ways of treating the land, whereas the second attempts to co-exist with rampant resource consumption and environmental destruction, trying to limit the costs and obtain some benefits. On another level, this divergence reflects differing responses to a history of language loss and forcible disconnection from traditional lands.

For the Algonquins of the Mississippi, Rideau, and lower Madawaska watersheds, resisting uranium exploration was rendered more difficult because the land claim divided Shabot Obaadjiwan and Ardoch. This has compromised the ability of the Shabot Obaadjiwan leadership to significantly challenge ongoing uranium exploration within a comprehensive claim negotiation based on *not* questioning provincial authority over the land. It has also isolated Ardoch's struggle, with Ardoch and, more recently, Pasapkedjiwanong on one side, and the Algonquins of Ontario and Shabot Obaadjiwan on the other.

For the leadership of Ardoch and Pasapkedjiwanong, as with the leadership of Kitchenuhmaykoosib Inninuwug and Mushkegowuk Council in James Bay, the basic issues involve the rights of land-based communities to *not* become "national sacrifice zones" for energy or other resource interests and to attempt to live on the land in ways that do not violate traditional values.[7]

This perspective is often considered unrealistic by those who suggest that modern living demands mining and that modern energy consumption requires the constant development of new energy resources. However, such views ignore the real costs of mining or energy resource development, which are absorbed by Indigenous people and therefore remain hidden.

As mining and energy development are needed for the technologies of modern urban life, it is important to consider what the true costs of developing these technologies would be if Indigenous homelands were *not* to be turned into national sacrifice zones. In such an approach, communities would be centrally involved in decision making about production processes, safety measures, treatment of waste, disaster relief funds to cope with unexpected contamination, and questions of *how* the land would be reclaimed, the timetables and safeguards to ensure that this took place, the measures to restore the health and ecological balance of waterways, how road building and other intrusive effects would be minimized, and most importantly, how these decisions would be made and what authority First Nations would have in the process. In other words, if mining or other resource developments are considered necessary for a society based on technology, the true costs must be paid from corporation profits and from funding supplied by governments who insist on the right to allow – and who enable – such resource development in the name of national interests.

By focusing on such questions of profit and sustainability, and the apparent determination of corporations and governments to continue downloading the real costs of resource development onto the Indigenous communities whose homelands are being devastated, we can see that the only reason Canada has been so wealthy and is so wasteful with its energy resources and its water is that the companies whose profits it enables are not compelled to pay the true costs of such resource use. Indeed, being forced to repair the damages from extractive industries (or being required not to incur the damages at all) would make corporate profits so minimal – and would make the violence and danger of such technologies so truly visible – that green technologies would certainly become the wave of the future.

The issue, then, about Indigenous people's relationship to land is not one that dichotomizes "modern" and "pre-modern" ways of life or insists that Aboriginal communities should live in pre-contact ways. Instead, the question relates to the ongoing colonialism hidden inside the status quo of resource development, the rights of Indigenous people to refuse resource development that destroys their lands, and the nearly unbridled power granted by Ottawa and the provinces to resource companies on Indigenous lands. Indeed, Aboriginal communities, when *not* shattered by corporate resource development, have been remarkably adept at producing new technologies to enable ways of "modern" living that do not require the sacrifice of the land.[8]

In this respect, the larger philosophical question – "What relationship do Indigenous people wish to have with their traditional lands?" – leads to the wider question, which the uranium struggle also raised: "What does it mean to be Algonquin?" As discussed in Chapter 5, after generations of land loss and silencing, many Algonquins are confused about what it means to *be* Algonquin. This question, though of intrinsic importance to Algonquin people, is again connected to the issue of colonial relations in highly specific ways.

Ardoch's guiding principles delineate the relationship between the land and being Omàmìwinini, asserting that Algonquins have a responsibility to protect the land. From this framework, contamination of surface and groundwater in particular violates Algonquin law, which holds waters to be sacred. Paula Sherman (2008a, 43) explains,

> The elders stated that *sah-kemah-wapoye,* which translates as "spiritual water," refers to the living water. In the spiritual sense, water is an entity that can be damaged by humans who are manipulators. We can make things happen, we can move things, we can throw things, and we can break things. They characterized water as more passive in that it will accept things done to its essence. Water will accept those changes and will undergo the same changes. It will mirror the climate or mood that we, as human beings, are in. It becomes the quality in which we shape it. We humans, in turn, are affected by the changing quality of water, and say that the water is "hurting us." It is only giving us what we have asked of it.

This understanding of being Algonquin is intimately concerned with the effects of human actions on land and water. In such a world view, there is no possible disconnection between humans and our reliance on the land, and especially on water.

Aboriginal people who have not learned about their heritage from their families and whose families were dispersed from their communities by land loss often find that a multitude of spiritual teachings can help fill the resultant "hole in our heart."[9] Although knowledge of identity that situates Native people in direct relationship to the land provides no option but to protect the land, those individuals whose families were dispersed usually acquire cultural knowledge through workshops and ceremonies in urban settings, often with elders from a range of traditions. Of necessity, these teachings focus primarily on immediate physical survival for urban Aboriginal individuals whose self-destructive behaviours often result from soul-destroying racism on top of intergenerational colonial violence and the loss of language, cultural knowledge, and connection to land. The teachings provide general instructions relating to Aboriginal values as a means for Indigenous people to develop pride in their identity.

And yet, relearning the Algonquin language or developing an in-depth understanding of community histories that remain largely unwritten, as well as learning about cultural values in relationship to the land, simply cannot be acquired overnight or fulfilled through workshops in urban settings (or through the Algonquin teachings featured on many of the ANTC community websites, for that matter). In the absence of knowledge of language and connection to the land, Aboriginal people are vulnerable to state-sanctioned notions of identity, such as focusing too much on what it means to be Indian rather than questioning what it means to be connected to the land. As Taiaiake Alfred (2005, 144) writes, "The domestication within the state of our formerly independent notion of ourselves – our being distinct peoples – the restriction of our identity and action to arenas built by Settlers, is maintained primarily by the limitation of our self-identification to the Settler State. Breaking out of this would generate enormous collective power in the unity of our voices and numbers, as well as resources. This expansive identity was woven through traditional teachings, but has been lost as restricted, colonial, narrow conceptions of self and community were imposed to break the solidarity of Onkwehonwe nations in their homelands." In most cases, the disconnection that so many Aboriginal people have experienced from their traditional lands and language leaves them ill-prepared to resist colonial encroachment.

This problem exists in *all* the communities that share the Mississippi, Rideau, and lower Madawaska watersheds. For example, the "cognitive colonialism" referred to by Paula Sherman (2008b, 121) addresses the confusion experienced at Ardoch about which traditional teachings would enable the community to define its relationship with the MNR. Teachings that express the need for honesty, respect, caring, and sharing may instill a basic framework of Aboriginal values, but they do not assist Algonquin people in understanding what it means to assert jurisdiction over their lands in defiance of provincial authority.

At the same time, this concern with protecting the land and trying to understand and apply traditional Algonquin values had prompted a number of individuals to leave Shabot Obaadjiwan and form Pasapkedjiwanong. In this respect, the resistance to uranium development in which both Shabot Obaadjiwan and Pasapkedjiwanong engaged required them to address these difficult questions about what it means to be Algonquin.

The nature of the answers depends on the stance of the leadership. The leader of Shabot Obaadjiwan has chosen to focus almost exclusively on the land claim. And though the community website contains a number of teachings – some by respected elders from a range of backgrounds, some by Aboriginal people who earn their living by developing such teachings for websites, and some that are frankly New Age ideas dressed up as Indian traditions – there is little focus on uranium development or what it means to be Algonquin.

A recent newsletter of Ardoch Algonquin First Nation contains a commentary titled "What Does It Mean to Be Algonquin Today?" (Ardoch Algonquin First Nation 2010, 5). It was written in response to a *Frontenac News* article that commented on the lack of cultural distinctiveness among Algonquins (as discernible to outsiders):

> The Algonquin language offers one way to approach the issue around identity. Who are we as people in the language spoken by our ancestors? We are

> not Algonquin that is for sure. In fact that term does not even originate from our homeland or our people, and yet we continue to use it. In the language we are called *Omamíwínini,* which translates as the people of the lower river. In the language it is not a noun oriented description of the lands we traditionally occupied but rather refers to a state of being and relating that is much more substantial. The term reflects the fact and reality that our collective identity as distinct people comes from the Land and those relationships that our ancestors established and maintained within the Kiji Síbí.
>
> Over those thousands of years of relating, our ancestors developed social and political structures based upon the natural law they observed. From that process our ancestors developed Omamíwínini Law and Guiding Principles which guided individual behaviour and interactions with the Natural World. Even language itself is thought to have emerged from the land and from those relationships with other parts of the Natural World. The term Omamíwínini, like the rest of the language, reminds us of that original relationship between our people and the land. It speaks to us about our responsibilities as human beings and how we need to maintain them to maintain our identity as Omamíwínini people.
>
> Elder William Commanda has offered guidance in this respect, reminding us that our ancestors know who we are and they recognize us when we speak to them as Omamíwínini people and use the language in our daily lives and practices. So the choice is up to us to make. Do we want our children and great grandchildren to be Algonquin or do we want them to be completely Omamíwínini?

In many respects, struggles about Native identity in response to the land claim have led Algonquin communities in the Ottawa River watershed to question what it means to be situated in the heart of an imperialistic technological society in the twenty-first century. This issue has assumed primary importance for Ardoch, Shabot Obaadjiwan, and Pasapkedjiwanong. In a sense, their territory has always been a battleground for such issues, from the rice war and legal struggles of the 1980s to the uranium resistance. And yet, the fact that these communities have had to work so hard to protect their lands may have enabled their identities as Algonquin people to seem less fraught with confusion. Most people whom I interviewed in the Mississippi, Rideau, and lower Madawaska River watersheds did not intensively question whether they were Algonquin. Their struggles related to deeper questions about what it means to be Omàmìwininiwak.

PART 3

The Bonnechere and Petawawa River Watersheds

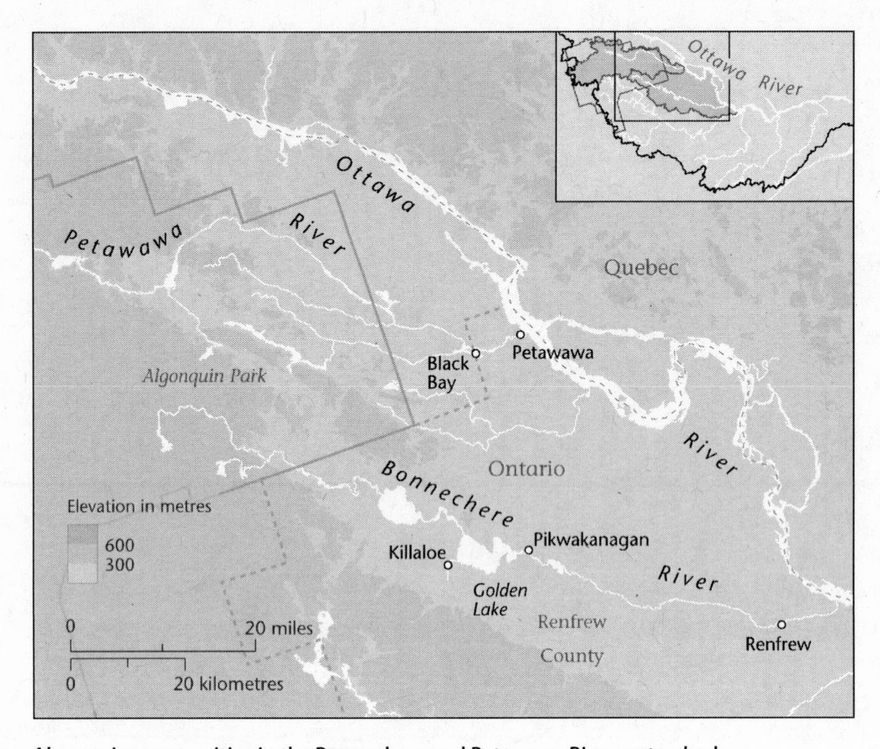

Algonquin communities in the Bonnechere and Petawawa River watersheds

9

The Bonnechere Communities and Greater Golden Lake

To explore more of the issues faced by non-status Algonquins in negotiating identity and nationhood, our focus moves to the busy central region of Algonquin activity in the Ottawa River Valley – the watershed of the Bonnechere and Petawawa Rivers. There, the only federally recognized Algonquin reserve in Ontario, Pikwakanagan, shares territory with three non-status Algonquin groups – the Bonnechere Algonquin Community (BAC), the Bonnechere Algonquin First Nation (BAFN), and the Algonquins and Nipissings of Greater Golden Lake.

For federally unrecognized communities in the Bonnechere-Petawawa region, a number of factors have rendered their assertion of their traditional territory far more complex than in other parts of the Ottawa River watershed. The federal government's actions in establishing the Golden Lake reserve in 1873 meant that a number of the families whose territories lay between the Bonnechere and Petawawa Rivers and who were attempting to farm there saw their settlement become the reserve. Others lost their lands to the reserve. For example, a member of the Pappin family, whose oral history was collected by the Bonnechere Algonquin Community History Project, recalled learning from his grandmother that some of her parents' land was taken to create the reserve (Bonnechere Algonquin Community 1999, 6).

Pikwakanagan became the primary community of affiliation for a great number of the Algonquins in the area. However, this straightforward picture was complicated by a number of factors. First, Algonquins throughout the territory were encouraged to move to Pikwakanagan, and although most Algonquins in other regions tried to survive on their own lands, some eventually moved either to Pikwakanagan or Maniwaki. Second, Pikwakanagan was tiny: it originally consisted of 1,561 acres. The reserve therefore could not support many families unless they relied on a mixed economy of hunting, trapping, and agriculture. Shortly after the reserve was created, logging intensified along the Bonnechere River as the Opeongo Colonization Road, midway between the Bonnechere and Madawaska Rivers, opened both territories to loggers. Logging was further accelerated by the building of the railways during the 1880s. As forests were destroyed, band members on the new reserve were forced to travel increasing distances to hunt and trap, including to Algonquin Park and even into Quebec. At the same time, despite the small size of the reserve and its general unsuitability for farming, the "civilization" project being asserted by Indian agents and religious authorities at Golden Lake focused on forcing Algonquins to remain on the reserve year-round. For example, after 1939, Indian Affairs increasingly followed the policy that Algonquins from the reserve who did not live full-time on the reserve were no longer entitled to recognition (Joan Holmes and Associates 1993, 2:235-36). The combination of these factors meant that some individuals, finding year-round residence on the reserve too onerous, ultimately drifted away and joined non-status relatives in other communities of the watershed. Others eked out a marginal existence near the reserve or attempted to work in tourism as guides or in parks. Their descendants comprise many of today's non-status Algonquins in the Bonnechere and Petawawa watersheds.

Finally, membership in the federally unrecognized communities along the Bonnechere and Petawawa Rivers has been rendered still more complex by various Indian Act policies that forced Pikwakanagan residents to leave the reserve: these applied to women who married non-Indians (including non-status Algonquins) between 1869 and 1985, to anyone who chose enfranchisement or was compelled to accept it before 1951, to those whose paternity was in question, and to those whose mother and grandmother had gained Indian status through marriage (after 1951). These multiple policies, which entailed loss of Indian status, had a profound impact on Pikwakanagan's membership. Indeed, with the passing of Bill C-31 in 1985, Pikwakanagan was one of a handful of Canadian reserves whose membership more than tripled overnight. According to Kirby Whiteduck, interviewed in 2005, the Pikwakanagan membership expanded from fewer than four hundred to thirteen hundred in the space of one year. In many respects, then, the three non-status communities of the Bonnechere-Petawawa watershed are closely tied to the history of Pikwakanagan.

And yet, to suggest that the memberships of the Bonnechere communities and Greater Golden Lake are limited solely to those whose traditional lands were situated in the Bonnechere-Petawawa watershed is to present a false picture. It belies the reality of nineteenth-century migration and displacement, particularly within this central region, as Algonquins travelled across the territory, seeking viable places to hunt, to fish, or to work. Whereas the Bonnechere Algonquin Community was made up of those whose families hunted and trapped between the Bonnechere and Petawawa Rivers and in Renfrew County, the Greater Golden Lake community gathered up Algonquins from throughout the Ottawa River watershed. Finally, significant intermarriage occurred between Ottawa River watershed communities, as even in times of crisis, Algonquins continued to do as they had always done – obtain marriage partners by travelling to other Algonquin communities.

In this chapter, I will explore the first organization created for non-status Algonquins in the region – the Bonnechere Metis and Non-Status Indian Association – and its subsequent incarnations as the Bonnechere Metis Association, the Bonnechere Algonquin Community (BAC), and the Bonnechere Algonquin First Nation (BAFN). I will also examine issues relating to the Algonquins and Nipissings of Greater Golden Lake, a community that originated as an area committee for the region. The following chapter will address Pikwakanagan perspectives on Algonquin identity.

My interviews revealed a persistent tendency on the part of people from Pikwakanagan to perceive non-status Algonquins as metis. In this part, I have capitalized "Metis" when referring to organizations funded as Metis. On the other hand, where local notions of "metisness" (as discussed in Chapter 5) refer purely to questions of blood quantum combined with absence of Indian status, I have not capitalized the word.

The Bonnechere Metis and Non-Status Indian Association

Formal representation for non-status Algonquins in the Bonnechere-Petawawa watershed, and increasingly throughout Renfrew County, has been in place since 1973, when Bernadette Bernard of Pikwakanagan lost her Indian status upon marrying Jack Bailey and was forced to leave the reserve. In conjunction with the Ontario Metis and Non-Status Indian Association (OMNSIA), she organized the Bonnechere Metis and Non-Status Indian Association. Its initial membership consisted of about fifty people, most of whom had lost their Indian status as well as their children. However, it soon expanded to include individuals who had never held status and whose traditional territories were in the Bonnechere-Petawawa watershed or who lived in Renfrew County.

According to Richard Zohr, the grandson of Bernadette Bailey, who became involved as a youth of eighteen with the Bonnechere Metis Association (as it subsequently became known), being affiliated as a Metis organization conferred a financial advantage. Certain funding, particularly after the Metis were officially recognized as Aboriginal people in 1982, was available to Metis but not to non-status Indians. In applying for this funding and in attempting to acquire other financing through the Ministry of Housing and other providers, the Bonnechere Metis Association was able to address the dire housing and impoverished circumstances that so many non-status Algonquins experienced in the region at that time.

In 2003, when I interviewed Richard Zohr, he described the Bonnechere Metis Association's success in providing services for non-status Algonquins in Renfrew County. The association had initially concentrated on assisting Algonquins with employment and training, but it later launched an extensive home-building program and constructed about a hundred houses in Renfrew County, particularly in the Pembroke area, where impoverished non-status Algonquins had endured substandard housing for so long. Because of this, it gradually developed a reputation for advocating Native self-empowerment. At its height, the association employed fourteen people, but government cutbacks severely curtailed its activities. It began laying off employees while at the same time initiating lawsuits to challenge the government to re-establish funding programs for Native people.

The Bonnechere Algonquin Community

As news of the land claim began to spread, addressing the Algonquin framework in which the Bonnechere Metis Association had operated became important as this would establish both the Algonquin rights and the location of the traditional hunting territories of its membership. The association therefore renamed itself the Bonnechere Algonquin Community and hired researchers to formally establish the genealogies of the membership.

It's worth noting that, despite the name change, the Bonnechere Metis Association continued to exist as a funding corporation. It could receive funds through the Metis Nation of Canada that were not available to a non-status Algonquin organization such as the BAC, whose funding came from the much more poorly financed Congress of Aboriginal People, which provided funding for non-status and urban Indians. The idea was that the BAC would function as the sociopolitical Algonquin governing body, whereas the Bonnechere Metis Association would control the allocation of funds for services while conducting genealogical research to enable members to establish their identities as Algonquins.

Through genealogical research, the BAC traced most of its ancestors to several main families, which it calls "core families" – the Aird-Partridge, Jocko, Kakwabit, Pappin, Stokwa, Turcotte, and Wajou families. These family histories appeared in the huge genealogical charts that graced the walls of the BAC's Petawawa office at the time of my 2003 interview, which make tangible the membership's rootedness in the area, regardless of whether it receives funding as Metis or as non-status Indians. The community also compiled oral histories of its membership, excerpts of which were printed in a booklet titled *The Bonnechere Algonquin Community History.*[1] In it, the members recounted stories from their grandparents – how they had lived by hunting, trapping, and farming. The oral histories frequently raised issues of classification, as individuals observed that their families had alternately been referred to as "Indian," "half-breed," or even "French" depending on whether they still hunted or had taken up farming. Interviewees also described the attitudes of religious authorities and the racism they faced as off-reserve Algonquins in a context where the presence of the nearby reserve heightened the everyday racism directed at all Native people.

Increasingly, however, as the genealogical work of the BAC wound down, the politics of the land claim gradually displaced the focus on services. Along with Ardoch and the Antoine First Nation in Mattawa, Bonnechere had to launch a court case to insist on its right to be involved in the claim, as Pikwakanagan and the area committees repeatedly denied its presence at the negotiating table. When Bonnechere was finally accepted into the claim in 1999, the community became divided; those who wished to continue the emphasis on services were dismayed by the manner in which the land claim was becoming the leadership's primary focus.

During my 2003 interview with Richard Zohr, who at the time was the chairman of the Bonnechere Algonquin Community, he reflected on the strength of being a community that predated the land claim, one that had a history, a structure, and a track record. He suggested that Ottawa believed that the non-status communities would probably disintegrate without the land claim and that some communities that existed because of it might not survive if it were abandoned. He felt that, with their long history of fighting for rights,

Ardoch and Bonnechere would always prevail, whether the claim existed or not. He did not feel that his job was simply to accept the dictates of Ottawa: if necessary, he would launch a court challenge, or Bonnechere would leave the table as a group. He noted that if the negotiations were to fail, the first step in inaugurating a new claim would be to involve the Algonquins of Quebec. As well, the international community might have to be engaged to apprise the United Nations of the Algonquin situation and to force Canada to take the treaty process seriously.

The Bonnechere Algonquin First Nation and the Land Claim

As involvement in the land claim continued to create pressures at Bonnechere, the community held a referendum in 2003 to vote on changing its name. Led by Zohr, a group of about three hundred formed the Bonnechere Algonquin First Nation (BAFN) and broke off from the BAC. However, a considerable number of people seemed undecided about this change as the BAC continued to exist, with a membership of about a thousand, maintaining its original mandate as a service organization for non-status Algonquins. Thus severed in two, Bonnechere was indisputably weakened in a number of ways.

First, as the chair of the BAC, Richard Zohr had functioned with a council of six people, who were also shareholders in the Bonnechere Metis Association and were responsible for ensuring that the finances were properly managed. The six councillors provided a more solid sense of collective leadership than could be created by one person alone. Moreover, Bonnechere also had an active elders' group, which provided guidance. In terms of governance, Zohr was community spokesperson, but he did not speak alone. Over its thirty years of existence prior to the split, Bonnechere had acquired a solid core of leadership.

When the Bonnechere Algonquin First Nation came into existence, Zohr became its Algonquin Nation Tribal Council (ANTC) chief, and in 2005 he was elected its Algonquin negotiation representative (ANR). As mentioned above, each non-status community sends only one individual, the ANR, to the land claim negotiating table. Community councils are not permitted to join the talks. By comparison, Pikwakanagan is allowed to send its whole council to the table along with its chief.

As discussed early in Chapter 7, this imbalance creates a uniquely undemocratic process for the non-status communities, in that a single person fills all their leadership roles (as well as being sworn to secrecy about the land claim negotiations). The process concentrates power in the hands of these people and insulates and separates them from their communities. For Bonnechere, formerly a large network of individuals with a full leadership structure that had existed for thirty years, to be reduced to three hundred people represented solely by one person constituted a profound diminishment of viability.

The BAFN does have a council of elders to advise the ANR, but under the mandate of the negotiations, its members cannot sit at the negotiation table: they can only advise and the ANR is not obligated to act on their advice. During their 2005 interviews, two BAFN elders remarked somewhat wistfully that they missed the band structure of the BAC, where Zohr's voice spoke in concert with others. They noted that Zohr sometimes disregarded the elders' decisions, prompting the sense that their influence on the land claim was negligible. Both elders were supportive of Zohr; they saw the problem as arising from the structure of the negotiations.

On the other hand, five individuals from the BAC, who were also interviewed in 2005, revealed that the BAC has been wracked with internal problems since the establishment of the BAFN. Some expressed ambivalent attitudes about Zohr's leadership prior to the break, but the reality is that the split represented the loss of a corporate history, of individuals who had stayed with the organization for nearly three decades. This severely destabilized the BAC and helped to produce a power vacuum that sometimes created genuine chaos in governance, a particularly unfortunate development given the large amount of funding administered by the organization. In subsequent stages, the BAC board of directors faced multiple turnovers and changes of mandate. Accusations of power hoarding were not unknown. At other times, attempts were made to rebuild the BAC's structure, but this simply limited its control of its finances and generated further chaos. In some interviews, the more vulnerable board members who had challenged certain proceedings spoke of being arbitrarily removed from the board; others mentioned being ostracized as "radicals"; and still others said that, when they began asking too many questions, they had been offered lucrative paid positions to remove them from the governance structure. They described incidents where decisions were ostensibly made by "elders" whose identities were unknown to the board and where financial records appeared to be deliberately withheld and minutes lost. When some attempted to hold meetings to reassert their authority, they were threatened with charges of trespass. Ultimately, certain members launched court actions against other members.[2] The departure of some three hundred core community members into the BAFN left a legacy of confusion in the BAC that members worked hard to stabilize, all the while attempting to administer significant levels of funding.

In 2006, the Ontario Metis Aboriginal Association, which funded the BAC through the Bonnechere Metis Association, was suspended by the Congress of Aboriginal People for failure to repay a loan of $163,245. On 18 January 2007, the congress board of directors unanimously voted to terminate the membership of the Ontario Metis Aboriginal Association, in accordance with its constitution and bylaws. The programs and services formerly administered by the Aboriginal association were transferred to the Ontario Coalition of Aboriginal Peoples. Because of this, the BAC is now affiliated within the structure of Ontario Friendship Centres and so is also known as the Renfrew County and District Aboriginal Friendship Centre.

In 2003, Richard Zohr had confidently assumed that the land claim would strengthen the community and that even if it were stopped, Bonnechere would survive because of its decades-long track record. However, the claim has significantly debilitated Bonnechere, at least in its organizational capacity, splitting a viable body with a solid history into factions and weakening both sides. An important question is whether the effects of the land claim will not ultimately undo Zohr's confident assertions of 2003.

With this in mind, we turn now to the situation of Greater Golden Lake, the area committee created by Pikwakanagan to replace the BAC at the start of the land claim proceedings when it refused to recognize the BAC at the table.

Algonquins and Nipissings of Greater Golden Lake

Greater Golden Lake has had a tumultuous history. Although the area committees established by Pikwakanagan were to be led by non-status representatives, Greater Golden Lake's chosen leader was Dale Benoit, a status Indian from Pikwakanagan. When Benoit subsequently surrendered her seat before her term ended, Patrick Glassford, whose family was affected by loss of status in complex ways, took charge, a change that prompted considerable opposition from some councillors.

When I interviewed Glassford in 2003, Greater Golden Lake was the largest of the ANTC communities, with nearly two thousand members (which included non-Native spouses). Indeed, Glassford described it as constituting "one-third of the nation." To some extent, he was operating in a vacuum, in that after he assumed power, Greater Golden Lake became almost a super-community, consisting of registered individuals who were distributed over a large region including outside the province or outside the country.

Lynn Gehl, a member of Greater Golden Lake interviewed in 2005, discussed the application of the word "community" to Greater Golden Lake: "I don't know if I'd call Greater Golden Lake a community. The word 'community' is used and the word 'region' is also used when its sole mandate has to do with negotiating a land claim. What I usually say to people is that these are constructed groups that have vast potentiality in terms of nation building, if that's where we're going."

She also explained why Greater Golden Lake became so large:

> There was a split within the Algonquin Nation Tribal Council a few years ago, when a number of representatives from communities walked away. The ANTC was having a lot of problems and Dale Benoit, who was the Greater Golden Lake leader at the time, was one of the representatives who decided to walk away. I was not happy about this and asked her, "What are you doing, leaving? You didn't ask us; you didn't consult your community members." There I was, in Toronto, not knowing why she did it, and in my mind, I'm with that idea of a dichotomy, being "Pikwakanagan versus the non-status." But I don't think it's that anymore – it's far more complicated than status versus non-status. But at that time I thought it was that issue, and there's still a lot of leaders who still play on that issue: "Oh, the problem is the status versus the non-status." And that is how [Patrick Glassford] took over Dale's position and refused to go away. Eventually he began calling himself chief. Indeed, part of this was masterminded.
>
> Now, what happened in the context of the land claim is that the ANTC takes care of the hunt. So in the communities where the representatives walked away from the process (and therefore from the ANTC), their membership came into the Greater Golden Lake office, now located in Killaloe, to get their hunting cards. These people were told, "You have to fill out this form for Greater Golden Lake membership in order to hunt." As a result, a lot of the hunters from many of the other communities signed up with Greater Golden Lake, not because they believed in [Glassford] as a leader but because they wanted to hunt. So what happened is [Glassford] ended up with a larger number of hunters in the community – and a huge community. That was the plan – as I said, it was all crafted. [Glassford] took advantage of the fact that hunting is the only interim benefit that non-status Algonquin people are entitled to. The use of hunting tags was an act used to entrench himself in the process ...

Within Greater Golden Lake, there's a lot of people who are also registered as band members with Pikwakanagan yet who are off-reserve and have no way of being represented as an off-reserve person. I think when Dale Benoit was leader, she was building a large community based on people from the reserve.

In addition to this, there's a lot of identification as Algonquin to your geographic region. Through the enfranchisement process, many Algonquins are now non-status and many still reside in that area. And many of these people, myself included, feel that Golden Lake best describes who they are. As such, a lot of people were choosing Greater Golden Lake. A lot of them are non-status or are off-reserve with status.

Heather Majaury, a member of the Ottawa community who worked at Pikwakanagan during the early days of the land claim, offered further background regarding the relationship between off-reserve Pikwakanagan members and Greater Golden Lake:

After Bill C-31, the *Corbiere* decision protected the rights of the Bill C-31-ers to participate in the politics of their communities even if they didn't live on-reserve[3] ... But after *Corbiere,* Pikwakanagan had an election and passed a rule that the chief would have to be a resident of Pikwakanagan. Okay? The off-reserve could still vote, but they couldn't run for chief. And they also said that to run for a council seat, you had to be a resident of Pikwakanagan. Now when you get into the bigger politics of the land claim ... if you're an off-reserve member of Pikwakanagan, you can't run. You can vote. But think about it. The band council at Pikwakanagan assigned themselves collectively to be the Algonquin negotiation representative. The off-reserve people from Pikwakanagan are not allowed to run for any position at the negotiating table. And that means they're not going to be consulted systematically or properly. There's no real representation for them. They are only allowed to vote.

Now, to make it even more exclusionary, in the last ANR election, off-reserve people were not given ballots unless they called the band council and asked for one. So maybe it's not surprising that if people actually want to be represented, they might want to register as a member of Greater Golden Lake instead.

My 2003 interview with Patrick Glassford demonstrated his sincere belief at the time that the land claim was vital for the future of non-status Algonquins.

During the interview, Glassford advocated what he called "One Algonquin": that there should be no status, no non-status, no Metis – only Algonquin – and that the emphasis on communities potentially detracted from building a nation. His analysis did not appear to include the idea that identity could also be developed and maintained organically through community building, through being part of an active structure that promoted the concerns of people's everyday lives, particularly in relation to the land. Instead, he envisioned that the negotiation of a treaty would validate identities collectively, from above.

Glassford characterized the non-status Algonquins as being the most concerned for knowledge of their identities, as being the thirstiest for traditional knowledge, and therefore pushing to be first "at the well." Indeed, of the four ANTC leaders and three independent community leaders whom I interviewed in 2003, he most clearly articulated the notion that the land claim would give the Algonquin people an identity – it would give them pride, and it would make them feel, finally, that they were truly Algonquins who had a right to the land. He suggested that even the possession of a hunting card that identified its owner as an Algonquin of Greater Golden Lake would validate the sense of identity.

However, Lynn Gehl expressed a different point of view:

> I think non-status Algonquins are disenfranchised in terms of their identity, and it's really unfortunate ... It's almost like the land claims will be ratified just because participating through a vote will validate their identity. I really think the federal and provincial governments are taking advantage of people that have had their identity denied. And now some of us are so desperate to have our identities affirmed, we will sign up to this process and participate in the nonsense of it. This is what I think is happening. They're taking advantage of that neediness for our Algonquin identity.

Glassford clearly brooked no opposition to his strong ideological stance that the land claim would give non-status Algonquins pride in their identities. His assumption seemed to be that, regardless of whether his constituents shared his vision, he had to pursue it for their own good. As he put it, complexity in community structure simply nurtured opposition. Having councils or heads of families would ultimately weaken the nation by diverting the focus to the community rather than the nation. Only those non-status communities that had a single leader were likely to survive. His vision did not admit that of the two processes mutually constituting each other, rebuilding a nation organically might mean working through these issues in the community while also working to build stronger connections between communities. Instead, Glassford advocated the quickest and most direct route – validation through a treaty. Unfortunately, this powerful image of what the claim could accomplish is not borne out by the reality of the comprehensive claims process.

Prompted by a desire to take her place and to move negotiations in a new direction, Lynn Gehl ran for election as Greater Golden Lake's ANR in 2005. Both she and Ray Pappin were defeated by Patrick Glassford in a process that highlights the difficulties and pitfalls encountered since that time by anyone who wishes to replace incumbent ANRs. In a context where every ANR is also an ANTC chief, has the membership lists and a communications budget as a result, and whose actions can be bolstered by other ANTC chiefs who share the same power and who similarly wish to retain their positions, the chances of ousting an incumbent are slim. The ongoing re-election of every incumbent ANR highlights the profoundly undemocratic nature of representation in the land claim negotiations, as each contender to replace existing ANRs is frustrated by built-in impediments.

Despite Glassford's opinion that Greater Golden Lake would be strongest if it were represented by a single person, the community had acquired a council as well as an elders' council by 2005, each of which met monthly. During that year, I interviewed a member of each council to understand how these changes had come about. Both men answered in-depth questions regarding how Greater Golden Lake was developing as a community and the specific issues that were important to it – for example, the effect of its preponderance of hunters – as well as questions of governance. Finally, given Glassford's view that the land claim negotiation should take priority over community building, I asked the two men about the extent to which Greater Golden Lake was becoming a community in the organic sense.

Both described the existence of the council and elders' council as "a thorn in Glassford's side," in that Glassford clearly preferred to concentrate power in his own position and therefore maintain his authority. The elder noted that, initially, Glassford had tended to bring preconceived ideas to the elders' meetings and did not generally listen to them; however, under pressure from the elders' council, he gradually began to heed their advice, although he did not always follow it. The council member observed that convincing Glassford to listen to the council required a long period of persistently challenging his decisions.

The two men differed in their appreciation for hunting. One believed that Algonquins hunted as a primary means of practising a traditional identity, whereas the other felt that too many of them hunted for recreation. However, both agreed that hunting played too large a role in the land claim process, particularly at Greater Golden Lake, where about 500 of its 1,057 Algonquins were actively involved with hunting. They also suggested that disagreement regarding hunting was shattering cohesion *between* Algonquin communities. Because of this, unless it was hunting season, only thirty people attended regular monthly community meetings. In terms of women's involvement, there was only one female elder, and less than 10 percent of those who attended community meetings were women. The fact that most meetings focused almost entirely on hunting issues tended to keep them away. They added that only about 30 percent of the electorate voted in the ANR elections.

The elder's greatest fear regarding Glassford (as with any politician) was that something he would sign would close the door to changes down the road. Knowing that Glassford tended to sign documents without community participation, the elder attempted to facilitate it himself by sometimes disregarding Glassford's wishes and inviting knowledgeable people to speak at council meetings.

Both individuals felt that more emphasis on traditions was needed and that many community members desired this. The elder remarked that the chief's eyes had recently been opened by the results of a mail-out on Native values that had been sent to the membership. Every response indicated that Algonquins had a right to exercise traditions other than hunting and that their heritage needed to be emphasized in the community.

The two men criticized the land claim process. The elder felt that most ANRs were working to reach a consensus between the government and their communities that would enable them to keep their jobs and that they rarely consulted with their communities. The council member was concerned about the negotiators' financial dependency on government loans. He also felt that the ANRs played too many roles at the same time – as ANND representatives, ANTC chiefs, and ANRs. He suggested that if the positions were divided among more people, a more diverse representation would result and communities might enjoy more involvement in the process than they currently had. He added that the tremendous apathy typifying most ANTC communities existed because the membership had no say in decisions and the current leaders held too much power.

When ANR elections were held in 2008, a number of individuals, including one of the individuals I interviewed, ran for the position of Greater Golden Lake ANR in an attempt to unseat Glassford. As with every ANR election since the positions were created, Glassford remained in power, as did all the current ANRs.

Both the elder and the councillor who were interviewed in 2005 spoke with confidence of their ability to make positive changes and clearly desired to do their best to build a good community. By 2009, however, they described a growing atmosphere of intimidation and reported that their experiences of the process had been so negative that they had left the community and wanted no further association with Greater Golden Lake. Indeed, by 2011, they requested that their words be paraphrased, rather than directly quoted, and that their identities remain anonymous. Clearly, at Greater Golden Lake, Patrick Glassford's power remains singular and entrenched.

10

Perspectives from Pikwakanagan

In conclusion, in our deliberations in the development of this submission, we were in many instances led to dwelling on threats and potential threats to the integrity and viability of First Nations and the Assembly of First Nations. Many of these come from our own experience in dealing with such issues as land claims negotiations, Metis, "non-status" people, self-government issues, and Indian Status, etc. ... There is no use in restructuring and renewal based on restructuring if you ignore real and impending threats such as the ones we have raised.

– Kirby Whiteduck, "Pikwakanagan's Presentation to the Assembly of First Nations Renewal Commission"

Like all reserve communities, Pikwakanagan has had to struggle to re-envision its identity and nationhood after their suppression and distortion by religious authorities, Indian agents, and the Indian Act itself. However, in the "total environments" of reserves, where all aspects of community life ricochet against one another, concerns about identity are frequently accompanied by other issues. These may range from struggles for clean water, good housing, or better infrastructure to re-envisioning traditional justice systems, developing traditional health models to counteract the phenomenal spread of diabetes and other diseases in First Nations communities, addressing the legacy of residential schooling, repatriating children lost to the sixties scoop, attempting to reclaim monies from resource use to develop economic viability, and above all, recovering the language and spirituality that can help to create a "blueprint" for genuine decolonization. Although questions of membership and citizenship are included within this framework, they have varying meanings and levels of urgency in different communities. Most of these issues are unique to reserve communities. In this respect, being "Indian" under the Indian Act has highly specific implications.

With this in mind, we should consider that Pikwakanagan's need to rediscover Algonquinness as central to decolonization was quite distinct from the efforts of non-status Algonquins to reclaim Algonquinness in order to recoup a denied identity. For Pikwakanagan, the need to replace Indianness with Algonquinness as part of a decolonization process relates to the manner in which the Indian Act forced it to accept significant controls on what it meant to be Algonquin. Among other things, this entailed accepting the authority of both the church and the Indian agent in daily life (which enforced habits of authoritarianism and passivity), accepting the diminishment of traditional governance patterns and their replacement with an elected chief and council, accepting patrilineal residence patterns and male dominance in marriage, rejecting extended family residences in favour of the nuclear family, and learning to take for granted that Indian status defines who is Indigenous. Of course, these pressures from both church and state were incompletely realized and were constantly resisted by many people at Pikwakanagan. Nevertheless, the fact that an "Indian" identity became the hegemonic means of understanding Indigenous identity in Canada has meant that Pikwakanagan was routinely forced to live in the world as Indian rather than Algonquin. Decolonization thus included not only learning about Algonquinness, but also attempting to deconstruct what Indianness signified.

At the same time, the assumption that hard-and-fast distinctions have always existed between status and non-status Algonquins is perhaps central to the problem that the land claim exemplifies. In actual fact, many people from Pikwakanagan endured a silencing about identity like that experienced by the federally unrecognized Algonquins. For example, during a 2000 interview with the *Kingston Whig-Standard,* Greg Sarazin, former chief negotiator for the Algonquin land claim, stated that he knew little about either Indianness or Algonquinness when he was a child (Hogben 2000d). Although he grew up at Pikwakanagan, he was "well integrated" into Canadian society. He knew he was Indian but had little idea of what that meant and less about being Algonquin. Only through the Native studies program at Trent University in Peterborough did Sarazin acquire an understanding of the histories and issues facing Native people and particularly the Algonquin people.

In other respects, however, because of the very different legal structures and material circumstances between the reserve and the off-reserve communities, the resurgence of Algonquin identity among federally unrecognized Algonquins in some respects disrupted the decolonization efforts that Pikwakanagan had envisioned through the land claim. When the land claim was first initiated, it was primarily focused, with tremendous clarity, on Pikwakanagan obtaining real compensation for past and ongoing resource theft and on claiming Crown lands unequivocally as Algonquin territory. The leaders from Pikwakanagan had very little concern with questions of rebuilding nationhood in that they viewed Pikwakanagan as unequivocally *being* "the Algonquin Nation," at least on the Ontario side of the nation. From that perspective, questions of rebuilding nationhood as a result of the land claim were seen as being part of self-government negotiations relating to a changing relationship with the Indian Act. However, for non-status Algonquins, who for the most part were being recognized for the first time as Algonquin *through* the land claim, rebuilding nationhood was generally viewed as the first and most fundamental step in the negotiations process. The reality is that the divergent visions of decolonization and nation rebuilding that were, and continue to be, generated by non-status Algonquins and the Pikwakanagan leadership represent a far more intractable problem than the question of what level of blood quantum confers Algonquin identity on non-status Algonquins. And yet, both issues intersect on profound levels.

Thus, it is important to consider what the land claim experience has meant for identity in terms of the Pikwakanagan membership. The groundswell of non-status presence, which began in the late 1980s with Pikwakanagan's first outreach to non-status Algonquins and attained massive proportions within a decade, until non-status Algonquins outnumbered Pikwakanagan Algonquins by almost three to one, was an unprecedented development for a close-knit community of about three hundred people who had perceived themselves as the only Algonquins in Ontario and who had assumed that being a status Indian was synonymous with being Algonquin. The ongoing efforts of Pikwakanagan's leadership to control the situation, through a citizenship code based on blood quantum and subsequently through challenging the registration process for non-status Algonquins, were therefore both a genuine intellectual problem and a visceral reaction to the presence of "difference" in experiences of Algonquinness.

On the one hand, the question "In the context of a land claim negotiation, how can we determine and reach consensus regarding who is Algonquin?" was an intellectual struggle. It addressed both the possibilities inherent in a *valid* non-status presence and the difficulties that would ensue if half the Ottawa Valley – including many who identified aggressively as white – were revealed to be of Algonquin descent and therefore eligible to be registered as Algonquin in order to obtain hunting rights. On the other hand, the process created a deep uneasiness among Pikwakanagan's members. Their identities had long been articulated both through and against a repressive body of legislation that sharply controlled who was and who was not an Indian. The influx of so many non-status Algonquins who displayed few of the markers associated with Indianness threatened to collapse this meaning of identity, as the standards that had shaped how Algonquins defined themselves were revealed to be somewhat nebulous. The cut-and-dried criteria of the Indian Act, then, functioned as something concrete that appealed to those whose identities might otherwise be swamped by the huge incursion of non-status Algonquins.

And yet, it is important to emphasize that these differences in meanings and experiences of Algonquinness would not have existed had the reserve never been created. Prior to 1873, all Algonquins in Ontario were simply Algonquins. Only through the establishment of the reserve at Golden Lake and the subsequent denial of land or recognition to off-reserve Algonquins did the categories of "status Indian Algonquin" and "non-status Algonquin" became meaningful. Thus, we will begin with a history of how the Golden Lake reserve was acquired. Paradoxically, although identities at Golden Lake have been created because of this history, they also represent an *organized forgetting* of this history, which was encouraged by church officials and Indian agents and the subsequent isolation and ghettoization that characterize many reserve communities.

History and Identity at Pikwakanagan

The Establishment of the Golden Lake Reserve

In 1834, eight years before Peter Shawinapinessi was petitioning for land in Bedford Township, Chief Ignatius Makwa complained that a trapper named Charles Thomas and his sons had set sixty steel traps on his hunting grounds along the Bonnechere River, which were killing beaver, muskrats, and otters. Makwa mentioned that he intended to settle and farm there (Joan Holmes and Associates 1993, 2:75).

In 1847, while surveying the Bonnechere River, J. McNaughton recorded that the survey party stopped at an Indian camp between the second and third falls below Golden Lake. He mentioned the existence of an Indian settlement at the base of the lake, and he described Makwa's house as being "further up" the river. He also noted the presence of an "Indian winter camp."

Ten years later, in 1857, Makwa sent a petition to E.P. Tache, the commissioner of Crown lands, reporting that the area he had settled and farmed was being surveyed and he was being asked to leave. The petition, which asked for a land grant at Golden Lake, was supported by a Mr. Egan, MPP, who stated that the Algonquins were farming the area and doing well. That same year, surveyor John A. Snow submitted an affidavit verifying that Makwa was an original "settler" who had improved his land (ibid., 144). E.P. Tache forwarded Makwa's petition to the governor-in-council, observing that for several decades a Native community had settled on the Bonnechere River at Golden Lake, now part of the new township of South Algona, and that it had turned from hunting and fishing to farming. Each family was requesting a free grant of 200 acres on the shores of Golden Lake (an amount similar to that granted to white settlers at the time). The petition had been signed by five individuals, who also noted the extent of improvements to the land, on a separate sheet. In communication with the governor-in-council, Tache denied the community's petition for public land as settlers but suggested that it might be purchased with Indian funds so as to be set aside as a reserve (ibid., 145).

A year later, Crown lands agent T.P. French visited the petitioners at Golden Lake and wrote to the superintendent of Indian Affairs, remarking that the Algonquins residing there had stopped going to Lake of Two Mountains eighty years earlier, in 1778. Their settlement consisted of thirty people, with five heads of families speaking for them. They had cleared twenty-five acres and complained that they were no longer receiving their royal presents (Joan Holmes and Associates 1993, 2:148).

In August 1860, Ignatius Makwa petitioned Superintendent of Indian Affairs Richard Pennefather regarding the taxes being charged on his 200-acre lot, which was now part of the newly surveyed Sebastopol Township. Asking that his property be exempted from taxation, he stated that he was incapable of paying the sum and added that Native chiefs were not usually taxed on their land grants. His petition was supported by affidavits from his neighbours, which were dated 1858 (ibid., 149). Makwa petitioned again in 1860, noting that his land was going to be sold. In 1861, the reeve of the United Townships of Wilberforce and Grattan, contiguous to North and South Algona Townships, wrote to Commissioner of Crown Lands Lawrence Vankoughnet in support of Makwa's petition.

In 1864, a memorandum was prepared for the local council of Algona, outlining the improvements completed by Indian "squatters" in the Township of South Algona and recommending that the land they occupied be sold to them at sixpence per acre, payable in five annual installments. This measure was approved by the council. The motion included the following comment: "These people are described by the Surveyor as 'half-bred half-civilized' Indians" (quoted in ibid., 152-53).

In 1866, Deputy Superintendent General of Indian Affairs William Spragge directed a request to Assistant Commissioner of Crown Lands Andrew Russell that certain lands in South Algona Township be permanently set aside for about sixty Native families, with other lands to be earmarked on the same terms. The families had lived in the area for some time, as long as forty years in some cases. The following day, Spragge informed the local chief, Michel Besdoront, that these lands would be set aside (Joan Holmes and Associates 1993, 2:156).

A reserve was therefore created for Algonquin families "resident or near Golden Lake" in September 1873. It consisted of 1,561 acres (only a quarter of the requested territory) in South Algona Township, Renfrew County. The federal government purchased this land from the Province for $156, and letters patent were issued in trust to the Crown (ibid., 160). Next year, the 1874 census listed ninety-seven Algonquins at the reserve, categorizing them according to sex and age but not listing their names. Because the reserve was so small, a number of local families decided not relocate there and thus did not become registered Indians; today, their descendants live around the perimeter of the reserve in the Bonnechere River watershed (Hanson 1986, 46).

In 1875, after the Golden Lake reserve was created, Chief Makwa again petitioned the superintendent of Indian Affairs for a patent to the land he occupied on lot twenty-one in concession thirteen, Sebastopol Township, having resided there for twenty-three years and having cleared fifteen acres. Statements from neighbours were attached (Joan Holmes and Associates 1993, 2:160-61). His patent denied, he was ultimately forced to move to the Golden Lake reserve some time between 1875 and 1880 (Hanson 1986, 46).

In subsequent years, when priests and Indian agents dictated the terms under which the community could live and in return interceded on its behalf with police and local governments, the distinctive and segregated life of a reserve became the norm at Golden Lake, particularly as residents were increasingly concentrated there after the turn of the century. As wards of the state, they were subjected to policies such as residential schooling and gendered laws concerning intermarriage and loss of Indian status. Their forms of government were controlled by the Indian Act. Surrounded by white settlers and incessantly encouraged by church and schooling to "leave Indianness behind," they resisted colonial control, networking primarily with other reserve communities, in grand councils with Maniwaki, Timiskaming, and Oka, and increasingly with the Grand General Indian Council of Ontario (the forerunner to the Union of Ontario Indians).

And yet, it is probable that on an everyday basis, the identities of status and non-status Algonquins began to diverge much more recently – probably with the generalized increase in modernization policies, and eventually in service provisions to on-reserve Indians after the Second World War. We can assume that until the war, non-status and status Algonquins in Ontario faced relatively similar circumstances: both lived in impoverished conditions, both relied on kinship networks (of status and non-status relatives), both struggled to maintain hunting despite ever-shrinking forests and intensive criminalization, both adapted to wage labour in the forest industry, and both gradually lost their language. However, from the post-war era onward, the distinctions around legal status gradually became much more meaningful for reserve residents, whereas a booming economy began to draw some non-status Algonquins away from the tight-knit clusters of families that had covertly maintained their identity. By the 1970s, the breakdown of a cohesive non-status identity became more pronounced as families in some regions pursued job opportunities and began to live apart from one another, whereas in others, alcohol and despair slowly destroyed community ties. In this manner, while pride in a Native identity was beginning to percolate through reserves across Canada, many non-status Algonquins were losing the family cohesiveness that had held non-status identity together for most of the century.

It is perhaps unsurprising that the residents of the Golden Lake reserve, which was subsequently renamed Pikwakanagan ("beautiful rolling green hills of evergreens"), learned increasingly to see themselves as status Indians and to forget about their connections with non-status relatives. At the same time, however, the laws controlling intermarriage, as well as enfranchisement, significantly affected Pikwakanagan. Successive generations of women lost their Indian status and, like their non-status kin, were declared legally non-Indian. The tripling of Pikwakanagan's membership after Bill C-31, from less than four hundred to thirteen hundred within a year, which enabled a generation of Pikwakanagan women and their children to regain their status, constituted the first shock to status Indian identity at the reserve. It was nothing, however, to the shock of discovering that almost five thousand non-status Algonquins were being recognized under the land claim.

Identity at Pikwakanagan

In 2005, I interviewed five Pikwakanagan members. In order to be able to speak freely in the intensely refracted world of a small reserve community, where issues of identity are highly polarizing, most interviewees requested confidentiality. Because of this, their comments will be paraphrased rather than quoted. Four of the individuals I interviewed lived on-reserve, and the fifth lived nearby. One had achieved status with Bill C-31, another was a product of the sixties scoop, and the remaining three, who had never lost their status, had always lived in the community.

The woman who attained status with Bill C-31 is now involved in Algonquin cultural recovery, though after she regained her status, her primary long-time interest was in women who had lost their own status. Gradually, however, as she became accustomed to having status, her ties to her old identity were replaced by the on-reserve histories and cultural referents that were central to her mother's life before she had married out.

Like the sixties scoop adoptee, this woman tended to problematize the Indian Act more than did the other interviewees. And yet, she subscribed to the basic assumption that hard-and-fast differences distinguished "metis" from "Algonquin," based primarily on blood quantum. She asserted that people whose ancestry was more non-Native than Native should consider themselves metis rather than Indian. She did not address the role of gender and Indian status in determining *which* mixed-bloods needed to measure their blood quantum and which could take Indianness for granted. Moreover, her definition of Algonquinness according to blood quantum kept sliding into issues of "culture," with the suggestion that lacking cultural knowledge was an *inevitable* aspect of having lower blood quantum. The idea that "full-blooded" people might have little cultural knowledge, whereas those with lower blood quantum might have been brought up traditionally did not fit into this unquestioned dichotomy.

On the other hand, the sixties scoop adoptee, who had later been repatriated to Pikwakanagan, had been forced to intensely explore what Algonquinness meant, which also caused her to question notions of Indianness more closely. For her, reclaiming an Algonquin identity meant reclaiming knowledge of Algonquin culture and history rather than relying on Indian status as a determinant of Algonquinness. However, because she had regained Indian status only as an adult, she tended to defer to the opinions of lifetime residents of the reserve for whom the Indian card was of prime importance. Although Indian status would never be central to her identity, she was very clear that for those who had always held it, the Indian card was essential to their very identity. For her, "culture" did not correspond to "blood quantum," so she did not regard non-status Algonquins as metis.

The three lifelong residents of Pikwakanagan were strongly critical of the tendency to dichotomize "status Indian" and "metis." Indeed, one challenged the common assumption that non-status Algonquins always had less blood quantum than status Algonquins. In doing so, he pointed out that though mixed-bloodedness had been more prevalent within non-status communities than on the reserve, *both* Pikwakanagan and non-status Algonquins had been strongly affected by the assimilative effects of intermarriage.

Two interviewees addressed the fact that although many non-status Algonquins had genuinely sought to reconnect with their heritage, a number of white-identified people of marginal Algonquin background, some of whom even had anti-Indian biases, desired to be counted as Algonquins solely to obtain hunting rights. One woman spoke about her experiences in working for the land claim, describing her intense feelings of disappointment in encountering people of Algonquin ancestry who were quite racist and yet who wished to be enrolled to acquire hunting rights. On the other hand, she also described her surprise at the numbers of non-status Algonquins who joyfully and even tearfully expressed their thanks for finally being acknowledged as Algonquin.

The other four recalled the days when Pikwakanagan was trying to pass the Algonquin enrolment law. One suggested that definitions of identity should have been arrived at early, not with the intent of excluding non-status people but to take Algonquin values into account and to determine whether minimally blooded individuals who simply wanted hunting rights should be defined as Algonquin. He felt that the current chaos was a result of *not* applying firmer standards earlier on, based on both values and a person's ancestry.

Most interviewees stressed that, for all the differences that exist between the goals, needs, and circumstances of the reserve as a corporate body, the actual lived differences between status and non-status *families* were minimal, particularly in the Bonnechere Valley, where so many non-status Algonquins were the grandchildren of former Pikwakanagan members who had lost their status. One individual pointed out that over two-thirds of the current Pikwakanagan membership had regained status only in 1985 under Bill C-31. Thus, many Pikwakanagan members were only one generation removed from the experience of lacking status. However, those whose Indian status had never been threatened did not easily recognize this.

Most interviewees observed that a number of people at Pikwakanagan retained their negative stereotypes regarding non-status Algonquins, a fact that often prevented them from realizing how much they had in common with their non-status counterparts. Although dismissive attitudes concerning non-status identity claims were no longer at the forefront in the community, a few interviewees remembered the backlash against non-status Algonquins that occurred in 2001, when Pikwakanagan walked away from the negotiation table. At that time, some Pikwakanagan members had disagreed with the rigid stance of the leadership, feeling that nation rebuilding must include *all* Algonquins regardless of whether they held status. However, they had kept silent, as anyone who spoke out in defence of non-status people was attacked and derided as a "metis-lover."

During my 2005 interview with Kirby Whiteduck, he suggested that the meaning of "metis" and "non-status" be clarified in the same manner that the Indian Act provides clarity in defining Indianness. He stated, very simply, that being metis was not the same as being Algonquin and that the land claim needed to delineate these differences.

In the realpolitik environment of the Pikwakanagan leadership, it appears that categories *must* be defined in a hard-and-fast manner. By comparison, most community members whom I interviewed were less concerned for clearly defined classifications than for organic connections. They felt that the identities of both status and non-status Algonquins were in many instances closer in experience than the labels allowed them to be. These individuals saw nation building as important. Whereas Whiteduck believed that nation building, in terms of naming beneficiaries, should wait until the conclusion of the land claim, the other Pikwakanagan interviewees believed that the nation needed rebuilding and that the land claim should not be negotiated until more clarity was achieved.

Two interviewees strongly asserted that, as it stands, the land claim violates Algonquin sovereignty and that the process needs to be rethought, particularly in connection with the involvement of Quebec. Both decried the superficiality of the claim and suggested that there was a strong need to recover traditions and language.

One woman felt that the process was flawed because it included so few women. She had been primarily involved with broader Anishinabe teachings and had conducted women's circles but remarked that few Algonquin women from the reserve joined them. In fact, most participants were Lakota and Mohawk women who had become community members because they married

Pikwakanagan men before 1985. She suggested that meeting with Quebec Algonquins was fundamental even if it meant giving French-language classes so that Ontario Algonquins could communicate with them. She saw a tremendous need to begin a youth movement between Ontario and Quebec Algonquins, status and non-status, as a form of rejuvenating the nation.

One individual with a far-reaching vision felt that the emphasis on the land claim was misplaced and that Pikwakanagan would be best served by a treaty that supplanted the Indian Act. He believed that the matter was urgent because Ottawa had persistently eroded the rights encoded in the Indian Act, using legislation to relentlessly pursue its assimilation agenda. A treaty for Pikwakanagan would be about protecting what it currently had as well as leading to a better future. In fact, this individual suggested opting out of the Indian Act and into an Algonquin Act.

In many respects, then, except for Kirby Whiteduck, most of the Pikwakanagan interviewees were relatively visionary and broad in their scope, somewhat sympathetic to non-status perspectives, and yet presenting a unique vision born of years of living under the Indian Act and an awareness of its implications. By comparison, the leadership was fundamentally pragmatic and concerned that non-status Algonquins lacked the necessary clear-cut definitions of identity.

In 2005, the Pikwakanagan leadership seemed ready to step away from the land claim simply because the process was so flawed, in that Ontario and Ottawa were determined that it should be defined by the comprehensive claims policy, whereas Pikwakanagan felt that a treaty between nations could not be constrained by a unilateral policy developed by one of them. Whiteduck indicated that Pikwakanagan would like to pursue many other initiatives, in terms of acquiring a larger land base, that could not be entered into because all business between itself and the governments had to be addressed through the claim. Indeed, he added that if talks broke off, Pikwakanagan would not be perturbed.

The reality is that Pikwakanagan, as a community, spans two worlds. On the one hand, it is connected organically, through bonds of family, to many of the non-status Algonquins in the Bonnechere Valley and elsewhere throughout the Ottawa River watershed, including Quebec. Particularly at the membership level, it is thus very much part of an Algonquin world, and, viewed organically, its connections need developing in those directions – connections that are hindered by the various legal regimes, both the Indian Act and the interprovincial boundary between Ontario and Quebec, that fracture the

Algonquin homeland. The land claim, from this perspective, is an additional complication, compounding the separation between Ontario and Quebec Algonquins, and maintaining Pikwakanagan in an ongoing adversarial relationship with non-status Algonquins that belies the ties of friendship and common history and that continues to shatter the bonds that once existed between status and non-status.

On the other hand, Pikwakanagan, as a status Indian community, particularly in its administrative capacity (in terms of chief and council and other administrators) sits within a much larger network of status Indian communities, and the bonds between these communities come from a common experience of living under the unique legal regime known as the Indian Act. Over the years, a number of organizations have been built to facilitate this networking. Examples include the provincial territorial organizations for those sharing a common treaty; the tribal councils, which address education, health, justice, policing, and other more local concerns; and finally, the provincial networks of chiefs and the national network of the Assembly of First Nations. These organizations connect Pikwakanagan to over 600 other First Nations – and indeed, the reality is that most of Pikwakanagan's official business and all matters relating to the administration of the community are conducted in concert with other First Nations rather than other Algonquins. Increasingly, this appears to be the direction that the leadership of Pikwakanagan is choosing in order to express its desires for sovereignty. The Union of Ontario Indians, in its capacity as the Anishinabek Nation, has recently undertaken strong moves to address issues of self-governance, control of education, and even citizenship. Because Algonquin peoples are part of a larger Anishinabek people, in many respects this appears to be the direction that the current regime is moving in. Whether this will entail an absolute disconnect from non-status Algonquins remains to be seen.

Indeed, Kirby Whiteduck has warned other First Nations of the problems that may result should they acknowledge their non-status relations without first carefully defining who will be included in the process. In Pikwakanagan's presentation to the Assembly of First Nations Renewal Commission on 26 February 2004, Whiteduck (2004) indicated that even contemplating the recognition of non-status Indians may be fundamentally dangerous for First Nations. Because of the importance of this perspective, I have included a number of paragraphs from his presentation:

> I guess up to this point and for the longest time, the Assembly of First Nations' foundation is First Nations under the Indian Act and Indian Act

Status Indians. While not disagreeing with this concept that we should be determining our own citizens, Pikwakanagan recommends proceeding very carefully on this matter. It is not just a simple matter of saying that it is our right, therefore just go ahead and do it. This is an issue that we must proceed very carefully on because this is, in our view, a case where it would be appropriate for anyone to say "Be careful what you wish for because you might get it."

We believe that there is an impending necessity to expand beyond or outside the parameters of the Indian Act. In some cases, this is more evident and immediate for some First Nations than for others. The atrophying aspects of the membership clauses of the Indian Act lead to increased differentiation between First Nations and this is one of the more impending and looming threats to the existence of the AFN as an organization ...

Our experience there is that we may want to recognize people or descendants of people who are outside of the Indian Act, but just analyze what the results would be if we do that. You try to forecast what the attitude of the people you recognize would be because people's attitudes change once they get some kind of recognition. They get a life of their own, then. "I am, therefore I am, and therefore I can do this, they have now recognized me" – and then you have something that you have to deal with. That's why we say be careful in how you proceed with citizenship, and even with organizations outside the formal First Nations ...

Pikwakanagan has concerns with the addition to the scope of responsibilities of the Minister of Indian Affairs to include "federal interlocutor for Metis and non-status Indians." We do not have so much of a concern with the reference to Metis as there is now some definition and criteria for who is considered to be Metis. We do have a concern with the reference to and inclusion of the term "non-status." In our opinion, it should be removed from the title and responsibilities as there is no reference to non-status in the constitution. Canada's constitution states that the Aboriginal Peoples of Canada include the Indian, Inuit and Metis. Do we have a clear or common idea of who may be considered non-status or even if we accept that category? Does Canada or its provinces have a constitutionally and therefore a legitimately recognized definition of non-status? It is our opinion that we do not and that to refer and address the minister as including responsibility for non-status Indians is to inadvertently recognize them or recognize an undefined category. I guess that goes back to recognizing either directly or indirectly a group of people that is undefined and to find a definition of it ... To recognize a group that is undefined will have its own repercussions. What I am saying

> is that before we recognize somebody, there should be some kind of definition of what it is and who they are.

Far from observing the organic vision of Algonquin identity and nationhood that some Pikwakanagan members espouse, Whiteduck's presentation views any recognition of non-status Indians as a danger to status Indians because there is no firm definition of what a non-status Indian is. It thus embodies the realpolitik vision held by the leadership of some reserves. And indeed, for Native communities at times of great vulnerability, survival has depended on the conservatism of leaders who cautiously evaluate the implications of every move before making it.

What this stance absolutely ignores, however, is that a *real* recognition of non-status Algonquins would not have entailed seeking to control and limit their membership and rights as Pikwakanagan did. Instead, it would have involved accepting non-status Algonquins as having the right that all First Nations demand: to determine their own membership. Had Pikwakanagan taken this position and conducted the necessary oral research to ensure that community recognition was completely addressed, true acknowledgment of non-status individuals as Algonquins would have ensued.

Ultimately, what all Algonquins, status or non-status, experienced with colonization was the desacralization of life and their relationship to the land. No room is made for this in the comprehensive claims policy, which means that observing the sacredness of the land cannot be brought to the negotiating table. Thus, rather than broadening the meaning of Algonquinness, the land claim constantly seeks to narrow it, reducing it to the neat-and-tidy categories to which the Indian Act has always been amenable.

Because of this, Pikwakanagan's current leadership seems unlikely ever to accept a common nationhood with non-status Algonquins until their identity has been defined by strict rules, through blood quantum. On the other hand, the directions advocated by some Pikwakanagan members (as opposed to the leadership) may lean toward a more organic vision, as my interviews demonstrated, or they may grow more polarized, as has taken place in the past. This suggests that non-status Algonquins need to begin thinking, in very clear terms, about forging their own nationhood as Algonquin people and about who should be considered part of that nation. This subject will be discussed more fully in the final chapter.

PART 4

The Upper Madawaska and York River Watersheds

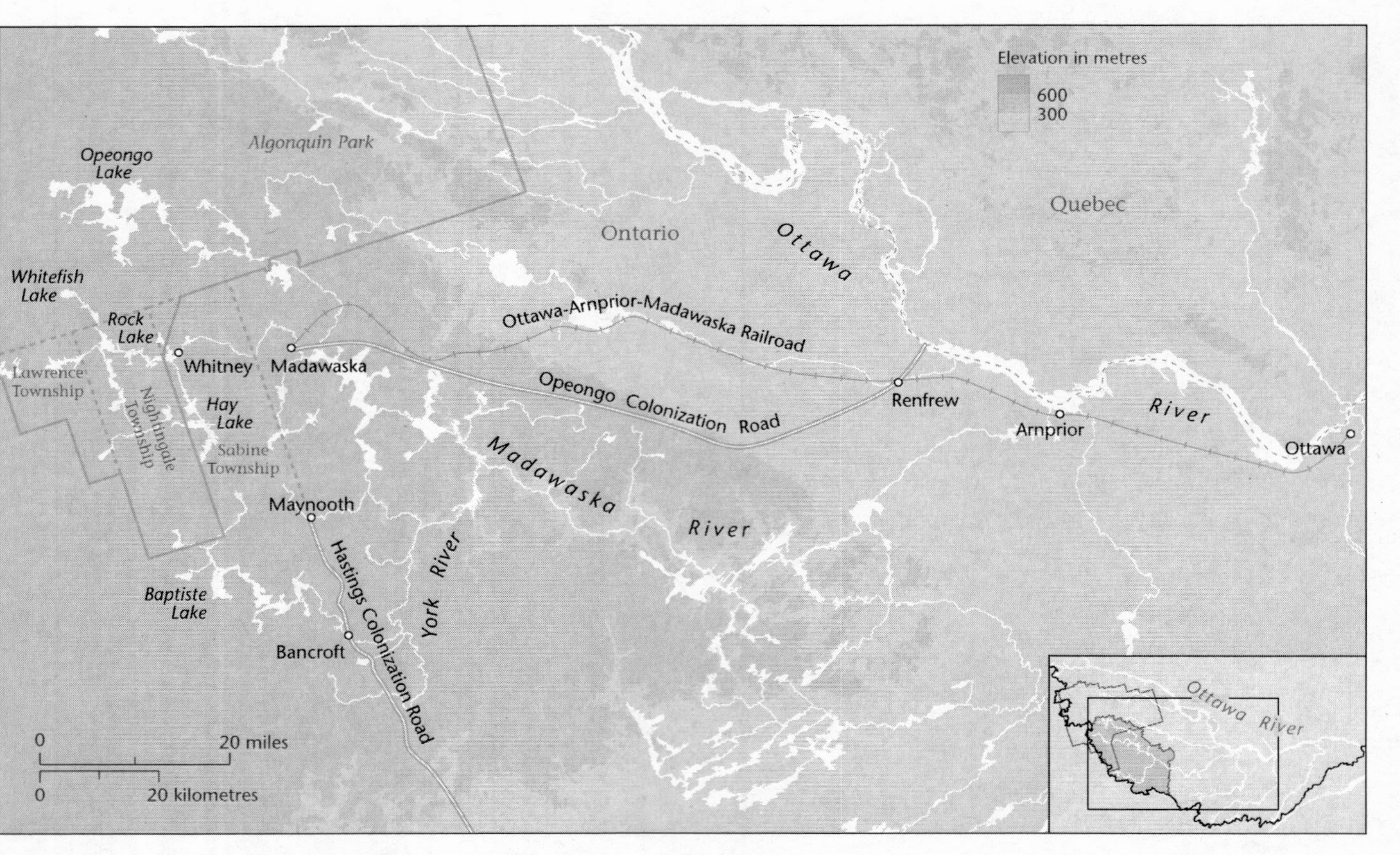

Algonquin communities in the upper Madawaska and York River watersheds

11

Whitney, Madawaska, and Sabine

The upper Madawaska River watershed is home to two groups of communities. At the westernmost edge of Algonquin territory and just to the south of Algonquin Park lie the communities of Whitney, Madawaska, and Sabine. Located further south, on the York River system, lies the historic Algonquin community of Baptiste Lake, whose citizens now form the modern Algonquin community of Bancroft. This chapter will focus on the communities of Whitney, Madawaska, and Sabine, whereas the next chapter will discuss issues facing the Bancroft community.[1]

Like Ardoch, the communities of Whitney, Madawaska, and Sabine have maintained a strong connection to the land; like Ardoch, they too have rejected the land claim, and though a small group formed to represent Whitney at the negotiating table, it did not assert that it spoke for all the Algonquins of the community, as happened with Ardoch. Furthermore, due to the communities' histories and relative isolation at the edge of Algonquin Park, the identities of many Whitney, Madawaska, and Sabine Algonquins do not appear to have been as submerged into settler frameworks as elsewhere. With an economy shaped by tourism and a major provincial park at their doorstep, the people of these three communities have had less need to hide their identities, and as a result, they appear clearer about being unambiguously "Indian."

Land Encroachment along the Madawaska River

The towns of Whitney, Madawaska, and Sabine form an inverted triangle on the southeast edge of Algonquin Park. Whitney borders the park, and

Madawaska lies about twenty kilometres further east. Approximately twenty-five kilometres south is the town of Lake St. Peter, which is near the Algonquin settlement of Sabine. About twenty kilometres south of Sabine is Baptiste Lake, the historic settlement where many Bancroft Algonquins once lived. Related in ancestry and the experience of losing their land, the Algonquins of these communities are descended from the Matouachkarini, who originally lived in the upper Madawaska watershed including areas that are now part of Algonquin Park. Both Algonquin Park and the Bancroft area appear to have been ancient gathering places for the Madawaska River Algonquins.

In the 1830s, when the lands further south had long been overrun by loggers and settlers, the upper Madawaska was still viable and the people lived well, trading for furs with the Hudson's Bay Company and other traders, as their ancestors had done since the first European incursion, and otherwise living unmolested. For a long period, the rugged topography of the upper Madawaska protected its Algonquin inhabitants from incursion by loggers and settlers. The river is relatively short – only 160 miles long – but it descends approximately 1,200 feet from Source Lake in Algonquin Park to Chats Lake, where it joins the Ottawa River. By comparison, the Ottawa itself drops only 1,100 feet in its 700-mile course (Kennedy 1970, 157). From Calabogie Lake a great geographical fault angles northwest across the country, with the result that the land along the Madawaska rises precipitously, about six hundred feet (ibid., 149). Because of this, while other Algonquin territories were being denuded of their beautiful pines, loggers were unable to drive logs down the upper Madawaska. Thus, when the Opeongo Colonization Road was built in 1859, its purpose was as much to facilitate log drives as to attract settlers. The logs were piled on huge carts and taken across country to shallower areas of the river, where they could be floated down to the Ottawa. Until the Opeongo Colonization Road was completed, Algonquins in the upper Madawaska survived relatively intact.

According to elder Jane Chartrand, during my interview with her in 2009, the Algonquin Park sites of Rock Lake and Whitefish Lake were important to the people of the upper Madawaska watershed. In 1939, 1948, and 1962, archaeologists uncovered "prehistoric" tools at Rock Lake (Kidd 1948) as well as petroglyphs and a series of pits and cairns assumed to be involved with vision quests (Noble 1968). At present, because of the sacredness of Rock Lake to the Matouachkarini, only Algonquin elders are allowed to visit it. The ancient gathering place of Whitefish Lake has now become the site of the Madawaska River Algonquin powwow. Chartrand describes this annual event: "It's a traditional powwow. We have a sunrise ceremony right on the lake facing over where our ancestors were and are still. And the women go there and have their circle right on the water, in amongst the trees, the cedar trees. Oh, it is a beautiful, beautiful place! And they call the high bluffs there Centennial Ridges, but my grandmother called it the Home of the Eagles. And the eagles are there, and they always circle our arbour and our grounds when we're having our powwow."

For years, park officials and local settlers have denied the importance of certain park lands to the Madawaska Algonquins and have also denied the extent of the historical Algonquin presence in the park.[2] This has been facilitated by what Patrick Brantlinger (2003) refers to as extinctionist discourse – the assumptions that still permeate many levels of settler societies that Indigenous peoples inevitably "die out" in the face of European presence. This obscures the fact that the diminishment and destruction of Indigenous communities was a deliberate process, brought about by policies of land loss, removal, and denial of basic means of living. To add insult to injury, the survivors of white encroachment, who have been forced to adapt to white society in order to survive, are then dismissed as not being "real Indians," like their ancestors, because they have become too acculturated.

In the case of the Madawaska River Algonquins, the tremendous reduction of their presence in and around Algonquin Park during the last century was effected by a combination of late-nineteenth-century land encroachment and a callous refusal on the part of Ottawa and Ontario to honour their promises to set aside land for the Madawaska Algonquins. The subsequent scattering of individuals to the villages near the park perimeter and further south to traditional lands near Maynooth and Bancroft or to jobs outside the territory follows a common trajectory.

Whitney, Madawaska, and Sabine

With its uplands, bluffs, lakes, and gorges, the Madawaska River is one of the most beautiful in the Ottawa River watershed. Once it was covered with abundant stands of white pine. However, the 1852-59 construction of the Opeongo Colonization Road provided an overland route that enabled timber to be shipped past the turbulent reaches of the river, and so logging the watershed began in earnest during the mid-1850s. In 1854, John A. Snow began surveying the Madawaska watershed into townships, concessions, and lots in preparation for settlement.

The Opeongo Line, as the colonization road was frequently called, began at Farrell's Landing, about two miles west of the mouth of the Bonnechere

River, ran to Renfrew, and then followed a course midway between the Bonnechere and Madawaska Rivers until it reached the Madawaska at Barry's Bay, on Lake Kamaniskeg (Kennedy 1970, 139-41). Intended as a wagon road to enable settlers to transport supplies, it frequently required repair during its construction due to the huge loads of timber that were dragged along it by horse sledge in winter and wagon in summer. By 1859, a branch of the Opeongo joined the Hastings Colonization Road, built from Madoc to Bancroft in 1864, which brought squatters and settlers into the area. By 1867, the seventy-eight-mile Opeongo would reach the present-day site of Madawaska, near Whitney. And from 1863 onward, surveyors moved north, followed by loggers, squatters, and settlers.

Because of this, in 1863, a petition by 8 Madawaska River chiefs and over 250 individuals whose territories spanned the Madawaska River system was sent to Governor General Charles Viscount Monk in 1863, requesting title to land at the Madawaska headwaters. The petitioners stated that their hunting territories were being ruined by logging and that they could no longer sustain their families. They therefore asked that 4,000 acres of land in Lawrence Township, adjoining Ayre Township, be set aside for approximately four hundred families. Lumber merchants had even agreed to erect a church for them and to observe their rights, should they settle there. The petition was forwarded to Indian Affairs by Robert Bell, the local MPP, who, as provincial surveyor, had surveyed the Opeongo Line (Joan Holmes and Associates 1993, 2:142).

Despite the petition, squatters and settlers followed hard on the heels of the lumbermen. In July 1866, after Indian Affairs failed to induce the Madawaska Algonquins to move to Maniwaki, Assistant Commissioner of Crown Lands Andrew Russell advised James Bangs, the Indian agent at Arnprior, that the commissioner had reserved the southeast quarter of Lawrence Township for an Algonquin settlement. The Algonquins were not to have the rights of merchantable timber and were not to stop lumbermen from cutting and carrying it off. Indian funds would be used to purchase the site at twenty cents an acre, and it was to be surveyed into 100-acre lots for each family (ibid., 54-55, 143-44).

Two years later, the Algonquins were still waiting for surveying to begin. Pon Sogmogneche, a high chief of the Algonquin and Nipissing Indians, addressed an inquiry to the commissioner of Crown lands in 1868, asking when surveying would commence. He requested that a document be drawn up as soon as possible to make it clear that the Algonquins could live in Lawrence Township without molestation and that the southeast quarter would be set aside for their use. The commissioner replied that there were no funds to subdivide the township, but if the Indians hired a surveyor themselves, he would consider setting the land aside. Ten years later, in 1878, when Nightingale Township was surveyed, the surveyors noted two "Indian clearings" in addition to the settlements in Lawrence Township (ibid., 203).

In the second half of the nineteenth century, the production of squared timber for British shipbuilding was gradually being succeeded by sawn lumber for the American market, which was more lucrative. In a way, this was better for the forests. Squaring timber was extremely wasteful because 30 percent of each squared tree was discarded, and the entire tree was often left to rot if it had too many knots. The technique used only the best trees and created huge amounts of debris, which affected vegetation and wildlife, and significantly increased the risk of forest fire. Debris that washed into the rivers, along with the bark of thousands of felled trees and logs abandoned in transportation, decomposed in the water and carved holes in the riverbanks, causing erosion that destroyed the spawning grounds of many species of fish. Indeed, many squatters who followed the loggers drew their entire winter's wood supply from the remnants floating in the river (Ottawa River Heritage Designation Committee 2005b, 92, 103).

But the trade in sawn lumber had two additional effects – it produced an industrial boom for settlers, as local sawmills had to be constructed and these in turn often required the damming of rapids and falls to generate the necessary hydroelectric power. But more devastatingly, it created the railroads that facilitated the settlement of Algonquin lands.

Between 1881 and 1883, seeking a quick route to US markets for the products of his mills, J.R. Booth built the Canada Atlantic Railway, which ran from Ottawa through Coteau Landing on the north shore of the St. Lawrence to the Canada-US border on Lake Champlain in Quebec, where his shipments could link with US railroads. Booth then turned his attention to connecting his vast holdings in eastern Ontario to the Canada Atlantic Railway. By 1888, he had incorporated two railroads – the Ottawa, Arnprior and Renfrew Railway Company, and the Ottawa and Parry Sound Railway Company – as well as two local lines, the Whitney and Opeongo Railway and the Egan Estates Junction Railway. Particularly between Madawaska and Whitney, this network of railways fed the white pines of the Madawaska watershed directly to the American markets (Kennedy 1970, 171-73).[3]

By 1886, the Algonquins in Lawrence and Nightingale Townships had been waiting twenty years for the land supposedly earmarked for them to be surveyed. Chief Nogonnaksukway continued petitioning for the land, stressing that the situation was urgent because the Algonquins were not recognized as a band and therefore did not receive benefits that would help them remain in the territory as a cohesive community. At that point, Indian Affairs once again began asserting that the Madawaska Algonquins should move to Maniwaki, hundreds of miles away (Joan Holmes and Associates 1993, 2:169-70).

Three pieces of Indian Affairs correspondence from February 1888 discuss another petition from the Lawrence Township Algonquins. Most of the four hundred families that had requested land in 1863 had dispersed, seeking survival in any way possible, as squatters moved into their territory. Only thirty families, or 150 people, remained in the settlement. Since the land in Lawrence Township was being logged and hunting was very poor, they requested that an alternative site be set aside for them near a market town, such as Maynooth, where some Algonquins were already settling. At this point, Indian Affairs recommended an investigation of their circumstances (ibid., 170).

Because logging was swiftly denuding entire townships, plans were made to create a forest and game reserve in the region. Five years later, in 1893, Algonquin Park was established. Although Lawrence and Nightingale Townships were not yet included within its boundaries, Peter Sharbot, who now represented the Lawrence Township families, requested that land be set aside elsewhere for them. He stated that the community had occupied the Lawrence Township land for forty-five years. However, Canada's long delay in responding to the community's needs had borne fruit. Faced with ongoing pressure from loggers and squatters, and uncertain whether they could keep their land, only forty-six Algonquins now remained of the initial four hundred families in the settlement.

Under pressure from the superintendent of Algonquin Park, it was decided that allowing Algonquins to settle so near the park, where they would surely hunt, would be "dangerous." The Lawrence Township Algonquins as well as thirty-two remaining in Nightingale Township, who had cleared land and established farms there forty-five years earlier, were told that they must move to Golden Lake, since they had no rights to the land they had cleared. Chief Peter Sharbot then suggested an alternative site at Hay Lake in Sabine Township. Indian Agent Bennett advised them to get the consent of the Algonquin Park chief ranger to settle in Sabine, although Sharbot replied that since the land was not in the park, the chief ranger's consent was surely irrelevant. Sharbot told the Indian agent that four families were already in Sabine Township and that others in the area would join them to make ten families if part of Sabine were set aside for a reserve. He noted that the proposed site was fifteen kilometres from the railroad, that the nearest white town was seven or eight miles away, that the land was arable and drained into Hay Lake, and that with 1,500 acres the community would be self-supporting as farmers. However, the Sabine Township land was included in a timber licence, so the government made no effort to obtain it. At the same time, Algonquin Park was being enlarged to include Lawrence and Nightingale Townships (Joan Holmes and Associates 1993, 2:173-76).

In 1899, an Indian Affairs report indicated that as the Province objected to the settlement of the Algonquins near the park, or in any township that might be thrown open for logging and subsequent settlement, their petitions were to be denied. Although land had long been promised to the Madawaska Algonquins, fifty years of logging, settler encroachment, and government inaction had repeatedly uprooted the hundreds of families who had built settlements in Ayre, Lawrence, Nightingale, and Sabine Townships, until their numbers had dwindled to a few handfuls of people who were now deemed "stragglers from other bands" connected to those from Golden Lake and Maniwaki. It was finally suggested that they join the Mohawks from Lake of Two Mountains, who had themselves been relocated to Wahta, a barren stretch of land at Gibson (ibid., 215).

Algonquins have their own stories about this history of dispossession. Below, elder Jane Chartrand, interviewed in 2009, recalled her grandmother's experience:

> I get so upset about these tourist brochures! They keep saying that there was "a smattering" of Algonquin people in the park. They called the place Algonquin Park for a reason – because the Algonquin people were there! And they never really did a study of how many people were there. But my grandma was very tiny, just a little girl, when she used to travel back up there with her parents. Her parents were part of the people who came out of Algonquin Park and settled in this area. They were Jack and Philomene Lavalley. She remembers as a little girl, going back up there in the canoes, and she said when they'd get to Rock Lake, they'd have such a feast! She had another name for it, though – what it was called by them, before it was called Rock Lake. She said your belly would just be sore from eating, and the men would go and do their men business, and she said her dad was always doing that. So they were there.
>
> Then they found that the archaeologists had gone in there and did a study. There are petroglyphs there, and we know where they are. And there have been some graves disturbed, but we found out about it too late. So the remains of some of our ancestors are scattered somewhere, where they filled in here

or filled in there. We don't know. But we do ceremonies for those ancestors when we come to the powwow.

Chartrand's own childhood experience reflected ongoing efforts to continue hunting in the park:

> Ayre Township was right next to Algonquin Park, so when they took the people out of Algonquin Park and said, "You're going to Golden Lake, take it or leave it," a lot went but the majority didn't go. So we have continuity with the land through our ancestry. And then when they took over the land, the Algonquin Park officials were saying, "Oh, no. Indians are too close to the park. They're poaching. They're doing this. They're doing that." Meanwhile, those poor people were just trying to eke out their living as they had always done. So they took over Ayre Township and Clyde-Bruton Township. And then they took over Lawrence and Nightingale Townships, too – all places where our people were living. So a lot of our people just spread out over the land, in Madawaska, Whitney, and Sabine ... places quite close to Algonquin Park.
>
> As a young girl, I used to go in with my dad to hunt, to trap – to poach – in the park. At Basin Depot, we'd go in. There was an old root house there, eh? An old place that was dug into the hill, and that's where an old logging camp was and where they kept their meat and their milk and everything. So my dad and I used to stay in there, and it's a good thing I was never afraid of spiders because it was all cobwebbed and the odd thing would look out a hole at you. But we used to go back there. The people still did what they did to earn a living; it was their way of life. But they had to go underground.
>
> If I were one of those white people, I'd be ashamed of myself. Because there are real old men, who, when they were trying to hunt, the Ministry of Natural Resources would take their rifle or they'd take their snowshoes. You know, they would do everything so they couldn't go in there. But meanwhile, they probably had a pair hid somewhere back in an old crevice in the rock or something. But that's what happened. They made it so hard. But our people stayed there. And that land is so important to me because my ancestors went up that river, because my ancestors were in that park. I can feel the pull of them when I go into the park, at Whitefish Lake, where the powwow is.

Chartrand's family stories also describe the ongoing assault on the land that occurred after people were forced out of the park, when their small settlements were devastated by forestry:

And then J.R. Booth came in ... He was a lumber baron and they had these people come in, the surveyors, and they saw the people living in Ayre Township, I think it was, and Lawrence and Nightingale – they had their wickiups. They didn't need a big home to live in like the Europeans.

So the surveyors who saw them said, "Well, it isn't fit for any white kind of people to live here because you've got Indians living in squalor in the bush with a pack of kids and ..." This is how we were described. When I read that, I get very angry. But they were ignorant. Not by choice, I guess, but they were ignorant. Indian people had no value to Europeans. So that's how we were looked at.

But what they said was ... that the Indians could stay there but they couldn't have the timber. They couldn't have the timber rights. Indians didn't cut logs. They didn't need them, so therefore they left the Standing People, as we called trees, alone, and that's what we always called ourselves as well – the Standing People. Back then, we knew that the trees purified the air. Pine, you can get your vitamin C from it. The trees were meant to be lived amongst. It broke the people's hearts when this J.R. Booth came and cut all the white pine. And my mom remembers, when she was about seven, Madawaska was a booming town because of the big pines they were taking out to build masts for the ships for the war.

My grandmother said, as a little girl, she'd watch and she could hear the click, clock, click, clock of the big flatcars going by, and she has pictures of those pines. Someone took a picture of the pine that was being loaded on these flatcars. And she said she'd count these three old puffing steam engines, eh, hauling about thirty cars, because that's all they could carry, and in those days that was a lot. All piled with white pine. J.R. Booth raped the white pine. We have a stand of pine in the interior of the park, and they're white pine and those are the grandfathers. They're the only ones left ...

This was a terrible injustice done to that town. And the more they would cut ... It's just like an animal, you cut into its space, it's still going to come to you but not in the numbers, and it'll adjust itself. So this is what happened and the Native people ... after that a lot went to the States ... They couldn't trap, couldn't hunt, there were no jobs available, and the land was becoming unlivable.

So then there was an influx of other people as settlers. There are places in Whitney that were given to homesteaders, 150 acres of Algonquin land! Land was *given* to them and there's one instance where the person sold it for a quarter million dollars. His family sold it to this other fellow who is in the process of losing it now, I think. There [was] a lot of backroom dealing going. The land was never ceded, and yet it was sold.

This history is tangible in the experiences of contemporary Algonquins in Madawaska, Sabine, and Whitney, as Chartrand, a head of family in the community, described:

> Today, in the three communities, I'd say we have six hundred to seven hundred Algonquin people, because most of them live off the reserve. There are dozens of people from these communities who live in Kitchener because that was the place to go for work – Kitchener, at Schneider's and all those places. So a lot of them, when they got out of school, they went there.
>
> But a few of them – like my brother and his son, and my partner and his son, they're working in the forestry industry ... It's something that came into place here about twenty years ago. They call themselves the Algonquin Forestry Authority. And the Native people who work with them work in accordance to their guidelines. So they'll go in and they'll mark a bunch of trees, and they'll say, "These have to go; this one's diseased" in order to make way for the new growth ...
>
> This is the best thing that's ever happened to Algonquin Park ... They have people from the rainforest who've come in here to see and to study this, and they say that this is the best-managed forest they have ever seen. It should be a model for the world.
>
> The Algonquin Forestry Authority works with plans and they'll develop a plan for ten years, and then when that plan is done, then they do another plan, for another ten years. And that tells you what volume of wood has to be cut and what areas have to be managed.
>
> They now have the Whitney Algonquin Aboriginal Loggers Association. I think there are twelve Algonquin men in it now, twelve loggers. Now, people are saying in the little villages, "Oh, them goddamn Indians. They get everything, you know." But take five hundred years of shit and abuse, then maybe you'll get a little break, at the end of it, in your own community.

The Communities and the Land Claim

The communities of Whitney, Madawaska, and Sabine represent the remnants of the upper Madawaska River people, those who had not been scattered when they were forced out of Algonquin Park. Although they had always had informal leaders, when the Ontario Metis and Non-Status Indian Association

(OMNSIA) approached them about organizing, they formed a group in Whitney – the Algonquin, Metis, and Non-Status Indian Association. According to Bob Lavalley, the Whitney association was one of the strongest in Ontario. Through OMNSIA, it managed to develop funding sources that made it relatively independent and highly successful for a number of years. However, as government guidelines increasingly controlled its ability to offer services, the organization became less effective.

When the land claim was instituted, Whitney, Madawaska, and Sabine were not invited to participate, and Bob Lavalley had to step forward and demand a place at the table for the communities. He had been involved in Native activism since the 1969 resistance to the White Paper and had worked for years with the Whitney Algonquin, Metis, and Non-Status Indian Association. As a result, he had acquired significant experience and was accustomed to dealing with governments. Lavalley had strong views on how the land claim should proceed. He suggested that, in order to build a nation, the leaders needed to clarify and pursue their own goals. Second, he noted that since authentic moves toward nationhood were impossible as long as government controlled the monies, the negotiators must initially arrive at a basic formula for compensation for resource use. With the resulting independent access to funds, Algonquins would be in a much better position for organizing.

At present, the communities that Bob calls "Whimasab" – for Whitney, Madawaska, and Sabine – are not represented at the land claim. When Pikwakanagan first began the break with the non-status communities, Whimasab walked away from the table. It subsequently refused to get involved with the Algonquin negotiation representative (ANR) system that was put in place when talks recommenced in 2004. On the other hand, an independent group of individuals from Whitney, primarily from one family, elected an ANR who now sits at the land claim table, representing Whitney alone. Whitney is therefore divided into two – the group at the land claim table and the rest, which organize with Madawaska and Sabine as Whimasab and no longer wish to be involved in the claim.[4]

The divisions created by the land claim also play out in hunting practices at Whitney. In her 2009 interview, Jane Chartrand explained the problems produced by differences between the tag system, which entitles the land claim families to hunt, and the traditional approach to hunting:

> Here's one of the big issues. When the ANR from Whitney gets those moose tags, you know there are certain people in Whitney that put in for them. Nobody from Madawaska puts in for them, but certain people from Whitney do.

> The Algonquin negotiation representative says that he's only supposed to be representing Whitney. But it's mostly all his family, and then there's people from Whitney that go to Golden Lake and go in that draw. Because they have Indian status.[5]
>
> You're supposed to hunt the traditional way. You go in with your family, regardless of tags or rules. We practise moose conservation ... People don't kill a cow because that's a producer. You go for what you need, and you share what you get.

Bob Lavalley is highly critical of the fact that so much of the land claim revolves around hunting and asserts that it should never have been put on the table, because an Aboriginal right to harvest is non-negotiable. On the other hand, particularly given the extent of corporate resource use in Algonquin territory, conservation should have been central to negotiations. Looking at the big picture, Lavalley believes that Whimasab should struggle for a land base of its own and should serve its own needs rather than following priorities that benefit Pikwakanagan. He suggests that, as long as they lack a land base and economic benefits, communities that lie outside federal or provincial control will remain marginalized. For Whimasab, then, a long-term goal is to resume the struggle for a community land base – the same struggle that so intensely occupied its leadership from the 1850s to 1899.

12

The People of Kijicho Manitou: Baptiste Lake and Bancroft

Although the geography of the upper Madawaska protected the Algonquins living around Algonquin Park from extensive logging until the 1860s, such was not the case for those whose territories extended down the York River, a tributary of the Madawaska. They faced encroachment much earlier, and by the 1840s, parts of their territory were already becoming unviable as lumbermen ceaselessly stripped the region of its white pine.

The Nipissing grand chief Jean Baptiste Kijicho Manitou was the first to establish a permanent Algonquin settlement at Baptiste Lake, the lake that the Algonquins called Kijicho Manitou, or "gentle spirit." In 1853, seeking to explore the unsurveyed country between Georgian Bay and the Ottawa River, Alexander Murray entered the Madawaska River at Lake Kamaniskiak and then proceeded to its southwest branch, the York River. Near Lake Papineau and the present-day town of Purdy, he met a leader whose name he recorded as "Kaijick Manitou," who told him that his people lived around the lake they had named after him and that lumbering operations had almost reached it (Joan Holmes and Associates 1993, 2:143).

The Bancroft Algonquins, the Anishinabe Baptiste Community Organization, refer to themselves as the people of the Algonquin Nation Kijicho Manitou. Although mining and settler incursion destroyed many signs of their early presence, archaeological evidence has revealed that Kijicho Manitou Lake was an ancient gathering place and an important spiritual area for Algonquins. A recent discovery of stone mounds, used in spiritual ceremonies, has highlighted this. Moreover, during my 2007 interview with him, Robin Tinney, a businessman who grew up in Bancroft and now lives in Toronto, recounted stories he heard from his great-uncles about stone "nests" in trees: "I can remember stories from my great-uncles; they were loggers working in the bush, and they would find stones, up in the middle of huge trees, nests of stones. Having never seen them because they cut the trees down, you don't know whether they were burial platforms or what they were." Through Ministry of Natural Resources funding, Tinney is attempting to map some of the known sacred sites and to have them designated as Native land use, either archaeologically or historically, under the land claim. This work is vital because so much of the Algonquin historical presence at Bancroft has been obscured or destroyed. However, in nearby places such as Maynooth, the extreme longevity of Algonquin presence is revealed by the existence of a number of "kettles" or "pot holes," sites where grains and seeds were ground, where years of use have worn holes in the bedrock.

Further evidence of ancient Algonquin presence may still exist, but as Tinney suggests, landowners may be reluctant to report it:

> Because so much of the land is private land, a lot of owners just don't want to say, "Well you know there's carvings on walls." If there's a lot in the way of markings, I'm not aware of it. But that's another thing that we want to do, is to encourage people in the Bancroft area, that if they know about these things, to let us know. I suspect a great fear is going to be, "Well they're going to try and claim my land." But there's ample evidence of it being around in long-term use. A lot of people up there [at Baptiste Lake] always found arrowheads, all that kind of thing.

For Bancroft Algonquins, however, silencing constituted a more profound erasure than the loss of ancient artifacts. Overwhelmed by settlers, forced into the wage economy, and pressured to keep silent about their identities, they survived at the cost of not passing on their extensive knowledge of Algonquin culture and history.

Jean Baptiste Kijicho Manitou's son, John Baptiste Dufond, was born at the Baptiste Lake settlement in 1842. Leader of the Bear Clan, he spent his life in the area. His generation was the last to live by hunting and trapping, and during that time they still travelled up the York in the summer to meet with other Madawaska Algonquins and share their ceremonies, as well as to harvest and gather food in the territories on the west side of Algonquin Park.

However, in 1854, work was begun on the Hastings Colonization Road, which ran from Bancroft to Madoc along the route of what is now Highway 62, to attract settlers to the region. Between 1858 and 1872, the government began offering 100 acres of free land along this road to settlers, provided they cleared 3 acres and constructed a house. Irish families fleeing the potato famine took advantage of the offer as did American emigrants seeking land. Most cleared their properties while working as loggers for the many logging companies in the region, including Rathburn, J.R. Booth, and Bronson and Weston. All too often the York River was clogged with logs as loggers and settlers spread throughout the territory.

In an attempt to protect his people's settlement at Baptiste Lake, John Baptiste Dufond developed a policy of being extremely obliging to the newcomers. He worked as a guide for the surveyors who sought out new stands of timber and other resources, and he and his wife, Madeline Benoit Dufond, supplied loggers with food, services, and medicines. When settlers began coming in, the couple also provided them with invaluable assistance (Fell 2008, 1). By the time the government was attempting to move the Baptiste Lake Algonquins to Golden Lake, Dufond had proved so valuable to local authorities and settlers that when 100-acre lots at Baptiste Lake were being given away to settlers, Algonquins were able to obtain fee simple title to certain tracts of land (ibid., 2).

Indeed, the Algonquins at Baptiste Lake are probably the last Native people who managed to obtain fee simple grants to parts of their former territory. In 1864, the assistant commissioner of Crown lands sent a letter to T.P. French, the local Crown lands agent, advising him that Indians were to be legally barred from obtaining fee simple grants (Joan Holmes and Associates 1993, 5:19); only European settlers were to be afforded that privilege. Clearly, the settler government would not allow Native people to independently adapt to settler society as landed individuals. From that point onward, the only two options left for Native people were to be on a reserve, under the legal controls of the Department of Indian Affairs, or to be landless and destitute, and therefore outside of the settler society without being legally recognized as Indians.

The Baptiste Lake Algonquins may have held fee simple title to their lands, but logging continued to affect them. In 1866, with the intent of shortening the log drives to the Ottawa market, the Bronson and Weston Company built a dam near the York River, flooding Baptiste Lake in order to connect its upper and lower basins (Fell 2008, 1). Although some of the Algonquins living there may have been flooded out, a number of Algonquin families stayed in the area after the flooding, including the Bernards, the Hunters, and the Yatemans (ibid., 2).

From the 1880s to 1920, as lumber operations gradually declined in key areas, mining provided an important additional source of income for settlers (Kennedy 1970, 170, 173). It brought more settlers to work in the mines and had a significant impact on the land, removing many signs of ancient Algonquin occupation. Iron was first discovered in 1882 and was mined in at least three sites until a profitable deposit was found in 1900, which was worked intensively until 1912, when the last iron mine closed (Reynolds 1979, 184). Sporadic and largely unsuccessful exploration for gold has taken place in the area, and copper deposits were found, although most were too small and too poor to mine (ibid., 186-87).

By the time the iron ore was becoming tapped out, extremely high-quality marble had been discovered in the area. Large slabs of Bancroft marble were used to construct the floors and walls of the Parliament Buildings in Ottawa and Queen's Park in Toronto, and as supports for the pillars of the Royal Ontario Museum, in addition to hundreds of other buildings. When the marble quarries eventually became depleted, uranium took over, although the last marble quarries closed only in 1977 (ibid., 189-91). Uranium was first discovered in the area in 1922, but deposits large enough for mining were not found until the 1950s, and most of these produced between 1956 and the late 1960s (ibid., 192-93).

As most of this mining was located in the Bancroft and outlying districts, it did not greatly intrude into Algonquin settlement areas. Although a European village had gradually surrounded the Algonquin settlement at Baptiste Lake, particularly when the Bancroft railroad was extended to the community, it remained relatively remote and quiet until the 1930s when a number of exclusive tourist resorts were developed for the wealthy. Furthermore, with the advent of the railroad, new US markets for sawn lumber became easily accessible. Pines that had not been large enough for the squared timber trade or were previously inaccessible were now cut, and barges towed the logs down the lake to newly built lumber mills (Fell 2008, 2).

John Baptiste Dufond's son, Sam, who built his own canoes and worked as a fishing guide and hunter for the new cottagers, is highly regarded by settlers in the area (ibid.). According to their accounts, he sold most of his family's land. Robin Tinney, however, gives the Algonquin version of this history, as the community faced increasingly hard times. Squeezed from all sides by encroaching settlers, loggers, and miners, and unable to pay the taxes on fee simple lands, individuals began to lose the land to settlers, often in exchange for food to prevent starvation. As Tinney put it, "What ended up happening with Chief Baptiste is that he slowly ended up giving up land. He traded it for beef or whatever he happened to need and eventually he had none left." Most of the Algonquins around Baptiste Lake appear to have lost their land at this time. Today, the beautiful land around Kijicho Manitou Lake, formerly owned by Algonquins, is some of the most expensive real estate in the Bancroft area.

Unlike in Whitney, Madawaska, and Sabine, where logging was not followed by the establishment of an industrial economy and where Algonquins attempted to survive as tourist guides in Algonquin Park and by hunting within its borders, the Baptiste Lake Algonquins faced waves of resource industries and other development, as settlers were followed by sawmills, a local furniture-making industry, and finally, mining. With almost no means of surviving on the land, the Bancroft Algonquins were forced into the wage economy and therefore into compliance with European norms. Robin Tinney explained how this affected Algonquin family dynamics, as Christianity and intermarriage began to change attitudes toward the value of children: "The history is that back then, there were all kinds of quietly kept secrets about various illegitimate children. I know through my grandmother, she was an illegitimate child, and so her brothers and sisters, her half-brothers and half-sisters, I never ever met them. They'd pretty much disowned her, which is sort of sad but typical of the day, quite honestly. So for us, where our line originates is that one of Chief Baptiste's sons was my grandmother's father."

Moreover, as the Algonquins struggled to survive in the wage economy, silencing of identity became the norm, in a context where being identified as Indian was a significant liability and where being Native inevitably meant being poor and marginalized. Those who evidenced pride in being Native also risked consequences. Robin Tinney recalled the subtle and not-so-subtle pressures to be silent about Indianness as he was growing up in the 1970s:

> I remember going to my aunt's once, before I started to think about the negative associations of being Indian. I had a headband on and probably, likely, my leather vest that I liked to wear. It was all Native stuff. And my brother and I were out there with knives, whittling; we were very into that then. The kids next door totally freaked out! And we weren't even aware of it. We didn't know, we'd never met the kids before. We'd sort of talked across the fence to them briefly and then went about our business, and then we left. And after we left, the next-door neighbour's kids were throwing stones through my aunt's window! Because we were Native! "There were Indians over there and they had knives and we were scared!" As a kid, I felt absolutely horrible that my

> aunt would have to deal with that, with her next-door neighbour. You sort of wake up at that point and start thinking, "Wow, you've got to be sort of cautious about where you let this out."

Tinney added that, in terms of re-empowerment as Algonquins, the Bancroft community still struggles with this history of silence – and with the costs of not remaining silent.

Like many towns founded on resource development, Bancroft can expect to decline significantly once the resources are exhausted, leaving little employment and a tiny tax base to maintain public services such as education. Unable to make a living in an area with little economic future, its young people are increasingly obliged to seek work in urban centres elsewhere. Tinney noted that between three and four hundred Algonquins live in Bancroft, representing about six extended families. Even so, attendance at Algonquin community meetings is a problem, in part because some families still feel the stigma of openly identifying as Algonquin. Others who may not share this reticence are nevertheless losing their children to the cities.

According to Tinney, about five Algonquin families regularly attended meetings, but the elders performed most of the related work. He frequently drove in from his Toronto home to attend, typically finding that, at age forty-four, he was among the youngest present. He voiced his frustration at this lack of involvement, where even those who were most visibly Algonquin-looking and who suffered the most stigma as Indian chose not to show up:

> Within our own community, getting projects done is just difficult because there's so few people that are willing to do the work. Until it comes time for handing out hunting tags – then it's like bugs in the woodwork. And why is that such a driving factor? I mean, I enjoy moose meat as much as anybody. I really like moose meat. But if doing this land claim properly meant that "fine for two generations there's absolutely no hunting," so be it. I still think it's worth putting the work in because it needs to be done. And sadly, very few people have that approach to it. And so when the sacred site work came up, Katherine [Cannon] said, "Well there's this opportunity; we could do this." Not a problem – I'm happy to work on it, because it's something that's of interest to me as well. But whether it was or not, if it means you go out and you slog up to your waist in cold water in the spring to do this, well then, that's still what you have to do. There's just so few people who apparently have the time or interest to do it. Everybody else is very much hands-off: "Well you know, when a settlement happens, then I'll step up to the plate."

Within our own community, there are probably four or five families that are represented by regularly attending meetings, and that's really it. My mother's family is fairly large, so most meetings I'm related to 90 percent of the people who are at the meeting. And then there's Katherine's family, but again she's typical – her kids are grown and living elsewhere, and so they really can't come to meetings. And there are a couple of other families, and that's it. Now there's a huge number of Native families in the Bancroft area, yet there is absolutely no representation whatsoever at meetings ... And I can think of people I went to public school with that I knew were Indians, simply because they really looked Indian. They're more than happy to go to the park and take the moose, but there's absolutely no efforts otherwise. And to a large extent, I'd like to say, "Well, if you don't want to take part in the work, you don't get the gravy." But you can't do that, sadly.

The reasons for this lack of involvement are unclear. It is typical in meetings that focus solely on the land claim to the exclusion of all other topics, including community development. Many who attend these meetings either do not understand the issues or feel no connection to them. And indeed, Tinney suggested that at the level of the community, many people lacked insight – or more properly, perhaps lacked the kind of empowerment that would enable them to take on the work of preserving cultural heritage:

I think in the whole land claim area, hunting and fishing has been a way of life for generations. And that's probably the only contact that most non-status people have with their history. I don't know anyone who does bark work any more. There are no basket-makers that I'm aware of. I don't know anyone who does handmade bows or anything like that. All of the old crafts and skills are no longer required. So the only real attachment they have to the old ways is hunting and fishing.

They don't see the big picture – or a big enough picture. And that's one of the things that really concerns me, going forward, is because there's so few Algonquins who can see beyond hunting or fishing – that they don't say, "Okay not only can we do that, but there's stumpage fees for timbering, there's money coming in from mining, and then all of that can go back into a pot and it can grow." And it's the growth concept that I think most people absolutely completely lack any idea of. They see trees, fish, and moose.

During my interview, Tinney discussed the land claim to a great extent. Although he is openly critical of many aspects of the land claim, in some respects his position is unique. Unlike individuals in many other communities, where the polarization is intense between those who are critical of the land claim and those who support it, Tinney's critiques have not estranged him from the community. Indeed, he is near the centre of the process; his mother, Ada Tinney, is an elder who works most closely with the Bancroft Algonquin negotiation representative (ANR), Katherine Cannon. The fact that he is close to the land claim process and yet has strong reservations gives his words all the more weight.

Tinney voiced two major concerns. As a successful businessman, he saw that many Algonquins were unprepared to shoulder the responsibilities that a treaty would entail and were not being trained to do so. His other concern related to the disregard manifested toward non-status Algonquins in the process itself. On the lack of preparedness, he recalled,

> At one of the last meetings I went to where they had Bob Potts attending, it was in Bancroft and they were talking about the state that the negotiations were at. They said that, looking ahead, in the next couple of years things will start to happen – and if that happens, it will happen quickly. And one of my big concerns was that – on the one hand, we're not ready, and on the other, one of the reasons we're not ready is that we don't have anyone in place or being groomed to take on the responsibilities that will occur. And Bob Potts, he's a very smart man, he's good at what he does, but I think his vision is a little clouded, because I think that from his perspective, his job is just to get the land claim done.
>
> Now, I'd like to see the land claim done, but I'd like to see the people who will be living with the land claim being prepared to take it on and shoulder it the moment that it turns over. We're going to need people to be trained in forestry, mining, and resource management. We're going to need people who are water specialists, environmentalists, and all that kind of stuff. And quite honestly, if this is going to go ahead, the people at the table should be saying to the government, "Fine, we want this to go ahead, but why should we be paying outsiders for the first ten years to be doing this?"
>
> That's when there's going to be the biggest flow of money – in the first ten years. That's when all of a sudden, all this stuff has to happen and you've got to hire specialists from outside the community, paying absolute top dollar to them, and you can guarantee when a Native finally steps into that job, they're not going to be getting the same money because they're not a specialist.
>
> So to have somebody doing a basic thing – like financial management – you've got to have Algonquin people who have some business savvy. So right

now, we should be saying, "You know what, we're happy to have Algonquins learn as much as they can in the next four years, so that when this happens, we'll have people that we can trust, who have a vested interest, more than just their pay cheques, to do the jobs and do them well."

But there's absolutely none of that going on in the negotiations. Which for me, because I'm in business, is really frustrating. I can look at it and say, "Okay, the easy thing is, we take whatever the cash settlement is going to be, and it gets dumped into a trust fund, so that it's dealt with between a lawyer and an investment counsellor, who is going to make his one hundred, two hundred, three hundred thousand dollars a year to say, 'Oh, well let's put it in a mutual fund.'" Quite honestly, you know, my fourteen-year-old could do that! So I don't see why I'm paying a half a million dollars to two specialists to do that.

As a community, to pick a number, if you end up with a hundred million dollar settlement, do most of these people realize what cash that will generate on its own, without ever touching the principal? And do any of them have the fortitude to say, "Let's not touch that principal; if it means we wait for a year so that we've got cash from our investment, then that's what we should do"? But I think ... what I'm afraid is going to happen, is the stereotypical cash rush, where everyone's going to have a new skidoo and a satellite dish. And that will be it – especially due to the fact that so many people have had so little for so long, that any possible opportunity to get a little extra is generally taken. It's sad to say, but it's true. And I know when I first was aware of the land claim and I started doing some background reading on things, the reality is that there's all kinds of tribes where when they get their settlement, there's two or three families that make out and are multi-millionaires, and everyone else has squat.

Since my interview with Tinney, I have spoken with other Algonquins in the territory who refute Tinney's assertion that Algonquins currently lack the skills to engage in high-level financial management and resource planning. They suggest that, instead, skilled Algonquins are being ignored by the land claim negotiating team who, as non-Natives, are more comfortable with the notion of hiring white expertise.

Tinney's focus on local control also extended to his concern for the land in the sense that Algonquins needed to be involved in determining how it would be treated, for both development and biodiversity:

When you're looking at the Ottawa Valley area, there are some absolutely huge tracts that are just government-held land. Domtar used to own the forestry

> rights on a lot of it, and it's in the middle of absolutely nowhere. Now, whether it's developed for cottages or whatever it's developed for, I don't see an overall vision from anyone to say, "Here's what's sustainable. Here's what we can do. Here's a huge chunk of land that we're going to absolutely keep and never ever touch." And we need to have big enough patches of land that are connected so that you maintain a decent biology in the area.

Tinney then addressed the deeper factors underlying this problem – that the process is entirely top down and that grassroots people have had little genuine opportunity to engage in discussions about their vision of Algonquin nationhood and Algonquin empowerment. Though not faulting his own ANR, who has distributed questionnaires and attempted to inform people, Tinney pointed out that such measures are not particularly effective in reaching people who have worked in resource industries all their lives and who have very little formal education.

He suggested that "kitchen table interviews" would be more useful: volunteers would visit with people and talk to them in a language they could understand about what was at stake, what could be done, and what their concerns were. However, the pace of the negotiations, and the secrecy in which they are shrouded, has made community involvement even more difficult:

> As you said, it's very much a top-down process, the way it's happening. We really have to find some way, preferably before the whole thing finalizes, to try and get a little more control. And it's difficult to do that with the way they've set it up. So much is done without community knowledge. Now, I understand the need for the secrecy – they don't want to let too much out of the bag before they go to negotiations. And being a community that's as fractured as the Native community in the Ottawa Valley is, there's always going to be a squeaky wheel that will look for grease elsewhere. So I do understand that, but at the same time, the reality is that I have no idea of what they're trying to negotiate! And I think I'm a fairly well-educated person. I like to think I'm at least on the ball enough that I can look at a situation and size it up relatively quickly, but I have no idea of what they think they're going to do. And it's not due to Katherine's inability to tell us – it's just that she can't.

Tinney's concerns, echoing those of Bob Lavalley in Whitney, also addressed the unwillingness of the Algonquins' own negotiators to insist that payment for *past* stumpage fees and other resource usage must come into consideration. He commented that if the issue of compensation were not forced onto the table, the Algonquins would be reduced to dining on crumbs after government and industry had enjoyed their feast:

> This is what annoys me in going to these meetings – you can go in and you can say to Mr. Potts, "Okay, with stumpage, what are we doing? Are we going to go from a certain date forward, or are we going to take into consideration the last hundred years of stumpage?" Because, you know what? We really need to. The government has made tremendous amounts of money from this resource, and they haven't done a good job managing it, quite honestly, and so what's left, they're going to hand to us and say, "Oh well, you do the best you can with that." It's like handing somebody half a fish and saying, "Well, breed that. And we expect you to survive on that fish from here on forward." I have some real concerns about where we'll end up. I'd love to be proved wrong on that, but this is a reality.

When asked whether he felt that the ANRs were genuinely aware of people's trepidations and fears, and were speaking to those issues at the table, Tinney differentiated between individual ANRs and stated that the intensity of opposition to the land claim was fuelled by those who did not listen to their constituencies. He observed that the experience of being voiceless in a process that will so fundamentally affect the future must be terrifying:

> At meetings that I've been at, I've heard some ANRs say, "Well, this is a concern from our community. This is what I keep hearing from our people." But I also think that there are certain representatives that are far more interested in their own agenda than their community's. Within our own community, Katherine has always made herself available. And it's not just because my mother helps out with her; she is more than willing to sit down and spend whatever time it takes with whomever is interested in talking to her. So, I'm very comfortable that our ANR is doing the very best she can to represent us.
>
> Because if I had a concern about that, I would be much more frustrated and probably tremendously fearful about where it's going. And I think that's an issue that results in creating some of the most vociferous critics of the land claim – because they know that they are not being heard.

In addressing his second major concern – the lack of respect accorded to non-status communities – Tinney mentioned that, in myriad ways, the communities "didn't really matter" in the land claim. He suggested that because Pikwakanagan had not allowed them to define their own membership, many sources who would have been able to accurately delineate which families were Algonquin had been lost. In the Bancroft area, and probably elsewhere, oral histories from both the Native community and local whites would easily have identified who was Native because everybody *knew* who was Indian and who wasn't. By ignoring those sources of oral history, which are now mostly gone, the land claim lost a good opportunity to clarify who was Algonquin. Tinney also commented on the fragility of the written record, noting that when churches or hospitals burn down, records of ancestries are often lost.

Moreover, relying on oral history would have validated the female Algonquin ancestors who often are omitted from written documents. This would have furnished a valuable means of more accurately assessing the blood quantum of the non-status Algonquins, a crucial issue with Pikwakanagan, because the female ancestors would be taken into account as well. Finally, in light of Canada's intense and continuous efforts to destroy Native people, Tinney suggested that Algonquins need to be as inclusive as possible:

> What I find really, really difficult in the whole negotiation process was the part in the time frame when they were wanting to decide, "Well, how do we determine who's an Algonquin – who is and who isn't, and should we have a blood quantum?" It's the short-sightedness of my own people! I'm having an argument at one meeting with a guy who's saying, "Well, if you're less than a quarter Indian, why should we even include you?" I said, "Well, you know what? It's sort of easy for you. You come from the group with Indian status!" I can remember having a similar conversation with Kirby Whiteduck. And his idea at the time was, "Well, if you're less than a quarter, why should we consider you?" And I said, "Well, Kirby, easy to say for you, but within your community, throughout your history, if a white woman married in, they were accepted and given status and so their kids were given full status. But despite that, you don't have that concern about blood quantum – because you don't have to have yours measured."
>
> It's Canada's attempt at eventually eliminating us. I don't see the point! From my perspective, if I choose to identify as being Native because I've got a bloodline, then that's my option! I can say I'm of Algonquin background as much as I can say I'm of English background. My kids ... my son's blond-haired and blue-eyed, not terribly Native-looking. As far as I'm concerned, if he wants to choose to be Algonquin – to follow that path – again, from my perspective, that means not just when it's convenient, it means that you do the slogging work too. But if he wants to, then he should be entitled to follow

> that path. Let's remember that at one time they gave us blankets laced with smallpox. Let's appreciate that, too! There's quite a history of them just trying to eliminate us.

Moving on to representation, Tinney stated that in many respects, even the chief negotiator did not see non-status Algonquins as *real* Indians:

> There's this whole notion of metisness that is mildly infuriating. And I say that from a number of different perspectives. I have no problem with Metis as a designation. Where I find it infuriating is that I would have more rights as a Metis than I do as a non-status Algonquin. I would have more rights, I would have more access to resources, funding, any number of things through that route than I do through my own nation, which is incredibly wrong. But welcome to the Canadian government and the way it's been set up! So I have issues with that. They're playing the old game of "Everyone keep them fractured." That way, it's a much easier bunch to deal with.
>
> It was a little disturbing in talking to, or hearing from, Mr. Potts during his updates. I guess part of my big concern is that the government is simply trying to say, "Well, we'll give you a *little* bit of land and a *little* bit of money – because, you know, you lost it a long time ago, and you're so inbred with the local populations now that it really shouldn't matter to you." And that was the impression I got, that this is where they're coming from. And I also got the impression that maybe that perspective is acceptable to Bob Potts, which, as my chief negotiator, I'm not sure I'm comfortable with. Sure, we're not living off the land, but so what? It ignores a responsibility. I think a prime example of how that responsibility is being ignored is that we have a lead negotiator who isn't Native. Personally, I think it's wrong.

When asked about his interests, hopes, and fears for his community, Tinney emphasized the need for cultural development and for the necessary time in which an Algonquin Nation could prepare itself to undertake the responsibilities of the land claim:

> In our community, one of the things that we've talked about would be to develop an Algonquin Centre in Bancroft. We could set it up, have sort of a learning centre, have a museum of artifacts, have some local artists who are encouraging people to go back to the traditional arts. I mean, personally, if I had the time and I could afford to take the time off to study, financially, it

would be lovely to go back and learn quillwork. As a man, it's not traditionally in our realm, but I find that absolutely phenomenal. I would like to try to learn how to do that. Or canoe making.

When I started out stone carving, my first piece was pathetic, and to think I spent twelve hours on it. Now I could do it in about an hour. But I have no training, other than sitting in my basement carving. And to be able to have a gallery where you can show people that kind of work, teach others how to do it – and if you want to sell it, that's fine, or even to create pieces to outfit a decent museum, or create with replicas of historical works.

And then, the other thing is – there's should be lots of artifacts out there – but we would need a curator to go to the ROM [Royal Ontario Museum] and various museums across Canada and the US, France, and England, and say, "We'd like our stuff back, please." Repatriation. Because we lost so much so early, there's so little left! I mean as far as artifacts, there's next to nothing here. Most of the Algonquin artifacts that exist are probably in France. Because of the initial French contact, I would assume that's where things went. I'd gladly spend hours looking for that stuff. Because people don't know our history, it's very hard to build identity without anything to fall back on, because almost everything we can access is so slim and spartan. If you've never been given the opportunity to think of yourself as Algonquin in a concerted way, and what it means to you – the reality is, that takes time, and traditional crafts help. When you've spent forty years thinking of yourself only as Canadian, then you can't expect in a day to change that thinking pattern.

For me, as much as there's hope, there's a tremendous amount of trepidation. I have great fears and reservations about the fallout from a forced settlement – that is, a settlement that's being constrained by time when, as a nation, I don't think we're ready for it. And I don't think that that needs to be a huge issue, except for the fact that the powers that hold the purse strings aren't allowing us to prepare properly. So we need to become experts in running our own show.

That's my perspective. It's very limited. I could be entirely wrong. But that's the feeling I get from the research I've done – that there isn't a lot being done to help make us successful. We've got to want to do it and be willing to do it, but to do that, we've got to have adequate training so that we can step up to the plate and do the job. And I don't see that happening. It makes me very frightened, quite honestly. I just have this horrible feeling that whatever financial monies that are given are going to be pissed away. I think the resources are going to get pissed away, and there's going to be a lot of back-room deals. And in twenty years, they're going to have absolutely nothing and no land claim left. So that, I guess, is my biggest concern. I guess my biggest hope would be that, at some point, somebody wakes up and says, "Okay, we need to deal with this and have a long-term perspective on it." It's the Native community that it needs to come from, and to do that requires time and it requires money, for people to get together and say, "Here's what I see, or what I'd like to see as a grand vision, but knowing my vision is from where I sit, I'd like to know what it looks like from where you sit over there." So hopefully we can all get a much better idea of the beast we're wrestling with and what can help out everyone the most.

PART 5

The Kiji Sibi – From Mattawa to Ottawa

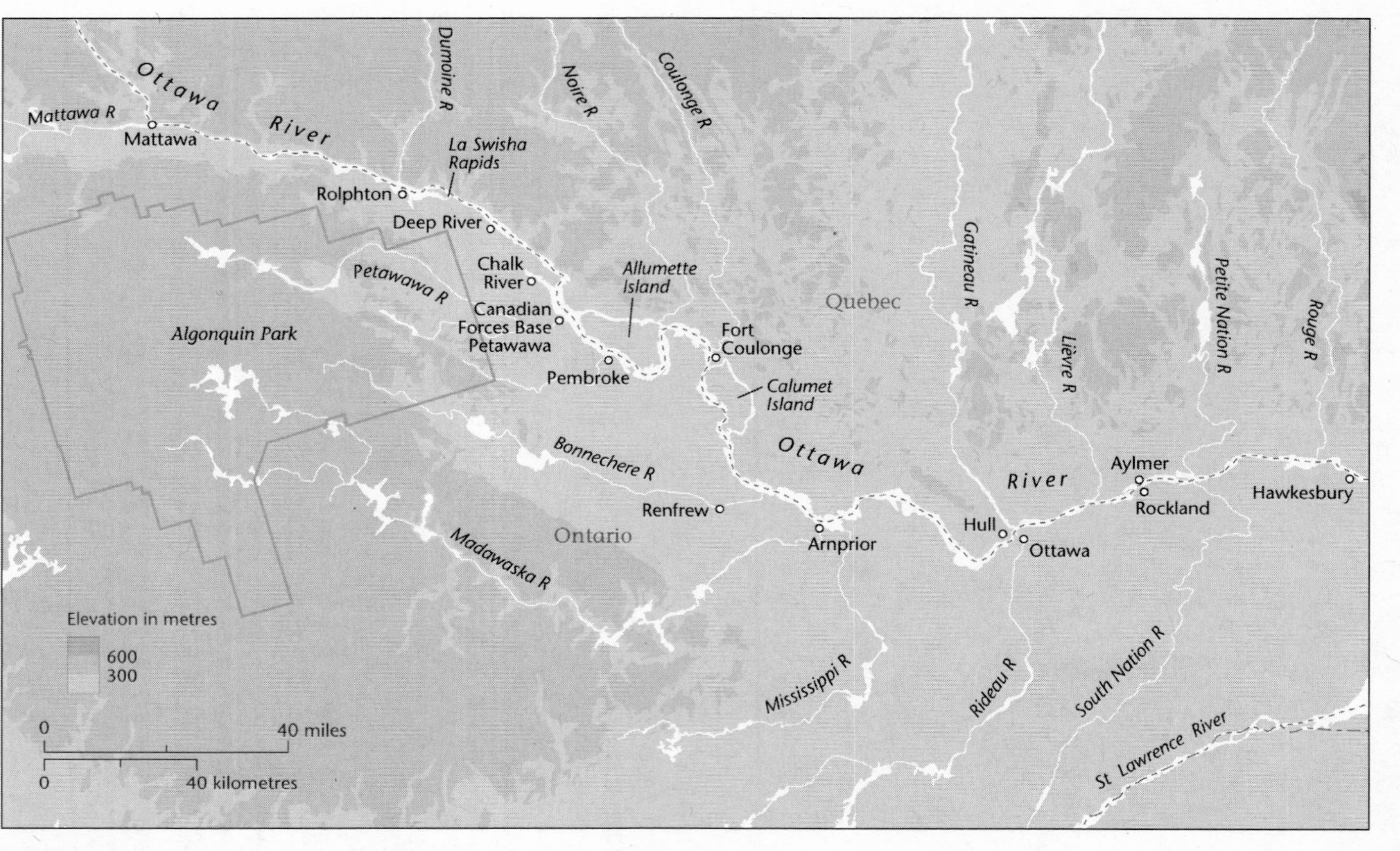

From Mattawa to Ottawa: Algonquin communities along the Kiji Sibi

13

The Ottawa River Communities

Nowhere is the bisection of Algonquin territory by the Quebec-Ontario boundary, coupled with a land claim that covers Ontario alone, more problematic than for the communities along the Ottawa River itself. From Mattawa to Ottawa, the membership of some Ontario-based Algonquin communities lives on both sides of the river. And in Pembroke, the Kichesipirini Algonquins, who live primarily in Ontario, must cope with the fact that the centre of their traditional territory, Allumette Island, is now part of Quebec. This is doubly problematic in that the Allumette Island people are descended from the ancient Kichesipirini, who once controlled the trade on the Ottawa River and therefore were the single greatest obstacle to European penetration of Algonquin lands. These communities, once central to Algonquin life, are now at the periphery of the land claim because of the colonial vision that is concerned only with Algonquin territory reaching to the Quebec border. And finally, in all these communities, the health of the Ottawa River is a major concern, and yet this is sacrificed to a narrow jurisdictional claim that makes the river simply an abstract dividing line on a map, not the living heart of Algonquin territory. In this chapter, we will focus on the river communities based at Mattawa, Pembroke, and Ottawa. But we will begin with the Ottawa River – the Kiji Sibi – itself. The river was essential to the lives of the ancient Algonquins, and it built the fortunes of fur trade companies. Indeed, it was central in building Canada itself. Thus, it is important to describe the river as it existed for millennia, before canals bypassed its rapids and dams virtually eliminated its steep falls.

The Ottawa River: An Overview

The source of the Ottawa River is Lac Capimichigama, also known as Lac Travers or Cross Lake, which lies north of Grand Lac Victoria in Quebec, near the height of land that divides the rivers flowing north into James Bay and the Arctic watershed from those flowing south into the Ottawa River watershed. Indeed, "Capimichigama" is an Anishinabe word that means "crossing from one watershed to another" (Morrison 2005, 21). From its source, the river follows a winding 150-mile-course westward through numerous bodies of water until it enters the long and narrow Lake Timiskaming. At that point, it abruptly changes direction southward to reach Mattawa, the boundary between the upper and lower Ottawa, and the northern edge of the land claim.

Here, the Ottawa is joined by the Mattawa, which links it to Lake Nipissing, the French River, and ultimately Georgian Bay and the Great Lakes system. Mattawa has thus been both the gateway to the west, via the Mattawa River, and to the north, via Lake Timiskaming. Now the Ottawa River turns east, flowing on to Allumette Island, with tiny Morrison's Island adjoining, and then Calumet Island. Below is Lac des Chats (known as Chats Lake in Ontario), which once fed the Chats Falls, where the river descended into Lac des Chênes, named for the oaks that once lined its shores. Lac des Chênes stretched thirty miles to the Des Chênes rapids, which, prior to hydroelectric development, once filled a four-mile stretch of the river, where a number of islands were also situated. At this spot, the channel dropped furiously into a cauldron-like basin, the falls of La Chaudière. Below La Chaudière, the south shore of the river is lined with limestone cliffs and here it is joined by the Rideau (the name means "curtain"), which once fell over the cliffs in a rushing curtain of water. On the opposite shore and a little lower, the fierce Gatineau River joins the Ottawa, adding its current to the main stream. At their confluence, where the river bends briefly northward, was an ancient meeting place that is now occupied by the city of Ottawa. After this, the river slows down and flows sluggishly for sixty miles until encountering what was once fifteen miles of rapids at Long Sault. Below Long Sault is the Lake of Two Mountains, near Oka. At this point, the river forms two channels around Île Perrot, Montreal Island, and Île Jésus, where it empties into the St. Lawrence (Bond 1966, 4-6).

For Native people, the Ottawa River was a vital part of a pan-continental trade network, replete with sacred sites and meeting grounds. For Europeans, the river was a gateway to the North American interior, the most direct route between the St. Lawrence and the upper Great Lakes. From there, a system of lakes and rivers gave access to the prairies and the northwest. Also, after

Mattawa, the Ottawa River turned north in a route that ultimately led to James and Hudson Bays.

The Ottawa made the Algonquins central to the affairs of other nations, in their ability to control passage through it. The Kichesipirini, who lived on both Allumette Island and the impenetrable fortress-like Morrison's Island next to it, blocked the French from setting up their own forts along the Ottawa River. For years, the Kichesipirini exacted a toll for every canoe that passed through their territory. Indeed, such was their control that nations further north, such as the Huron/Wendat, were not permitted to use the route unless they observed Algonquin restrictions on allowing European passage along the river.

In the mid-seventeenth century, desiring to break the power of the Kichesipirini, the French made a secret treaty with the Iroquois to go to war with the Algonquins. Armed with a deadly new weapon – guns supplied by the Dutch – the Iroquois massacred the Kichesipirini in 1647, after which the entire river lay open. The Iroquois drove many of the Algonquins from the Ottawa River watershed and kept them out for approximately twenty-five years. With the destruction of the Kichesipirini, the French were finally able to establish trading posts in Algonquin territory.

The Fur Trade on the Ottawa River

One of the first French trading posts on the Ottawa was Fort Coulonge, established in 1649 at the mouth of the Coulonge River, itself a gateway to a vast network of northern trade in the Quebec interior. Other posts were established near the site of present-day Rockland on the south shore of the river, at Allumette Island (during the nineteenth century, the post became Fort William), at Chats Falls, and at Lake of Two Mountains (Bond 1966, 8). As the trade reached northward and westward, posts were also established at Des Joachims, Mattawa, and Timiskaming.

At this time, the fur trade was dominated by two rival enterprises – the North West Company, based in Montreal, whose trade networks, via the Ottawa River, extended across the prairies into the north, and the Hudson's Bay Company, which shipped furs and supplies via Hudson Bay and had a network of subarctic trading posts across Canada. As the trade network expanded, the North West Company's routes extended in two great arcs that spanned much of the continent and connected its outposts to its Montreal-based factors. The first arc stretched from the mouth of the Ottawa River, at Montreal, to Lake Superior, and the second continued west and north via prairie rivers to the northern territories at Athabasca and Great Slave Lake. The company's voyageurs generally left Montreal in the spring, paddling huge Indian-made birchbark canoes capable of carrying up to six thousand pounds together with crews ranging from sixteen to sixty men. Through the connection with Lake of Two Mountains, Iroquois men commonly worked as voyageurs as did French Canadians (St. Onge 2007, 109). As fur traders married into Native families in order to establish the trade network, their mixed-blood sons increasingly entered the trade and soon became central to it.

Commonly, the arc to Lake Superior was made by "summer men." Laden with supplies, they completed a round trip in one season, paddling along the Ottawa, Mattawa, and French Rivers to Georgian Bay, thence to Thunder Bay (Fort William) on Lake Superior, and on to Lac la Pluie, or Rainy Lake, where they deposited the supplies for the "hivernants" (traders who wintered in the interior), collected the furs the hivernants had left for them, and returned to Montreal. The other trade arc, maintained by the hivernants, involved a huge and exhausting journey. Bringing furs from Great Slave Lake, Athabasca, or the Peace River, the hivernants left them at Lac la Pluie and returned to the north before winter set in (ibid., 109-11). In addition, furs were brought down the rivers of the Ottawa watershed to be traded at the posts along the Ottawa.

In 1821, the North West Company merged with the Hudson's Bay Company. With this, the fur trade was reorganized into two administrative units: Based at York Factory on Hudson Bay, the northern department managed the trade from the Pacific Ocean to Rainy Lake and the Severn River in northwestern Ontario. The southern department, based at Moose Factory on the tip of James Bay, handled the trade on the northern shores of Lakes Superior and Huron, the James Bay area, and the posts in Upper and Lower Canada including the Ottawa River post at Timiskaming. Independent traders along the Ottawa River, who had struggled to survive by trading for furs with the Algonquins and other Native people, were quickly driven out of business by a Montreal firm known as McGillivrays, Thain and Company, which administered the remaining posts on the Ottawa (Bond 1966, 4, 8).

At this point, as the fur trade on the lower Ottawa began to wane, the timber trade accelerated, and hundreds of rafts of squared pine logs were floated down the Ottawa every year to be loaded onto ships bound for England. Because of this, transportation along the Ottawa River began to change. After the 1821 merger of the North West and Hudson's Bay Companies, the canoe routes had become shorter and more truncated. Gradually, as settlers arrived, they built roads along some portage routes, using wagons to haul goods. Canoes were slowly replaced by horse-drawn sleighs that brought supplies on the ice in winter. Even so, the fur trade continued to use flotillas of canoes well into the 1830s (ibid., 12).

The Ottawa experienced a transportation revolution in 1826, when Colonel John By of the Royal Engineers arrived at the La Chaudière falls to begin constructing a canal to Kingston via the Rideau River. The town that sprang up there would eventually become the city of Ottawa. Other engineers built a canal along the fifteen-mile stretch of rapids at Long Sault. Soon a steamer, partially financed by fur traders, was operating from the north side of Montreal Island to La Chaudière. From there, goods were carried by road to Aylmer and then by steamer to Chats Lake (ibid.).

As the fur trade began to fall off, the trading posts on the lower Ottawa were gradually transformed into supply depots to take advantage of the growing timber trade. Ultimately, however, many of them closed during the 1840s, with the exception of Fort William, on Allumette Island, which handled much of the local Indian trade (in furs and other goods), and Fort Coulonge, which continued its involvement in the timber trade. When the British preferential duties that favoured colonial timber over Baltic timber were dropped in the 1840s, it drastically reduced the British squared timber trade and brought about the transition to the sawn lumber trade with the United States, facilitated by the construction of railroads.

Fort Timiskaming remained a viable part of the fur trade, though furs were increasingly shipped out from Moose Factory, on James Bay, and supplies were brought up the Ottawa River. The Allumette Island post survived until 1864, when it was closed and much of its business transferred to the fort at Des Joachims (Bond 1966, 11-12). After the 1830s, the Mattawa fur trade was increasingly disrupted by loggers and settlers, but with the construction of railroads, Mattawa's importance as a depot in the railway trade became even more pronounced. When the Timiskaming trading post closed in 1891, only the Mattawa post remained. It is here, at the "gateway to the west," that we will begin our look at the river communities at the border of the Ontario land claim.

Mattawa

Mattawa has long been a meeting place for Algonquins and Nipissings, as well as other Native people who travelled from east and west to trade, socialize, engage in diplomacy, and address issues of mutual importance. As the gateway to the west, it became an important voyageur route to the Great Lakes, with Europeans first entering the region as early as 1610.

In 1686, the Chevalier de Troyes mentioned a sizeable Indian settlement at Mattawa (Morel 1980, 21). However, not until the early eighteen hundreds did travellers mention the names of the bands in the region. Chief Antoine Kiwiwisens's Algonquins lived on the north side of the Mattawa River, whereas Chief Commanda's Nipissings had land to the west. Chief Beaucage's Nipissings lived north of Lake Nipissing, and the lands of Chief Amable Dufond were south of the Mattawa (Gravelle 1963, 69-70). For years, all travellers, voyageurs, and missionaries paused at Mattawa to repair canoes, repack supplies, or trade with local Algonquins and Nipissings. Indeed, although the Hudson's Bay post at Mattawa closed in 1908, individuals in the region still trap commercially, trading their furs at North Bay (Chrétien 1996, 74).

Missionaries from the Red River settlement were the first to extend their outreach to the local Algonquins and Nipissings as well as the growing population of Metis voyageurs who had settled at Mattawa. Although the first Mass was held at Mattawa in 1843, the Hudson's Bay Company refused the Oblates' request to permanently settle missionaries in the region until 1869. By that point, lumbering was slowly replacing the fur trade, and loggers, most of them Irish, began to enter the area. A church was built in Mattawa in 1863 to serve the fifty French Canadian and Irish families in the area as well as two thousand Algonquins and Nipissings, and the Metis. Mattawa also became a centre for two sets of missions: one to James Bay including Timiskaming and Abitibi, the other extending from Mattawa to what became Ottawa (Joan Holmes and Associates 1993, 2:109). Mattawa's first school was organized in 1871, teaching classes in French, English, and Algonquin (Chrétien 1996, 77).

In 1881, the railroad route extending from Ottawa via Pembroke reached Mattawa, and roads were built to encourage settlement in the district. By the turn of the twentieth century, Mattawa had become a major distribution centre for the logging industry, with thousands of loggers in the region. In fact, logging remains its main industry (ibid., 79-80).

Native Identity at Mattawa

Mattawa is unique among the Algonquin communities in that its proximity to North Bay means that it is located relatively close to the territory of Nipissing First Nation, a status Indian reserve. The reserve is also the headquarters of the Union of Ontario Indians, the political territorial organization representing status Indian reserves in the areas covered by the Robinson-Huron, Robinson-Superior, and other pre-Confederation treaties in southern Ontario. Because so many non-status Algonquin communities also have people of

Nipissing ancestry, there is a potential for tension between Indian reserves that politically represent status Indian Nipissings and federally unrecognized communities who represent Nipissings as well as Algonquins.

However, unlike Pikwakanagan, the leadership and community at Nipissing First Nation do not seem intent on denying the Indianness of non-status Algonquins and Nipissings. Although the primary reason may be that the Nipissing First Nation is not involved in the Algonquin land claim, it is also true that a strong federally unrecognized Algonquin and Nipissing presence has always existed in Mattawa; because of this, their "Indianness" cannot be denied as it has been elsewhere in the Ottawa River watershed.

During the 2005 interview conducted with the late Mattawa elder Bob Ferguson, he recalled that Algonquins have always lived in the Mattawa area:

> About being Algonquin – well, there were no two ways about it. It was pretty obvious ... from my grandfather and my dad. Back then, we hunted for our own meat and stuff ... and fishing on the river ... that was a lot of it. And then, we had to watch for game wardens more than anybody else because they didn't treat you the same as everybody else. But they never seemed to catch us, so – we were always one step ahead of them. You had to be. Back in them days, too, there sure wasn't much work around, at all.
>
> We lived in the valley, across the river here. Used to call it Squaw Valley ... used to be pretty much all Indian people lived there. Just across the bridge there. Up the hill, and down, and you see the big valley there. It was pretty much all log houses in there when I was a kid. Now, it's all built up here. It's changed. A lot of the people moved away, from there, the younger people, Native people, moved away, eh? Lot of them headed down south. They're out in Milton, Hamilton, and areas round there.

The strength of the Algonquins' presence in Mattawa is also evidenced by the fact that they retained their language for longer than any other Algonquin group in Ontario. Indeed, the grandparents of today's Mattawa Algonquins tended to speak the language fluently and more or less openly, unlike in the southern parts of the territory, where the use of the language had diminished by the late nineteenth century.

In 1988, there were approximately twenty-five hundred people in Mattawa. At the time, the Ontario Metis and Non-Status Indian Association, which was intent on organizing there, estimated that between 150 and 350 Metis and non-status Indians lived in Mattawa during the 1980s (Chrétien 1996, 80-81). However, though the Mattawa Algonquins and Metis worked together tactically, they remained distinct; when Metis researcher Annette Chrétien conducted a number of oral histories with Mattawa Metis in the early 1990s, she found that though the groups acknowledged each other, they recognized the boundaries between them.[1]

Mattawa has a tightly-knit network of Metis families that have been established there since the time of the fur trade. The older people whom Chrétien interviewed differentiated between themselves and local Algonquins, primarily on the basis of their family networks. The distinction between Algonquin and Metis had nothing to do with blood quantum; instead, it was about the cultural expression and histories of each group. The Mattawa Metis whom Chrétien interviewed during the 1990s spoke of having borrowed a range of practices from various Native traditions, all mixed together and frequently expressed in French Michif. In general, they saw their Aboriginal roots as hybrid, originating in the multiple communities of mixed-blood voyageurs of Iroquois, Cree, Dakota, and other backgrounds who had passed through Mattawa for centuries – although the Metis community is dynamic and constantly changing. The differences between the Metis and local Algonquins appear to reflect a long history of co-existence in the "Indian" parts of Mattawa, with an awareness that though both were Aboriginal, both had a distinct history and approach to life.

However, assimilatory pressures and loss of Native language (either Algonquin or Michif) have diminished this awareness for some of the younger people, with a corresponding lack of respect for either cultural background. For example, in March 2009, the hunting update on the Mattawa/North Bay Algonquin website indicated that, since the *Powley* decision affirmed Metis hunting rights, people have begun to hunt under both regimes. Apparently, seventy-six individuals held harvesting cards from both the Algonquins of Ontario and the Metis Nation of Ontario, and forty-three others with Algonquin cards had applied for Metis cards as well. Although the concentration of Algonquins is higher in this region than in the southern parts of the Ottawa River watershed, cultural loss and disrespect for traditional protocols are growing problems in Mattawa as they are elsewhere in the watershed.

In discussing the retention of Native values, Bob Ferguson mentioned the importance of considering the implications should communities become filled with people whose Algonquin ancestry is minimal and who continue to intermarry with settlers:

> I feel sorry for all the old people there, that passed on. They never got nothing. Should have been looked after years ago. I guess, today the government just

> figures they wait long enough and they'll be all gone. That's the attitude they had toward the Indian people ... When I was young – like I said, in the valley up there it was mostly all Indian people. Everybody got along together pretty good. Small community. Everybody knew one another. But now ... you gotta be careful, too; there's a lot of wannabes, too, you know. Because anybody that thinks they're gonna get something out of the land claim is gonna try and get in there. I think that they're keeping it pretty well screened, though, with people's ancestry.
>
> The trouble is, that you get people with not enough names in them, and then you start building communities, and these people start having families and everything else. After a while, the breakdown is gonna be complete – there's gonna be no more Indian people left. I guess it's something that a whole community has got to decide. Because you gotta think down the road.

There are currently two non-status Algonquin communities in Mattawa: Antoine First Nation, consisting of the Antoine extended family, existed informally as a group before the land claim. The local area committee, organized under the claim, refers to itself as the Mattawa/North Bay Algonquin First Nation. According to the Antoine leader, Dave Joannise, its members are descended from the Matawasi'bi people of the area and are connected through marriage to Quebec bands such as the Kipawa First Nation as well as to other Ontario communities such as the Algonquins of Bonnechere and Pikwakanagan. I experienced difficulty in interviewing Antoine members, so most of my information about Mattawa comes from interviews with the Mattawa/North Bay Algonquin First Nation.[2] Both groups claim descent from the Amable Dufond band, whose territories lay south of the Mattawa River. However, Gilbert Labreche, chief of the Mattawa/North Bay Algonquins, has suggested that Antoine's members also descend from the Antoine Kiwiwisens band, whose territories were north of the Mattawa in Quebec. This would suggest that the original exclusion of Antoine from the land claim and the creation of the Mattawa area committee related to the fact that some of Antoine's traditional territories were not in Ontario.

The land claim negotiators, who have named themselves the Algonquins of Ontario, assert that they will "settle" all outstanding claims between Ontario Algonquins and the federal and provincial governments. Of crucial importance here are the jurisdictional "sacrifices" that may result for the Ottawa River communities. Two such sacrifices exist simply due to the boundaries established by the land claim process. The first is the Ottawa River itself. As we will learn from the experiences of the Mattawa community and from

Algonquins living along the banks of the river, the health of the Ottawa is a key concern – including development schemes that displace Algonquins from waterfront properties, large-scale interprovincial projects of the past such as damming and nuclear facilities, and the ongoing problem of toxic effluent. These issues cannot be considered within negotiations that follow the colonial boundaries and reduce a huge living river to a line on a map. The second jurisdictional sacrifice, which involves the communities and individuals whose lives and traditional territories span the Quebec-Ontario border, addresses issues that the Antoine community has faced and will also be discussed later in this chapter in connection with the Kichesipirini Algonquins.

Mattawa/North Bay Algonquin First Nation

When a researcher for the project interviewed Gilbert Labreche in 2005, Mattawa/North Bay Algonquin First Nation was a unique land-claim-affiliated band in that it had a chief and council structure that was separate from its Algonquin negotiation representative (ANR).[3] Labreche suggested that ANR representation was inherently contradictory: the Algonquin Nation Tribal Council (ANTC) had been established to give a political voice to non-status communities at the negotiating table but had been bypassed by the creation of the ANR system, which ultimately prevented the communities' leadership from representing them in the claim.

And yet, having a chief and council that were not part of the land claim negotiations furnished the Mattawa/North Bay Algonquins under Labreche with a structure and a direction that did not simply focus on the claim – and that therefore could address community concerns *regarding* the claim.

For example, Mattawa/North Bay has a separate economic arm, the Madadjiwan Economic Development Corporation, with its own board of directors, to handle economic development for the membership. Its work is facilitated by having a chief and council who are independent of the Algonquins of Ontario. Furthermore, Labreche's focus on his community has enabled him to address the fact that during the negotiations, development has proceeded at a heightened pace along the Ottawa River without any Algonquin input at all.

As we saw in Chapter 3, a central problem with the comprehensive claims process is that Indigenous nations find themselves trapped in negotiations while resource development continues unchecked in their traditional territories. Labreche's main concern was that no freeze on development had been instigated pending completion of the claim, an essential requirement for any serious consideration of Algonquin rights in the territory. He had repeatedly spoken with the ANTC regarding a general moratorium on development, but the ANTC had been advised by its legal team that, due to the *Bear Island* decision, this would not be possible. *Bear Island* had concerned the Teme Augama Anishnabeg, an Indigenous nation in northern Ontario that was seeking recognition of its territory in the Temagami region and that froze all development in its entire claim area by applying legal cautions through the courts. As a result of *Bear Island,* Indigenous groups could no longer follow the Teme Augama Anishnabeg example. Instead, they must place specific cautions relating only to certain developments in an area. As Labreche noted, Ontario is proceeding in an unrestrained manner in the meantime:

> My fear is that all the while we're sending ANR representatives to the table trying to negotiate a final settlement, Ontario and Canada are going to go ahead and continue to displace Algonquins from their traditional territory, and certainly we've seen evidence of that under the Ontario Living Legacy, and there's many, many other initiatives that are being put in place.[4] It seems they are making every effort to try and get Algonquins who are situated anywhere near the Ottawa river, away from it. Or the Mattawa river, or any other prime real estate property in Algonquin territory. It's basically hands-off right now to Algonquins.
>
> So while the negotiations are going on, there is no protection whatsoever. And what I've done in the past, having the role of chief, is every possible chance that I've got, to try and oppose these land grabs, or what appears to me like a land grab, while the negotiations are ongoing. My problem is that any time something is designated, under the Ontario Living Legacy, for example, it's very difficult to get it back afterwards, and in this particular case, the whole territory is Algonquin traditional territory for which we're supposed to be negotiating. Now, if huge tracts of territory – and it basically follows the watershed, so it includes the riverbeds and so on – if these huge tracts of territory are only designated for specific purposes, it can infringe on our Aboriginal rights to use those territories for what we see fit, whether it involves setting up a hunting camp or whatever. Although they're saying Aboriginal rights are not impacted, maybe directly they're not impacted, but indirectly they certainly are. By creating a type of park or other development, certainly it restricts our ability to do certain things on those watersheds.
>
> Unless there's substantive negotiations or discussions with the Aboriginal groups that are involved, meaning the Quebec Algonquins as well as the

Ontario Algonquins, and an agreed-upon settlement, none of these policies and programs should be implemented while we're negotiating for those same tracts of land.

Although development on the Ontario side of the Ottawa waterfront is a real concern for the river communities, a larger issue involves the health of the river itself and the fact that, with separate land claims proceeding for Quebec and Ontario, the river is effectively cross-jurisdictional. This is particularly important in connection with resource development on the river, such as hydroelectric projects.

Hydro development along the Ottawa River took place between 1902 and the 1970s. Dams were built at most of the river's great cataracts, flooding and silencing them, harnessing their power for the benefit of cities such as Ottawa, and causing great misery for both wildlife and local Algonquins. By the 1970s, over two thousand megawatts of electricity were being pulled from the main river and thirteen hundred megawatts from its tributaries (Whitlock 1997).

Bob Ferguson described the effect on Mattawa of the hydro dams, particularly the Otto Holden Dam, known as La Cav by people in Mattawa, and the La Swisha dam at Rolphton:

When I was young, you could go out down the river here in the evening and sit there, where they put a bridge here, and with just an old alder rod and a line about ten, fifteen feet long, you'd go home with all the fish you wanted to take home with you. Now, I don't know, with all the pollution and everything else, there's nothing left. It's from the dams here. There used to be weed beds, and everything else, on the shore. But all the bulrushes are gone, everything else ... Small fish and that, that's their safety net. The weeds. They get in there, and they hide in there. And now there's hardly any weeds, and the only place the little fish got to go is up along the shoals, little hollows, the shallow places, and when the water level goes down, they're all separated, and then they die. The La Swisha dam is below here, and La Cav dam is only about five miles upriver.[5] And with the dams, it's nothing for the water to drop five, six feet here at night. It has a huge impact on everything that's alive in the river.

I remember I was only a kid when they put the dam in there. There was a bunch of Indian people along the Ottawa River here; well, everybody was pretty poor. They had little shacks around there. So the hydro come along and said, "Here, we'll give you twenty-five dollars for your shack." And they had to move out. Just like that. If they evicted somebody from there, they should have built them another place somewhere. Build them houses someplace else. But that's what they did ...

To me now, personally, I don't think you should be eating them fish at all any more. You catch some fish here, they got lumps on 'em. Tumours. They're pale, they're not good gold colour, or they're not blue gold, like we used to get 'em ... When you get a pickerel, they don't even look like pickerel any more. When you get them, they're smaller and skinny, and they're pale – no, it's not right.

Others have been affected by even more intensive development on the Ottawa River. At the end of the Second World War, Canada built a nuclear reactor complex on the river, selecting a twenty-four-mile straight stretch where the water was remarkably deep (which would allow for cooling the reactor) and where the nearby Petawawa military base provided security. The hundreds of non-Native families that were brought in to operate the support laboratory that produced the reactor were housed in a hidden townsite later named Deep River. Meanwhile, the Algonquins who lived in the area were forced to move. A number of research reactors were built until the world's first CANDU power reactor went into operation at a site near Rolphton in 1962.

In 2005, an interview was conducted with the late Janet Hoffman, her sister Helen King, and her daughter Cathie Dupuis. Hoffman and King were children when the nuclear plant displaced their family from their home. Below, they talk together about the way of life that ended with nuclear development and how their family survived its displacement:

Helen King: I remember quite a bit before Atomic Energy of Canada came in.
Janet Hoffman: When we used to live there, we used to go down the river in a wagon, all of us, and pick blueberries, wild chokecherries, and wild strawberries. We'd pick berries all day, come down, have a lunch, and then go back, and then the next day, whatever they did, preserves, can them or whatever. Oh, they were sweet! We used to pick cranberries in the marshes. They'd be high bushes, kind of raised above the marsh, so you'd go in where it was wet and you'd just walk through. The adults did the canning.
Helen King: We had a root cellar in the house – it was a log house. The families there lived off what they gathered and what they caught.
Janet Hoffman: Gardens had a big part in it. They'd grow carrots, turnips, beets, potato, squash ... We had our own hens, cattle, and pigs. We had the

milk, the cream, the buttermilk. Everything was used up – if they killed a pig, every part of that pig was used. Used to make sausages ... blood pudding ...
Helen King: But we didn't tan the hides.
Janet Hoffman: There was an Indian family lived up nearby that were really traditional. Like the furs, and all home remedies and all stuff like that. They lived up the river, about five or six miles. We'd take the hide up, or they'd come down. And maybe you'd be there helping them to slaughter a pig or the cattle. And they'd all go hunting and fishing together and stuff like that. You know? And they'd share with everybody else, the same whenever they killed even a beef or something, it was all distributed.
Helen King: And maybe the next time, the next guy did one, he'd share it, you know? Everyone did all their farming with the horse. And always in the fall, at trapping time, they'd all go from one place to the other and trap ... They shared all their equipment that they had. The women made all the clothes. My mother had a little sewing machine. She made all the clothes and the bedding. And she quilted, the ladies all quilted. And I remember them making feather ticks, mattresses, pillows ... Always, when plucking birds, it was "Save the feathers! Save the feathers!" Everything was saved.

But when the plant came through, the whole community got moved out. The families got split up. Dad went to work in the bush for Stewarts, a big logging company. They used to cut logs across on the Quebec side. He cut the wood. He'd go for a week and then he'd come home, like on the weekend.
Janet Hoffman: And then in the spring, he'd be on the drive, with the logs, on the river. And I remember him saying that whenever they had a jam – you know, like when the logs would all pile up on the river and they had to dynamite the logs, he was one of the guys that went out and had to light the fuse and then get the hell out of there! It was dangerous. And Mom would do the laundry and we'd sell milk and bread to the boats, too, on the river, for when they'd be towing the booms of logs down. She would do their laundry on a scrub board; she'd get the water from the river.
Helen King: And you know, when they used to go into camp? Mom would be knitting stockings and mitts, and Daddy would take them into camp and sell them to the guys.

Dad cut wood for about fifteen years. He worked up at Mattawa for a while there, at a mill. And then he worked at night at Deep River. Firing the boiler. Then he went on plumber ... He only worked there about eight years, and then he went back to Stewarts and cut wood. And I worked at a restaurant and at a hotel, the Chalk River Hotel. I was only fourteen. I was doing the rooms and making the beds and helping in the kitchen.

Janet Hoffman: When we were small, we'd go down for a swim – we could just, if we were thirsty, we'd just take a drink of water. Now you wouldn't dare. You know like, you wouldn't even think of drinking the Ottawa River.

Nuclear development has heavily affected the condition of the Ottawa River. By the 1970s, the combined water usage of the power and research reactors along the Ottawa exceeded that of the entire city of Ottawa and constituted one-quarter of the river's total usage (Whitlock 1997). In recent years, a major concern in Pembroke has been that a private company, SRT Technologies, was granted a licence to develop the use of waste tritium from the Rolphton plant to power off-grid lighting devices.[6] In an unprecedented move, however, in February 2007, the Canadian Nuclear Safety Commission refused to renew the SRT Technologies licence. Stephen Salaff (2007) attributes this success to the manner in which environmental and anti-nuclear activists were joined by the Pembroke-based Kichesipirini Algonquin First Nation.

If the Ottawa River is the first jurisdictional sacrifice of the land claim, the second sacrifice involves the communities whose territories are considered "cross-jurisdictional" in a comprehensive claims process that divides Quebec Algonquins from Ontario Algonquins. Kichesipirini Algonquin First Nation has also been central to this struggle.

Jurisdictional Sacrifices: The Kichesipirini

In 2006, the Algonquin negotiation representatives (ANRs) denied the Kichesipirini Algonquin First Nation a place within the land claim as a separate party, citing the difficulties posed by interprovincial jurisdictions (LaPierre 2006b). This refusal reveals that the Algonquins of Ontario are ill-prepared to deal with a reality that affects many First Nations whose territories have been bisected by an imposed border: the traditional territory of the Kichesipirini Algonquin First Nation lies on both sides of the Ottawa River.

From the Ottawa River shoreline at Riverside Park in Pembroke, Allumette Island, which was arbitrarily included on the Quebec side of the boundary, seems almost close enough to touch. The people of Allumette and Morrison's Islands, now largely displaced to the town of Pembroke, are nevertheless the descendants of the Kichesipirini, who occupied the islands for over six thousand years and yet are currently invisible in the official discourses of both Ontario and Quebec. So, whereas the name of their seventeenth-century chief, Tessouat, is appropriated at Pikwakanagan as a symbol of successful Algonquin resistance to European incursion, their ancient remains are appropriated by Quebec

First Nations organizations. For example, artifacts and skeletal remains of ancestors unearthed on Morrison's Island and once displayed in the Museum of Civilization have recently been repatriated – not to the people of the island but to Algonquin leaders in Quebec (Naumetz 2007, 3).

And yet the Kichesipirini have a powerful history among Algonquins – from their primary role in excluding Europeans from the Ottawa River throughout much of the seventeenth century, to their long struggle to retain cohesion as a people despite the presence of logging, damming, and nuclear power plants along the river. It is also clear that the Kichesipirini have a unique potential, by virtue of their trans-jurisdictional position, to function as a bridge between provincial jurisdictions that are dividing a homeland and their people. Indeed, when they attempted to enter the land claim, they proposed to the Algonquins of Ontario that because of jurisdictional complexities they needed to enter as a discrete community, like Pikwakanagan, rather than joining the ANTC. However, they were prevented by the ANRs from joining the table.[7] Instead, the Algonquins of Ontario suggested that Kichesipirini members could simply join existing communities as Ontario-based individuals (LaPierre 2006a).

The short-sightedness of this position is perhaps symbolic of all the weaknesses demonstrated by the Algonquins of Ontario. Even a comprehensive claims process that follows provincial boundaries would be expected to have a mechanism to address "overlap areas" – in this case, the border communities whose concerns span both sides of the Ottawa River.

The Ottawa Community

Whereas both the Mattawa/North Bay Algonquins and the Kichesipirini have been disregarded in their efforts to protect the land along the river, such is not the case for the Ottawa community, a fact that reveals the strategic and hegemonic place occupied by Ottawa as the National Capital Region. In Ottawa, government bureaucrats and a large, fairly well-educated, and nationalistic segment of the Canadian public are on hand to observe events, with the result that a different picture has emerged. On two occasions, lawyers working for the land claim succeeded in halting plans for the National Capital Region waterfront – a light-rail project on federal land in Ottawa's greenbelt and the sale of the former Canadian Forces Base Rockcliffe to a Crown corporation to build residences. The lawyers won their cases by asserting that, because of the *Haida* decision, governments were required to consult with Native groups regarding land that was subject to a claim.

The blocking of these projects by lawyers acting on behalf of the land claim was extensively discussed in the Ottawa press, and the *Ottawa Citizen* accorded the claim serious, thoughtful, and ultimately supportive coverage. Had the two projects been situated in Mattawa or even Pembroke, their outcome, and thus the land claim itself, would have remained largely invisible to the Ottawa press. Thus, halting the two National Capital Region developments appears to be a highly strategic move by the non-Native lawyers who control the negotiation process on behalf of Algonquins.

This contrast is all the more apparent because the Ottawa community is the smallest in the claim, representing Algonquins who live and work in Ottawa. During my 2007 interview with Bob Majaury, who is now a member of the Ottawa community, he described how Pikwakanagan established the first area committee at Ottawa in 1991 to represent the Algonquins who worked and lived there as part of its general outreach to non-status Algonquins. Dan Kohoko, the first leader, gathered a handful of individuals, including Paul Lamothe, and built a community in Ottawa until the land claim negotiations broke down in 2001. When the talks resumed, the community re-formed, and Paul Lamothe became the ANR for Ottawa.[8]

Some Ottawa members, such as Bob Majaury, believe that Ottawa should not try to be a "local" community and should instead be the site for the government of the Algonquin Nation. This would provide the numerous communities of the territory with a gathering place to negotiate their own governance issues at a national level and would counteract the manner in which the non-status Algonquins are represented at the land claim negotiations solely as "communities" in ways that bypass nationhood at the most fundamental level. Indeed, in fulfilling this role, Algonquins in Ottawa would be hearkening back to the area's earliest function as a meeting place.

Located at the point where the Gatineau and Rideau Rivers meet the Ottawa, the site of what is now the city of Ottawa was an ancient gathering place where Algonquins from the northern and southern parts of the territory could meet. However, Ottawa's hegemonic identity as the capital of Canada has largely obscured the ancient Algonquin presence. Although one burial ground was discovered during the building of the Canadian Museum of Civilization, for almost two hundred years Ottawa has not only erased the presence of ancient Algonquins but has denied Algonquin nationhood in both the past and for the future.[9] Indeed, many Algonquins believe that, both literally and metaphorically, the Parliament Buildings are founded on Algonquin remains.[10]

Since 2006, the Ottawa Algonquin community has had a tumultuous existence. As its ANR, Paul Lamothe helped to create the Ottawa Algonquin First

Nation Cultural Organization in 2006, a corporation intended to promote the best interests of the community. However, during land claim negotiations, he began asking pointed questions regarding the power structure in the claim and the lack of fundamental representation at many levels for non-status Algonquins. In April 2007, he left the table and called for a moratorium on the claim until the terms of negotiation were revisited (Lamothe 2007). Since then, there have been two subsequent ANRs at the table; however, Lamothe continues to challenge aspects of the claim from outside the negotiations.

Lamothe's break with the negotiations came at a time when the *Ottawa Citizen* coverage appeared quite sympathetic to the land claim and presented an overwhelming vision of the power that affiliating with the claim could give to Algonquins – to stop major developments, to address the dispensation of lands, to put Algonquins "on the map" for mainstream Canada, and above all else, to end the poverty and powerlessness of their communities. This vision made it difficult for a sympathetic public to see the disparities in representation for those sitting at the table that Lamothe was attempting to address, the absolute lack of community development and training for most of the six thousand people who will benefit from any agreement brokered in these high-powered negotiations, and the outright dismissal of the question as to whether such a settlement would truly be a treaty or just another real estate deal.

And yet, despite the resources that the Algonquins of Ontario can command, Algonquins can draw strength from other sources. The late William Commanda, venerated as "the Grandfather" by many Algonquins on the Ontario side – and indeed their most visible sign of nationhood – had long called for Victoria Island to become the site for an international gathering of nations, with Algonquins as the host nation. One of his last actions prior to his death in July 2011 was to call Algonquins together in defence of the South March Highlands in Ottawa.[11] The response from Algonquins in both Quebec and Ontario resulted in the creation of a new organization, the Algonquin Union, established to unite Algonquin communities while allowing them to maintain their independence in managing their own internal interests. The Algonquin Union hopes to empower the communities by giving them a strong, united voice for dealings with non-Algonquin entities. It also strives to embody the Algonquin traditional culture in a manner that promotes understanding and respectful co-existence with sympathetic non-Algonquin participants.

There have been other Algonquin cultural associations, such as Omàmìwininì Pimàdjwowin, which was initiated by Aimee Bailey of Pikwakanagan. However, since it has become an "official" cultural organization in the land claim, many see it as a site where no Algonquins of any affiliation can assemble.[12]

The Algonquin Union, on the other hand, has held a number of cultural teaching events, always in connection with the land, and thus it promises to offer Algonquins a new venue for cultural renewal. It may well be that Ottawa can become an Algonquin gathering place again.

Conclusion: Algonquin Identity and Nationhood

> First of all, it must be said that the responsibility for defining Algonquin identity rests solely with Algonquin people. Secondly, it is important that Algonquin culture and traditions be transmitted to Algonquin children and youth before anyone else ... As a people with a history in this place, we have a choice to make. We have to decide who we want to be in the future as human beings. Do we want to carry forward an identity that has been created by the province and federal government, or do we reject that colonial construct and begin to challenge ourselves to regain and restore our true identity as spiritual beings? It's an important question that must be answered by each Algonquin person as they move forward with their life and existence in this homeland that we inherited from our ancestors.
>
> **– Ardoch Algonquin First Nation, "What Does It Mean to Be Algonquin Today?"**

This book has focused on questions relating to identity and nationhood for federally unrecognized Algonquins during an eight-year period when a major land claim negotiation was under way. Through years of conducting interviews in the Ottawa River watershed, I have attempted to learn about historical and contemporary Algonquin experience. I wanted to discover how unrecognized Algonquins continued to survive as a people during a time when their very existence was ignored and denied, and being "Indian" was intensively defined by the Canadian government. I also wanted to focus on how being "invisible" as a people had shaped non-status identity, in the past and today. More broadly, I wanted to understand how the land claim affected them. Over the course of the research, these questions led to the issue of Algonquin nationhood itself and how federally unrecognized Algonquins are struggling to re-create the nationhood that was so relentlessly dismantled by colonial encroachments across their homeland. In many respects, the interview process began to answer some of these questions as well as pointing to directions where other answers may be found. Below, I will address these issues.

The historical record of how the ancestors of today's non-status Algonquins endured the loss of their lands and the transformation of their ways of life is of immense importance in bridging the rupture of identity that so many federally unrecognized Algonquins discussed. In many ways, this is a collective history. And yet, identity is always personal. Immersed in a settler society that simultaneously devalues Indigenous identity and belittles Algonquins for not being "Indian enough," today's non-status Algonquins need to reach past the silencing to trace the personal connections between their own lives and those of their ancestors. For the most part, this knowledge lies in the childhood experiences of those who are now elders.

Some elders mentioned these experiences, albeit briefly. For example, Harold Perry's childhood reminiscences of life at Ardoch in the 1930s, and the stories he heard dating back to the First World War and the 1920s, of people progressively losing their sugar bush stands, their manoomin, their fishing spots, and their hunting grounds to the hostile or indifferent settlers who now had deeds to the lands they had always used, are a valuable link between past and present. Another set of important experiences concern those who managed, during this time of dispersal, to acquire fee simple land in their own territories – at Baptiste Lake, near Bancroft, in the Bonnechere Valley, or at Ardoch, and elsewhere – only to lose it to taxes. Marginalized in the settler economy, those who did acquire fee simple land were almost never able to keep it. The histories recounted by elders whose family lands were lost in this manner, represent yet another bridge between the present and the past, as do Jane Chartrand's recollections of her grandmother's stories from her own childhood, of watching the Madawaska River pine trees being logged and hauled away on flatcars. Although they speak of land loss and the reasons *why* individuals became silent about their identities, these memories connect today's Algonquins tangibly to those who lived through the painful experience of dispossession.

The next generation's experiences also anchor the present to the past – as encoded in the late Bob Ferguson's memories of the building of the La Cav and La Swisha hydroelectric dams and how deeply it changed life for local Algonquins, or in the stories of Pembroke elders Janet Hoffman (now deceased) and Helen King of how their family survived being forcibly removed from their homes at Deep River so that Atomic Energy of Canada could build a nuclear plant. These and other stories that were shared with me have demonstrated that most of today's elders can furnish important connections between past and present. Their accounts are significant because they establish non-status Algonquins as *rooted* where the stories took place – that their ancestral territories were there, that collective ways of life were being maintained there. They give the lie to the hegemonic logic that non-status Algonquins have no connection to place and that only Indian status – or recognition through a land claim – can secure an Algonquin identity.

In many ways, these stories are the only true foundation on which Algonquin nationhood can be reborn. And if for the most part they are about dispossession, they are also about the survival of people who were not *expected* to survive – not as individuals and certainly not as a people. I believe it is vital for Algonquins to begin or to continue to record the stories of their elders, of what their own grandparents told them, how they lived as children, the changes they saw, the migrations and dispossessions they experienced, how they adapted, and how they endured. The difficulty is that these elders are passing away every day. A land claim can provide a legal identity card, but a people's true presence on the land is ultimately established by stories, and it is those stories that will provide a foundation for the renascent nationhood of federally unrecognized Algonquins.

And yet, ironically, the ability for many people to begin telling their stories *has* been shaped in part by having their Algonquin lineage proved. And this relates to the effects of silence on identity. Whereas the people who went to Golden Lake or Maniwaki encountered intense interference in their traditional ways, those who refused to leave faced the brunt of settler racism and violence at a time when extinctionist discourse was in full flower and the life of "an Indian" was held very cheap. For many non-status Algonquins, particularly those who lost their lands early in the process, being barely tolerated outsiders living in close proximity to a newly establishing settler society meant always being at risk of having their homes burned down so that settlers could expand their own farms, of being physically attacked for attempting to fish on land that was now "private property," or of losing children to child welfare authorities when their fathers were arrested for "illegal" hunting. For many, it meant being used as child labour, being a source of cheap labour, being sexually exploited by employers, or simply being considered a local social problem that should be driven out of town. For individuals in these circumstances, skin colour could not be changed, but other signs of external difference could. From forcing their children to speak English rather than Algonquin, to refusing to tell their traditional stories, to eventually attempting to network with settlers by joining their churches and attending their community gatherings, many non-status Algonquins did their best to remove the obvious external traces of Algonquinness from their lives in hopes of ensuring the survival of their children. Over the past fifty years in particular, intermarriage with settlers began to take place, but this did not erase the legacy carried by their mixed-blood descendants.

It is important to conceptualize these experiences of forced adaptation not as countless individual aberrations from Algonquinness but as *part of* federally unrecognized Algonquin experience. The pressures faced by Algonquins in attempting to survive, landless, in a largely hostile settler society, and the survival processes of their ancestors, are as much a part of Algonquin history as the efforts of earlier leaders to negotiate treaties in the interests of survival.

In regions where settler influence and industry arrived late or were less prevalent, such as in the upper Madawaska River and at Mattawa, Algonquins were less pressured to hide their identity. In those areas, the forced changes and adaptations were less extreme, federally unrecognized Algonquins were more visible, and the language was more frequently spoken. However, constant dispersal in search of work shaped the histories of Algonquins in these areas, and those who left faced their own pressures to be silent about their identity.

This legacy of silence has meant that many of the grandchildren and great-grandchildren of nineteenth-century Algonquins have grown up with a deep sense of cultural confusion in a society where extinctionist discourse has been transformed into a range of assumptions and stereotypes, positive or negative, about "the Indian," which insist, above all, that the only valid Indianness is "pure" Indianness. For many non-status Algonquins, even hearing or valuing the stories passed down in their families has been difficult in the face of such stereotypes. The result for many was long years of disempowerment.

The reality is that how a person is identified determines which histories he or she can access and make claims on. For example, when Metis writer Greg Scofield learned that his previously unknown father was Jewish, it was a profound moment for him. Through this heritage, he became connected to the experience of surviving the Holocaust as well as a range of contemporary Jewish cultural and social practices. This led Scofield to explore what it meant to be both Jewish and Metis, to reject categories that are considered unilateral and mutually exclusive, to become a Jewish Metis or, indeed, a Metis Jew.

For many Algonquins, the disjuncture between family histories that situated them as Indian and the daily actualities of life in a settler society that continuously erased Algonquin presence meant that they had little means of connecting themselves to their own stories. As a result, the stories gradually began to minimize Indianness or to reflect its presence in disjointed ways. On several occasions, in conducting these interviews, the people I interviewed spoke about how older Algonquins, when their identities were finally validated as Indian, almost immediately began to access stories of loss and dispossession that were profound. In a sense, the validation of their Algonquin identity meant that they could finally make sense of the stories they had been told as children and interpret their grandparents' stories in a new light. Accessing proof of lineage has, in many respects, meant being able to finally make sense of family stories.

Because of this history, for many Algonquins, accessing family stories also has to mean understanding how living in a society that constantly erases Algonquinness has affected their own family stories about the past. For example, in a society where individuals are taught to think of themselves as white, their family stories will almost inevitably position their Native heritage as marginal to the family's life. Those stories need reinterpretation – carefully and honestly, but with an eye to the constant minimizing effect of living in a society that considers "the Indian" to have essentially vanished. Learning about family histories therefore also means learning to understand being Algonquin in contemporary ways – in essence, to re-imagine Algonquinness to make it an identity that is about the future, and not just a marginalized part of the past.

Up to now, I have focused on histories of erasure of Algonquinness. The other side of the picture, however – which the interviews demonstrated remarkably well – was the tangible evidence that even if language use vanished, ceremonial life was transformed, external practices were modified, and visible appearance changed, federally unrecognized Algonquins did not vanish as peoples. Instead, the interviews suggest that they maintained the values and collective practices that kept them together as a people—whether or not those practices were understood as Algonquin practices.

Collective practices were demonstrated most clearly in the stories told by Janet Hoffman and her sister Helen King about the extended family network that was displaced when the nuclear facility was built at Deep River. From farming to trapping to berrying and fishing, tasks were shared collectively as were the products of their labour. At a time when each isolated settler family looked after its own winter needs by slaughtering a farm animal and potting the meat or storing it on ice in a root cellar, the people at Deep River simply shared both abundance and scarcity as part of their daily life, as Algonquins have always done. Whether it was time to slaughter a cow or kill a moose or deer, everything was shared, and every part of the animal was used. What they could not use, such as the hide (because they had lost the practice of tanning), was given to Algonquins living nearby who still knew how to work it. Nothing was thrown away and everything was shared.

It is equally obvious what happens to community members when the collective ethic is shattered by alcohol. As some of the interviews in Pembroke demonstrated, the lives of Algonquin families who have struggled with alcoholism are marked by lateral violence, the breakdown of family ties, tremendous internalized racism, and the loss of kinship knowledge.

Before we consider how collective practices were maintained among non-status Algonquins, it's important to understand the extent to which sharing was an ethic among them (as it is with most Native people who still retain their traditions). For example, the wild rice seed that Mary Buckshot, the great-grandmother of Harold Perry, brought from Rice Lake and sowed at Mud Lake flourished so well that Ardoch frequently invited the Mississaugas of Alderville and Curve Lake to take part in its harvesting. Similarly, during the Depression, when the settlers who had displaced the Ardoch people were themselves going hungry, Ardoch provided the neediest families with the parched and prepared rice for them to cook.

The interviews showed that the ethic of sharing was neither accidental nor a product of innate goodness – it was created and sustained by deliberate socializing. Across the territory, I interviewed people who spoke about the regular get-togethers held by their families. Some noticed merely that their settler neighbours did not follow those practices, whereas others explained what the family gatherings had taught them. Reflecting on the regular family gatherings of his Bancroft childhood, Robin Tinney stated that they taught relatives how to "get along with each other," so that internal cohesion and the values of hard work and sharing were impressed on everyone. The Pembroke families interviewed for the project also showed this pattern of systematic family gathering, except in the families where alcoholism had wrought social breakdown and destroyed ties.

For the families who met habitually, the results of such socializing were palpable. While visiting individuals in Pembroke, I was struck by the cordiality of their relationship and by the manner in which they established their connection by talking about their lineages. Clearly, these values are taught and are as intrinsic to most Indigenous people as the more obvious collective practices such as cooking meat or fish by burying it in the ground and covering it with wet leaves and hot rocks. A number of federally unrecognized

Algonquins appear to have upheld these practices for many years, which allowed them to maintain their values regardless of how invisible they were to settler society.

Intensive socializing to preserve collective values also seemed to assist families in retaining ties to place and community. Connections to place are strong in many non-status Algonquin families and are linked to a sense of community. In Sharbot Lake, for example, the presence of "natural" leaders – community people who visit the elders simply to sustain relations and share information with them – helps to explain why so many Algonquins live in this community, in that collective ties reinforce ties of place.

This history suggests the importance for communities of strengthening these practices, which in many cases are breaking down as children leave to find work in cities. Now that the lineage of each Algonquin has been established in order to qualify him or her for the land claim, re-creating ways that extended families can regularly gather may be an important means of rebuilding a collective ethic. It may also be central to forms of governance, which will be addressed later in this chapter.

The relationship to the land, which has been strengthened by practices on the land, has also enabled federally unrecognized Algonquins to survive as a people. This is often expressed through an attachment to hunting. The deep connection to hunting that so many Algonquins continue to maintain has become a complex issue because of the extent to which the politics of hunting have become implicated with the politics of the land claim, and the tensions that many Algonquins are currently struggling with, between hunting for food and hunting as an expression of a collective *right*. For all these reasons, there is little consensus over the question of hunting at present. But what *is* obvious is the intense relationship to the land of some Algonquin hunters and trappers, a deep familiarity that approaches stewardship, as Art Cota Jr. explained during his 2007 interview:

> But this is our land and we need more people protecting it, more people looking after it ... I just love in the wintertime to go out after a snow and you see all the different tracks and you see everything and it just makes me feel whole, as a person ... to be able to go back in the woods. Like in the fall of the year, when the ice freezes, you can walk on, like, an inch of ice. You can walk right across it and it'll go crack, bang ... But in the spring of the year, you can walk on it and she won't make a noise. I don't have to kill anything. Just the quiet of it is what I like.

I learned most of my skills from my dad. And after that, the more time you put at something the better you get at it ... I know every rock and hill there is for a few square miles around here. I'm here all the time in the winter. I know where I'm going. And you just get so attached to it. In the spring of the year, I'd have my dad drive me down and I'd have a set of chest waders and I'd walk in a great big huge circle, all around all these big floods and this and that. And he'd drop me off around nine o'clock and he'd say, "OK what time do you want me to come and pick you up?" I'd say three o'clock. And I'd walk that whole big circle, all the way around there, and I'd get back there three o'clock. My dad would be sitting there waiting for me and I'd have ten, fifteen, or twenty muskrats, and the next day I'd do it again. You see, in the spring, that's when the muskrats mate. So that's when you catch your muskrats, is in the spring.

My dad and I, we had a lot of good times. Like we'd have a fall that would get really cold, maybe, this time of year, and you could walk on the pond so I'd strike down my trapline, carry a bunch of traps down, set the traps and I'll be darned, two or three days later a mild spell would come. You can't walk on the ponds any more, but my traps are out there. So I would say, "Well, if it's going to be mild again tomorrow, I think I can still walk on the ice." So I would go down and I'd walk on the ice. And you'd get down there two or three miles in the bush and you've got two or three great big beaver. And I'd say, "With those guys on my back, the ice is not going to hold me." So I'd take a knife and I'd sit up on a rock and I'd skin them and I'd take the carcasses and I'd hang them up and maybe set a snare for a wolf, or whatever, and then hang my traps up in a tree because it might stay mild for a week. You can't have your traps set for a week. So I'd hang my traps up in the tree and maybe set a snare for a wolf, or whatever, and put the hides in my backpack, carry them out, and then as soon as it was froze up, that'd be the first place I'd head back to, to fix things up. So I have a lot of memories of that.

When I was young, all I wanted to do was catch beaver. A herd of otter could go by and I'm beaver trapping. I went one day and I lifted my beaver trap up. I had a muskrat. "Aah muskrat." My dad says, "Why don't you set that? Skin that muskrat out and set it for a mink?" Then I just grumbled away, you know. A kid, you know, I knew everything. I said OK. I skinned the muskrat and I put the hide in my backpack and I got a little trap out and he took some rocks, and they're still piled there today and that would be over thirty years ago. Right down alongside of the pond, he took the rocks and he made like a little house, back maybe sixteen inches, just a little wee door, at

> the front. He put the muskrat carcass back there, put the trap in front of it, and tied the trap to a big long pole. We went back the next day. I was eager to get to the beaver house. I had to check my beaver trap. My dad walks over. "Hey bud, you've got a mink." Yeah, OK. I got the mink. I got seventy-five dollars for the mink. The muskrat carcass is still inside the little cubbyhole there. My dad reset the trap. Went back the next day, I got another mink. All of a sudden mink trapping isn't so bad, you know ... I can go back to that same place, and when I go by there I still see those rocks that my dad put there over thirty years ago.

It is clear that a dialogue about hunting needs to take place across the Ottawa Valley. This needs also to engage the *Perry* decision (as discussed in Chapter 6) and how signing agreements with the Ministry of Natural Resources damages the rights of non-status Indians to hunt as were established in *Perry.*

And yet, this issue leads to the question of the land claim, of how discussions of Algonquin nationhood or of hunting – or any discussion that threatens to interrogate the claim – are subverted in many of the land claim communities. Before examining this, however, we must scrutinize the issue of connections to the land and ties to place.

The communities outside the land claim all emphasize that their members have particular ties to the land in their watershed. Both Ardoch and Whimasab (Whitney, Madawaska, and Sabine), as well as Kichesipirini, Pasapkedjiwanong, and probably many more of the newer unaffiliated communities base their existence on the fact that their members have historical and specific ties to the lands of their ancestors (indeed, this is undoubtedly part of the reason why they left the claim or were never admitted in the first place). In every region, reclaiming stories of the land will organically connect Algonquins to it, even as their ancestors' remains make up the land. These stories are the foundation upon which an Indigenous nation stands, with or without a comprehensive claim to "recognize" the process.

And though the membership of some of the ANTC communities also clearly consider themselves rooted to the land (as do some of the ANRs), the Algonquins of Ontario assert that all Algonquins have a stake in the entire territory. To create an undifferentiated claim to all of the territory in this manner is to deny the existence of any specific ties to the land by any of the communities that continued to occupy the territories where their ancestors had always lived. To proceed in this way is to create a nation "on paper" but not a nation on the land. Moreover, it is to endlessly be vulnerable to arguments about blood quantum with respect to who belongs and who doesn't within the legal structure of the nation. Connecting peoples' histories to specific lands clarifies that being Indigenous is not about blood quantum – it is about establishing connections to the ancestors.

A particularly troubling feature of the Algonquins of Ontario stance is the insistence that any non-status Ontario Algonquin can affiliate with any ANTC community. The effect of this position is to blur the actual histories of Algonquins in specific territories and to reduce Algonquinness to finding an ancestor's name on a list and being slotted into an ANTC community. And though this strategy may seem adequate in a comprehensive claim, it does not allow for the stories that connect families and communities to specific places. More troubling still is the manner in which this implicitly (and officially) detaches the membership of the ANTC communities from any real ties to any specific territory at all other than the land claim area in general.

Rebuilding Algonquin Nationhood

Most of the individuals I interviewed expressed a desire for an organic process of nation rebuilding. They envisioned this primarily with respect to a reinfusion of traditional values and practices, so that leaders could be trusted to be free of corruption, accompanied by a rebirth of genuine kindness and caring for one another. Part of this entailed a reconnection with Algonquins in Quebec and an end to the barriers between status and non-status Algonquins. Others emphasized that notions of the sacred needed to be brought back – the sacredness of the land, of life, of women, and of the relationship between Algonquins and their land. And as Algonquin scholar Lynn Gehl has suggested, a genuine treaty with Canada would require bringing this reinfused traditional process into the negotiations, so that Algonquin paradigms and the comprehensive claims policy are accorded equal weight and treaties are once again seen as part of a sacred trust that is to be maintained between peoples and with the land.

Many Algonquins at the grassroots level believe that the people need a deep spiritual awakening, and certain communities and organizations outside the land claim are focusing on this goal. For example, Pasapkedjiwanong was established specifically to engage with traditional teachings and to emphasize the importance of relearning the language. Similarly, the Algonquin Union, which formed to protect specific land from development, is also about promoting spiritual growth in Algonquins. Some Algonquins who belong to ANTC communities also speak to the need for spiritual renewal. And yet, for many of them, a fundamental contradiction exists in that any spiritual awakening that might occur at the ground level will be overshadowed by a land claim process that most resembles a real estate deal. However, certain facts – that many Algonquins in the Ottawa River watershed are poor and that their children will continue to migrate to cities to work no matter how much they attempt to reinfuse traditional values into daily life – are also a concern. Given these circumstances, it may not be unreasonable to combine a desire for spiritual awakening with a pragmatic hope that the economic changes brought by the claim will enable young Algonquins to stay home and live well there. Whether the claim is capable of *delivering* on such promises and whether alternative economic strategies could address regional poverty without surrendering Aboriginal title are questions that the ANTC leadership will not permit its membership to discuss.

Without such discussion of what non-status Algonquins stand to gain, given the limitations of what can be obtained under the comprehensive claims policy, and of how an organic nation can be restored with a comprehensive claim that regularly violates the principles of nation building, many Algonquins are having to define precisely how they see their own relationship to the land. Across the Ottawa River watershed, profound spiritual and philosophical divergences in world views between land-based people and technological society are being played out both *within* Algonquin communities and *between* them. As uranium mining at Robertsville, clear cutting in the South March Highlands, hydroelectric projects, pulp and paper mill effluent, and waste tritium put their stamp on the land and profoundly affect the communities of the Ottawa River watershed, many Algonquins are struggling to come to terms with the implications of constantly accelerating corporate-driven resource development and the costs of resisting it, even as they attempt to solidify a sense of themselves as Algonquins. In this context, they are caught between the "rock" of needing to reclaim a sacred connection with the land as integral to being Algonquin and the "hard place" of attempting to do so while the lands and waters are assaulted by corporate-driven resource extraction.

At present, the comprehensive claims process is pre-empting discussion among Algonquins as to *alternative* ways of making a good living on the land without simply allowing it to be logged out or mined. Instances of sustainable community-driven resource development are few and far between in this region, yet two examples do exist: the Algonquin Forestry Authority and the Whitney Algonquin Aboriginal Loggers Association are community initiatives that enable the Algonquins of Whimasab to engage in sustainable, community-organized, and relatively low-tech logging in Algonquin Park outside of corporate or provincial control. This involves Algonquins maintaining the forest while making a living from it. Other endeavours are possible, including eco-tourism, canoe making, traditional and ecological alternatives in housing, solar and wind power cooperatives to enable people to get "off the grid," arts or crafts cooperatives, small-business ventures, marketing cooperatives with other First Nations, and programs to train youth in sustainable practices relating to wildlife. In all cases, the goal would be to allow Algonquins to live sustainably on the land while making a comfortable enough living for the next generation that the youth would not need to take jobs elsewhere. All these alternatives require networking and pooling of resources implicit in community building, and none are possible without challenging the corporate-fuelled resource extraction that pre-empts all other activity on the land. This means challenging the manner in which the Ministry of Natural Resources and the Ministry of Northern Development and Mines facilitate corporate resource development. Following Ardoch's example, communities can stake a number of claims through direct action, including rights to the land that would enable them to engage in alternative economic strategies or to reclaim and develop traditional and ecological technologies. But at present, the land claim negotiations supersede everything else, including engaging knowledgeable Algonquins who might have much to contribute to alternative forms of development. Ultimately, however, under the comprehensive claims policy, Algonquins must submit to provincial authority in every aspect of their relationship to the land. And it is this feature of the claim, along with the implicit surrender of title, that has made communities such as Ardoch and Whimasab so vehemently opposed to the process. At this point, the claim is actively interfering with communities' attempts to protect their land.

With its unique experience of fighting so openly and in so many arenas to defend its territory and to assert its jurisdiction, and in its determination to resist further resource rape in the Ottawa Valley, Ardoch has produced the most sustained and thoughtful critique of the land claim process. During a 2003 interview, Bob Lovelace detailed what he had learned through his long association with Harold Perry – that the comprehensive claims process is about removing Aboriginal title:

> I think for a lot of the people who've lived on the land and haven't separated from the land, it's not real hard for them to figure out what's going on. Because they've lived with that legacy, there's not been any interruption ... If you were born in the 1970s, you would have grown up knowing that land claims are a fact of life in Canada. If you were born in the 1930s, you would scratch your head and wonder what the hell is this all about. Because the land claim was

really born out of the White Paper, along with a whole lot of other stuff that came out of the White Paper. Because you need processes to implement termination of title and termination of responsibilities, traditional responsibilities. Do you know of any land claim that has actually asserted Aboriginal title? Or even recognized title? Comprehensive land claims are never settled in favour of the Indian people. The process was never intended to.

Interviewed in 2005, Ardoch elder Carol Bate voiced the perspective of many in her community that values can be too easily abandoned when individuals are too eager to proceed with a land claim at any cost, particularly given the assaults on identity that Algonquins in Ontario have already experienced. Bate believes that because of this history, too many Algonquins are insecure about their identities and are therefore susceptible to what the land claim professes to offer. She points to the basic values that Algonquin people need to consider before uncritically accepting a real estate deal that will permanently settle their rights as Algonquin people to their traditional land:

I have seen elderly men with tears in their eyes because they got a card that said they were Algonquin ... What they wanted was that one piece of European paper that said according to the European records they were Algonquin. Now, they always knew that, but without a piece of paper to prove it, they haven't got a chance in the world of getting their balance ...

Here's my favourite thing to say: What do we own? What are we responsible for? And what would we sell? And until every member of my band knows that, I'm not happy. If they can't draw me a picture of what they own, the shape and size and the location ... and if they can't tell me that that was theirs, and if they can't tell me that they feel some responsibility to the waterways and to the earth that was theirs and that maybe still is theirs legally ... then I want them to tell me what they'd sell it for – now what do they want for it? And if they say to me, "Oh, I'd sell it for a hundred dollars," well, okay – that's your answer, eh? What do you own? What are you responsible for? What would you sell for it?

Bate's words speak to the concerns of many Algonquins, that the individuals involved in the land claim are being driven by their need to see their identities recognized via the process and that they have not thought out the value systems that underlie the negotiations.

During her 2004 interview, Paula Sherman, a co-chief of Ardoch and a professor of Native studies at Trent University, voiced the need for a different approach, in which Algonquins simply claim their rights, regardless of colonial jurisdictions:

> We're far better off to just articulate our autonomy and sovereignty in different ways, and if that ends up in court, then it ends up in court. I mean, that's the way we have hunting and fishing rights, it's through Harold [Perry] and all those things that were brought through the courts. And I think that it's better than us being forced to negotiate for a treaty from an inferior position with the Canadian government. As I said, we shouldn't have to go to court with them at all; they should be coming to us. They are on our land illegally. Ottawa, the capital of Canada, sits in our territory that we never gave them. Not to mention the fact that all the buildings, all the mortar that's in Parliament, has Algonquin remains in them. All of the buildings that Parliament was made from in the nineteenth century, they took the sand for the mortar from an ancient burial ground there in Ottawa. So they're conducting their business on our land, the capital of Canada is on our land. And in buildings that are built with the human remains of our people.

The leaders of Whimasab, which is also seeking its own future away from the land claim, have expressed their frustration at the ongoing erosion of whatever gains Aboriginal people make and the need for Algonquins to be aware of this reality in the negotiation process. As Whimasab leader Bob Lavalley states, without the ability to take a tough stance, to really know the extent of the robbery perpetrated on Algonquin people, and to respond with a unified front, Algonquins will remain poor and will have to accept whatever crumbs are handed to them – not as compensation for the rape of their land but so that their rights to it can be terminated. He also reminds us that Ottawa's largest concern with respect to Native people has always been to terminate them as Indians and that the land claim must be understood on that basis.

Proponents of a middle ground in the land claim process often critique its corruption and negativity but are not opposed to comprehensive claims in principle. Grounding their views in realpolitik rather than idealism, they often fail to see the possibility of a large-scale repossessing of traditional Algonquin ways or of a fundamental power shift between Algonquin people and Canada. However, they accept no aspect of the claim without carefully examining all its implications.

Bob Majaury, who has struggled with the difficulties of occupying a principled middle ground in such a chaotic and divided environment, has long been a proponent of a national government for Algonquins, which he believes will enable Algonquins to overcome the flawed processes that many of the land claims communities are experiencing. He has spoken out strongly and continuously against the corruption of the process and has expressed his distress regarding the disrespectful behaviour of some Algonquins toward each other in their conflict around the land claim. He has also frequently decried the lack of information being disseminated regarding the process, noting that most Algonquins learn more from newspaper articles than they do from their erstwhile representatives, despite the fact that large amounts of funding are available for communication but are apparently not being used.

In January 2010, the Algonquins of Ontario announced that they had opened a centre in Pembroke "to co-ordinate a wide variety of consultation activities with government departments, ministries or agencies" (Algonquins of Ontario 2010). With the opening of this office, Majaury offered his insight that such a centre would not work as a government-Algonquin enterprise and that the only way in which it could be useful would be for it to function as a centralized information site for Algonquin people.

In many ways, Bob Majaury's position points most strongly to the need for Algonquins to begin practical processes of nation rebuilding without waiting for the outcome of the comprehensive claim. However, given the polarization among many Algonquins who are grappling with this process, I believe it is important to suggest that a land claim *cannot* create – or rather re-create – a nation, not in the organic sense that many Algonquins appear to be seeking. The original attempt by Pikwakanagan to claim the Ontario side of the Ottawa Valley *did* entail a vision of an organic nationhood. The first chief negotiator, Greg Sarazin, subscribed to the powerful if utopian idea that the claim could rebuild the nation despite the profound fracturing of the Algonquin homeland by provincial boundaries and Indian Act policies. Conflict regarding Indian status derailed this vision of the land claim as restoring justice to Algonquins, and the barriers that separate Algonquins along lines of Indian status are now deeper than ever because the land claim regime implemented in 2004 simply entrenched them. Moreover, these divisions concerning Indian status cannot be reduced to a matter of local prejudice; they are tied to national policies in which definitions of Indianness function to set Native people apart.

The fact that status Indian communities presently enjoy rights and benefits that are not shared by other differently defined Aboriginal people is central to the colonialist logic of division that, in so many different ways, hived off so many people from their nations. Nevertheless, those First Nations who have *not* lost their recognition as Indian also view themselves as the last bastion for the protection of Indigenous land and nationhood in Canada. And given the ongoing attempts by Ottawa to force assimilation on status Indians through the constant eroding of the protections offered in the Indian Act, First Nations are increasingly unlikely to negotiate agreements with anyone whose identities as Indian are not secured by firm defining legislation. To do so is to potentially invite further attrition of their rights and recognition as Indigenous nations, since under this logic, being Indigenous depends on being Indian.

Changes in the definition of other categories of Aboriginal people – of "Metis" and "non-status Indians" – are also of relevance in entrenching divisions. The multiple currents of Metis discourse on nation building are too complex to explore in depth here. For the most part, however, the Constitution's 1982 inclusion of the Metis as Aboriginal people resulted in an intensive effort to formalize the various meanings of "Metisness," particularly relating to questions of Metis land rights. Generally speaking, Metis land rights are addressed in two capacities. On the one hand, as articulated by Patricia Sawchuk (1996), Larry Gilbert (1996), and a host of others, the definition of "Indian" in the Constitution Act of 1867 was broader than that of the Indian Act, and as a result "Metis" land rights flow from Indian rights.

On the other hand is the emphasis, particularly from many Western Metis historians, that the formation of the Red River settlement and the political engagement of the Metis under Louis Riel constituted a struggle for a distinct Metis nationhood with accruing rights, including land. The recent *Powley* decision points to this direction and indeed not only delineates the distinct rights of Metis in relation to harvesting but defines Metisness in non-restrictive ways.

In a sense, it is not surprising that Metisness would increasingly be seen as distinct from Indianness and any rights relating to it. The colonialist logic that originally defined Indianness demands categories of racial difference to justify the existence of such definitions and to ensure that Aboriginal people remain at odds and therefore disempowered. To emphasize the Indian rights of Metis people would be to maintain Indianness as the common ground that establishes entitlement for Metis, non-status, *and* status Indians, making forms of unity at least conceivable. But to present the Metis as a nation that by definition must *always* be distinct from Indianness is to generate multiple unconnected ways of asserting Indigeneity, all separately defined and without possibility of creating alliance. Indeed, rather than facilitating alliances, such definitions invite competition between the various Indigenous categories – for land, resources, and recognition.

Moreover, if definitions of Metisness irrevocably separate Indianness and Metisness, no space is left for non-status Indians. Although it does include "Metis" as a category of Aboriginal people, the Constitution does not explicitly mention non-status Indians. The boundaries between Metis and non-status Indians were mutable and ill-defined for many years, but the declaration of a separate Metis Nation has increasingly prompted Metis associations to suggest that their non-status Indian members must look to Indian organizations for their support, since they are not Metis (Joe Sawchuk 1986).

However, status Indian bodies normally do not recognize the rights of non-status people, which has certainly been the experience of those who attempted to claim Indian rights, as was the case in the Maritimes. In 1999, the *Marshall* decision recognized the right of Mi'kmaq people to fish commercially, a right based on treaties of 1760-61, which certainly predated the Indian Act. But when non-status Mi'kmaq attempted to fish under *Marshall*, many New Brunswick and Nova Scotia First Nations viewed them as doing so illegally (Palmater 2000).

Furthermore, even though First Nations are attempting to take over their own citizenship, local circumstances play a major role in defining the relations that many are willing to strike with non-status people. Kirby Whiteduck's (2004) exhortation to the Assembly of First Nations Renewal Commission (addressed in Chapter 10) should be revisited here:

> Pikwakanagan has concerns with the addition to the scope of responsibilities of the Minister of Indian Affairs to include "federal interlocutor for Metis and non-status Indians." We do not have so much of a concern with the reference to Metis as there is now some definition and criteria for who is considered to be Metis. We do have a concern with the reference to and inclusion of the term "non-status." In our opinion, it should be removed from the title and responsibilities as there is no reference to non-status in the constitution. Canada's constitution states that the Aboriginal Peoples of Canada include the Indian, Inuit and Metis. Do we have a clear or common idea of who may be considered non-status or even if we accept that category? Does Canada or its provinces have a constitutionally and therefore a legitimately recognized definition of non-status? It is our opinion that we do not and that to refer and address the minister as including responsibility for non-status Indians is to inadvertently recognize them or recognize an undefined category. I guess that goes back to recognizing either directly or indirectly a group of people that is undefined and to find a definition of it ... To recognize a group that is undefined will have its own repercussions. What I am saying is that before we recognize somebody, there should be some kind of definition of what it is and who they are.

For many First Nations leaders, the problem with the category of "non-status Indian" is its poorly defined nature. For Pikwakanagan in particular, the reluctance of non-status Algonquins to pigeonhole themselves according to the cut-and-dried blood quantum definitions that it recognizes is what makes the problem so intractable.

It's important to understand that if connections to land are ignored and blood quantum alone is taken into account, non-status Algonquin identity will then run the gamut between "almost fully Indian" and "almost white." Thus, when applied to non-status Algonquins, blood quantum definitions of identity can never confer enough Indianness for Pikwakanagan even to consider any form of *direct* political connection with them as part of an Algonquin nation-rebuilding project.

Other factors make it impossible for a land claim to rebuild Algonquin nationhood. Almost all completed comprehensive claims involve groups who share a common category under Canada's definitions of Aboriginal people. That is, they are either status Indians or Inuit, categories that are recognized as land-based peoples to whom Canada has a fiduciary obligation. Only one agreement departs from this pattern: the Sahtu Dene and Metis Comprehensive Land Claim Agreement of 1994 applies to both Metis people and the Sahtu Dene, status Indians who had not been assigned reserves even though they came under Treaty 8. Thus, the claim involved two landless groups who together would be melded into a new Sahtu Council, in the process losing the definitional distinctions between them.

Given this, how can a comprehensive claim consider the rights of two groups who, though they are both Algonquin, differ in such crucial aspects? The larger part of the group is non-status and therefore landless, whereas the much smaller part has both Indian status and a reserve. Furthermore, Canada has denied a fiduciary obligation to non-status Indians, accepting it only for status Indians. Indeed, there have been no comprehensive claims to date where the majority of claimants have lacked federal recognition.

As Bob Lavalley put it, Canada is *not* in the business of creating more Indians. Indeed, its policy has always been to limit the number of recognized Indians and to deny any requirement to pay compensation for past losses (as with Bedford Township, Lawrence Township, and Allumette Island). Thus, after a settlement, Canada can be expected to attempt to maintain the status quo – that non-status Algonquins will continue to lack both intrinsic territory-specific rights and a fiduciary relationship with Ottawa. As Robin Tinney has observed, even the non-Native leaders of the negotiation team appear to accept this distinction between Algonquins. The claim's own organization suggests that since differing rules apply to non-status and status Algonquins in the negotiations, the two groups will continue to be classified differently once the land claim is completed.

Prior to 2000, for all its faults, the negotiations team as led by Greg Sarazin had at least created a means of ensuring identical structures for status and non-status communities under the Algonquin Nation Circle, which claimed land rights for the entire nation. However, the current negotiations are bifurcated: Pikwakanagan is one partner to the claim, and the non-status representatives, who form one body, constitute the other partner. Each non-status community has one negotiator, but the communities do *not* address intrinsic land rights to the region. In fact, as the example of Kichesipirini's attempt to join the land claim demonstrated, non-status Algonquins resident in Ontario can enrol in any community they wish, even if their traditional lands lie in Quebec. There is no requirement that community members must have traditional lands in that community. In fact, non-status communities who attempt to enrol while insisting on their claims to their traditional land base are denied entrance.

If the specific territorial rights of federally unrecognized communities are not addressed, negotiable lands or compensation will be minimized. In addition, once the claim is resolved, Pikwakanagan may be able to retain its distinct position, with a concomitant entrenched non-recognition of nationhood for the federally unrecognized groups. Most signatories to land claims relinquish their status as a reserve under the Indian Act in exchange for lands and monies. Thus, Pikwakanagan would be expected to surrender its Indian status; its reserve, which would become part of the territory claimed, would belong to all claimants. Ostensibly, Pikwakanagan would then be expected to enter into a formal body of governance with non-status Algonquins, a step it would almost certainly refuse to take as long as the non-status Algonquins remained unwilling to define themselves (and limit their numbers) by blood quantum. Tacitly, then, the non-status Algonquins could lack formal land rights and have a separate structure of governance. Pikwakanagan could conceivably be recognized as a nation, whereas the non-status Algonquins would be "communities of beneficiaries" rather than part of a nation.[1]

Although this scenario is speculative, it does address the way in which the parties are being positioned at the table. Only now, as an agreement in principle is being sought, is the question of beneficiaries being sorted out. And the Pikwakanagan leadership is still attempting to remove non-status

Algonquins from the beneficiary list. These two factors relate to questions of the compensation that might accrue to a group that has been situated in the claim as lacking distinct land rights.

Regardless of the politics of the claim, the reality is that most of the approximately five thousand federally unrecognized Algonquins in Ontario, who are not privy to the information being shared at the negotiation table, must decide for themselves how they will be treated. In many respects, their position would be immensely strengthened if they could envision an alternative form of representation rather than the land claim. For example, the Algonquin communities that have opted out of the claim and that see it with some clarity could slowly undertake a process of nation rebuilding that ignores and bypasses the divisions in the Algonquins of Ontario, and begin to address who they are as Omàmìwinini in Ontario today.

Federally unrecognized Algonquins who still hope for a settlement would be wise to consider the great risk they run in not attempting to actualize their nationhood *before* the claim is concluded. This is particularly the case where settlement monies are concerned. A number of Algonquins have pointed out that many federally unrecognized Algonquins are either unprepared or unconnected to the land claim regime and therefore will not be invited to fill the jobs that will be generated during the early days of the claim's resolution. In addition, except for Mattawa and the Bonnechere Algonquin Community, none have a community infrastructure of any kind *or* an economic development corporation capable of managing settlement monies. Indeed, Robin Tinney, of the Bancroft community, also suggests that most funding will pour into the pockets of the non-Native consultants who are being encouraged to "step up to the plate." And an article in the *Ottawa Citizen* about the planned sale of the former Canadian Forces Base Rockcliffe to a Crown corporation, which was scuttled by the land claim lawyers (Cook 2007, 2), is highly instructive about how Pikwakanagan hopes to profit from a resolved claim. In discussing the Rockcliffe project, the article revealed that Pikwakanagan had hoped to manage or own a quarter of the site to develop housing for Algonquin people, presumably those who held status. Regardless of the difficulties posed by living under the Indian Act, being a discrete community with a governance structure and a collective history as a reserve dating back more than a hundred years has positioned Pikwakanagan to take advantage of any economic developments that might accrue once a treaty is signed.

Moreover, after the loans are either forgiven or paid out of the settlement monies and non-Native consultants and Pikwakanagan have taken the lion's share, a truly frightening scenario might arise if negotiations conclude before federally unrecognized Algonquins engage in real nation building outside the land claim. At present, most communities are represented at the table by just one individual, the ANR, who controls all information, holds membership lists of up to two thousand individuals in some instances, and occupies their only real official positions. The potential for corruption is already great, simply because ANRs are privy to knowledge that is not available to their communities – even without the reality that many community members are poor and lack the education to fully understand the negotiations. For a number of years, the sense of bitter helplessness expressed by many articulate and concerned Algonquins about corruption in the negotiation process has been palpable. Once a settlement is reached, there will be nobody else, other than the ANRs, to take charge of whatever monies remain to be divided among ANTC communities. The ensuing bitterness, hostility, and schisms might make the current rupturing of federally unrecognized Algonquin communities seem minor by comparison. Algonquins who hoped that the land claim would at least provide them with economic options might find such options extremely elusive – unless they work on building a structure for themselves outside the comprehensive claims process, which could then be factored in as part of the distribution and organization of proceeds.

Nation Building: Issues to Consider

There are several issues to consider when speaking of nation building. Many individuals involved with the land claim have assumed that an Algonquin Nation entails a centralized state structure whose citizens are subordinated to both it and Ottawa – the model of "domestic dependent nations," which enjoy far greater powers on an everyday level than bands do in Canada. Multiple difficulties stem from this model, not the least of which is that blood quantum will remain central to the definition of citizenship. Nor is it possible even to conceive of such a model without a legal regime to support it. In Canada, unlike in the United States, there is no "third order" of government to enable Indigenous nations to hold semi-autonomous status. In the United States, tribes may be domestic dependent nations that are subject to the plenary power of Congress to negate their rights, but they are not subordinated to states. Indeed, many assert that they have more power than the states.

Perhaps the most viable option that Algonquins might pursue – and the only one that is possible given their lack of funding and the lack of a third order of government in Canada to provide a viable governance structure beyond the level of a municipality – is a loose network of affiliated communities, a form of nationhood that is in essence a confederacy, capable of drawing on the strengths of the collectivity in a centralized manner and yet allowing each community to set its own priorities. Governance would be managed by family groups, a structure that can consolidate communities in powerful and organic ways. In this confederacy, Algonquinness would be defined by family relations and community membership, not by citizenship based on blood quantum.

Algonquins who wish to form such a confederacy could learn from other nations that have faced dilemmas similar to their own. For example, the process developed by MoCreebec to re-create itself as a community might be useful to them. MoCreebec consists of Ontario-based Cree in Moose Factory who, like Algonquins, were drastically affected by the imposition of the Quebec-Ontario border. Their traditional territories are in Quebec, whereas they themselves have resided in Ontario for the most part since their grandparents attended residential school there. Like Algonquins, they occupy an anomalous position: They are not signatories to Treaty 9, which governs the part of Ontario where they live. Nor were they included in the James Bay and Northern Quebec Agreement of 1975, the "first modern-day treaty," which was signed on the Quebec half of their territory. To re-form as a community, MoCreebec began with the empowerment of individuals. It developed a constitution, which might be useful as a means of providing both an organizational framework for new Algonquin communities and a prototype for the constitution of an Algonquin confederacy.[2] The MoCreebec constitution was then signed by *each individual,* who declared his or her affiliation with the group, affirmed a desire to be self-determining, and assumed responsibility for re-creating the nation. Those individuals subsequently chose the leaders who would represent them as heads of families. In combination, the heads of families work to bring their members' concerns to the larger circle. Ardoch opted for a similar heads-of-families structure as its mode of governance, as did Whimasab, though more informally.

For Algonquins, a confederacy form may be the style of governance that comes most naturally. The large and fairly autonomous communities encountered by Champlain, from the Kichesipirini to the Matouachkarini, who gathered at various times in parts of the watershed to sort out details that mutually affected them, were functionally a confederacy of Algonquin people. Even with the subsequent development under the British regime of a series of grand chiefs who represented all the territories, no chief spoke on behalf of his community until it had expressly indicated its wishes in the matter. For Algonquins at present, each community in the various watersheds faces its own set of issues. Clearly, they need a way of both pooling their resources and setting their own priorities, with a view to both collective and local goals. Should an Algonquin confederacy come into being, it would represent a first real expression of collective nation rebuilding undertaken by those whose ancestors have been formally erased as a people for over a hundred years.

Indeed, many hopeful factors exist. The Algonquin Union, which coalesced at the beginning of 2011 around the need to protect the South March Highlands in Ottawa, is intended to enable member communities to pool their strengths while maintaining local autonomy. At present, some Algonquins have suggested that there are probably at least ten unaffiliated communities. Some, such as Ardoch and Whimasab, have been formally organized for years, whereas Pasapkedjiwanong formed so that its members could separate themselves from the Sharbot Lake community and engage in positive community building and cultural reclamation. Few of the newer unaffiliated groups, struggling to maintain themselves in the difficult climate of a land claim, have formally joined the Algonquin Union. Nonetheless, this body has tremendous potential to provide a framework whereby communities can maintain their own autonomy while banding together for strength and to celebrate the spiritual processes related to the land that so many Algonquins are seeking.

Undertaking this kind of nation building achieves other functions as well. It represents a definitive acknowledgment that Algonquins do not need to seek validation from either external governments or status Indian organizations to know that they are Algonquin. Indeed, engaging with confederacy building through the Algonquin Union or other structures allows Algonquins to move beyond the fruitless politics of recognition in which the comprehensive claims process has mired them.

I believe that the land claim currently exists in a contradictory space for Algonquins. Although it has enabled people to certify their Algonquin genealogies, it has also blighted the development of further community efforts at self-empowerment. This is partially because of the authoritarian control exercised by most ANRs over their communities (itself the fruit of the negotiating team's authoritarianism) and the way in which such leadership promotes passivity and resignation among already disempowered people as well as massive divisions between those who oppose the land claim. But fundamentally, the claim impedes Algonquin development because those involved in it must accept the infantilization and belittling of Indigenous societies that occurs when colonizers define the "integral" aspects of their "special cultures," delegate self-government that permits no real Indigenous control, and manage land claim negotiations so tightly that any expression of real nationhood is curtailed. And this form of blighted "recognition" has a hegemonic power that makes it all the harder for Algonquins to resist, unless a new structure is built to bypass it.

A viable confederacy, for which the Algonquin Union appears to be a healthy prototype, would accomplish more than a thousand arguments for or against the claim. It would offer an alternative to land claim community members who can express no sense of real nationhood within those communities. In a sense, even a fledgling framework for an Algonquin confederacy would be much *larger* than the claim, rooted in the histories and collective presence of Omàmìwinini in their own homelands, who have the right to rebuild their governance models regardless of the social entrenchment (through the claim) of those who seek recognition according to federal government rules.

Ironically, more than any identity card signifying Algonquin heritage, the growth of an Algonquin confederacy would probably generate forms of recognition from other Indigenous governments, including status Indian governments, that at present regard non-status Algonquins as less than Indigenous. It might help to develop discussions and exchange programs with Algonquin communities in Quebec. Mutual self-help between Ontario and Quebec Algonquins would be another means of rebuilding a nation across provincial boundaries.

Algonquins who are engaged in retrieving their historical and cultural traditions can probably learn much by studying the efforts of Indigenous people in other regions, particularly by examining what is gained and lost when groups struggle for recognition from colonial powers as part of decolonization. Ultimately, however, nation rebuilding will need to be a slow and thoughtful process, a concerted exploration on the part of Algonquins about what it means to be Omàmìwinini in the twenty-first century and what this can teach them about working toward a future in a homeland that is no longer fractured.

Notes

Introduction

1 The Indian Act pertains to registered Indians, their bands, and the system of Indian reserves in Canada. Ottawa first enacted it in 1876 under the provisions of section 91(24) of the British North America Act, 1867, which provides the federal government exclusive authority to legislate in relation to "Indians and Lands Reserved for Indians." The Indian Act defines who is legally an Indian; it therefore contains certain legal rights and legal disabilities for registered Indians. For over a hundred years, it has also specified which Indigenous groups are excluded from Indianness; moreover, it has painstakingly delineated the means through which those individuals registered as Indian can become legally non-Indian. Since its inception, the Indian Act has been administered by the Department of Indian Affairs and Northern Development. Since the Constitution Act of 1982, two other categories of Native peoples – "Metis" and "Inuit" – have been defined, and the label "Aboriginal" for all three categories has become commonly used. Accordingly, in 2011, the Department of Indian Affairs became the Department of Aboriginal Affairs and Northern Development. However, this new Department of Aboriginal Affairs continues to maintain specific controls through the Indian Act only for status Indians; for that reason, in this book, the federal agency responsible for the Indian Act will continue to be referred to as "Indian Affairs."

2 In 1869, Canada passed the Gradual Enfranchisement Act, which stipulated that any Indian woman who married a man who lacked Indian status would lose her own status and any right to band membership. Accordingly, for 116 years, the Indian Act removed the status of all Indian women who married men who did not themselves hold status (including non-status Canadian and American Indians, as well as white men) and forced them to leave their communities. The same act gave Indian status to white women who married status Indians. Additional sections of the Indian Act often compounded this gender discrimination by introducing other processes such as regulations removing the status of Indian children with undisclosed paternity, and other regulation involuntarily enfranchising the wives of men who enfranchised (gave up their Indian status to gain Canadian rights). This legislation would remain part of the Indian Act until 1985.

3 The *Powley* decision set out the foundations for the interpretation of Metis Aboriginal rights within the meaning of section 35 of the 1982 Constitution Act. The case dealt with hunting rights, which were granted to First Nations but not to Metis. In October 1993, Steve Powley and his son killed a moose outside of Sault Ste. Marie, Ontario, tagging it with Powley's Metis affiliation card number. Charged with violating Ontario's Game and Fish Act, the Powleys asserted their right to hunt as Metis people. After winning at the provincial court level as well as a Crown appeal of that decision, the Supreme Court decision in *Powley* in 2003 affirmed the Aboriginal rights of Metis as Aboriginal people (Teillet 2007, 55).

4 The Tri-Council Policy Statement was developed in 1998 by the three research councils who fund most academic research in Canada, to serve as a single reference document for all research involving humans conducted under the auspices of institutions eligible for agency funding. The agencies subsequently established an Interagency Advisory Panel on Research Ethics to ensure that the policy evolves to keep pace with changes in research and society at large. Updated in 2010, the Tri-Council Policy Statement includes new chapters on research involving First Nations, Inuit, and Metis peoples. Information about the statement can be found at http://www.pre.ethics.gc.ca/.

5 I had been in touch with both individuals sporadically over the years but had been unable set a time for interviews. By 2006, my attempts to reach both leaders constantly met with no response; they would no longer return my calls or even answer my e-mails. Their silence became explicable only after I read a July 2007 article in the *Ottawa Citizen*, which stated that Robert Potts, the chief negotiator for the land claim, was the sole person authorized to speak on behalf of the Algonquins involved in the claim negotiations (Naumetz 2007, 1-2).

Chapter 1: Diplomacy, Resistance, and Dispossession

1 In order to avoid confusion, it's important to distinguish between two similar words: Algonquian (or Algonkian) refers broadly to a language group and the people who speak those languages, whereas Algonquin (or Algonkin) applies to the nation whose homeland is the Ottawa River watershed. Algonquians include the Abenaki, Cree, Delaware, Malicite, Mi'kmaq, Montagnais, and Anishinabeg (Hessel 1993, 2), as well as, of course, the Algonquins themselves. Algonquins are also part of a larger group of Anishinabeg people who include Ojibways, Pottawatomis, and Odawas. Algonquians are generally categorized as "hunter-gatherers" by anthropologists, as opposed to the more sedentary agriculturalists who speak Iroquoian languages (the other language group of northeastern North America).

2 Algonquin oral traditions are supported by archaeology, which indicates that human occupation in the northern part of Algonquin territory dates back at least four thousand years. Along the Ottawa River itself, the oldest sites, at Morrison's and Allumette Islands, date back six thousand years (Council of the Algonquins of Pikwakanagan and Kirby J. Whiteduck 2002, 9).

3 The term "Anishinabeg" refers first of all to the people whom colonizers have called "Ojibwa/Ojibway" or "Chippewa"; Native people also use it to refer to the relatives of the Ojibways, the Pottawatomis, and the Odawas. The spelling of Anishinabemowin (the Anishinabe language) has not yet been standardized so that spellings can vary from "Anishinaabe" to "Anishnawbe" or even "Nishnawbe." In general, throughout this text, I will be using the term "Anishinabe" to denote the singular form of this word and "Anishinabeg" to denote the collective name of the people.

4 Côté (1996) notes that even 4000 years B.P., evidence existed of trade networks extending both to the west and southwest and to the east and north, that Onondaga chert was used extensively from about 2900 B.P. to 2400 B.P., and that Algonquins may have influenced the Ontario Iroquoian ceramic tradition, prevalent after 750 B.P. Hessel (1993, 27) asserts that the Ottawa River was a central route for trade in copper, flint, obsidian, and even whalebone, suggesting that trade routes

extending from Lake Superior to the east coast all centred on the Ottawa. Diane Delorme (cited in Joan Holmes and Associates 1993, 2:2) states that Algonquins regularly exchanged birch bark, medicinal herbs, and furs for the agricultural products of Native peoples from the south.

5 According to James Morrison (2005, 21), "Asticou" is actually a misprint in the original text since the Algonquin word for small cauldrons or boilers is actually akikok; the full name for the Chaudière rapids is Akikodjiwan, or "place where the water falls into stone basins whose rounded form resembles a boiler."

6 As summarized in Biggar (1922-36).

7 Sagard's journals were gathered together in Wrong (1939). For the writings of the Jesuits, which have been compiled into a seventy-three-volume work known as *The Jesuit Relations and Allied Documents,* see Thwaites (1901).

8 The next chapter, as well as the chapters that focus specifically on the various federally unrecognized communities, will describe the ways in which Algonquins who were not registered as Indians were routinely ignored, considered not "bona fide Indians" whenever Indian Affairs addressed issues related to status Algonquins. Ultimately, as assimilative pressures took their toll, Indian Affairs no longer addressed even the existence of non-status Algonquins.

9 For example, at Ardoch, the wild rice beds planted by Mary Buckshot in the mid-nineteenth century are still tended by her great-grandson Harold Perry, a respected elder with Ardoch Algonquin First Nation. For years, Mitchell Shewell, also of Ardoch, has assisted Bob Lovelace in sweat lodges on land situated just north of the bridge on Canoe Lake/Bedford Road, where Shewell's great-grandfather had a hunting camp. The land not only sustains part of Ardoch's livelihood, it bears the family histories of community members and therefore strengthens who they are as Algonquins today.

10 They were beset from all sides. For example, in 1800, the lands at Hull, in Lower Canada, were settled and cleared by a party of Massachusetts loyalists led by Philemon Wright. When challenged by Algonquin chiefs, Wright replied that the Quebec authorities had assured him that there was no proof that the land belonged to the Algonquins. While the Algonquins were still voicing their concerns to Lord Dalhousie, the governor of Lower Canada, 2 million acres of Algonquin land in eastern Ontario were ceded illegally to the Crown by the Mississaugas in a treaty known as the Rideau Purchase, which was finalized in 1822 (Joan Holmes and Associates 1993, 3:4). And while protests regarding the Rideau Purchase continued, white trappers had begun to invade northern Quebec Algonquin land by 1825 to the extent that every family territory was encroached upon (Davidson 1928, 73-74).

11 In 1839, two squatters on islands in the Ottawa River, Mr. McNab and Mr. Morson, petitioned as to the legality of a ninety-nine-year lease granted in 1818 by certain Algonquin chiefs to Eleazar Gillson. Under Sir J. Colborne, the executive council declared that the lease was null and void, and that Indians had no rights to grant leases or dispose of the lands situated within their ancient hunting grounds – that indeed, they had no property rights in the lands (Joan Holmes and Associates 1993, 6:17).

12 In 1898, when Ontario addressed its brief to the tribunal to settle accounts between itself and the Province of Canada, A. White, assistant commissioner of the Department of Crown Lands of Ontario, concluded that the Algonquins at Golden Lake "were not in a position to make any claims against the province of Ontario, because they were a few families who seemed to have belonged to indigent tribes resident in Lower Canada, with no annuities of interest accruing from lands, who had squatted in South Algona. While land was sold to them by the Indian Department, this did not constitute them making claims against the Province of Ontario" (quoted in Joan Holmes and Associates 1993, 2:72-73).

13 For a description of the petitions, see Joan Holmes and Associates (1993, 2:43-148, 6:2-6).

14 This is most clearly demonstrated in the earliest petitions. In a 1795 meeting with Alexander McKee at Lake of Two Mountains, the Mohawk chiefs addressed McKee, but the Algonquins were not prepared to state their claims until they had consulted with other Algonquins in council (Joan

Holmes and Associates 1993, 6:1-2). The last collective petition, submitted in 1851, reveals that consensus had been sought; however, it was signed on behalf of some three to four hundred families. From the 1840s onward, individual families petitioned for certain lands, and these final petitions speak only for them, no longer for the entire territory.

15 In 1884, Deputy Superintendent General of Indian Affairs Lawrence Vankoughnet described the claims of the Lakes Huron and Simcoe Chippewas and certain Mississauga bands as improperly incorporated into the Robinson-Huron Treaty of 1850. Despite the 1881 letter from the chiefs, he ascertained that the bands did have an interest in the Ottawa River watershed. As a result, the Chippewa and Mississauga bands were awarded four dollars per head, retroactive to 1850, when their lands had been erroneously included in the Robinson-Huron Treaty (Joan Holmes and Associates 1993, 2:169). Subsequently, in 1923, the lands, including those remaining on the Ontario side of the watershed, were formally included in the Williams Treaties with the Chippewa and Mississauga bands. In many respects, the Williams Treaties were the most cynical of the treaties: Ontario exploited its opportunity to formally acquire all unceded territory, including seven townships running south to Lake Simcoe, which were valued at $30 million. It also obtained the region between the Bay of Quinte and Toronto, which had not been part of the Crawford Purchase and which, even in 1923, was of phenomenal value. Ultimately, after taking evidence at the Alderville, Christian Island, Georgina Island, Mud Lake, Rama, Rice Lake, and Scugog reserves, A.S. Williams and commissioners concluded that $700,000 would be a fair and equitable compensation for the entire group (ibid., 170).

Chapter 2: The Fracturing of the Algonquin Homeland

1 Squatters were settlers who moved into territories before the land was surveyed and deeds of occupation were awarded; although their presence created chaos for the British, they repeatedly served the needs of empire in that they ensured that land claimed from Native people would be immediately occupied by Europeans and therefore permanently alienated from Native hands.

2 It is not clear which belts these were. They may have been associated with treaties that the Algonquins maintained with their neighbours.

3 The little people are part of the epistemological framework of many Algonquian peoples. The Mi'kmaq, for example, tell stories of the *booglatomoojt,* the little people who often appear when humans are not behaving properly. With the Anishinabeg people, the Bagwajinini are the little people of the forest, sometimes behaving mischievously but generally good. For an individual to shoot one of the little people suggests an extreme estrangement from traditional values.

4 It should be noted that, at this time, in different parts of eastern Ontario, settlers were being *given* between 100 and 200 free acres each, with the stipulation that they clear a certain portion and remain full-time on the property. With these terms in mind, the Golden Lake reserve should have held only ten to fifteen families.

5 For example, in 1985, Maniwaki was forced to erect a barricade in order to block a principal access route to one of the ZECs created by the Province in direct disregard of Indigenous presence; the Province had refused to pay the access fees required to enter Maniwaki's traditional territory (Joan Holmes and Associates 1993, 2:xx).

6 Long before the sixties scoop, which removed almost an entire generation of status Indian children from many reserve communities, the children of non-status Algonquins were being apprehended into children's aid because their parents were impoverished and their fathers were criminalized or had to migrate to work (Bob Lovelace, pers. comm., 2003).

7 The use – or loss – of the Algonquin language in many ways typifies the growing distinctions between Quebec and Ontario Algonquins. For example, in 1940, the Indian agent in Senneterre protested the development of a fish and game reserve on the hunting grounds of the Grand Lac Victoria band, not only because the band's traplines would be lost, but because band members would

not be able to work as guides since most spoke only Algonquian (Joan Holmes and Associates 1993, 2:238-39). At this point, Ontario Algonquins had faced intensive settler pressure for over a century and had experienced profound loss of language; increasingly, the majority spoke only English.

Chapter 3: Aboriginal Title and the Comprehensive Claims Process

1 The notion of a fiduciary obligation developed with *Guerin,* a Supreme Court case in 1984. Before this, the Department of Indian Affairs, which controlled all rents and monies obtained from lands belonging to Indians, had no recognized legal responsibility for the way in which it administered these funds. *Guerin* dealt with land on the Musqueam Indian reserve that Indian Affairs had leased to the Shaughnessy Golf Club. The terms of the lease were misrepresented to the band, and it did not receive a copy despite its requests over the years. When the band finally took the federal government to court, it discovered that if it were to secure a remedy, it had to demonstrate that an existing legal obligation had prohibited Indian Affairs from procuring less favourable lease terms. But because the band had not been not party to the lease, and the golf club had not been party to the band's surrender of its territory to Canada, no possibility of securing a remedy existed. Justice Brian Dickson resolved this legal impasse by asserting that a fiduciary relationship existed between the band and Ottawa (as represented by the Department of Indian Affairs), a *sui generis* (unlike all else) arrangement in which the federal government was required to observe a trust relationship since Indian land is alienable only to the Crown under the terms of the Royal Proclamation of 1763. All eight Supreme Court judges were unanimous in awarding relief to the Musqueam band. Both the fiduciary doctrine and the notion of *sui generis* thus flow from the *Guerin* decision; moreover, *Guerin* states that the nature and scope of the relationship between the Crown and Native people is what renders it fiduciary. Due to the nature of the powers vested in Ottawa under the Indian Act, bands that take the federal government to court for mishandling the monies derived from their estates are not required to prove the existence of the fiduciary relationship (Monture-Angus 1999, 77-80).

   The *Guerin* decision thus made the federal government potentially liable for charges of mishandling any of the large sums of money that it had acquired over the years via logging fees, royalties for minerals or oil, hydroelectric development, or allowing Indian lands to be settled for minimal rents or to be sold for a minimal price. Indeed, since *Guerin,* Ottawa has seemed increasingly anxious to devolve control over Indian lands and to implement self-government or land claim agreements that would diminish or end the fiduciary relationship. If the Crown's discretionary power over Aboriginal lands were diminished due to self-government, so too would its fiduciary obligation.

2 The Nunavut Agreement involved an entire territory where the Inuit were a majority population and therefore received some jurisdictions similar to provinces. For the terms of the agreement, see Government of Nunavut (1993).

3 Although the origin of the term "Gisday" is not clear, it relates to Indigenous people's assertion of rights: the Gisday process takes the stand that if Natives believe their title to exist, they should simply enjoy its benefits rather than waiting for governments to approve. Mohawk philosopher Taiaiake Alfred has called this type of activity "self-conscious traditionalism" (De Costa 2002b, 10).

4 More information on the BC treaty process is available at the British Columbia Treaty Commission website: http://www.bctreaty.net/.

Chapter 4: The Algonquin Land Claim

1 For example, in *Tanakiwin,* the negotiations newsletter, Greg Sarazin (1998, 2) wrote, "In 1986, Paul Williams, Tom Vincent and Kirby Whiteduck went traveling in the Sharbot Lake area to 'find' Algonquins. All they managed to find was one elderly aboriginal man, who turned out to be from

British Columbia, and a gas station which was known locally as 'the Indian reserve.' In 1986, a second 'expedition' was undertaken, by then Chief Greg Sarazin and Paul Williams in the area south of Lake Nipissing, again without significant success."

2 In 1990, Pikwakanagan undertook a current use data collection project to find the non-status Algonquins, to survey them as to their historical and continued land use activities, and to provide maps and documentation of its findings. The project revealed that concentrations of Algonquin people lived in certain identifiable areas and that Algonquins resided throughout the territory.

3 The complexities of non-status Algonquin identity and the reality that, during the negotiations, Ottawa's image of Algonquinness consisted largely of stereotypes, will be explored more generally in Chapter 5.

4 In Chapter 6, it will become apparent that the rights of non-status Algonquin hunters were secured by the *Perry* case; however, for strategic reasons, which will be explored in Chapter 7, the leaders of the communities involved in the land claim refused to acknowledge this.

5 For non-status Algonquins, the protocol indicated that, for the first time, a provincial body had recognized them as Algonquin, independent of Pikwakanagan. However, as communities who left the land claim discovered, this recognition was confined solely to the claim. Thus, because the recognition did not extend beyond the negotiation process, I will continue to refer to them as "federally unrecognized Algonquins."

6 Since the 1985 changes to the Indian Act, a number of individuals in the federally unrecognized communities whose ancestors once were registered at Pikwakanagan have regained their Indian status; nonetheless, many feel little loyalty to Pikwakanagan, and most have chosen to remain part of their original federally unrecognized communities.

7 Heather Majaury (pers. comm., July 2011) has characterized the desire to be named "chief" as "chief fever," a disorder in which people believe that the title of chief will confer power, money, and prestige, despite the fact that the position does not tend to be highly remunerated. Majaury struggles with the loss of local political organizing ability that appears inherent in the authority of this value system. For her, chiefs are simply spokespersons; their status does not surpass that of anyone else in the community, and their responsibility is to communicate to outsiders the community position on any issue, negotiation, or agreement. In situations where financial remuneration is not controlled by the grassroots community that named the chief, this responsibility will be undermined because the chief will be serving two masters. Majaury believes that work done on behalf of the community should be remunerated, but she questions the route by which payment reaches the community leader. This contradiction was not resolved by electing ANTC chiefs as ANRs, since the process for electing ANRs is virtually identical to that for electing ANTC chiefs.

8 When Lynn Gehl ran for ANR of Greater Golden Lake in the 2005 election, she encountered numerous procedural violations (which are documented in Chapter 7) and had difficulty in acquiring the membership list. She also paid $1,354.25 out of her own pocket for printing, postage, gas, and other expenses to reach the membership (Gehl 2005a). The existing representatives, on the other hand, have e-mail access to members, per diems for travelling, and budgets of $225 for every day that they work on the land claim (which can include the campaign process). And finally, they can maintain community loyalty by resorting to patronage with respect to the moose tags they receive. Because the Ministry of Natural Resources controls hunting for all communities registered with the land claim, its moose tag system controls how moose are hunted. Within this system, only those individuals possessing a moose tag can hunt for moose. Since only a handful of tags are issued per community, and the leaderships of the communities control how the tags are allocated, leaders can attract votes simply because they have the power to allocate moose tags (which the person running for ANR lacks).

9 The beneficiary list was finally drawn up in 2011; during the process, many previously accepted non-status Algonquins were carved off the list after their identities were challenged by the council of Pikwakanagan. Their names were excluded from the list through unilateral action by the ANRs. This issue will be explored more closely in Chapter 5.

10 This information comes from my observations at the 28 April 2004 Algonquin Nation Information Meeting at Sharbot Lake.

11 This information comes from e-mail discussions among concerned Algonquins, particularly between 2005 and 2008, during the early years of the Potts regime.

Chapter 6: The Development of Ardoch Algonquin First Nation

1 According to Marijke Huitema (2000), the registry at St. Killam's Roman Catholic Church in Ardoch recorded Algonquin families attending as early as 1886. Many were listed as being from Lake of Two Mountains, whereas others were described as Indians of Bedford. The records also show that Indian children might be born or die in the bush months before their parents returned to the parish to have them baptized or buried by the church. This suggests that people retained the practice of living in the bush as much as possible but sought out the church when they returned to town.

2 In the years when the harvest was plentiful, Ardoch had allowed the Alderville and Curve Lake Mississaugas to share in it, since their own wild rice stands had not survived development on the Trent River system. Settlers at Ardoch were heavily dependent on tourism for their livelihoods; the fact that ducks and other wild birds fed on the rice meant that the region attracted hunters.

3 As Randy Cota explained during a 2005 interview, the word "allies" came from the rice war: "We had Tyendinaga there, we had Curve Lake, we had Alderville, and all the different communities were there. They were our allies. Then, also, our allies were the non-Native people of the area that were bound with us, so that made us even stronger. But our registration, our community of who we are, does not involve the allies. The word 'allies' was to show we had allies."

4 Indeed, Chief Robert Whiteduck of Pikwakanagan had been brought into the *Perry* case as an intervenor on the side of the government. Although he agreed with Ardoch that Aboriginal rights did not depend upon Indian status, he asserted that the application against the enforcement policy was harmful to the greater Algonquin Nation because it invited a narrowing of Charter rights. This should not be done without the consent of status Indians, whose rights might be affected. As Harold Perry noted during an interview conducted with him in 2004, the reason that the ANTC communities intervened against him in the court case was that if Perry won, the ANTC might lose a good part of its membership since those non-status Algonquins who enrolled simply to acquire hunting rights would not have to enroll in the communities to hunt.

Chapter 7: The Effect of the Land Claim in This Region

1 LaRocque (2010, 15) suggests that the civilization-savagery discourse, in which white civilization is continually juxtaposed with Native "savagery," is Canada's "master narrative." Through its use, white people elevate themselves as rational and masterful, whereas Native people are viewed as primitive or childlike. In the context of the Ottawa River Valley and the Algonquin land claim, local whites perceived the institutions of white society, such as the MNR, as eminently rational and scientific, and therefore capable of properly "managing" natural resources. Native people, on the other hand, were portrayed as untrustworthy and incapable of shouldering responsibilities. Given control of the natural resources, they would over-hunt and over-fish like greedy children, never taking thought for the future, until all the resources were gone.

2 In particular, Gehl (2005a) notes the ways in which the practice and application of the protocol agreement covering ANR elections made it difficult for non-ANTC candidates to run in 2005. For example, their meetings were poorly advertised despite a huge communications budget, and ANTC candidates had access to mailing, telephone, websites, and electronic mailing lists. In dozens of ways, they disregarded the needs of the new candidates who were seeking election. Not surprisingly, they defeated their rivals (thus becoming ANRs as well as ANTC chiefs and ANND reps). In subsequent elections, existing ANRs have continued to carry the field.

Chapter 8: Uranium Resistance

1 The legal duty to consult in instances where title has not been extinguished flows from *Haida* and *Taku River*, two Supreme Court decisions of 2004. *Haida* addressed the replacement of a tree farm licence by the BC minister of forests against opposition from, and without the consent of, the Haida Nation. *Taku River* involved approval by the BC minister of the environment of the construction of a 160-kilometre mining access road despite objections from the Taku River Tlingit First Nation. In both cases, the Province argued that it had no obligation to consult with Aboriginal groups where their Aboriginal rights and title had not been proven. The Supreme Court disagreed, ruling that the government's duty to consult arises whenever it knows of the potential existence of Aboriginal rights or title and is considering measures that might adversely affect them. The scope of consultation required is proportionate to the strength of the asserted right or title and the seriousness of the potential adverse impact.

2 MELT and ART existed as a result of the Ipperwash Inquiry, which investigated the death of Indigenous rights protestor Dudley George. In September 1995, George was killed by an Ontario Provincial Police officer after the Labour Day weekend occupation of disputed land in Ipperwash Provincial Park. Twelve years later, a long-overdue provincial inquiry into George's death concluded that the single biggest source of frustration, distrust, and ill feeling among Aboriginal people in Ontario was the Province's failure to deal in a just and expeditious manner with breaches of treaty and other obligations to First Nations. The inquiry report stated that if Ontario and Ottawa wished to avoid further confrontations, they must deal effectively and fairly with treaty land. The inquiry revealed that the provincial government had ordered the OPP to remove the protestors from the park and that the police had done so despite their own better knowledge of the situation "on the ground." The OPP desire to ensure that neither the public nor police officers were endangered was put at risk by this ill-conceived order. As a result of the Ipperwash Inquiry, the OPP set up the MELT and ART units to assist in ensuring that protests relating to Aboriginal peoples were maintained peacefully.

3 Due to the recommendations of the Ipperwash Inquiry, the Ontario Provincial Police have increasingly made public safety their overriding concern. Thus, if a protest remains peaceful, they will not endanger public safety by removing protestors and will not serve the interests of a government that has not fulfilled its duty to negotiate with protestors.

4 The document via which federal officials fulfill their legal obligation to consult, titled "Aboriginal Consultation and Accommodation" (Canada 2011), specifies that consultation must entail sorting out which federal department should be involved and gathering information on the Aboriginal groups in the area, their current and past uses, indicators of established or potential Aboriginal rights and of pre-1982 extinguishment, interests or concerns relating to the proposed project, and potential adverse impacts on established or potential Aboriginal and treaty rights (rather than on the communities themselves). Ottawa has a duty to consult if an established or potential section 35 right exists and if that right could potentially be adversely affected by the project (ibid., 42). In such cases, a sliding scale is employed, in which weak claims to section 35 rights are accorded less consultation and possibly no accommodation, whereas established claims require more consultation and possible accommodation. This scale also applies to adverse effect and is determined by the potential seriousness of its impact (ibid., 44-45). The consultation process itself should clarify which departments or agencies have the authority to consult on behalf of Canada, and, notably, should attempt to integrate Crown consultation with an existing regulatory process (such as an environmental assessment or consultations in a comprehensive claim). Companies involved in projects might also have their own consultation process that the Crown must examine. And though these guidelines pertain to Ottawa, they establish the processes that provincial Crowns must also undertake.

5 Since 1994, diamond exploration has taken place throughout the James Bay Lowlands. According to DiaMine Explorations (2007), the De Beers Victor open mine established the James Bay Lowlands as potentially producing world-class diamond deposits. In 2009, a mining magazine chose Victor

as mine of the year. It has an expected life of twelve years and a total project life of seventeen years. Annual revenue from the mine is expected to be between $200 million and $300 million, with a per carat value of $500, one of the highest in the world. The Ontario Geological Survey has documented twenty-nine kimberlite pipes in the James Bay Lowlands, nineteen of them containing diamonds. Much of this activity is in the Moose River basin, which could significantly affect the coastal communities drained by the basin, all along the west coast of James Bay.

6 Throughout the 1980s, the Province of Alberta allowed more than twenty-six hundred oil and gas wells to be drilled on Lubicon Cree land in northern Alberta. Instigated against the wishes of the Lubicon, this has had tragic consequences for their society and livelihoods. There are fears that even more destructive forms of extraction are planned for the future. International human rights bodies have long been critical of the poverty, widespread ill health, and culture loss that resulted from the near total destruction of the Lubicon economy and way of life. Until 1979, hunting, trapping, and other traditional activities had made the Lubicon largely self-sufficient (Amnesty International n.d.). For an account of Alberta's and Canada's disregard of Lubicon Cree efforts to hold them accountable, see Martin-Hill (2004).

Often dubbed the Saudi Arabia of the uranium industry, northern Saskatchewan supplies most of Canada's uranium, which was discovered in the area during the 1950s. By 1984, Canada had become the Western world's top exporter of uranium. The northern Saskatchewan deposits are the richest in the world – where most uranium deposits are only a few tenths of a percent in ore grade, the Cigar Lake ore body is the richest undeveloped uranium deposit in the world, with an average ore grade of 18 percent U_3O_8 (uranium oxide). It is also one of the largest, with geological reserves totalling 103,000 tonnes of uranium oxide. Whereas most mining in northern Saskatchewan is open-pit due to the shallow nature of many ore bodies, the Cigar Lake deposit will be mined from tunnels above and below the ore zone. It was discovered in 1981, and construction started during the summer of 1997. Although the mine flooded due to a rock fall in October 2006, measures to pump out the water were put in place during mid-2008 (Canadian Nuclear Association 2010).

7 The term originates with the US government, which stated that certain Indian reservations where considerable uranium mining has taken place should be designated "national sacrifice zones." The areas included the Navajo reservation in Arizona and New Mexico, Acoma and Laguna Pueblos in New Mexico, the Yakima reservation in Washington, and the Pine Ridge Lakota Reservation in South Dakota (Churchill 1992, 54, 78).

8 Of greatest relevance here are the efforts at Pine Ridge to harness *tate* (the wind) in developing wind generators (LaDuke 2005, 240) and the Native-SUN project at Hopi Pueblo to rely on solar panels. The latter project fits well with Hopi traditionals, who do not allow power lines into their villages so as to limit the access of power facilities and their potential to appropriate Hopi land. In 1999, one-third of Hopi villages did not allow electrical power lines into their communities (LaDuke 1999, 187).

9 This wording comes from Jackson (2001, 189), which addresses the feelings of loss experienced by many urban Native people whose families remained silent about Native identity.

Chapter 9: The Bonnechere Communities and Greater Golden Lake

1 Many of these oral histories are now available on the Bonnechere Algonquin First Nation website at http://www.bafn.

2 Due to the highly controversial and legal proceedings that have taken place, the names of all of the BAC individuals interviewed in 2005 are being withheld.

3 In 1999, John Corbiere and three other individuals from the Batchewana band on their own behalf and on behalf of all non-resident members of the Batchewana band sought a declaration that section 77(1) of the Indian Act, which requires that band members be "ordinarily resident" on-reserve in order to vote in band elections, violates section 15(1) of the Charter. Fewer than a third of the registered members of the band lived on-reserve. The Federal Court, Trial Division, found that, as

it related to the disposition of reserve lands or Indian monies held for the band as a whole, section 77(1) infringed on the rights guaranteed by section 15(1) and that the infringement was not justified under section 1 of the Charter. On the basis of this ruling, off-reserve band members were entitled to vote in band elections.

Chapter 11: Whitney, Madawaska, and Sabine

1 Although my interview process for the Madawaska and York River communities was affected by the fact that I was not allowed to approach the ANRs and lacked extensive connections in the communities, the people whom I interviewed were either close enough to traditional governance (as heads of families) or to ANR leadership to provide strong insights. These perspectives were not comprehensive, but in many cases, they were unique to the specific circumstances of the Madawaska and York River Algonquins, thus providing a snapshot of their histories and concerns as they existed in 2007.

2 This is particularly the case in the reading material available at the Algonquin Park Museum. The museum's unpublished compilation, titled "Indians of Algonquin Park at the Time of Contact – 1600 A.D.," which refers to seasonal movements of Algonquins in and out of the park, suggests that "no direct evidence" shows the use of defined hunting territories by Algonquins prior to the arrival of Europeans. Moreover, while referring to research about Algonquin traditions, it makes no mention of possible sacred sites in the park. Indians are present, but only as ancient figures in a timeless past rather than as viable communities whose rights to the park need acknowledgment. Still more problematic is Roderick Mackay's (1991) "Supplementary Report on Indian Occurrences in Algonquin Park." Available at the museum, it details hundreds of hours of interviews carried out in the mid-1970s with former park rangers, visitors, guides, lumbermen, and trappers, offering these as "evidence" of Algonquin non-presence in the park. The interviews barely mention Indians, except to dismiss them as "commercial fur poachers" or "licensed trappers" who are therefore assumed to have no traditional ties to the territory. It is unclear whether Mackay compiled the interviews as a response to the Algonquin land claim, which includes Algonquin Park, or whether his compilation simply speaks to the long-term denial that the creation of the park displaced the Algonquins who had always lived there.

3 Amalgamated as the Ottawa, Arnprior and Parry Sound Railway, the railroad was extended to Georgian Bay, with the intention of cashing in on the export of wheat from the west shipped via the Great Lakes once the timber stands were depleted. When the lumber trade became less profitable, the Booth family divested itself of its railways and sold them to the Grand Trunk Railway, which became part of the Canadian National Railway in 1923 (Kennedy 1970, 172).

4 Because the chief negotiator, Bob Potts, handles all dealings between the Algonquins of Ontario and the public, I was therefore unable to interview Robert Craftchick, the Whitney ANR, or the Whitney community members whom he represents.

5 Although they are Madawaska River Algonquins and prefer to identify with Whimasab, a number of Whimasab individuals have Indian status because their ancestors settled at Pikwakanagan and were accorded status as a result.

Chapter 13: The Ottawa River Communities

1 Annette Chrétien is a northern Ontario Metis ethnomusicologist and researcher. Her master's thesis on the Mattawa Metis community, with its detailed nuances addressing Metis identity, was instrumental in advancing recognition of Ontario Metis and ultimately the *Powley* decision, which promoted the further development of the Aboriginal rights of Metis people.

2 I first spoke with Dave Joannise in April 2003, on the telephone, seeking to arrange an interview. At the time, although somewhat reluctant to talk to a researcher, he did speak a little about his community. He suggested an interview later that summer but subsequently never returned my calls,

either in 2003 or 2004. In 2005, he agreed to meet with one of the researchers working for this project, but when she went to Mattawa, he did not show up for the interview. In 2007, I again attempted to interview him, without success. Afterward, I interviewed two students in Toronto who were from the Antoine family but who had enrolled with the Mattawa/North Bay Algonquin group because they felt better represented there. An elder who was interviewed by a researcher for this project had also made the switch from Antoine to Mattawa/North Bay. My information about Antoine is based entirely on these sources.

3 At the time of the interview, Labreche had just lost the 2005 ANR election, which the community was disputing.

4 Ontario's Living Legacy Land Use Strategy (Ministry of Natural Resources 2001) was the result of an extensive planning process that was carried out in the late 1990s. Outlining the intended strategic direction for the management of 39 million hectares of Crown lands and waters in an area covering 45 percent of the province, it encompassed forests, mineral and aggregate resources, fish, wildlife, hydro power, provincial parks and conservation reserves, and the beds of lakes and rivers. The strategy focused on four specific objectives, including the creation of parks and protected areas, the land use needs of the resource-based tourism industry, providing resource industries (such as forestry and mining) with greater certainty relating to land and resource use, and enhancing fishing, hunting, and other recreation activities on Crown lands. The strategy set a framework for future land and resource management, providing guidance and direction on what activities are proposed and permitted in certain areas. Notably, almost every objective involved land use for everybody but Native people.

5 The dam at Rolphton is more commonly known as Des Joachims, but many people refer to it as La Swisha, an old name that is preserved in other local landmarks. For example, Highway 635, which leads from Rolphton to the Ottawa River, is also called Swisha Road. And the nearby island of Rapides-des-Joachims was once called La Swisha. With thanks to George Ferguson for explaining this to me.

6 Tritium is a radioactive form of hydrogen that cannot be removed from drinking water by any existing water treatment plants. In the body, tritium irradiates living cells and damages organic molecules, including DNA. Such damage can manifest itself later in the form of cancers as well as defects in reproductive and embryonic cells. The Tritium Awareness Project, which consists of antinuclear and environmental organizations, citizens groups, and scientists, is concerned that Chalk River authorities have routinely dumped tens of trillions of becquerels of liquid tritium into the Ottawa, with the permission of the Canadian Nuclear Safety Commission. A becquerel is a unit of radioactivity; it corresponds to one radioactive disintegration every second. When tritium-contaminated water is ingested, this disintegration occurs in the body.

7 The response of a number of ANRs to Kichesipirini's proposal to be included in the claim as a distinct community included attacks on the veracity of its claim, a "breaking ranks" attempt to open the table to all excluded groups, subsequent threats and counter-threats between various ANRs through e-mail discussions that were circulated far and wide to concerned Algonquins whose only access to information was through such e-mail, and the formation of a group that broke away from the Bonnechere community, claimed to represent the historical Kinouchepirini band, and asserted rights based on ancestors shared with the Kichesipirini (Hendry 2006). Overwhelmingly, it is obvious that LaPierre's proposal presented unique challenges to the ANRs.

8 Because Paul Lamothe did not respond to my requests for an interview, I gathered most of my information from Ottawa community documents from his website and from documents and interviews shared with me by Bob Majaury, who was briefly Lamothe's alternate as ANR.

9 During the 1840s, according to the *Ottawa Citizen* (2002), the human remains of about twenty Aboriginal ancestors were dug up from Algonquin burial grounds near the present location of the Canadian Museum of Civilization in Ottawa-Hull. In December 2002, the museum announced that it would return the bones to local Algonquins.

10 In 1916, the Parliament Buildings were destroyed by a huge fire that claimed everything except the library. Construction of the new Parliament Buildings used soil taken from a landfill across the river where the Museum of Civilization currently sits. Many Algonquins believe that the Parliament Buildings include fragments of Algonquin bones in their structure.

11 The South March Highlands have been described as a "wild island" of natural landscape in the city of Ottawa. No other major city in the world includes a vigorous old-growth forest with endangered species. The closest is perhaps Vancouver's Stanley Park, which is a third of the size, contains half the variety of vascular plants, and has no species at risk. Until recently, the highlands remained largely untouched because their rugged landscape was unsuitable for agriculture. Yet even though various regional, Kanata, and Ottawa city official plans have "protected" the highlands since 1972, less than a third of the original area remains. The land north of the Beaver Pond in Kanata is an accessible portion of the highlands and an example of their richness and beauty. In fall 2010, Kanata Northlands/Urbandale Construction received permission to start clearing this area to build about thirty-two hundred houses, preserving only eight hectares of forest lining the Beaver Pond.

On 6 January 2011, Grandfather William Commanda wrote to the mayor of Ottawa, requesting that city council initiate an immediate and comprehensive archaeological survey of the construction site. He spoke of the South March Highlands not only as a potential national heritage but as a place of significant importance to the Algonquin people, as a living temple, a place of Manitou, and he cited numerous reasons why Ottawa should stop its plans to clear-cut the Beaver Pond area. Kanata Northlands had intended to start cutting on 17 January but was delayed in order to conduct an archaeological survey. On 19 January 2011, Algonquin Daniel Bernard "Amikwabe" set up a camp at the entrance to the Beaver forest, where he kept a sacred fire burning round the clock. This was a personal initiative to address the destruction of the wildlife and the forest, in response to Commanda's declaration that the forest was sacred. Bernard camped out and kept the fire burning until 23 January. When clear cutting started shortly afterward, he and Robert Lovelace tied themselves to trees in the path of the clear-cutters. Protests continued throughout the spring and summer until Ottawa City Council agreed to conduct a vote to acquire the seventy-two acres north of the Beaver Pond that had been sold to Kanata Northlands.

12 In 2007, Omàmìwininì Pimàdjwowin commenced management of the Manido Chiman Museum at Pikwakanagan and subsequently transformed it into the Algonquin Way Cultural Centre. Along with the museum, the cultural centre has an art gallery, a gift shop, a reference library, a meeting room/classroom, a temporary artifact repository, and a head office.

Conclusion: Algonquin Identity and Nationhood

1 The post-settlement entrenchment of such differences between Native people certainly has a precedent. Though not arising from a comprehensive claim, the situation of the Newfoundland Mi'kmaq is nonetheless instructive in this respect. Because Canada did not bring Newfoundland's Indians under the Indian Act when Newfoundland joined Confederation in 1949, an organization known as the Federation of Newfoundland Indians fought long and hard for their recognition as status Indians. During the 1980s, Canada finally selected a small community situated in a remote area of the province, one with recent ties to Nova Scotia status Indian communities, and bestowed status and a reserve on it. Miawpukek First Nation, at Conne River, was thus created. The other Newfoundland Mi'kmaq, already organized into nine non-status communities reflecting their ties to land in various regions, continued the struggle for recognition. But because they had had to live in non-Native communities for years and had engaged in some intermarriage, Canada deemed that they lacked the "distinctiveness" required of status Indians on reserves. It eventually offered to gather the nine communities across western Newfoundland into one landless band, the Qalipu Mi'kmaq band. Under its terms, not only are off-territory Mi'kmaq prevented from joining the band, but the band itself will never be able to make land-based claims on Canada. Thus, the

Miawpukek First Nation Mi'kmaq at Conne River are status Indians with a reserve, whereas no other Newfoundland Mi'kmaq are recognized as having any regional ties to specific territories, and though they are status Indians, they are landless, with far fewer rights than Conne River (Lawrence 2009).

2 For highlights of the constitution, see MoCreebec Council of the Cree Nation (2005). Readers who are interested in the process can contact the MoCreebec Council at http://www.creevillage.com/11252_MoCreebec.pdf.

References

AAND. 2011. "Self Government." Aboriginal Affairs and Northern Development. http://www.aadnc-aandc.gc.ca/.

Alfred, Taiaiake. 1999. *Peace, Power, Righteousness: An Indigenous Manifesto.* Don Mills: Oxford University Press.

–. 2005. *Wasáse: Indigenous Pathways of Action and Freedom.* Toronto: Broadview Press.

Algonquin Golden Lake First Nation. 1992a. Letter to Harold Perry. 26 October.

–. 1992b. "Press Release: Federal Government Joins Ontario and Algonquin Golden Lake First Nation Governments at Negotiation Table." 7 December.

–. 2001. "21st Century Algonquin Moose War: Recommendations concerning the 2001/2002 Moose Harvest." http://www.greatergoldenlake.com/.

Algonquin Nation Negotiations Directorate. 2002. "The Algonquin Accord." 6 March. http://www.greatergoldenlake.com/.

Algonquin Nation Tribal Council. 2002. "Algonquins/Ontario Sign Historic Agreement." Press release, 9 August.

Algonquins of Ontario. 2010. "Algonquins of Ontario Officially Open Consultation Office in Pembroke." *Tanakiwin,* 11 January. http://www.tanakiwin.com/.

Amnesty International. N.d. "Justice for the Lubicon Cree." http://www.amnesty.ca/.

Ardoch Algonquin First Nation. 1999. "Algonquin Rights Are Being Negotiated Away." Unpublished flyer.

–. 2004. "Greetings from the Chief." *Point of Contact,* June-July, 1.

–. 2008. Press release, 9 December.

–. 2010. "What Does It Mean to Be Algonquin Today?" *Point of Contact,* May-June, 5. http://www.aafna.ca/AAFNA_Newsletter_May,_June,_July_2010_Electronic_C.pdf.

Ardoch Algonquin First Nation and Allies. 1993. "Self Government Model." *Point of Contact,* 15 December, 3-5.

–. 1996a. Results of members poll. 2 May. Unpublished document.

–. 1996b. "To All Members of the Ardoch Algonquin First Nation and Allies." 7 February. Unpublished document.

Armstrong, Frank. 2006. "Land Grab? Members of Ardoch Algonquin First Nation Are Clearing Land for a Cultural Centre." *Kingston Whig-Standard,* 8 July.

Aronson, Stephen, and Ronald C. Maguire. 1996. "Federal Treaty Policy Study." In Canada, *For Seven Generations: An Information Legacy of the Royal Commission on Aboriginal Peoples,* 1-106. Ottawa: Libraxus. CD-ROM.

Asch, Michael, and Patrick Macklem. 1991. "Aboriginal Rights and Canadian Sovereignty: An Essay on *R. v. Sparrow.*" *Alberta Law Review* 29,2: 498-517.

Barsh, Russell, and James Youngblood Henderson. 1997. "The Supreme Court's *Van der Peet* Trilogy: Naïve Imperialism and Ropes of Sand." *McGill Law Journal* 42: 993-1009.

Bartko, Patricia. 1999-2000. "Lesser Slave Lake Aboriginal Population circa 1899: 'The Community Quandary – Choosing between Treaty and Scrip.'" In "Treaty 8 Revisited: Selected Papers on the 1999 Centennial Conference," ed. Duff Crerar and Jaroslav Petryshyn. Special issue, *Lobstick: An Interdisciplinary Journal* 1,1 (Winter): 259-76.

BC Treaty Commission. 2006. Maa-nulth First Nations Final Agreement. 9 December. http://www.bctreaty.net/nations/agreements/Maanulth_final_intial_Dec06.pdf.

Biggar, H.P., ed. 1922-36. *Works of Samuel de Champlain.* Toronto: Champlain Society.

Black, Meredith Jean. 1980. *Algonquin Ethnobotany: An Interpretation of Aboriginal Adaptation in Southwestern Quebec.* Ottawa: National Museums of Canada.

–. 1993. "A Tale of Two Ethnicities: Identity and Ethnicity at Lake of Two Mountains, 1721-1850." In *Papers of the Twenty-Fourth Algonquian Conference,* ed. William Cowan, 1-7. Ottawa: Carlton University.

Blackwell, Tom. 1997. "Non-Status Indians Denied Casino Profits." *Toronto Star,* 7 June, A10.

Bond, C.J. 1966. "The Hudson's Bay Company in the Ottawa Valley." *The Beaver* (Spring): 4-21.

Bonnechere Algonquin Community. 1999. "Bonnechere Algonquin Community History." Unpublished document.

Borrows, John. 1997. "Wampum at Niagara: The Royal Proclamation, Canadian Legal History, and Self Government." In *Aboriginal and Treaty Rights in Canada: Essays on Law, Equality and Respect for Difference,* ed. Michael Asch, 155-72. Vancouver: UBC Press.

–. 2002. *Recovering Canada: The Resurgence of Indigenous Law.* Toronto: University of Toronto Press.

Brantlinger, Patrick. 2003. *Dark Vanishings: Discourse on the Extinction of Primitive Races, 1800-1930.* Ithaca: Cornell University Press.

Brethour, Patrick. 2007. "Tiny Band Votes down Historic Land Treaty." *Toronto Globe and Mail,* 2 April, 1.

Canada. 1987. *Comprehensive Claims Policy.* Ottawa: Minister of Supply and Services Canada.

–. 1995. "The Government of Canada's Approach to Implementation of the Inherent Right and the Negotiation of Aboriginal Self-Government Policy." Aboriginal Affairs and Northern Development Canada. http://www.aadnc-aandc.gc.ca/eng/.

–. 1996. *For Seven Generations: An Information Legacy of the Royal Commission on Aboriginal Peoples.* Ottawa: Libraxus. CD-ROM.

–. 2011. *Aboriginal Consultation and Accommodation: Updated Guidelines for Federal Officials to Fulfill the Legal Duty to Consult.* March. http://www.aadnc-aandc.gc.ca/eng.

Canadian Nuclear Association. 2010. "Uranium Mining in Northern Saskatchewan." http://www.cna.ca/.

Carrière, Gaston. 1957-75. *Histoire documentaire de la Congrégation des missionaires oblate de Marie-Immaculée dans l'est du Canada.* Ottawa: Éditions de l'Université d'Ottawa.

Chrétien Annette. 1996. "'Mattawa, Where the Waters Meet': The Question of Identity in Metis Culture." Master's thesis, Department of Music, University of Ottawa.

Churchill, Ward. 1992. *Struggle for the Land: Indigenous Resistance to Genocide, Ecocide and Expropriation in Contemporary North America.* Toronto: Between the Lines Press.

Cobo, José Martínez. 1987. *Study of the Problem of Discrimination against Indigenous Populations.* Vol. 5. New York: United Nations.

Conseil Attikamek Montagnais, Council for Yukon Indians, Dene Nation, Métis Association of the N.W.T., Kaska-Dena, Labrador Inuit Association, Nishga Tribal Council, Taku River Tlingit, and Tungavik Federation of Nunavut. 1986. "Key Components of a New Federal Policy for Comprehensive Land Claims." 30 October. http://www.carc.org/.

Cook, Maria. 2007. "Native Land Claim Halts Huge Rockcliffe Development: Negotiations Block Sale of Former Airbase." *Ottawa Citizen,* 1 May, 2.

Coon Come, Matthew. 2004. "Survival in the Context of Mega-Resource Development: Experiences of the James Bay Crees and the First Nations of Canada." In *In the Way of Development: Indigenous Peoples, Life Projects, and Globalization,* ed. Mario Blaser, Harvey A. Feit, and Glenn McRae, 153-65. London: Zed Books.

Côté, Marc. 1996. "Prehistory of Abitibi-Témiscamingue." In *The Algonquins,* ed. Daniel Clément, 5-29. Mercury Series, Canadian Ethnology Service 130. Hull: Canadian Museum of Civilization.

Coulthard, Glen. 2008. "Beyond Recognition: Indigenous Self-Determination as Prefigurative Practice." In *Lighting the Eighth Fire: The Liberation, Resurgence, and Protection of Indigenous Nations,* ed. Leanne Simpson, 187-204. Winnipeg: Arbeiter Ring.

Council of the Algonquins of Pikwakanagan, and Kirby J. Whiteduck. 2002. *Algonquin Traditional Culture: The Algonquins of the Kitchissippi Valley – Traditional Culture at the Early Contact Period.* Golden Lake: Algonquins of Pikwakanagan.

Culhane, Dara. 1998. *The Pleasure of the Crown: Anthropology, Law and First Nations.* Burnaby, BC: Talonbooks.

Darwell, Marcus Thomas. 1998. "Canada and the History without a People: Identity, Tradition and Struggle in a Non-Status Aboriginal Community." Master's thesis, Department of Sociology, Queen's University, Kingston, ON.

Davidson, D. Sutherland. 1928. "Family Hunting Territories of the Grand Lake Victoria Indians." In *International Congress of Americanists 22nd Congress,* 69-95. Rome: Riccardo Garroni.

Day, Gordon. 1979. "The Indians of the Ottawa Valley." *Oracle* 30: 1-4.

De Costa, Ravi. 2002a. "Agreements and Referenda: Recent Developments in the British Columbia Treaty Process." Paper presented at "Negotiating Settlements: Indigenous Peoples, Settler States and the Significance of Treaties and Agreements," Institute for Postcolonial Studies, Melbourne, 29 August. http://www.atns.net.au/.

–. 2002b. *Treaty Now? First, A Closer Look at the British Columbia Treaty Process.* Institute for Social Research Working Paper 5. Victoria, Australia: Institute for Social Research, Swinburne University of Technology.

–. 2008. "History, Democracy, and Treaty Negotiations in British Columbia." In *The Power of Promises: Rethinking Indian Treaties in the Pacific Northwest,* ed. Alexandra Harmon, 297-320. Seattle and London: Centre for the Study of the Pacific Northwest in association with University of Washington Press.

Delisle, Susan B. 2001. "Coming Out of the Shadows: Asserting Identity and Authority in a Layered Homeland: The 1979-82 Mud Lake Wild Rice Confrontation." Master's thesis, Geography Department, Queen's University, Kingston, ON.

Deloria, Vine, Jr., and Clifford M. Lytle. 1984. *The Nations Within: The Past and Future of American Indian Sovereignty.* Austin: University of Texas Press.

DiaMine Explorations. 2007. "James Bay Lowlands." http://www.diamineexplorations.com/.

Dickason, Olive P. 1985. "From 'One Nation' in the Northeast to 'New Nation' in the Northwest: A Look at the Emergence of the Metis." In *The New Peoples: Being and Becoming Metis in North America,* ed. Jacqueline Peterson and Jennifer S.H. Brown, 19-36. Winnipeg: University of Manitoba Press.

Eganville Leader. 2002. "Confused Community." Letter to the editor, 17 April.

Fell, Lorraine. 2008. "History of Baptiste Lake 2008." http://www.baptistelake.org/articles/lakehistory.pdf.

Forte, Maximilian C. 2006a. "Introduction: The Dual Absences of Extinction and Marginality – What Difference Does an Indigenous Presence Make?" In *Indigenous Resurgence in the Contemporary Caribbean: Amerindian Survival and Revival,* ed. Maximilian C. Forte, 1-17. New York: Peter Lang.

–. 2006b. "Searching for a Center in the Digital Ether: Notes on the Indigenous Caribbean Resurgence on the Internet." In *Indigenous Resurgence in the Contemporary Caribbean: Amerindian Survival and Revival,* ed. Maximilian C. Forte, 253-69. New York: Peter Lang.

Frontenac Ventures. 2009. "Frontenac Ventures Corp. Announces a New Alaskite Type Uranium Discovery, in the East Bancroft Area of Ontario." *Marketwire,* 26 February. http://www.marketwire.com/.

Gehl, Lynn. 2003. "The Rebuilding of a Nation: A Grassroots Analysis of the Aboriginal Nation-Building Process in Canada." *Canadian Journal of Native Studies* 23,1: 57-82.

–. 2005a. "Election Process Fair?" *Anishinabek News,* June, 5. http://www.k.ca/download/news/2005-6.pdf.

–. 2005b. "What Is a Contemporary Treaty?" Unpublished document, Trent University, April.

–. 2006. "Land Claim Deals Have Paid Pittance for Huge Acreages." *Anishinabek News,* March, 24.

–. 2009. "Land Settlements Not Improving." *Anishinabek News,* July-August, 5.

Gilbert, Larry. 1996. *Entitlement to Indian Status and Membership Codes in Canada.* Scarborough, ON: Thompson Canada.

Government of Nunavut. 1993. *Agreement between the Inuit of the Nunavut Settlement Area and Her Majesty the Queen in Right of Canada.* http://www.gov.nu.ca/hr/site/doc/nlca.pdf.

Gravelle, Abbe J.E. 1963. "Mme Noah Timmins a été la première femme blanche à s'installer à Mattawa." In Chrétien, 1996, "'Mattawa: Where the Waters Meet,'" 69-70.

Green, Jeff. 2009. "Diamond Driller Confirms 15 Drill Holes at Frontenac Ventures Exploration Site." *Frontenac News,* 12 February, 1.

Hanson, L.C. 1986. "Research Report: The Algonquins of Golden Lake Indian Band – Land Claim." Ministry of Natural Resources, Office of Indian Resource Policy.

Havard, Gilles. 2001. *The Great Peace of Montreal of 1701: French-Native Diplomacy in the Seventeenth Century.* Translated by Phyllis Aronoff and Howard Scott. Montreal and Kingston: McGill-Queen's University Press.

Hendry, Barry. 2006. "ANR Election Issues Uncovered." *Bancroft Times,* 2 July. http://www.greatergoldenlake.com/.

Hessel, Peter D.K. 1993. *The Algonkin Nation: The Algonkins of the Ottawa Valley: An Historical Outline.* Arnprior, ON: Kichesippi Books.

Hogben, Murray. 1996. "Non-Status Natives Demand More Rights." *Kingston Whig-Standard.*

–. 2000a. "Natives Experience Revitalization of Their Heritage." *Kingston Whig-Standard,* 1, 4.

–. 2000b. "Native Hunters Discover New-Found Alliance." *Kingston Whig-Standard,* 1.

–. 2000c. "Chamber Hands Out Community Awards." *Kingston Whig-Standard,* 3.

–. 2000d. "Discovering Pride Half the Battle." *Kingston Whig-Standard,* 3.

Huitema, Marijke E. 2000. "'Land of Which the Savages Stood in No Particular Need': Dispossessing the Algonquins of South-Eastern Ontario of Their Lands, 1760-1930." Master's thesis, Department of Geography, Queen's University, Kingston, ON.

Hurley, Mary C. 2009. "Settling Comprehensive Land Claims." Parliamentary Information and Research Service, Library of Parliament. 21 September. http://www2.parl.gc.ca/Content/LOP/ResearchPublications/prb0916-e.pdf.

INAC (Indian and Northern Affairs Canada). 2003. *Resolving Aboriginal Claims: A Practical Guide to Canadian Experiences.* Ottawa: INAC.

Jackson, Deborah Davis. 2001. "'This Hole in Our Heart': The Urban-Raised Generation and the Legacy of Silence." In *American Indians and the Urban Experience*, ed. Susan Lobo and Kurt Peters, 189-206. New York: Altamira Press.

Joan Holmes and Associates. 1993. *Algonquins of Golden Lake Claim*. 8 vols. N.p.: Ontario Native Secretariat.

–. 1995. "Ardoch Algonquins." Draft report, prepared for Chris Reid in anticipation of litigation. September.

Joly de Lotbiniere, Pauline. 1996. "Of Wampum and Little People: Historical Narratives Regarding the Algonquin Wampum Record." In *The Algonquins*, ed. Daniel Clément, 93-121. Mercury Series, Canadian Ethnology Service 130. Hull: Canadian Museum of Civilization.

Jury, Elsie McLeod. 2000. "Tessouat." In *Dictionary of Canadian Biography Online*. Vol. 1, *1000-1700*. University of Toronto. http://www.biographi.ca/.

Kanatiio, ed. 1998a. "Algonquin Enrolment Law: What's the Point?" *Tanakiwin* (Our Homeland) 1,2: 3.

–. 1998b. "Report of the Algonquin Government Task Force." *Tanakiwin* (Our Homeland) 1,3: 1-4.

–. 1998c. "Towards an Algonquin Citizenship Law." *Tanakiwin* (Our Homeland) 1,2: 3-4.

Kelly, Jim. 2009. "First Nations Attack Mining Act Changes." *Thunder Bay Chronicle Journal*, 1 May, 1.

Kennedy, Clyde C. 1970. *The Upper Ottawa Valley*. Pembroke, ON: Renfrew County Council.

Kidd, Kenneth E. 1948. "A Prehistoric Camp Site at Rock Lake, Algonquin Park, Ontario." *Southwestern Journal of Anthropology* 4,1 (Spring): 97-106.

Kingston Whig-Standard. 2008. "First Nation, Mining Company, Open Dialogue." 13 June.

Koschade, Bettina. 2003. "'The Tay River Watershed Is Our Responsibility': The Ardoch Algonquins and the 2000-2002 Environmental Review Tribunal Hearings." Master's thesis, Geography Department, Queen's University, Kingston, ON.

Koschade, Bettina, and Evelyn Peters. 2006. "Algonquin Notions of Jurisdiction: Inserting Indigenous Voices into Legal Spaces." *Geografiska Annaler: Series B, Human Geography* 88,3 (September): 299-310.

LaDuke, Winona. 1999. *All My Relations: Native Struggles for Land and Life*. Cambridge, MA: South End Press.

–. 2005. *Recovering the Sacred: The Power of Naming and Claiming*. Toronto: Between the Lines Press.

Laflamme, Jean. 1979. "Le marquis de Vaudreuil et l'Abitibi-Témiscamingue (seconde partie: 1724-1731)." In *De l'Abitibi-Témiskaming 5*, ed. Maurice Asselin et al., 1-20. Rouyn, QC: Collège du Nord-Ouest.

Lamothe, Paul. 2007. Letter to Brian Crane, Robin Aitken, and Robert Potts. 23 April. Ottawa Algonquin First Nation. http://www.ottawaalgonquins.com/index_files/Ottawa%20Algonquin%20Update%20April%2023%2007.pdf.

LaPierre, Paula. 2006a. Letter to Bob Potts, Principal Negotiator, and to the Algonquin Negotiation Representatives. 3 May.

–. 2006b. Letter to Bob Potts, Principal Negotiator, and to the Algonquin Negotiation Representatives. 8 May.

LaRocque, Emma. 2010. *When the Other Is Me: Native Resistance Discourse 1850-1990*. Winnipeg: University of Manitoba Press.

Lawrence, Bonita. 2002. "Rewriting Histories of the Land: Colonization and Resistance in Eastern Canada." In *Race, Space and the Law: Unmapping a White Settler Society*, ed. Sherene Razack, 23-46. Toronto: Between the Lines Press.

–. 2004. *"Real" Indians and Others: Mixed-Blood Urban Native Peoples and Indigenous Nationhood*. Vancouver: UBC Press.

–. 2009. "Reclaiming Ktaqumkuk: Land and Mi'kmaq Identity in Newfoundland." In *Speaking for Ourselves: Environmental Justice in Canada*, ed. Julian Agyeman, Peter Cole, Randolph Haluza-DeLay, and Pat O'Riley, 42-64. Vancouver: UBC Press.

Lawrence, Bonita, and Enakshi Dua. 2005. "Decolonizing Anti-Racism." *Social Justice: A Journal of Crime, Conflict and World Order* 32,4: 120-43.

Leonard, David, and Beverly Whalen. 1999. *On the North Trail: The Treaty 8 Diary of O.C. Edwards.* Calgary: Alberta Records Publication Board.

Leslie, J., and R. Maguire, eds. 1979. *The Historical Development of the Indian Act.* 2nd ed. Ottawa: Indian and Northern Affairs Canada.

Lovelace, Robert. 1982. "Manomin." *Ontario Indian* 5,89 (August): 28-39.

–. 2006. "An Algonquin History." Ardoch Algonquin First Nation. http://www.aafna.ca/.

–. 2008. Teaching circle, Maberley Community Centre. January.

–. 2009. "Prologue – Notes from Prison: Protecting Algonquin Lands from Uranium Mining." In *Speaking for Ourselves: Environmental Justice in Canada,* ed. Julian Agyeman, Peter Cole, Randolph Haluza-DeLay, and Pat O'Riley, ix-xix. Vancouver: UBC Press.

Maaka, Roger, and Augie Fleras. 2005. *The Politics of Indigeneity: Challenging the State in Canada and Aotearoa New Zealand.* Dunedin: University of Otago Press.

Mackay, Roderick. 1991. "Supplementary Report on Indian Occurrences in Algonquin Park." Unpublished compilation, Algonquin Park Museum.

Mainville, Robert. 2001. *An Overview of Aboriginal and Treaty Rights and Compensation for Their Breach.* Saskatoon: Purich.

Majaury, Heather. 2005. "Living Inside Layers of Colonial Division: A Part of the Algonquin Story." *Atlantis* 29,2: 145-47.

Marshall, Donald, Sr., Alexander Denny, and Putus Simon Marshall. 1989. "The Covenant Chain." In *Drumbeat: Anger and Renewal in Indian Country,* ed. Boyce Richardson, 73-103. Toronto: Summerhill Press and the Assembly of First Nations.

Martin-Hill, Dawn. 2004. "Resistance, Determination and Persistence of the Lubicon Cree Women." In *In the Way of Development: Indigenous Peoples, Life Projects, and Globalization,* ed. Mario Blaser, Harvey A. Feit, and Glenn McRae, 313-30. London: Zed Books.

Matachewan, Jean-Maurice. 1989. "Mitchikanibikonginik Algonquins of Barriere Lake: Our Long Battle to Create a Sustainable Future." In *Drumbeat: Anger and Renewal in Indian Country,* ed. Boyce Richardson, 139-66. Toronto: Summerhill Press and the Assembly of First Nations.

McCaslin, Wanda D. 2005. "Introduction: Reweaving the Fabrics of Life." In *Justice as Healing: Indigenous Ways – Writings on Community Peacemaking and Restorative Justice from the Native Law Centre of Canada,* ed. Wanda D. McCaslin, 87-92. St. Paul, MN: Living Justice Press.

McNeil, Kent. 2002. "The Inherent Right of Self-Government: Emerging Directions for Legal Research." A research report prepared for the First Nations Governance Centre, Chilliwack, BC. November.

Meyer, David. 1985. *The Red Earth Crees, 1860-1960.* Mercury Series, Canadian Ethnology Service 100. Ottawa: National Museum of Canada.

Meyer, David, Terrance Gibson, and Dale Russell. 2008. "The Quest for Pasquatinow: An Aboriginal Gathering Centre in the Saskatchewan River Valley." In *The Early Northwest,* ed. Gregory P. Marchildon, 47-71. History of the Prairie West Series 1. Regina: Canadian Plains Research Center, University of Regina.

Meyer, David, and Dale Russell. 2004. "'So Fine and Pleasant, Beyond Description': The Lands and Lives of the Pegogamaw Crees." *Plains Anthropologist* 49,191: 217-52.

Meyer, David, and Paul C. Thistle. 1995. "Saskatchewan River Rendezvous Centers and Trading Posts: Continuity in a Cree Social Geography." *Ethnohistory* 42,3 (Summer): 403-44.

Miller, Bruce Granville. 2003. *Invisible Indigenes: The Politics of Nonrecognition.* Lincoln: University of Nebraska Press.

Miller, J.R. 2009. *Compact, Contract and Covenant: Aboriginal Treaty-Making in Canada.* Toronto: University of Toronto Press.

Ministry of Natural Resources. 2001. *Ontario's Living Legacy.* http://www.ontla.on.ca/library/repository/mon/2000/10281337.pdf.
MoCreebec Council of the Cree Nation. 2005. "25th Anniversary Commemorative Report." http://www.creevillage.com/11252_MoCreebec.pdf.
Monet, Don, and Skanu'u (Ardythe Wilson). 1992. *Colonialism on Trial: Indigenous Land Rights and the Gitksan and Wet'suwet'en Sovereignty Case.* Gabriola Island, BC: New Society.
Monture-Angus, Patricia. 1999. *Journeying Forward: Dreaming First Nations Independence.* Halifax: Fernwood.
Morel, Leo. 1980. *Mattawa: Meeting of the Waters.* Mattawa: Mattawa Historical Society.
Morrison, James. 2005. "Algonquin History in the Ottawa River Watershed." In *A Background Study for Nomination of the Ottawa River under the Canadian Heritage Rivers System,* ed. Ottawa River Heritage Designation Committee, 17-32. Petawawa: Ottawa River Heritage Designation Committee. http://www.ottawariver.org/pdf/05-ch2-3.pdf.
Naumetz, Tim. 2007. "Never Surrendered." *Ottawa Citizen,* 8 July, 1,3.
Noble, William C. 1968. "'Vision Pits,' Cairns and Petroglyphs at Rock Lake, Algonquin Provincial Park, Ontario." *Ontario Archaeology* 11 (June): 47-64.
Nuttall, A.J. 1980. "The Success of Government Settlement Policy in the Ottawa-Huron Territory, 1853-1898." Master's thesis, Geography Department, Queen's University, Kingston, ON.
–. 1982. "Pushing Back the Frontier." In *County of a Thousand Lakes: The History of the County of Frontenac, 1673-1973,* ed. B. Rollason, 48-68. Kingston, ON: Frontenac County Council.
Olthuis, John, and H.W. Roger Townshend. 1996. "Is Canada's Thumb on the Scales? An Analysis of Canada's Comprehensive and Specific Claims Policies and Suggested Alternatives." In Canada, *For Seven Generations: An Information Legacy of the Royal Commission on Aboriginal Peoples,* 63174-63877. Ottawa: Libraxus. CD-ROM.
Ottawa Citizen. 2002. "Museum of Civilization to Return Algonquin Bones," 31 December.
Ottawa River Heritage Designation Committee. 2005a. "Hydroelectricity on the Ottawa River." In *A Background Study for Nomination of the Ottawa River under the Canadian Heritage Rivers System,* ed. Ottawa River Heritage Designation Committee, 118-28. Petawawa: Ottawa River Heritage Designation Committee. http://ottawariver.org/pdf/11-ch2-9.pdf.
–. 2005b. "Logging in the Ottawa Valley – The Ottawa River and the Lumber Industry." In *A Background Study for Nomination of the Ottawa River under the Canadian Heritage Rivers System,* ed. Ottawa River Heritage Designation Committee, 89-103. Petawawa: Ottawa River Heritage Designation Committee. http://www.ottawariver.org/pdf/09-ch2-7.pdf.
Ottawa River Regulation Planning Board. 1984. *Managing the Waters of the Ottawa River.* Gatineau: Ottawa River Regulation Planning Board. http://www.ottawariver.ca/.
Owens, Louis. 1998. *Mixedblood Messages: Literature, Film, Family, Place.* Norman: University of Oklahoma Press.
Ozawanimke, Lisa. 2001. Letter to Members of Algonquins of Pikwakanagan First Nation. 19 December. http://www.greatergoldenlake.com/.
Palmater, Pamela D. 2000. "An Empty Shell of a Treaty Promise: *R. v. Marshall* and the Rights of Non-Status Indians." *Dalhousie Law Journal* 23,1 (Spring): 101-48.
Pawlick, Thomas. 1982. "The Siege of Mud Lake." *Harrowsmith* 40, 32-41.
Peplinskie, Tina. 2002. "United Voice Needed for Algonquin Claims." *Pembroke Daily Observer,* 8 April. http://www.greatergoldenlake.com.
Persky, Stan. 1998. *Delgamuukw: The Supreme Court of Canada Decision on Aboriginal Title.* Vancouver: Douglas and McIntyre.
Platiel, Rudy. 1996. "Judge Tells Province to Talk with Indians." *Toronto Globe and Mail,* 16 April, 5.
Potts, Robert. 2004. "Open Letter to All People in Ontario of Algonquin Ancestry." 26 August.
–. 2005. "Algonquins Selecting Negotiation Representatives." *Anishinabek News,* April.

Province of Ontario. 2008. "Building Relationships through Consultation: Ontario, First Nations and Industry Reach Agreement on Mineral Exploration in Eastern Ontario." Press release, 28 November.

Ratelle, Maurice. 1996. "Location of the Algonquins from 1534 to 1650." In *The Algonquins*, ed. Daniel Clément, 41-67. Mercury Series, Canadian Ethnology Service 130. Hull: Canadian Museum of Civilization.

RCAP (Royal Commission on Aboriginal Peoples). 1996a. *Report of the Royal Commission on Aboriginal Peoples.* Vol. 1, *Looking Forward, Looking Back.* Ottawa: Ministry of Supply and Services.

–. 1996b. *Report of the Royal Commission on Aboriginal Peoples.* Vol. 2, *Restructuring the Relationship.* Ottawa: Ministry of Supply and Services.

Reynolds, Nila. 1979. "Bancroft Gems and Minerals: So Rich, So Rare." In *Bancroft: A Bonanza of Memories*, ed. Bancroft Centennial Committee, 183-86. Bancroft: Bancroft Centennial Committee.

Roseberry, William. 1994. "Hegemony and the Language of Contention." In *Everyday Forms of State Formation: Revolution and the Negotiation of Rule in Modern Mexico*, ed. Gilbert Joseph and Donald Nugent, 355-61. Durham, NC: Duke University Press.

Salaff, Stephen. 2007. "License Renewal Refused to Nuclear Waste Polluter in Pembroke." *ACTivist Magazine*, 25 February. http://activistmagazine.com/.

Sarazin, Greg. 1989. "220 Years of Broken Promises." In *Drumbeat: Anger and Renewal in Indian Country*, ed. Boyce Richardson, 169-200. Toronto: Summerhill Press and the Assembly of First Nations.

–. 1997. "Algonquin Members Asked to Act in Nation's Best Interest." *Anishinabek News*, November, 2.

–. 1998. "Consultation, Enrolment and Representation." *Tanakiwin* (Our Homeland) 1,2: 1-2.

Sawchuk, Joe. 1986. "The Metis, Non Status Indians and the New Aboriginality: Government Influence on Native Political Alliances and Identity." *Canadian Ethnic Studies* 17,2: 133-46.

Sawchuk, Patricia. 1996. "The Historic Interchangeability of Status of Metis and Indians: An Alberta Example." In *The Recognition of Aboriginal Rights: Case Studies*, ed. Samuel W. Corrigan and Joe Sawchuk, 57-70. Brandon, MB: Bearpaw Publishing (University of Brandon).

Sherman, Paula. 2008a. *Dishonour of the Crown: The Ontario Resource Regime in the Valley of the Kiji Sibì.* Winnipeg: Arbeiter Ring.

–. 2008b. "The Friendship Wampum: Maintaining Traditional Practices in Our Contemporary Interactions in the Valley of the Kiji Sibi." In *Lighting the Eighth Fire: The Liberation, Resurgence and Protection of Indigenous Nations*, ed. Leanne Simpson, 111-26. Winnipeg: Arbeiter Ring.

Smith, Linda Tuhiwai. 1999. *Decolonizing Methodologies: Research and Indigenous Peoples.* London: Zed Books.

St. Onge, Nicole. 2007. "Early Forefathers to the Athabasca Metis: Long-Term North West Company Employees." In *The Long Journey of a Forgotten People: Metis Identities and Family Histories*, ed. Ute Lischke and David T. McNab, 109-62. Waterloo: Wilfrid Laurier University Press.

Sturm, Circe. 2002. *Blood Politics: Race, Culture, and Identity in the Cherokee Nation of Oklahoma.* Berkeley: University of California Press.

Teillet, Jean. 2007. "The Winds of Change: Metis Rights after *Powley, Taku*, and *Haida*." In *The Long Journey of a Forgotten People: Metis Identities and Family Histories*, ed. Ute Lischke and David T. McNab, 55-78. Waterloo: Wilfrid Laurier University Press.

Tennescoe, George. 2002. "More Moose Details." Letter to the editor, *Eganville Leader*, 6 November, 8.

Thwaites, R.G., ed. 1901. *The Jesuit Relations and Allied Documents.* Cleveland: Burrows Brothers.

Tolley, Sara-Larus. 2006. *Quest for Tribal Acknowledgement: California's Honey Lake Maidus.* Norman: University of Oklahoma Press.

Trigger, Bruce G. 1985. *Natives and Newcomers: Canada's "Heroic Age" Reconsidered.* Montreal and Kingston: McGill-Queen's University Press.

–. 1994. "The Original Iroquoians: Huron, Petun, and Neutral." In *Aboriginal Ontario: Historical Perspectives on the First Nations,* ed. Edward S. Rogers and Donald B. Smith, 41-63. Toronto: Dundurn Press.
Turtle Island Native Network. 2001. "Comprehensive Claims Policy and Status of Claims." 29 October. http://www.turtleisland.org/news/comp.pdf.
Union of Ontario Indians. 2009. Press release, 1 May.
Whiteduck, Kirby. 2004. "Pikwakanagan's Presentation to the Assembly of First Nations Renewal Commission." 26 February.
Whitlock, Jeremy. 1997. "Algonquins to Atoms along the Ottawa: A History of Life and Development along the Ottawa River, from Copper Kettles to Nuclear Reactors." *Canadian Nuclear Society Bulletin* 18,1 (Winter): 31-33. http://www.nuclearfaq.ca/.
Wilkins, Kerry. 1999. "... But We Need the Eggs: The Royal Commission, the Charter of Rights, and the Inherent Right of Aboriginal Self-Government." *University of Toronto Law Journal* 49,1 (Winter): 53-121.
Willsey, Ralph. 1981. "Mud Lake Protestors Block Launching of Rice Harvester." *Kingston Whig-Standard,* 22 August, 44.
Windspeaker Business Quarterly. 2007. "A New Report Has Recommended That British Columbia Return Half of Its Forest Revenues to First Nations." Spring, 9.
Wong, Christine. 1996. "Metis to Share in Casino Rama Profits." *Windspeaker,* 1 September, 1.
Wrong, G.M., ed. 1939. *The Long Journey to the Country of the Hurons*: The Collected Works of Gabriel Sagard. Toronto: Champlain Society.

Index